# HANDBOOK OF THE INTERNATIONAL POLITICAL ECONOMY OF AGRICULTURE AND FOOD

HANDBOOKS OF RESEARCH ON INTERNATIONAL POLITICAL
ECONOMY

**Series Editors:** Matthew Watson, *Department of Politics and International Studies,
University of Warwick, Coventry, UK* and Benjamin J. Cohen, *Louis G. Lancaster
Professor of International Political Economy, University of California, Santa
Barbara, USA*

This highly original *Handbook* series offers a unique appraisal of the state-
of-the-art of research in International Political Economy (IPE). Consisting
of original contributions by leading authorities, *Handbooks* in the series
provide comprehensive overviews of the very latest research within key areas
of IPE. Taking a thematic approach, emphasis is placed on both expanding
current debate and indicating the likely research agenda for the future.
Each *Handbook* forms a prestigious and high quality work of lasting significance.
The *Handbooks* will encompass arguments from both the British and American
schools of IPE to give a comprehensive overview of the debates and research
positions in each key area of interest, as well as offering a space for those who feel
that their work fits neither designation easily. Taking a genuinely international
approach these *Handbooks* are designed to inform as well as to contribute to
current debates.
   Titles in the series include:

Handbook of the International Political Economy of Governance
*Edited by Anthony Payne and Nicola Phillips*

Handbook of the International Political Economy of Monetary Relations
*Edited by Thomas Oatley and W. Kindred Winecoff*

Handbook of the International Political Economy of Trade
*Edited by David A. Deese*

Handbook of the International Political Economy of Production
*Edited by Kees van der Pijl*

Handbook of the International Political Economy of Agriculture and Food
*Edited by Alessandro Bonanno and Lawrence Busch*

# Handbook of the International Political Economy of Agriculture and Food

*Edited by*

Alessandro Bonanno
*Sam Houston State University, USA*

Lawrence Busch
*Michigan State University, USA*

HANDBOOKS OF RESEARCH ON INTERNATIONAL POLITICAL ECONOMY

Cheltenham, UK • Northampton, MA, USA

Published by
Edward Elgar Publishing Limited
The Lypiatts
15 Lansdown Road
Cheltenham
Glos GL50 2JA
UK

Edward Elgar Publishing, Inc.
William Pratt House
9 Dewey Court
Northampton
Massachusetts 01060
USA

A catalogue record for this book
is available from the British Library

Library of Congress Control Number: 2014954936

This book is available electronically in the **Elgar**online
Social and Political Science subject collection
DOI 10.4337/9781782548263

ISBN 978 1 78254 825 6 (cased)
ISBN 978 1 78254 826 3 (eBook)

Typeset by Servis Filmsetting Ltd, Stockport, Cheshire
Printed and bound in Great Britain by T.J. International Ltd, Padstow

# Contents

*v*

# Contributors

**Gilberto Aboites** is Professor at the Center of Socioeconomic Research at the Autonomous University of Coahuila and in the Department of Agricultural Economics at Antonio Narro Autonomous Agrarian University, Mexico. He is the author of numerous refereed publications that have appeared in Spanish and English.

**Carmen Bain** is Associate Professor in the Department of Sociology at Iowa State University, USA. Her research interests include the political economy of food and agriculture; the socio-political dimensions of biotechnology as it relates to food and agriculture; and gender, social change and development. Her current research focuses on understanding and analyzing societal acceptance and governance issues related to genetically engineered foods, especially as it relates to labeling. She has conducted research in Chile, Ghana, New Zealand, Uganda and the United States. Her work has been published in the journals *Agriculture and Human Values, Biomass and Bioenergy, Food Policy, Gender and Society, International Journal of Sociology of Agriculture and Food, Rural Sociology* and *Signs: Journal of Women in Culture and Society* and several edited volumes including *Gendered Commodity Chains: Bringing Households and Women into Global Commodity Chain Analysis, Rural America in a Globalizing World: Problems and Prospects for the 2010s, Sustainable Development of Biofuels in Latin America and the Caribbean, Calculating the Social: Standards and the Re-configuration of Governing* and *Agricultural Governance: Globalization and the New Politics of Regulation.*

**Josefa Salete Barbosa Cavalcanti** is Researcher of the Brazilian CNPq and Professor of Sociology and Anthropology at the Federal University of Pernambuco, Brazil. She has a PhD from the University of Manchester, UK. She is the author of numerous publications that have appeared in English, Portuguese and Spanish and the co-author with Alessandro Bonanno of *Labor Relations in Global Agri-food* (2014) and *Globalization and the Time–Space Reorganization* (2011).

**Manuel Belo Moreira** is an Agronomist and Professor at the Instituto Superior de Agronomia, University of Lisbon, Portugal, from where he retired in 2012. He holds a PhD in economics from the University of Grenoble (France) and was on the staff at the Portuguese Ministry of Agriculture during the 1975 land reform process. He has published numerous books, refereed articles and book chapters that have appeared in English, Portuguese and other major languages. He organized domestic and international conferences such as the International Rural Sociological Association World Congress of Rural Sociology, which was held in Lisbon in 2012 and co-edited various issues of the *International Journal of Sociology of Agriculture and Food* (*IJSAF*). He served on the advisory board of the journals *Sociologia Ruralis* and *IJSAF*, on a number of European Commission technical teams appointed to assess EU legislation and as President of the International Sociological Association's Research Committee on Sociology of Agriculture and Food (RC-40) (2002–2006).

**Bettina Bock** is Associate Professor of Rural Sociology in the Department of Social Science at Wageningen University, the Netherlands. She holds a PhD in rural sociology based on a study of gender and rural development policy and practice defended in 2002. She teaches social theory, sustainable development, food policy and health and supervises PhDs in the field of gender and rural development, sustainable food and animal welfare policy. She is editor in chief of *Sociologia Ruralis* and has been a board member of the European and International Society for Rural Sociology (ESRS and IRSA). Her research projects include farm animal welfare, rural development and social innovation, and rural gender relations, as well as sustainable food consumption and production. Recently she has coordinated the EU funded project FOODLINKS, which aims to develop new modalities of linking research to policy making in the field of sustainable food consumption and production. She has also been a member of the coordinating team of EUWelNet, an interdisciplinary (EU funded) study of implementation of farm animal welfare legislation across Europe. She has published on social equality, rural gender issues, rural development governance and animal welfare policies in a number of international journals.

**Alessandro Bonanno** is Texas State University System Regents' Professor and Distinguished Professor of Sociology at Sam Houston State University, USA. His research focuses on the globalization of the economy and society with particular emphasis on agri-food. His most recent books discuss labor relations in agri-food and the crisis of neoliberalism.

**Barbara Brandl** is a PhD candidate in the Department of Sociology at the University of Munich (LMU), Germany. During the 2012–2014 academic year she was a visiting scholar in the Department of Agricultural Economics, Sociology, and Education at Penn State University, USA. Her doctoral research is in the field of the institutional embedding of seed systems in the United States and Germany.

**Lawrence Busch** is University Distinguished Professor of Sociology at Michigan State University, USA, and a recent visiting scholar at CIRAD, Montpellier, France. His research interests include the growing role of formal standards in neoliberal governance globally, with particular concern for agri-food, and higher education and research. His most recent book addresses neoliberal notions of knowledge: *Le Marché aux Connaisances* (Éditions Quea, 2014).

**Clara Craviotti** is Researcher at the National Council of Scientific and Technological Research (CONICET), Argentina and is a Principal Teaching Fellow at the Master's of Agrarian Social Studies Program of the Latin American Faculty of Social Sciences (FLACSO), Argentina. She holds a degree in sociology, a Master's degree in social studies and a PhD in geography. Her main areas of research are the new profiles of family farming and enterprise agriculture and the dynamics of delocalization and relocalization in food production and its impacts on rural spaces and agrarian structures. She has recently edited and co-authored *Agricultura familiar en Latinoamérica. Continuidades, transformaciones y controversias* (Buenos Aires: Ed. CICCUS, 2014) and *Tramas productivas y agentes sociales en la fruticultura globalizada* (Buenos Aires: Miño y Dávila, 2012). Some of her recent articles are: Craviotti, Clara, "Agricultura familiar-agronegocios: Disputas, interrelaciones y proyectos," *Territorios*, no. 30 (2014); Craviotti, Clara and Paula Palacios, "La diversificación de los mercados como estrategia de la agricultura familiar," *Revista Brasileira de Sociologia e Economía Rural*, vol. 51, supl. 1, S063–S078 (2013); Craviotti, Clara "Producer Relationships and Local Development in Fresh Fruit Commodity Chains: An Analysis of Blueberry Production in Entre Ríos, Argentina," *Regional Studies*, vol. 46, no. 2, pp. 203–215 (2012).

**Ivan Cucco** is a postdoctoral research fellow in the Department of Economics and Statistics at the University of Naples Federico II, Italy. His current research project brings theoretical and methodological insights from social network analysis to the field of innovation studies. Dr. Cucco obtained his PhD in 2012 at Macquarie University with a neo-Marxist class analysis of inequality in a Chinese New- and High-Technology Development Zone. Beyond innovation and inequality, his research interests include rural development, the transformation of global food regimes and the political economy of alternative food networks. He spent several years doing fieldwork in rural and urban areas of China and Vietnam.

**Tamera Dandachi** is a graduate student in the sociology department at Iowa State University, USA. She completed her BA in sociology and anthropology at the University of Michigan-Flint. Her research interests are the political economy of agri-food systems, food production and distribution, social movements, and gender, class and race inequalities.

**María del Rosario Castro Bernardini** is a first year graduate student in rural sociology in the Department of Agricultural Economics, Sociology and Education at Penn State University, USA.

**Jane Dixon** is Senior Fellow at the National Centre for Epidemiology and Population Health, Australian National University, Australia. Her research takes place at the intersection of sociology and public health, with a focus on the cultural, social and health impacts of food system transformations. She has advised numerous bodies on adopting a food system perspective, including the International Union on Health Promotion and Education and WHO Western Pacific Regional Office. Recent books include *When Culture Impacts Health* (Elsevier) and *Weight of Modernity* (Springer). In agri-food studies, she has written on the cultural economy of poultry commodity systems, the nutrition relations which underpin food regimes and the exercise of authority by supermarkets. She is currently researching for a new book, *The Culinary Footprint* (Bloomsbury), which examines how consumer demand shapes food security.

**Miren Etxezarreta** holds a PhD in economics from the London School of Economics, UK. She is Professor Emeritus of Applied Economics at the Autonomous University of Barcelona, Spain and has researched and published in agricultural economics and rural development, development economics and economic policy.

**Madeleine Fairbairn** earned a PhD from the joint Sociology/Community and Environmental Sociology graduate program at the University of Wisconsin-Madison, USA, in 2014 and is now a postdoctoral fellow at Goucher College, USA. Her work explores transformation in the global agri-food system through the lens of political ecology. Her previous research projects have focused on the global food sovereignty movement and on land concessions to foreign investors in Mozambique. Her current work explores growing interest in farmland on the part of the financial sector, as well as the policy debate that surrounds foreign farmland investment in Brazil. Her work has been published in *Development and Change, Agriculture and Human Values* and the *Journal of Peasant Studies*.

**Maria Fonte** is Associate Professor of Agricultural Economics in the Department of Economics, Management and Institutions at the University of Naples Federico II, Italy. Her teaching and research topics include political economy of agriculture, rural development, local agriculture, knowledge systems and local knowledge, agri-food systems, territorial development and biocultural diversity, agricultural innovation and biotechnology. Her recent publications include numerous articles on rural development and civic food networks in Italy and the volume *Naming Food after Places: Knowledge Dynamics in Rural Development*, co-edited with Apostolos G. Papadopoulos.

**Leland Glenna** is an Associate Professor of Rural Sociology and Science, Technology, and Society in the Agricultural Economics, Sociology, and Education Department at Penn State University, USA. His research interests are in the areas of social and environmental impacts of agricultural science and technologies, the role of science and technology in agricultural and natural resource policy making, and the social and ethical implications of democratizing science and technology research.

**Lummina Horlings** is Associate Professor of Rural Sociology in the Department of Social Science at Wageningen University. the Netherlands. She has studied human geography and holds a PhD in policy sciences, based on a study of innovative farmers groups and the role of national policy, defended in 1996. She teaches in sustainability leadership, sociological theories of rural transformation, place-based development and sociology of food and place, and she supervises PhDs. Her research deals with the question of how people contribute to sustainable place-shaping, including aspects such as leadership, self-organization, coalitions, values and sense of place. She has also published on these issues and on sustainable food production in international journals. She is involved in several European networks such as the RSA research network on "The Place of Leadership in Urban and Regional Development," the Interreg IVB project on "Rural Alliances" and the COST Action "Investigating Cultural Sustainability."

**Kristal Jones** holds a PhD in Rural Sociology and International Agriculture and Development from Penn State University, USA, where she currently is a postdoctoral scholar. Her research focuses on agricultural development, with a specific emphasis on Francophone West Africa and seed systems.

**Evander Eloi Krone** holds a Master's degree in anthropology and is currently completing his doctorate degree in anthropology at the Federal University of Pernambuco, Brazil.

**Geoffrey Lawrence** is Emeritus Professor of Sociology at the University of Queensland, Australia. His current research examines the financialization of food and agriculture, the political economy of supermarkets and agri-food supply chains, and the causes and contours of food security/ insecurity. He is the author/co-author/editor of some 30 books and 500 journal articles and book chapters. He is President of the International Rural Sociology Association (2012–2016) and is an elected Fellow of the Academy of Social Sciences in Australia.

**Francisco Martínez** is Professor at the Center of Socioeconomic Research at the Autonomous University of Coahuila and in the Department of Agricultural Economics at Antonio Narro Autonomous Agrarian University, Mexico. Dr Martínez's work focuses on globalization of the economy and society; plant genetic resources and rural development; and globalization and the poultry industry. Dr Martínez is the author of numerous publications that have appeared in Spanish and English.

**Mara Miele** is Reader in Human Geography in the Cardiff School of Planning and Geography at Cardiff University, UK. Her research addresses the geographies of ethical foods consumption and the role of animal welfare science and technology in challenging the way farmed animals are used in current agricultural practices and policies. Over the last decade, Dr. Miele has worked with a large interdisciplinary network of social and animal welfare scientists to develop innovative forms of critical public engagement with animal production and animal welfare science. She was the coordinator of the EU project Dialrel (2006–2010), which was dedicated to establishing a dialogue between religious authorities and scientists about the welfare of animals in practices of religious slaughter, and a member of the steering committee of the EU funded project Welfare Quality (2004–2009), which was dedicated to developing standardized protocols for monitoring and assessing animal welfare on farms and in slaughterhouses. In 2012 Dr. Miele received the Ashby prize for her 2011 article "The Taste of Happiness: Free Range Chicken," published in *Environment and Planning A*, 43 (9): 2070–2090.

**Gerardo Otero** is Professor of Sociology and International Studies at Simon Fraser University, Canada. Author of *Farewell to the Peasantry? Political Class Formation in Rural Mexico* (Westview, 1999), he has published numerous scholarly articles, chapters and books about political economy of agriculture and food, civil society and the state in Mexico and Latin America. His latest edited book is *Food for the Few: Neoliberal Globalism and Biotechnology in Latin America* (University of Texas Press, 2008, reissued in paperback in 2010), which was published in a revised and updated version in Spanish as *La dieta neoliberal: Globalización y biotecnología agrícola en las Américas*, co-published in Mexico by Simon Fraser University, Universidad Autónoma Metropolitana-Xochimilco and M.A. Porrúa. During Fall of 2014, Otero was Tinker Visiting Professor at the University of Wisconsin-

Madison, affiliated to the Department of Community and Environmental Sociology.

**Anouk Patel-Campillo** is Assistant Professor in the Department of Agricultural Economics, Sociology and Education at Penn State University, USA. From a critical development studies perspective, Dr. Patel-Campillo's research examines the socio-economic and political processes and impacts of agri-food system restructuring at the local, national and international scales and across distinct institutional and developmental contexts. Her research program falls within three broadly defined areas: (1) the investigation of agri-food systems restructuring and its impacts on workers, communities, regional food security and national development; (2) the examination of organization, structure and competitive position of value-added chains across scale, space and time; and (3) the analysis of the role of geopolitics, the state, regulation, civil society and production–consumption relations related to the practices of economic actors in value-added chains.

**Gabriela Pechlaner** is the author of *Corporate Crops: Biotechnology, Agriculture, and the Struggle for Control*, published by the University of Texas Press in December 2012, reissued in paperback in December 2013. Her research focuses on the sociology of agriculture and food, with a particular emphasis on the legal and regulatory aspects of new technologies. She has published a number of solo and co-authored articles in this and related areas in scholarly journals such as *Anthropologica, International Journal of the Sociology of Agriculture and Food, Rural Sociology, Sociologia Ruralis* and *Canadian Journal of Sociology*. She has also contributed to a number of chapters in edited volumes, such as the *Routledge Handbook of Poverty in the United States* (Routledge, 2014), and *Seeing Ourselves: Classic, Contemporary, and Cross-Cultural Readings in Sociology* (Pearson, 2013). Pechlaner is a permanent faculty member in sociology at the University of the Fraser Valley, Canada.

**Elizabeth Ransom** is an Associate Professor of Sociology at the University of Richmond, USA. Her primary research interests are in international development and globalization, agriculture and food systems with an emphasis on Southern Africa, and science and technology studies especially in relation to agriculture and food. She has two ongoing research programs. The first program focuses on the linkages between Southern African (South Africa, Botswana and Namibia) red meat industries and global food systems. The second program analyzes international agricultural development assistance in developing countries with an emphasis on the ways in which agricultural assistance targets women and focuses on gender empowerment.

**Jordi Rosell** holds a PhD in economics and is Senior Lecturer in Applied Economics at the Autonomous University of Barcelona, Spain. Dr. Rosell's primary areas of investigation are rural development, the Common Agricultural Policy and world and Latin American economics.

**Carolyn Sachs** is Professor of Rural Sociology at Penn State University, USA. Dr. Sachs' research examines issues of gender and agriculture and gender and environmental issues. In particular she studies the new women agricultural entrepreneurs and the opportunities and barriers to success. She is engaged in a comparative international project on gender and climate change in India in collaboration with the Food and Agriculture Organization. Dr. Sachs also focuses on gender and the food system, exploring gendered work in the food system from farm to table.

**Kae Sekine** is Lecturer of Rural Economics at Aichi Gakuin University, Japan. She holds a PhD (2011) in economics from Kyoto University, Japan, and studied at the French National Institute for Agricultural Research (INRA) in Montpellier, France, from 2007 to 2010. Dr. Sekine has researched transnational agri-food corporations and the consequences of, and reactions to, their actions in rural society. Her current research focuses on adoption of, and resistances to, neoliberal policies in agri-food.

**Lourdes Viladomiu** holds a PhD in economics and is Senior Lecturer in Applied Economics at the Autonomous University of Barcelona, Spain. Her primary areas of expertise are rural development, the Common Agricultural Policy, development economics and Latin American economics.

# Acknowledgments

We would like to thank Megan Boone, Debbra Vogel and Giovanni Bonanno for their assistance in the preparation of this volume.

Alessandro Bonanno and Lawrence Busch

# The international political economy of agriculture and food: An introduction
*Alessandro Bonanno and Lawrence Busch*

In his illustration of the virtues of neoliberalism and the functioning of the free market, Friedrich von Hayek (2011[1960]; 2007[1944]) denounces the perils associated with attempts to politically direct the economy. Referring to politically selected economic objectives and measures as "intelligent design," Hayek contends that they can never be replacements for the highly desirable solutions offered by the autonomous functioning of the market. Political plans of any type, he contends, need to be eliminated from the managing of the economy. Accordingly, for Hayek and likeminded neoliberals, political economy should be confined to nothing more than the free functioning of the market. This neoliberal position stands in sharp contrast to the manner in which the political economy of agri-food has been interpreted and evolved for virtually the entire modern era and, certainly, throughout the 20th Century. Keynesian, radical, socialist, social democratic, but also beginning of the century laissez-faire approaches have interpreted and managed agriculture and food in terms of the interplay of a variety of factors pertaining to the economic, social, cultural, political and geopolitical spheres. These and other factors have been considered central in the directing of agri-food development and the achievement of the specific goals assigned to this sector.

In this context, for the greatest part of the 20th Century, agriculture and the production and distribution of food around the world were highly planned activities supported and coordinated by the intervention of the nation-state. Continuing practices initiated in previous centuries, the capitalist nation-states of advanced countries directed the organization of agriculture and food not only in terms of the economic growth and social stability of the sector, but, above all, in terms of the overall balanced development of the entire society. The production of affordable food for the growing urban lower and middle classes, the controlled migration of agricultural labor to manufacturing jobs and cities and the creation of a reliable system for the production of food for the domestic market and security became the period's fundamental objectives of virtually all nations. Indeed, both democratic and authoritarian regimes understood that cheap food limited social unrest. The insistence on the use of a social planning approach found support in theory and practice. The popularity of Keynesian economic theory justified state-sponsored deficit spending as a system to stimulate demand and reignite economic growth. Simultaneously, the acceptance of Henry Ford's (1988[1926]) industrial policy of high wages was central for the development of mass consumption, employment growth, social stability and the enhancement of profit. As pointed out by Antonio Gramsci (2011[1945]) in his classical essay "Americanism and Fordism," state intervention in the economy was complemented by the promotion of cultural patterns that provided legitimacy to state planning and regulation.

The political economy of agriculture of this Fordist era featured state promoted intervention in a variety of areas, including land redistribution, infrastructure building, publicly sponsored research and development, and price control and commodity programs. The declared goal was to increase production and productivity in order to generate abundant food to feed the growing domestic and world population. This overt objective was to be achieved through the enhanced use of machines, chemicals, improved plant varieties and the application of productivist industrial plans. Latent objectives included the containment of labor reproduction cost and the establishment of pacified labor relations through the availability of affordable consumer goods. Geopolitically, food remained an important tool in the shaping of international relations. While class differences and inequality continued to be sharp and the growth of agricultural regions occurred at a lower rate than their urban counterparts, the objective of ensuring rural communities' social stability and sustainability featured centrally on the agendas of many governments. Reacting to the Fordist high level of state intervention in agriculture, the neoliberal theorist Milton Friedman (1982[1962]:181) argued that agricultural special interests controlled the US Congress and that rural districts were overrepresented in the electoral system. He saw this as distorting prices such that the free market could not work according to the model. Far from representing reality, this view concealed the significant socio-economic differences within agri-food and the struggle of small farm holders and farmworkers to keep their farms and jobs vis-à-vis a process of structural and productive concentration.

In less developed countries of the South, Fordism translated primarily into the application of modernization policies to peasant-dominated sectors. Legitimized by functionalist arguments about the necessity to apply the US model of development (Parsons 1971; Rostow 1960), state intervention in agriculture took a form that favored corporate investment and presence, the outflow of wealth and the exploitation of natural resources and labor. Simultaneously, however, modernization also involved measures that favored land redistribution, reclamation and irrigation programs, infrastructure building and schemes in support of small farm holders and peasant agriculture. Facing mounting contradictions and a legitimation crisis, many countries in the South experimented with import substitution policies whose results, however, fell short of intended outcomes and often increased economic and political dependency.

In the late 1970s, limited corporate profitability and the fiscal crisis that affected virtually all major nation-states ushered the final crisis of Fordism. Propelled by the strong political movements that led to the elections of Ronald Reagan in the United States and Margaret Thatcher in Britain, neoliberalism emerged as the new dominant ideology and political economic strategy. Finding strength in the crisis and eventual collapse of the Soviet system, the weakness of the political left and unions, arguments about the ineffectiveness and inefficiency of state intervention and claims about the neutrality and benign nature of the market, neoliberalism offered an appealing solution to global social and economic problems. Declaring the end of the historical contraposition between capitalism and socialism, Francis Fukuyama (1992) stressed that free market capitalism was the only possible way to govern the world. Lacking an alternative vision, left leaning theorists and political groups yielded to the hegemonic power of neoliberalism. Writing from a leftist position, Thomas Friedman (1999; 2005) lauded the consequences of the application of neoliberalism at the global scale by contending that it flattened historical differences and obstacles and allowed large segments of previously marginalized groups to benefit from the growth of neoliberal globalization. Relinquishing historically held objectives, parties of the left moved to centrist positions. In the United States, the Democratic Party led by President Clinton restructured and downsized the welfare system and contributed to the establishment of the so-called Washington Consensus: a convergence of interests in support of neoliberal views of political economy.

The reduction of trade barriers and nation-state regulations promoted the creation of networks of production and consumption that feature spatial decentralization, global organization and economic concentration. Supported by the dominant view of the desirability of free market solutions, a selected number of large corporations established quasi-monopolistic control of key commodity markets. Similarly, large food retailers began to control the distribution industry and exercise power over production processes as well. This shift was aided by the growth of information technology and containerization that opened up numerous new commercial options. State regulation was replaced by third party programs that privatized control, imposed production strategies and prescribed behavior to producers, hired labor and consumers worldwide. The enhanced global circulation of commodities and capital became accompanied by the establishment of stronger forms of control and exploitation of labor. The creation of precarious and poorly remunerated jobs was implemented through, and justified by, the desirability of higher levels of competitiveness and cost containment and the presumed convenience that the availability of these jobs entails for workers. These conditions led to the current control of wages and labor resistance through the creation of a large reserve army of labor established through the mobilization of previously untapped labor pools, production decentralization and massive processes of migration whereby the use of migrant labor is controlled through the criminalization of migratory processes and immigrant status. As debates on immigration often center on political conditions, humanitarian aspects and the suffering and resilience of immigrants, dominant discourses conceal the economic relevance of the presence of a docile and inexpensive labor force worldwide (Bonanno and Cavalcanti 2014).

Neoliberalism promoted processes that resulted in the economization of society, politics and the individual (Foucault 2004; Dean 2010; Rose 1996). The economization of society refers to processes whereby the organization of social relations is decentered from the state to the market. Market relations and profitability become the core conditions for desirable social arrangements. In this context, the distinction between society, regulated and governed by the actions of the state, and the economy, defined by the search for profit and the satisfaction of individual interests, is erased. Accordingly, market-based rationality becomes the entity that guides the regulation of society. In the economization of politics, political institutions employ "economic rationality" and operate in a corporate-like manner, transforming the search for profit into a social value and primary regulatory criterion. Simultaneously, corporations take up charges and regulate matters (such as ethics and morality) that once were the exclusive prerogative of the state (Ronen 2008). The displacement of the state as the political regulatory authority allows corporations to assert greater power in defining rules of regulation as control is shifted to those close to the problem (Busch 2014). The economization of the individual refers to processes whereby individual actors assume moral responsibility for all of their actions (responsibilization) (Ronen 2008). Dismissing structural constraints and power relations, individuals are seen as endowed with the ability to fully define their actions. And solutions to problems are increasingly assigned to the individual sphere (individualization). In this context, the organization and management of agri-food is increasingly placed in the hands of private corporate actors while solutions to problems and alternatives are shifted to the initiative of individual consumers.

Opposition to these dominant conditions and the creation of alternative production and consumption systems have been shaped and contained by the ideological and political power of neoliberalism. The crisis of organizations (parties and unions) that traditionally represented the working class is extended by the mobilization of the reserve army of labor and the presentation of the functioning of the market as a neutral and objective process. Simultaneously, agri-food production and distribution alternative systems (e.g., organic farming, farmer markets, civic agriculture, Slow Food and more), while otherwise successful, have been charged with reproducing elitism, failing to improve the conditions of the working class and the poor and accepting dominant values and the fundamental tenets of the very neoliberal ideology that they try to counter. More importantly, they have been criticized for offering limited resistance to the expansion of corporate agri-food as the latter has been even often able to colonize these alternative initiatives.

Salient aspects of the political economy of agriculture and food are reviewed by the authors included in this volume. They are organized into two parts. The first presents the cases of selected countries and world regions. This geographical organization of the book is complemented by a second part that analyzes selected themes. Without claiming to be exhaustive, the selection of areas and themes is designed to provide instances of relevant features and changes that characterize agri-food. The first part of the volume opens with two chapters that illustrate examples of the evolution of agri-food in Africa and Oceania. In the opening chapter, Elizabeth Ransom analyzes the evolution of agri-food in the Southern portion of Africa. This region includes Botswana, Lesotho, Namibia, South Africa and Swaziland, whose development contends with the consequences of past colonial rule and declining access to the European market. The dual system of large export oriented farms and peasant agriculture has been impacted by the establishment of the World Trade Organization (WTO) that, along with other factors, contributed to the neoliberalization of these agricultures and the limited availability of alternative policies. The economic weakness of the large number of small units overexposes these farming sectors to climate change that often translates into both droughts and floods. Additionally, gender and racial inequality produce problems that are difficult to address. The search for regional alternative policies, Ransom concludes, appears as a locally supported solution to this region's dependence on global market forces. In the following chapter, Carmen Bain and Tamera Dandachi examine the dairy sector in New Zealand. In particular, they probe the contradictory situation of dairy in a context characterized by a neoliberal approach to environmental regulation. They contend that the image of New Zealand as an environmentally clean and ecologically pristine country has legitimized lax environmental laws and a voluntarist approach to environmental regulation. This limited regulation, they continue, has been instrumental in the growth of the dairy sector and international competiveness. The contradiction between a clean and environmentally sound image and the actual limited protection of the environment, the authors conclude, remains an unresolved problem that will continue to characterize the evolution of agri-food in New Zealand.

The next set of five chapters deal with agri-food in Latin America. The first of these chapters explores the case of Mexico. Francisco Martínez and Gilberto Aboites analyze the evolution of an increasingly polarized agri-food sector that is formed by an economically strong and numerically small sector of agri-food firms and a poor and numerically large small farm/peasant sector. They contend that the Fordist period in Mexico was characterized by the expansion of domestic consumption that favored the growth of agriculture and food production. Simultaneously, state support for the small farm/peasant sector allowed the persistence of a large number of small farm holders. The introduction of neoliberal policies in the 1980s and the membership in NAFTA (North American Free Trade Agreement) in the early 1990s changed this situation, fostering a restructuring of the sector and its orientation toward the production of fruits and vegetables for export. This reorientation of the sector affected the production of commodities for domestic consumption such as corn. High priced imports replaced locally produced corn, creating significant increases in the prices of basic food items and, ultimately, dissatisfaction among the local population. The authors conclude by highlighting the current contradictory conditions of Mexican agri-food whereby integration into the global market and, particularly, enhanced commercial relations with the United States are accompanied by a delegitimation of the actions of the government.

The chapter by Clara Craviotti explores the conditions of agri-food in Argentina. One of the largest word suppliers of the food–feed–energy complex, Argentina has experienced a significant process of change following the development of globalization and the insertion of the country into the new global division of labor. Technical innovations associated with deregulation and the growth of financialization, Craviotti contends, created new systems of agri-food production. Particularly relevant is the establishment of *pools de siembra*, or networks of production management based on contractual relations that supplanted traditional forms of production based on property in land, machines and inputs. In this new form of production, limited fixed capital is employed along with the flexible use of labor and equipment. This reorganization of agriculture has reintroduced the export-based growth model that was dominant during the immediate pre-World War II decades. As this new development model remains susceptible to commodity market fluctuations, it makes Argentina particularly vulnerable to market downturns. Also relevant are the environmental consequences of the extensive production of global crops, such as soya, that increase Argentina's instability and future uncertainties.

The significantly different case of Colombia is discussed in the chapter by Anouk Patel-Campillo and María del Rosario Castro Bernardini. Employing David Harvey's concept of accumulation by dispossession, the authors illustrate the evolution of social relations in agriculture, focusing on the processes of land concentration and redistribution. Patel-Campillo narrates the growth of Colombian agriculture by dividing it into three periods. The first covers the years from the post-independence era to 1960. During this long period, efforts to distribute land to peasants and family farm holders were accompanied by processes of land consolidation in the hands of large landowners (latifundistas). This contradictory situation led to social instability that contributed to the emergence of a period of overt violent confrontations (1947–1964). The second period was characterized by the implementation of modernization and land redistribution (land reform) policies. Their failure radicalized conflict that was characterized by the emergence of armed guerrilla factions and the creation of pro-rural elite vigilante groups. While the escalation of violence delegitimized political processes, it also allowed the repression of peasants and farmers and the further concentration of land ownership by rural elites. The third and final period coincided with the liberalization of agricultural policies. Drug lords used land to recycle profit from their illegal trade and found in land ownership a vehicle for social legitimacy and political clout. Simultaneously, the insertion of Columbian agriculture into global networks weakened domestic food production and food imports increased dramatically. The strengthening of the power of the rural landed class and the further displacement of small farm holders and peasants define a complex and contradictory situation that can be hardly addressed by neoliberal measures.

The case of Brazil is analyzed by Josefa Salete Barbosa Cavalcanti and Evander Eloi Krone. The authors stress the continuity of the export oriented agricultural policy that has characterized Brazil since colonial times and the concomitant prominent role played by large landowners and the overt exploitation of labor. Recent decades have not altered the emphasis on export oriented policies that are mitigated by state promoted pro-family farm measures and investment. The current situation sees a growth of the corporate presence in agri-food not only at the level of production but also at the level of retailing. Large supermarket chains have a firm grip on agri-food production in the country, dictating the conditions of production as well as the use of labor. Vulnerability to market fluctuations remains highly relevant for the family farm and peasant sectors. While contradictory, their involvement in the production of quality products for export and membership in global networks of production are seen as fundamental conditions for growth.

The fifth of this group of chapters, by Gabriela Pechlaner and Gerardo Otero, probes the effects of NAFTA on the participating countries of Mexico, Canada and the United States. These authors contend that NAFTA is an excellent example of the types of changes that resulted from the neoliberal globalization of agri-food. Original predictions, they argue, stressed that the liberalization of markets and borders would have created the homogenization of production and diets. In reality, the authors demonstrate, NAFTA has generated a "differentiated convergence" in which the most negative consequences are disproportionally experienced by Mexico, the least economically developed of the three partner countries, and by members of the lower classes. As agricultural trade has increased among these three countries, the United States has retained its hegemonic position while import dependence has increased for Mexico with significant negative consequences for local consumers. Pechlaner and Otero further contend that there has been a "class differentiated convergence" of diets featuring an increase in the consumption of meat and fruits that does not involve the lower classes. This socio-economic divergence has negative consequences not only on social inequality but also on food security and health. While the positive view of liberalization remains dominant, the authors conclude, the negative consequences of NAFTA are increasingly evident in Mexico and among the poorer social strata.

The first part of the book concludes with three chapters that discuss the agri-food sectors of countries of the advanced North. In her chapter on Japan, Kae Sekine maintains that agri-food was shaped by the country's post-World War II rapid growth. Based on the export of selected consumer goods, Japanese developmental policy assigned a complementary yet important role to agri-food. Particularly relevant was the role played by the farm sector as a reservoir of excess labor. This surplus labor eventually migrated to urban areas and was key to the development of manufacturing and the overall success of the Japanese growth model. The post-war reorganization of agri-food was based on democratic principles that stressed the importance of family farming and collective decision making. Significant changes, Sekine illustrates, occurred in the 1980s and 1990s as Japan embraced neoliberal reforms. The family farm orientation that characterized the sector was reversed in favor of the corporatization of agri-food. Deregulation policies were implemented to promote corporate investment in the hope of a revitalization of the sector. Despite this move, Japanese agri-food, the author concludes, remains much less developed than other economic sectors, while the corporatization of agri-food generates discontent among the rural and also general population.

The evolution of the European Union's Common Agricultural Policy, or CAP, is analyzed in the chapter by Manuel Belo Moreira. Moreira divides the development of the CAP into four periods. The first covers the first 30 years since the implementation of the CAP (1962). During this time, agri-food policy was aimed at the modernization of agriculture through a productivist approach that, however, contained strong provisions for the preservation of family farms. This latter objective was pursued through an extensive system of price support and trade protection programs. This period ended in the early 1990s as the MacSharry reform reoriented the CAP away from productivist policies toward a multifunctional view of agriculture. Central in this new orientation was the objective of rural development, which was decoupled from the expansion of production and productivity. A further reorganization of the CAP characterized the third period that began in 2003. This new period saw the decoupling of support programs from production levels and the creation of a single payment scheme. In this contest, not only rural development but also a strong pro-environment posture became features of the agri-food policy of the European Union. The fourth and current period continues the move toward the neoliberalization of agri-food that has shaped the CAP over the previous three decades. However, due to the fiscal crisis of this supranational organization, Moreira contends that a move toward the renationalization of policy and its focusing on agriculture, rather than on the environmental and rural development, will increasingly characterize the CAP.

Miren Etxezarreta, Jordi Rosell and Lourdes Viladomiu probe the development of agri-food in Spain. Among the most relevant characteristics of the evolution of the agri-food sector of Spain are its integration into the global system, the modernization of its farms and significant modifications of its labor market and structure. This rapid change has generated a current situation in which the overall importance of farming has declined significantly in terms of its contribution to the economy, employment and the quantity of farmland employed. A significant portion of this land has been redirected to other and more lucrative uses as the financialization of the sector and of the economy has contributed to this outcome and the overall reorganization of agri-food. The internationalization of production, these authors maintain, has increased the role that it plays as exporter of key commodities such as fruits, olive oil and wine, but it has also exacerbated the dualism of the local farm structure. The large farm-dominated export sector, the authors conclude, will likely continue to grow. Yet, the resilience of the family farm sector and pressure from urban consumers and groups for better quality agri-food products and environmentally friendly production processes will also condition future developments.

The second part of the volume opens with the chapter by Geoffrey Lawrence and Jane Dixon that discusses the role of supermarkets. The authors stress that supermarket chains are powerful transnational corporations that not only control food retailing but also food supply. In this context, supermarkets have emerged as major regulators of the agri-food system and gatekeepers of food consumption. Their actions define food choice and quality and are legitimized by the convenience that they provide to consumers. Their attention to more rigorous food standards and regulation has been instrumental to the achievement of this hegemonic position. However, through the implementation of these standards, they have been able to affect farmers and the farming sector often to the detriment of small farm holders, farmworkers, the environment and the health of consumers. Resistance to this supermarketization has forcefully emerged, as the authors document. Yet, the creation of alternative agri-food systems decreases pressure on supermarkets to respond to alternative claims and has not been an obstacle to these organizations' continuous growth. In their concluding remarks, these authors call for greater clarity in the regulation of supermarkets and, ultimately, for ways that can counter their growing concentration and power.

Often mentioned in the previous chapters as one of the major phenomena of the neoliberal global era, the financialization of agri-food is reviewed by Madeleine Fairbairn. Financialization refers, first, to the increased importance of financial capital over manufacturing and agricultural capital in the overall generation of profit and, second, to the fact that a large and growing share of profit is made through the buying and selling of financial products. In her illustration of the growth of financialization in agri-food, Fairbairn stresses that some financial products, such as derivatives, have been long standing features of the sector. Items such as contracts that establish future prices of agricultural commodities to be sold at harvest have been popular since the 19th Century. However, the financial deregulation that occurred as part of the neoliberalization of the economy changed this situation drastically, allowing the trading of financial products independently from production trends and outcomes. In this context, agri-food commodities have been transformed into assets subjected to financial trade and speculation, products that interest a large spectrum of investors and entities that are primarily used to increase shareholder value. Financialization, this author maintains, has transformed the economy into a system that is centered on the generation of shareholder returns. Financialization, Fairbairn continues, has been extended to all components of agri-food including supermarkets and land. In the case of supermarkets, financialization decouples investment from quality of service as supermarkets are purchased and restructured primarily to increase their resale value rather than service efficiency. Simultaneously, large food retail corporations, the author documents, have become active actors in the financial sector as they now offer financial services to consumers, such as banking, credit cards, insurance programs and home mortgages, and hold more financial assets than real assets. In the case of land, while often justified in terms of production needs and food security, its purchase as a financial asset and an item to be employed in speculative moves has become one of the major global phenomena. Fairbairn concludes by stressing the growing importance of financialization in the shaping of agri-food regimes.

In the chapter entitled "The political economy of labor relations in agriculture and food," Alessandro Bonanno discusses the recent evolution of labor relations. He contends that the 20th Century Fordist era was characterized by stable and pacified labor relations regulated by the tacit, yet effective, "management-labor accord." In this context, agricultural labor represented a fundamental factor in the increase of production that generated abundant and inexpensive food for urban dwellers and a reservoir of labor for the growth of urban manufacturing. While agricultural employment remained seasonal, more unstable and less remunerated that its urban counterpart, Fordist wealth redistribution mechanisms allowed a progressive betterment of labor's living and working conditions. Neoliberal globalization changed this situation. The author discusses this change by stressing seven relevant aspects. First, there is a flexibilization of labor relations that consists of reduced wages, precarious and unstable employment, enhanced exploitation and the political weakness of agri-food workers. Second, the mobilization of a large reserve army of labor allows the enhanced control of labor's wages and claims. Through decentralization of production and global sourcing, distant labor pools are placed in direct competition with each other resulting in the creation of a docile and inexpensive labor force. Third, similar results are accomplished through the use of immigrant labor. As neoliberalization promotes the free circulation of goods and services, labor mobility remains highly controlled mostly through political mechanisms (i.e., citizenship, residency, work permits and work programs). Moreover, the criminalization of immigrant labor further allows the control of this component of the global reserve army of labor. Fourth, agri-food labor is feminized. The use of female labor is promoted not only in terms of the use of inexpensive workers but also in terms of a discourse that legitimizes labor exploitation. The presentation of flexible labor as "convenient" for women conceals the many disadvantages associated with this form of employment. Fifth, the development of third party production contracts allows firms to circumvent labor laws and regulations and further the exploitation of labor. Sixth, the crisis of labor unions weakens resistance. This crisis, it is argued, is not only the result of a deliberate corporate attack on unions but also the result of ineffective union strategies. Finally, the author contends, resistance centers on spheres that do not consider labor as a central component. While successful in some instances, overall, these efforts have not been able to halt the power of corporate agri-food and the worsening of the conditions of labor.

In the following chapter, and focusing on the case of Italy, Maria Fonte and Ivan Cucco address the theme of alternative agri-food movements. The authors highlight the characteristics of the development of agriculture in Italy since the immediate post-World War II years, stressing the changes in objectives of agri-food movements. They contend that Fordist labor-based, union-led movements were replaced by consumer centered, quality oriented organizations in the post-Fordist neoliberal globalization era. In particular, they review the objectives, discourses and actions of four movements: Campagna Amica, the organic movement, Slow Food and the Solidarity Purchasing Group movement. Campagna Amica, or CA, is an organization of the Coltivatori Diretti, a post-World War II Christian Democratic Party (CD) directed farmer organization. During the Cold War era, CD continuously ruled Italy. However, it dissolved, along with other era political parties, after the fall of the Communist bloc and the end of the Cold War. A strong supporter of modernization and productivist strategies, CA followed changes in EU policy to transform itself into a fervent advocate of quality, made-in-Italy agri-food products. This combination of quality production and protectionism has allowed CA to achieve significant economic visibility, as its products are now widely available through major supermarket chains. The organic movement, the authors contend, counted on the participation of a number of small groups that contributed to the establishment of an important, yet fragmented, movement. In the early 1990s, it reached a significant level of popularity, propelled by the introduction of pro-organic EU legislation. This recognition, the authors continue, translated into a "conventionalization" of the organic sector that was co-opted by mainstream agri-food and its products sold by corporate retailers. Slow Food is described as a complex social movement with significant clout in Italian food politics. Born out of the dissolution of Cold War politics and resistance to the expansion of corporate fast-food, Slow Food became the symbol of culturally rich and locally oriented food production and consumption. Stressing the convivial dimension of food, this movement does not necessarily oppose capitalism and corporate food, but it struggles for the recognition, persistence and growth of artisan food in all its forms and varieties. Solidarity Purchasing Groups (or GAS as per the Italian acronym) emerged as a response to the conventionalization of other alternative movements and the growth of globalization. Inspired by the international civic agriculture movement, the GAS movement grew dramatically from its first appearance in the mid-1990s. Its horizontal form of coordination contemplates the creation of direct contacts between producers and consumers, framed by a discourse that emphasizes the relevance of the local, agro-ecological sustainability, civic responsibility and solidarity. The authors conclude by stressing that the significant presence of alternative agri-food movements in Italy is partially a by-product of the niche- and local-production-based historical development of this sector and country. They further indicate that the conventionalization of these movements has significantly limited the construction of effective alternatives, but the emergence of GAS represents a likely alteration of this pattern.

In their chapter entitled "Animal welfare: The challenges of implementing a common legislation in Europe," Mara Miele, Bettina Bock and Lummina Horlings discuss the implementation of animal welfare legislation in the European Union. Paying particular attention to the implications that it has in terms of the economization of values in agri-food, they stress that EU directives that support animal welfare have been introduced to address growing concerns voiced by pro-animal welfare organizations and the general public. Through a multi-nation study that focuses on the case of the Netherlands, the chapter documents the conditions that determine differences in the implementation of EU legislation. It also stresses that the implementation of value oriented legislation is framed in a context of marketization (economization) of agri-food products whereby animal welfare is transformed into a factor that promotes the commercialization of agri-food products. Simultaneously, the case of the Netherlands is described as an example of a new form of governamentality in which "best practices" are implemented by a private–public expert group. In this context, the state remains the political regulatory authority. Yet, it is part of a neo-corporatist collaboration that includes a variety of stakeholders such as agro-business, researchers and civic organizations.

In their chapter, Leland Glenna, Barbara Brandl and Kristal Jones tackle the issue of the international political economy of research and development (R&D). They contend that throughout the 20th Century, state directed R&D was an irreplaceable component of the evolution of agri-food, the introduction of technical innovations and increases in food production and farm productivity. In recent decades, and because of the adoption of neoliberal policies, stagnant public expenditures and the concomitant increase of private investment created conditions that are viewed as threatening to the ability to produce food and the food needs of developing countries and regions. In particular, the authors show that reliance of private-sector funding in advanced countries fosters research on crops that are relevant to agri-food corporations but do not necessarily address food needs at the world level. While differences exist among major developed countries, the neoliberalization of R&D is a common trend. In emerging countries, however, public investment in R&D is growing as a result of the adopted neo-Fordist postures. Yet, even in these countries, the emphasis on commercially relevant crops generates doubts as to the adequacy of this solution. The authors conclude by stressing the importance of publicly directed R&D that could generate a more environmentally sound, just and sustainable agri-food development.

In the final chapter of this volume, Carolyn Sachs probes the very important issue of the role of women in agri-food. She documents that women provide the majority of labor in contemporary agriculture in many regions of the world. This is an important fact given the common understanding of agriculture as a "male" sector. Discussing regions of the global South, Sachs underscores the importance of the role of women in the production of export crops, as the flexibilization of female labor is one of the most decisive factors in the organization of this type of production. Precarious employment, low pay, harassment and sexual violence characterize the lives of these workers. Female labor also constitutes an important component of migrant labor that from regions of the global South is displaced to work in rich nations of the North. Its immigrant and female statuses make it the most vulnerable segment of the agri-food labor structure. In the case of family farms, Sachs continues, the difficulties that this sector encounters as corporate agriculture expands are particularly felt by women. The proportion of women that operate family farms has significantly increased in recent years along with these farms' weak economic situation. Despite these adverse conditions, Sachs concludes, women have emerged as a formidable force in global struggles for a more democratic and sustainable agri-food.

# REFERENCES

Bonanno, Alessandro and Josefa Salete Barbosa Cavalcanti (eds.). 2014. *Labor Relations in Globalized Food*. Bingley, UK: Emerald Publishing.

Busch, Lawrence. 2014. "How Neoliberal Myths Endanger Democracy and Open New Avenues for Democratic Action." Pp. 32–51 in Steven A. Wolf and Alessandro Bonanno (eds.) *The Neoliberal Regime in the Agri-food Sector: Crisis, Resilience and Restructuring*. New York: Routledge.

Dean, Mitchell M. 2010. *Governamentality: Power and Rule in Modern Society*. London: Sage.

Ford, Henry. 1988[1926]. *Today and Tomorrow*. New York: Productivity Press.

Foucault, Michel. 2004. *The Birth of Biopolitics*. New York: Picador.

Friedman, Milton. 1982[1962]. *Capitalism and Freedom*. Chicago: University of Chicago Press.

Friedman, Thomas. 1999. *The Lexus and the Olive Tree*. New York: Anchor Books.

Friedman, Thomas. 2005. *The World Is Flat: A Brief History of the Globalized World in the Twentieth-First Century*. New York: Allen Lane.

Fukuyama, Francis. 1992. *The End of History and the Last Man*. New York: The Free Press.

Gramsci, Antonio. 2011[1945]. *Prison Notebooks*. Translated by Joseph A. Buttigieg. New York: Columbia University Press.

Hayek, Fredrick A. von. 2007[1944]. *The Road to Serfdom*. Chicago: University of Chicago Press.

Hayek, Fredrick A. von. 2011[1960]. *The Constitution of Liberty*. Chicago: University of Chicago Press.

Parsons, Talcott. 1971. *The System of Modern Societies*. Englewood Cliffs, NJ: Prentice-Hall.

Ronen, Shamir. 2008. "The Age of Responsibilization: On Market-Embedded Morality." *Economy and Society* 37 (1): 1–19.

Rose, Nikolas. 1996. *Inventing Our Selves: Psychology, Power and Personhood*. Cambridge: Cambridge University Press.

Rostow, Walter W. 1960. *The Stages of Economic Growth*. Cambridge: Cambridge University Press.

# PART I

# THE INTERNATIONAL POLITICAL ECONOMY OF AGRICULTURE AND FOOD: SELECTED COUNTRIES AND REGIONS

# 1. The political economy of agriculture in Southern Africa

*Elizabeth Ransom*

## INTRODUCTION

Agriculture remains the primary source of employment and income for most of the rural populations of Southern Africa (Hachigonta et al. 2013). When focusing on the political economy of agriculture and food in the region, Europe and European legislation have played a dominant role in both the past and the present. All the countries under discussion were impacted by colonial rule, and at present there is a significant disparity between commercial and smallholder agriculture. While the disparity is one of the consequences of colonialism and South African apartheid policies in the region, this disparity is exacerbated by current European Union (EU) trade policies. With future challenges related to climate change, combined with declining EU market access and struggles to better integrate smallholders into income generating activities, the Southern African region is in need of a new map with which to navigate towards a future that ensures a vibrant agricultural sector.

### Defining the Scope

Depending upon the year and political organization one references, the Southern Africa community consists of anywhere from five to fifteen countries. For example, the Southern African Development Community (SADC) now considers fifteen countries as falling within the region. However, the United Nations (UN) defines Southern Africa as consisting of five countries: Botswana, Lesotho, Namibia, South Africa, and Swaziland (see Figure 1.1). For the purposes of this overview the following discussion will largely be limited to the UN defined countries, although with occasional references to other SADC countries.

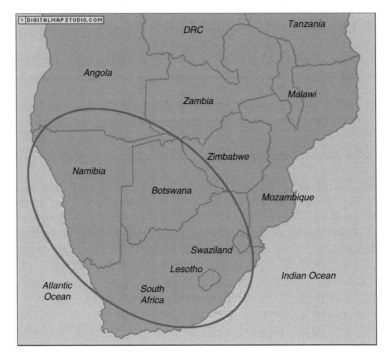

*Source:*   http://www.CustomDigitalMaps.com/.

*Figure 1.1    Map of Southern African countries*

## AGRICULTURE IN SOUTHERN AFRICA IN THE PAST AND THE PRESENT: COMMON LINKAGES

Geography and climate play critical roles in shaping the agricultural land-scape of the region. The average rainfall in Southern Africa is low, with the least amount of rainfall occurring in the west (Namibia) and increasing incrementally as one moves east (the eastern coast of South Africa and portions of Swaziland and Lesotho receive the most). However, rainfall is episodic and vast regions of Southern Africa experience regular droughts (Hachigonta et al. 2013).

Rainfall is important because of the prevalence of rain-fed crops and the role that livestock, particularly cattle, play in the region's agricultural system. For the vast majority of Africa, irrigation does not play a sig-nificant role in agriculture. A 2010 International Food Policy Research Institute (IFPRI) report notes that "irrigated area as a share of total cultivated area is estimated at only 6 percent for Africa, compared with 37 percent for Asia and 14 percent for Latin America" (You et al. 2010: 1). Within Africa, the bulk of irrigation is actually located in Northern Africa, whereas the only country in Southern Africa with approximately 1 million hectares irrigated is South Africa, and this represents less than 10 percent of agricultural lands within the country (You et al. 2010). In sum, Southern African producers are highly dependent on rainfall for growing crops. This dependency, when combined with weather patterns that are expected to become more erratic due to climate change and increasing water needs for other economic sectors, will significantly impact agricultural productivity in the future.

Rainfall also impacts the amount of grasses available for grazing cattle. Historically, cattle populations have increased or declined based on the amount of rainfall. For example, in Botswana the peak cattle population, due to the availability of grass, has hovered around 3 million (in 1979 and 2002), with dramatic declines in cattle populations during periods of drought (BIDPA 2006). Rainfall also affects the ability for farmers to rear cattle using more intensive methods of production (feedlots as opposed to pasture) due to limited availability of water for cattle and for growing the crops used for cattle feed. Water constraints, in combination with cultural traditions, have limited the number of producers in Southern Africa that have adopted the industrial model of cattle farming.

In the past, and into the present, cattle have played a critical role in Southern African agriculture. Scholars of Southern Africa history have long been interested in exactly when domesticated livestock began to appear in Southern Africa, because their appearance would signify a shift from hunter-gathering societies to food producing societies. Cattle are thought to have appeared in Southern Africa approximately 2,000 years ago (Sadr 2013). Sadr (2013: 171) summarizes that many, including the popular author Jarrod Diamond (1998), view this shift to food production as a "first step towards the rise of economically, socially, and politically more complex societies, and ultimately of civilization." However, Sadr counters that the archeological evidence is far from conclusive about such grand results. He argues that the introduction of domesticated cattle approximately 2,000 years ago does not correlate with significant changes in other domains of material culture (Sadr 2013: 179). Regardless of when hunters transitioned to pastoralists, the historical record does reveal that cattle were crucial for obtaining wives among the Early Iron Age Bantu-speaking farmers and herders (Sadr 2013). The multi-dimensional importance of cattle continues to this day for many indigenous ethnic groups in Southern Africa.

Cattle as "a bank on hooves" is a phrase often used to describe the use of cattle by indigenous populations in Southern Africa. This phrase refers to the fact that many smallholders view cattle as their investment, which can be turned into cash as needed, in addition to providing fresh milk for home consumption (see Schwalbach, Groenewald, and Marfo 2001; Ferguson 1990). There is also the view that cattle ownership lends status or prestige (i.e., the more cattle one owns the higher one's status) and, as previously mentioned, is important for *lobola* (the negotiated number of cattle a groom's family gives to the bride's family). The degree to which various indigenous smallholders subscribe to the use of cattle as prestige, and for the purposes of *lobola*, varies by ethnic group, geographical location (e.g., urban versus rural), and, based on the author's own observations, socio-economic status among people within the same community (e.g., those with higher socio-economic status having the ability to purchase cattle; also see, Schwalbach et al. 2001). However, the practice of keeping cattle for cash-related reasons generally persists among most of the indigenous ethnic groups in Southern Africa. A consequence of this is that while there are large commercial cattle operations in South Africa, and to a lesser extent Namibia and Botswana, the vast majority of cattle in Southern Africa are located in smallholder, subsistence agricultural systems.

Despite the rather long history of cattle ownership and the social, cultural, and economic significance associated with cattle, the rise of colonialism in Southern Africa marked a period of removal of indigenous people and their cattle from their lands. Indigenous Southern Africans were confined to a limited amount of land, also known as reserves, beginning in the colonial period, which contributed to overcrowding. Depending upon the government in power and the time period, little to no government support for developing infrastructure or facilitating appropriate land management occurred in the reserves,[1] which when combined with overcrowded conditions further contributed to highly degraded soils.

As the region under discussion is diverse and involves different colonial and post-colonial histories, it is beneficial to briefly review each country's agrifood sector. Common concerns across the five countries are then examined. Finally, the challenges for the future are discussed in the conclusion.

## INDIVIDUAL COUNTRY AGRICULTURAL OVERVIEWS

### South Africa

Due to the sheer size of the economy, South Africa plays a dominant role on the continent and in shaping the agricultural economies of the other countries in Southern Africa. South Africa is a major producer of sugar, maize, dairy, chicken, grapes, apples, and beef among many other commodities. South Africa is the only country in this region that is currently capable of producing all its own basic foodstuffs (Agritrade 2011). The country also has a large food processing sector and a number of well-developed export markets, with agriculture accounting for 4.5 percent of GDP and the food processing sector accounting for an additional 10 percent of GDP (Agritrade 2011). The size of both South Africa's economy and their population relative to the other nations means that regional agricultural production and policy debates "take place in the shadow" of South African dominance (Agritrade 2011: 1). South Africa's population represents 35 percent of the entire SADC region and 73 percent of GDP for the region (Hachigonta et al. 2013). In addition, there are many historical linkages between South Africa and the larger region, in particular in policies that encourage economic interdependency and a demand for migrant laborers, especially for mining (Botha 2013; O'Laughlin et al. 2013). Thus, all four of the other countries under consideration in this discussion are dependent on South Africa as an export market for specific commodities (in the case of Lesotho, a primary export to South Africa is water) and for imports of basic foodstuffs. Despite the seemingly "successful" agricultural sector of South Africa, the sector has been critiqued for the degree to which it has imitated the United States and Canada in terms of its resource intensiveness and environmental degradation (Mather 1996). In addition, South Africa and Namibia share a postcolonial agricultural history which contributes to both countries having dual economies within the sector (see Lipton and Simkins 1993).

South Africa and Namibia each have a well-developed, predominantly white commercial agricultural sector alongside an indigenous smallholder, subsistence agriculture sector. The dual economies found within the agricultural sector are directly linked to past colonial and apartheid policies, which among other things included removal of indigenous people from much of the better agricultural lands and policies that "encouraged" indigenous populations to seek work in formal, white-controlled, labor markets. At present, reducing the dual economies to a minimum requires land reform, as most smallholders suffer from insecure land tenure and/ or access to land that is inadequate in size or soil quality to allow them a competitive advantage.

In the case of South Africa, land reform has largely been unsuccessful. The lack of success is beyond the scope of this discussion, but it is important to note that in general, along with the significant social and political changes that South Africans have experienced in the past two decades, farmers were significantly impacted by economic liberalization policies. State support to farmers was dismantled and import tariffs reduced in the 1990s, which left many farmers unable to compete with farmers from developed countries in specific commodity markets, like those for milk and wheat, but increased opportunities for some farmers in other sectors, particularly high-value export markets, like citrus and game meat (Goldblatt 2004). The social, cultural, and economic changes have contributed to a significant decline in the number of farmers (31 percent decrease, or 40,000 fewer farmers from 1993 to 2008) and farmworkers in South Africa (1.6 million in 1971 to approximately 800,000 in 2007) and an increase in concentration within the commercial agricultural sector (Goldblatt 2004; O'Laughlin et al. 2013). Ultimately, larger, commercial South African agricultural production may feed much of Southern Africa, but it does so using industrial agricultural techniques that are resource intensive (especially in terms of water) and without employing large tracts of rural labor and, therefore, without providing an income source for the large number of rural inhabitants in the region (O'Laughlin et al. 2013).

**Namibia**

The dual agricultural economy in Namibia is directly linked to the decimation of the indigenous populations under German rule and the imposition of South Africa's governance, particularly apartheid policies. The indigenous people of what is now known as Namibia, were first brutally colonized by the Germans (1885–1915), and then controlled by South Africa for more than 70 years, finally achieving independence in 1990. Botha (2013) recounts that from the 1920s to the 1950s the South African government was especially preoccupied with resettling whites onto lands, which expanded upon resettlement practices that Germans had begun prior to 1915. After the end of German rule, Botha claims that indigenous Africans briefly hoped for the opportunity to become pastoralists again, by restoring their herds and reclaiming access to land. However, South Africa viewed indigenous African men as a ready labor supply for the mines, thus local Africans' hopes were short lived (*Ibid.*: 236). In addition, after 1950 South Africa began to counter previous German initiatives of mixed-farming operations and equitable water supplies (with the goal of food self-sufficiency) and instead moved to the narrow pursuit of "karakul or meat monocultures – heavily capitalised industrial ranches" among white, commercial producers (Botha 2013: 234 citing Lau and Reiner 1993: 58). Despite Namibia gaining independence in 1990, Botha (2013: 249) observes that most indigenous communal farmers "continue to be hamstrung by limited stock numbers, lack of quality grazing land, inadequate support services and recurrent drought."

As of 2010 Namibian agriculture represented 7.4 percent of the overall GDP, which includes fishing and hunting (AfDB 2012). Cattle remain one of the most important sub-sectors within agriculture, but other significant exports include fish, karakul sheep pelts, and live sheep to South Africa (although the government regulates live sheep sales). Despite a few well-developed commercial agricultural sub-sectors, the majority of population in Namibia is rural and relies upon subsistence agriculture. The dual agricultural economy reflects, at least in part, the fact that Namibia, despite being considered an upper middle-income country, is among the most inequitable societies in the world in terms of income distribution (World Bank 2014). In fact, along with Namibia, South Africa and Botswana rank among the highest countries for average levels of development on the African continent, but all three also have some of the highest rates of inequality (McKeever 2008).[2] Thus, the Namibian government is interested in trying to expand formal labor market opportunities in all sub-sectors of the economy. In the case of agriculture, the government has focused on the fishing industry (e.g., improved resource management) and redistribution of lands for the purposes of resettling smallholders.

## Botswana

Botswana, Lesotho, and Swaziland, in contrast to South Africa and Namibia, can all be characterized as having primarily smallholder agriculture, and they all share the unique status of having been considered British protectorates up until they gained independence from the British in the 1960s (thereby evading formal rule by South Africa and the imposition of apartheid policies). However, similar to Namibia, a large percentage of young indigenous men in all three countries have migrated out of rural areas to find work in mining. Many of those mines are located in South Africa, although mines exist throughout the region. Thus, rural areas often became repositories of women, children, and the elderly, who lacked steady incomes. Ferguson (1990), in his detailed study of Lesotho, also argues that the cattle economy stayed strong in many of these rural spaces because men working in the mines could buy cattle with their mine wages and keep the cattle in their home spaces as a mechanism for securing their money (ensuring it would not be spent while they were away) and as a way of maintaining connections to their homes.

Botswana's agricultural sector as a portion of GDP is quite small (2.94 percent in 2012), but agriculture, particularly livestock farming, remains an important activity for the purposes of diversifying the economy (the bulk of Botswana's GDP comes from mining). The agricultural sector is also a source of jobs and food security in rural areas, and livestock ownership is culturally highly valued. The dominant Tswana group (comprising 79 percent of the population) is one of the ethnic groups in Southern Africa that value cattle for social, cultural, and economic reasons.

Due to climate, Botswana is very limited in terms of the amount of land that is suitable for crop production. At present crop production is limited to 1 percent of a possible 5 percent of land suitable for cultivation (Zhou et al. 2013). This means that the vast majority of commodities (e.g., maize, wheat, sorghum) are imported primarily from South Africa. Cattle production is the only significant agricultural export commodity for the country (Zhou et al. 2013: 52). In recent years the amount of beef exported to Europe has steadily declined, and since 2010 it has experienced periods of interruption due to European concerns over disease control and lax enforcement of traceability requirements (Ransom 2011). Botswana is unique in that the vast majority of cattle are reared on communal lands (85 percent), and cattle reared in both communal and commercial production are exported (whereas in most Southern African countries only cattle reared on commercial farms qualify for export). This unique aspect of the industry has to do with longstanding government support for communal production and an elaborate system of fences and traceability technology put in place (with government funding) to meet the export criteria set by European governments.

**Lesotho**

Agriculture accounts for about 10 percent of Lesotho's GDP and is the main source of employment in rural areas (Gwimbi et al. 2013). The majority of the country lives in rural areas (82 percent), and 58 percent of the population engaged in agriculture are female (World Bank 2013). The majority of the population remains dependent on subsistence agriculture, and there has been an uptick in droughts, which has increased food insecurity. It is estimated that Lesotho grows approximately 30 percent of its own food (Gwimbi et al. 2013). The amount produced has declined over the past several years, which is attributed to increasing number of people settling on arable land near cities, erratic weather patterns, soil degradation, and declining productivity (e.g., due to lack of fertilizer) (Frenken 2005; Gwimbi et al. 2013). Part of the declining productivity has to do with declining remittances from mine workers. Historically, people living in rural areas have relied on remittances from men working in South African mines to purchase inputs for farming (World Bank 2013). However, in the past few decades remittances have declined due to a decline in mine employment.

Cultivable land is limited to approximately 11 percent of the total area of the country, of which the most common crops are maize (60 percent), sorghum (10–20 percent), wheat (10 percent) and beans (6 percent) (Frenken 2005). Despite the popularity of growing maize, Lesotho must import an estimated 65 percent of the population's maize requirement and 80 percent of the population's annual wheat requirements (Frenken 2005). Livestock, particularly cattle, sheep, and goats, are prevalent, although they primarily exist as part of subsistence agriculture, and cattle are considered a major contributor to land degradation in the country (Gwimbi et al. 2013).

Water is considered Lesotho's most important natural resource, but the amount of rain received is erratic and scientists predict that water resources will be increasingly scarce with climate change. Irrigation projects in Lesotho have long been a priority, but most projects over the past 40 years have not been successful. The lack of success has been attributed to a "top-down and supply-driven approach on the part of government and donors and little consultation with, or participation by, farmers" (Frenken 2005: 303). Supposedly, the government is now pursuing irrigation projects that are "farmer- and market-led" and "based on small-scale schemes provided for and managed by the farmers themselves" (Frenken 2005: 308).

## Swaziland

Agriculture accounts for approximately 8.4 percent of Swaziland's GDP (Thwala 2011), with 70 percent of the labor force engaged in agriculture. Unofficial unemployment is estimated at approximately 40 percent, and it is even higher in rural areas (Manyatsi et al. 2013). Similar to Lesotho, some of the rising unemployment is due to retrenchment in South African labor mines.

Swaziland's agricultural sector is bifurcated into a commercial, largely export sector focused on sugarcane, citrus, and forestry and a large subsistence sector marked by declining productivity. As such the country imports approximately 60 percent of all its food requirements, with almost all the imports coming from South Africa (Manyatsi et al. 2013). Sugarcane is the main export crop (95 percent of all sugarcane produced is exported). Moreover, 85 percent of irrigated lands are dedicated to sugarcane (Manyatsi et al. 2013). The African Growth and Opportunity Act (AGOA)[3] has been important for bolstering Swaziland's apparel industry and cotton production, which supplies the apparel industry. However, cotton production declined significantly during the drought from 2002 to 2007, and currently not enough cotton is grown to support the apparel sector – so cotton is imported (Manyatsi et al. 2013).

Within subsistence agriculture, livestock is an important sub-sector. Similar to Lesotho, Botswana, and portions of Namibia and South Africa, cattle as a sub-sector is often associated with high stocking density, overgrazing, and soil erosion (Thwala 2011). Unlike cattle, poultry are viewed as primarily a women's domain and they are viewed as providing a much needed source of food.[4] According to a report by Thwala (2011), Swaziland does not import any broiler meat and eggs as the local production meets demand.

## ISSUES FOR FURTHER CONSIDERATION: MARKET ACCESS, SMALLHOLDERS, LAND TENURE, AND GENDER

### Market Access: Economic Partnership Agreement Negotiations and the EU Market

Since the advent of the World Trade Organization (WTO) in 1995, Africa has increasingly lost market share in Europe for their agrifood products (Daviron 2008). Gibbon and Ponte (2005) argue that with the advent of the WTO, developing countries lost some of their autonomy in trade negotiations. Whereas previously developing countries were able to ask for concessions in recognition of the qualitatively different challenges they faced, current trade agreements do not allow for a recognition of qualitative differences between countries. Instead there is an assumption that developing countries are simply at a "lower" stage of development and need more time to implement the new requirements.

Part of the impact of the WTO on Southern Africa has been long-term loss of preferential market access for specific goods (e.g., beef, sugar) that was assured under the Lomé Convention, which was negotiated in 1975 between the European Community and 46 African, Caribbean, and Pacific countries (Hurt 2012). Preferential access was deemed as not in compliance with the WTO's "no special and differential treatment" stipulation[5] and the EU has moved to negotiating free trade agreements, or what are called Economic Partnership Agreements (EPAs). Initially the EU pursued regional EPA negotiations, but overtime more negotiations have been occurring between individual countries. This approach has been problematic for Southern Africa countries, in part because the EU is attempting to negotiate for what are considered "behind the border" issues, like "transparency in government procurement, national treatment for foreign investors, and trade facilitation measures" (Hurt 2012: 502)[6] – all items that developing countries resisted at the WTO Doha Rounds.

In addition, Hurt (2012: 496) argues that the EPA negotiations in Southern Africa are a means for the EU to "lock in" the neoliberal development model and thus advance the EU's hegemonic position within the region. This is taking place by limiting the policy options available to developing countries' governments for pursuing their own development. Finally, the EPA negotiations are said to be potentially undermining the political legitimacy of several Southern African political and economic organizations, including SADC and the Southern Africa Customs Union (SACU). This is because many of the EPA negotiations between individual African countries and the EU are contradictory to existing SADC and SACU agreements, thereby challenging the continuing legitimacy of these organizations (Hurt 2012). Many leaders in the Southern African region believe a regional approach is needed to tackle complex social and economic problems that are beyond the abilities of any one nation-state (e.g., increasing food security, reducing unemployment through the promotion of wildlife tourism, tackling HIV/AIDS) (McKeever 2008). It is within this framework that the potentially negative consequences of EU EPA negotiations which directly contradict regional institutional agreements must be understood.

Increasingly, some "behind the borders" issues built into the EPAs that shape agricultural production in Southern Africa focus on technical specifications, for example related to animal welfare and traceability policies. The increasing focus on technical specifications has contributed to mounting pressure on smallholder agriculture. The pressure on smallholders occurs because many technical specifications favor systems of production already in place among larger, commercial producers, and/or due to economies of scale, smallholder agriculturalists cannot afford to implement new specifications as dictated by the EU (see Ransom 2011). In combination with economic policies that have pushed for market deregulation in the region, smallholders exist in a production environment that is extremely competitive, and those wishing to expand generally exist in a hostile environment (Lahiff and Cousins 2005: 127).[7]

**Smallholders**

In all five countries under examination here, there is a preponderance of smallholder agriculture. The percentage of the population that can be identified as smallholders varies widely between countries, with an estimated 61 percent of producers being smallholders within the broader SADC community (SADC 2008). Despite significant efforts on the part of governments and technical experts (e.g., economists, agricultural scientists) to reduce smallholder agriculture and encourage more market integration, smallholders remain important throughout the region in that they provide household food security and rural employment, and more generally provide buffers against periods of economic downturns (Bayer, von Lossau, and Feldmann 2003). Many studies have focused on small-holder agriculture in Africa (Collier and Dercon 2014; Jayne, Mather, and Mghenyi 2010), though not all have focused on the countries in this analysis. Nonetheless, the themes and issues that emerge inform debates and policies for this region.

First, despite the label, smallholders represent a diverse group, with some evidence of growing disparities between smallholders in terms of land and asset holdings (see Jayne et al. 2010). In the case of Botswana, it appears that cattle ownership is increasingly concentrated among a small number of communal farmers (Ransom 2011).[8] Second, the productivity levels of smallholders are highly variable. In all five countries under consideration, smallholders are usually dependent on other forms of income (e.g., remit-tances, state welfare). Thus, if these forms of income decline, there is gener-ally a decline in the inputs smallholders are able to purchase (e.g., fertilizer), which can impact productivity. All smallholders throughout the region are also highly vulnerable to climatic shocks, particularly drought. In the case of livestock ownership, this usually means many cattle are sold off at lower prices during periods of drought. Finally, smallholders are increasingly vulnerable to what Jayne et al. (2010) refer to as governance issues. This includes declining donor support for smallholders, as well as economic trade agreements that disadvantage smallholders, and land tenure policies. In conclusion, Jayne et al. (2010: 1394) argue, "most small farms in Africa are becoming increasingly unviable as sustainable economic and social units. Unless government policy is changed radically, the world may see increas-ingly frequent and severe economic and social crises in Sub-Saharan Africa."

**Land Tenure and Reform**

As previously noted, land tenure issues tend to go hand-in-hand with smallholder agriculture. South Africa and Namibia are both countries formally grappling with the issue of land redistribution. In South Africa, as of 2000, Black South Africans comprised 75 percent of the population, but were limited to 13 percent of the land, which comprised the former homelands. As of 2004, land reform in South Africa had managed to only transfer an additional 2.9 percent of total agricultural land outside of the former homelands (Lahiff and Cousins 2005). Similarly, in Namibia land reform has been slow and heavily criticized. For example, in 2013 the Namibian government announced that 345 farms have been acquired since 1991 for a grand total of 2.4 million hectares, and 5,000 families have

*Table 1.1    Land distribution in Southern Africa as a percentage of total land*

|  | Individual tenure | Communal lands | Other public lands |
|---|---|---|---|
| Botswana | 5 | 70 | 25 |
| Lesotho | 5 | 90 | 5 |
| Namibia | 44 | 41 | 15 |
| South Africa | 72 | 14 | 14 |
| Swaziland | 40 | 60 | 0 |

*Source:*    Adapted from Garcia (2004).

been resettled on these farms (Immanuel 2013). While the government viewed these efforts as a sign of progress, many question the likelihood of agricultural success in the context of increasingly competitive and concentrated global agricultural markets. The questionable likelihood of success is due to the small farm size relative to the harsh environment that these families are being settled upon. The dry environment means that the number of animals that can be supported on approximately 450 hectares is low. In addition, the amount of technological support and agricultural extension many of these newly resettled farmers will need to farm success-fully is viewed as largely lacking.

Botswana, Lesotho, and Swaziland have to contend with issues of land reform, but for significantly different reasons. These three countries have an abundance of smallholders situated on communal lands, as opposed to land owned privately. Table 1.1 provides a comparison of communally owned lands in contrast to privately owned lands. All five of the countries in this analysis have debated the role of communal lands, but Botswana, Lesotho, and Swaziland's governments have received significantly more pressure (by outside donor agencies and development experts) to consider privatizing communal lands. For example, there is growing pressure from outside experts for Swaziland to implement land reform. Population pres-sures, increasing water scarcity, and rising poverty rates are all contribut-ing to academics and donor institutions, like the International Monetary Fund (IMF), recommending privatization so that smallholders have incentives for improving the land (e.g., installing irrigation systems) (see IRIN 2013). Generally, there are many reasons for encouraging privatiza-tion of communal lands across the region, but the most common reasons include arguments for increasing the productivity of agriculture and the belief that communal lands suffer from higher rates of land degradation relative to privately held lands.

Land reform and redistribution is a complex topic, which demands contextual specificity within Southern Africa. Nonetheless, a few over-arching points can be made. First, reform of communal lands needs to pay special attention to the legal status and economic activities of women and the poor, as they are the ones who disproportionally depend upon the commons (Adams 2003; Wily 2011). Moreover, in this era of global land grabs and corporate consolidation of agriculture, Wily (2011) argues that the weak legal status of communal rights allows national governments to take undue liberties with their citizens' lands, which is another reason that government land reform activities demand scrutiny.

Finally, low agricultural productivity and environmental concerns are very real for many in Southern Africa, but land reform has often been used as a means to try and insert pastoralists into formal legal systems of land tenure. Specifically, support for land reform often rests on an assumption that pastoralists do not fit within the dominant economic, legal, and sci-entific paradigms of global agriculture. Building on the work of Douglas North (1990), Galaty (2013: 477) observes that communal "systems of tenure are undergoing formalization, with various parties gaining legal rights to land long held by pastoral societies, whether the state, local elites, foreign companies, conservation entities or communities themselves." Many economists, public policy officials, and scholars believe formaliza-tion of land tenure arrangements is a prerequisite for increasing economic efficiency (Galaty 2013), though this belief is not fully supported by the existing data. For example, Feeny et al. (1990) argue that evidence gath-ered over a 22 year period (1968–1990) reveals that private, state, or com-munal property are all potentially viable resource management options. Rather, a more complete theory of land tenure should incorporate institu-tional arrangements and cultural factors to provide for better analysis and prediction of effective resource management. Despite the counterevidence, the dominant belief of economic efficiency being gained through privatiza-tion means that land tenure reform that targets communal lands should simultaneously be viewed as a political and economic project within the current globalizing agrifood system.

Of course, land reform in South Africa and Namibia rightly has a substantial amount of political currency among the vast majority of the population due to the persistence of extremely inequitable landholdings. However, land reform alone will not solve some of the bigger issues facing Southern Africa. Tackling increasing inequality, especially in Botswana, Namibia, and South Africa, and the problem of rural and urban poverty throughout the region will require a much more integrated approach than simply focusing on land reform and land tenure (O'Laughlin et al. 2013). Nor should it be assumed that improved land tenure equates with increased agricultural production, as Ferguson (2013) argues rural people use lands in a variety of ways only one of which is for agricultural production.

**Gender**

Women form a substantial percentage of smallholders in Southern Africa. They tend to face constraints similar to the larger smallholder population in terms of maintaining food security and incomes (FAO 2013). Constraints include lack of: secure land tenure, access to adequate financing, extension services, production inputs (e.g., genetic diversity, fertilizer), and up-to-date technology and training (see Ransom and Bain 2011). However, women tend to experience these constraints more deeply and "as a result it is far more difficult for rural women than for rural men to reach their full potential as farmers and livestock keepers" (FAO 2013: 9). In addition, poverty continues to be concentrated within rural areas, with the poorest and most vulnerable disproportionally being "young, female and black" (O'Laughlin et al. 2013: 2).

Small ruminants (goats and sheep) are an important source of livelihoods for smallholders throughout the developing world (FAO 2013), and women tend to be the people charged with managing them. The Food and Agriculture Organization of the United Nations (FAO) estimates that in Africa as a whole, goats represent about 30 percent of the ruminant livestock and contribute about 17 percent of the continent's meat and 12 percent of the continent's milk (*Ibid.*). Among the countries in this analysis, sheep and/or goat meat rank in the top ten agricultural commodities produced by value for all five countries (FAOSTAT 2012). However, similar to the slaughter of cattle, men tend to oversee the slaughter and sale of small ruminants, thereby reducing some of the potential earnings of women. In general, there continues to be a need to focus on gender inequality within agriculture in Southern Africa.

## ALTERNATIVE PATHS FORWARD

Noticeably absent from this discussion is HIV/AIDS, especially since the countries in this discussion have among the highest infection rates in Southern Africa and the world. For example, Swaziland is considered to have the highest prevalence rate, 26 percent of the population, while South Africa is considered to have the most HIV infected people in the world, with 5.6 million people infected, which is 17.3 percent of the population (UNICEF 2009). While earlier studies argued that the loss of an adult would be devastating to smallholder production, more recent studies suggests HIV/AIDS has not impacted smallholders as much as previously predicted (Jayne et al. 2010; McKeever 2008). Deaths of adults are occurring, but households for the most part appear to be able to offset the loss of the family member (see Jayne et al. 2010; McKeever 2008 for references to recent research). Jayne et al. (2010: 1392) suggest that a better approach might be to acknowledge that many African countries are "facing a serious development crisis, driven by various trends – of which HIV/AIDS is but one – which together are making smallholder livelihoods and welfare more and more tenuous, particularly for the large percentage of smallholders with highly constrained access to land and education."

Sustainability of the agrifood system of Southern Africa will become increasingly urgent due to climate change. However, adopting sustainable approaches to agrifood production is not a foregone conclusion. For many in Southern Africa, including producers, processors, and government officials, the current economic system encourages the pursuit of industrial production methods, which tend to be resource, particularly water, intensive. It cannot simply be assumed that sustainable approaches to food production will be adopted.

At present, the commercial producers in Botswana, Namibia, Swaziland, and especially South Africa all utilize industrialized, resource intensive agricultural models of production. Changing these models of production will prove difficult. The combination of a food insecure region and a neoliberal global trade environment that increases uncertainty for producers can stall policy makers and producers' willingness to experiment with more sustainable approaches (Mather 1996). Moreover, the ongoing negotiations between the EU and individual Southern African countries, do not privilege more sustainable production techniques. Rather, many of the "behind the border" issues being negotiated either maintain the status quo, or further instantiate more industrial modes of production, with little attention to long-term environmental suitability or the impact on smallholders.

Furthermore, it should not be assumed that commercial or smallholder producers are aware of or thinking strategically about the impact of climate change on agriculture in Southern Africa. At present, there is a lack of data about producers' attitudes towards and knowledge about climate change in Southern Africa. Antidotal evidence from the author's own research suggests that there are a range of attitudes among commercial livestock producers in Botswana, Namibia, and South Africa. While some are aware of likely changes, at least a few do not believe in climate change, and few of the commercial livestock producers interviewed in these three countries appear to have a strategy for dealing with drier and more sporadic weather patterns in the future. This lack of knowledge or adaption strategies suggests the need for more institutional engagement, particularly among the government ministries of agriculture and private sector or non-governmental trade associations.

There are clearly also opportunities for working with smallholders to pursue more sustainable production techniques. As smallholders continue to be a sizeable portion of the population in all five countries, this would *not* be an insignificant accomplishment. However, successful engagement with smallholders will require an increased recognition of the heterogeneity of smallholders in the region. Specifically, recognizing smallholders better positioned to adopt capital intensive projects or consider adopting more collaborative approaches, such as hybrid models where smallholders work with larger farmers and vertically integrated enterprises (Collier and Dercon 2014; Mather 1996; Jayne et al. 2010). Such efforts will require not only a renewed investment in resources, but also increases in knowledge co-construction (e.g., Newsham and Thomas 2011), where techniques for sustainable production are informed by the actual practices of smallholders. The institutional support for such measures will likely need to come from collaborative arrangements between national governments, non-governmental organizations, international donors, and smallholders.

Finally, there are opportunities for increasing urban and peri-urban agriculture. One study conducted in Namibia found that with the increasing migration of rural people to major cities in search of work there has been a significant increase in gardening (Dima, Ogunmokun, and Nantanga 2002). Rural to urban migration will continue to occur in the coming decades. Facilitating the growth of urban gardens could be one mechanism for decreasing food insecurity in urban spaces. Some of the challenges that would need to be dealt with in order to promote urban and peri-urban gardening include limited access to water; a lack of regulatory oversight, such as access to land and reporting of problems such as theft; and a lack of extension service personnel in urban spaces. Extension personnel could assist in improving urban gardens through increased knowledge related to types of plants grown and improved growing techniques.

In sum, there are many challenges facing Southern African agriculture. Climate change, international trade agreements, particularly with the EU, and a large percentage of subsistence smallholders are some of the principal issues shaping agricultural development at present. Pursuing solutions that are sensitive to the needs and cultures of smallholders, including women, who largely rely on communal lands, will take ingenuity and perseverance. However, without a sustained effort to engage with the issues reviewed here, the rural populations of Southern Africa will increasingly be vulnerable to political, economic, and climatic shocks to the agricultural system, and these shocks will likely have unique spillover effects for the Southern African region (e.g., increased rural to urban migration, added pressure on the existing welfare safety nets, growing environmental degradation).

## NOTES

1.  Botha (2013: 247) claims Rhodesia (present day Zimbabwe) and South Africa both had interventionist strategies in homelands, the lands upon which indigenous communities were confined, before 1960.
2.  The reasons for the high rates of inequality across the three countries are diverse, but McKeever (2008) argues that one common reason is the reliance of each country on mineral wealth. He argues that while mineral wealth increases the overall size of an economy, "only a few people reap the benefits of these industries, as most workers in most of these countries work in agriculture" (McKeever 2008: 460).
3.  The AGOA was signed into law on May 18, 2000 by the US government, and initially 34 Sub-Saharan African countries were identified as eligible for the trade benefits from AGOA. Swaziland's AGOA status was revoked by the Obama administration in June 2014 due to concerns over governance in Swaziland. Swaziland officials are currently appealing to the Obama administration to reconsider the revocation, scheduled to go into effect in January 2015 (AGOA.info 2014).
4.  This was also the case for women in the United States prior to the industrialization of the poultry industry prior to World War II (Neth 1994; Sachs 1996).
5.  See WTO, http://www.wto.org/english/tratop_e/devel_e/dev_special_differential_provi sions_e.htm.
6.  Botswana, Lesotho, and Swaziland signed an interim EPA on June 4, 2009, while Namibia initiated negotiations, but has not signed; South Africa does not qualify for an EPA and it has its own trade agreement with the EU (see Hurt 2012).
7.  This is particularly true in South Africa, where extensive deregulation of the agriculture sector has occurred and current policies tend to favor more capital intensive operations.
8.  As the next section explains, communal farmers are usually considered smallholders.

## REFERENCES

Adams, Martin. 2003. "Land Tenure Policy and Practice in Botswana: Governance Lessons for Southern Africa." *Austrian Journal of Development Studies* XIX (1): 55–74. Retrieved November 2, 2003 (http://www.mokoro.co.uk/files/13/file/lria/land_tenure_policy_and_ practice_botswana.pdf).

AfDB (African Development Bank). 2012. "Namibia." African Economic Outlook 2012. Retrieved October 10, 2013 (http://www.afdb.org/fileadmin/uploads/afdb/Documents/ Publications/Namibia%20Full%20PDF%20Country%20Note.pdf).

AGOA.info. 2014. "AGOA.info: African Growth and Opportunity Act." Retrieved June 25, 2014 (http://agoa.info/).

Agritrade. 2011. "SADC: Agricultural Trade Policy Debates and Developments." Technical Centre for Agricultural and Rural Cooperation (ACP-EU). Retrieved December 6, 2013 (http://agritrade.cta.int/en/layout/set/print/Agriculture/Topics/EPAs/ SADC-Agricultural-trade-policy-debates-and-developments).

Bayer, W.A., A. von Lossau, and A. Feldmann. 2003. "Smallholders and Community-Based Management of Farm Animal Genetic Resources." Pp. 1–12 in *Proceedings of* the *Workshop on Community-Based Management of Animal Genetic Resources: A Tool for Rural Development and Food Security*. Mbabane, Swaziland, May 7–11, 2001. Rome: FAO.

BIDPA (Botswana Institute for Development Policy Analysis). 2006. "Consultancy on the Viability and Long Term Development Strategy for the Livestock (Beef) Subsector in Botswana." Final report submitted to the Government of Botswana, March 2006, internal document.

Botha, Christo. 2013. "Pastoralism, Commercial Ranching and the State in Namibia." Pp. 230–255 in *Pastoralism in Africa Past, Present and Future*, edited by Michael Bollig, Michael Schnegg, and Hans-Peter Wotzka. New York: Berghahn Books.

Collier, Paul and Stefan Dercon. 2014. "African Agriculture in 50 Years: Smallholders in a Rapidly Changing World?" *World Development* 63: 92–101.

Daviron, Benoit. 2008. "The Historical Integration of Africa in the International Food Trade: A Food Regime Perspective." Pp. 44–78 in *Globalization and Restructuring of African Commodity Flows*, edited by N. Fold and M.N. Uppsala. Nordic Africa Institute.

Diamond, Jared. 1998. *Guns, Germs and Steel: A Short History of Everybody for the Last 13,000 Years*. London: Vintage.

Dima, S.J., A.A. Ogunmokun, and T. Nantanga. 2002. "The Status of Urban and Peri-urban Agriculture in Windhoek and Oshakati, Namibia." Windhoek, Namibia: University of Namibia and the Ministry of Agriculture, Water and Rural Development. Retrieved May 12, 2014 (http://www.fao.org/fileadmin/templates/esw/esw_new/documents/IP/5b_The_status_of_urban_and_peri.pdf).

FAO. 2013. "Understanding and Integrating Gender Issues into Livestock Projects and Programmes: A Checklist for Practitioners." Rome: FAO. Retrieved October 13, 2013 (http://www.fao.org/docrep/018/i3216e/i3216e.pdf).

FAOSTAT. 2012. "FAOSTAT." Rome, Italy: Food and Agricultural Organization.

Feeny, David, Fikret Berkes, Bonnie J. McCay, and James M. Acheson. 1990. "The Tragedy of the Commons: Twenty-Two Years Later." *Human Ecology* 18 (1): 1–19.

Ferguson, James. 1990. *The Anti-Politics Machine: "Development," Depoliticization, and Bureaucratic Power in Lesotho*. Cambridge: Cambridge University Press.

Ferguson, James. 2013. "How to Do Things with Land: A Distributive Perspective on Rural Livelihoods in Southern Africa." *Journal of Agrarian Change* 13 (1): 166–174.

Frenken, Karen. 2005. "Irrigation in Africa in Figures: AQUASTAT Survey – 2005." FAO Water Reports No. 29. Rome, Italy: FAO.

Galaty, John G. 2013. "The Indigenisation of Pastoral Modernity: Territoriality, Mobility and Poverty in Dryland Africa." Pp. 473–510 in *Pastoralism in Africa Past, Present and Future*, edited by Michael Bollig, Michael Schnegg, and Hans-Peter Wotzka. New York: Berghahn Books.

Garcia, C.T. 2004. "Land Reform in Namibia: Economic versus Socio-economic Rationale." Pp. 40–53 in *Land Reform, Land Settlement and Cooperatives*, edited by P. Groppo. Rome, Italy: FAO.

Gibbon, Peter and Stepfano Ponte. 2005. *Trading Down: Africa, Value Chains, and the Global Economy*. Philadelphia: Temple University Press.

Goldblatt, Amy. 2004. "Agriculture: Facts and Trends South Africa." South Africa: WWF. Retrieved November 11, 2013 (http://awsassets.wwf.org.za/downloads/facts_brochure_mockup_04_b.pdf).

Gwimbi, Patrick, Timothy S. Thomas, Sepo Hachigonta, and Lindiwe Majele Sibanda. 2013. "Lesotho." Chapter 4 in *Southern African Agriculture and Climate Change: A Comprehensive Analysis*, edited by Sepo Hachigonta, Gerald C. Nelson, Timothy S. Thomas, and Lindiwe Majele Sibanda. Washington, DC: International Food Policy Research Institute.

Hachigonta, Sepo, Gerald C. Nelson, Timothy S. Thomas, and Lindiwe Majele Sibanda. 2013. "Overview." Chapter 1 in *Southern African Agriculture and Climate Change: A Comprehensive Analysis*, edited by Sepo Hachigonta, Gerald C. Nelson, Timothy

S. Thomas, and Lindiwe Majele Sibanda. Washington, DC: International Food Policy Research Institute.

Hurt, Stephen. 2012. "The EU–SADC Economic Partnership Agreement Negotiations: 'Locking in' the Neoliberal Development Model in Southern Africa." *Third World Quarterly* 33 (3): 495–510.

Immanuel, Shinovene. 2013. "5,000 People Have Benefitted from Land Reform since 1991." *The Namibian.* Retrieved November 18, 2013 (http://www.namibian.com.na/indexx.php?archive_id=115133&page_type=archive_story_detail&page=1).

IRIN. 2013. "Swaziland: IMF Recommends Land Reforms." Irinnews.org. Retrieved April 15, 2014 (http://www.irinnews.org/report/96742/swaziland-imf-recommends-land-reforms).

Jayne, T.S., David Mather, and Elliot Mghenyi. 2010. "Principal Challenges Confronting Smallholder Agriculture in Sub-Saharan Africa." *World Development* 38 (10): 1384–1398.

Lahiff, Edward and Ben Cousins. 2005. "Smallholder Agriculture and Land Reform in South Africa." *IDS Bulletin* 36 (2): 127–131.

Lau, Brigitte and Peter Reiner. 1993. "100 Years of Agricultural Development in Colonial Namibia." *Archeia* 17. National Archives of Namibia, Windhoek.

Lipton, Michael and Charles Simkins, eds. 1993. *State and Market in Post Apartheid South Africa.* Boulder, CO: Westview Press.

Manyatsi, Absalom M., Timothy S. Thomas, Michael T. Masarirambi, Sepo Hachigonta, and Lindiwe Majele Sibanda. 2013. "Swaziland." Chapter 8 in *Southern African Agriculture and Climate Change: A Comprehensive Analysis,* edited by Sepo Hachigonta, Gerald C. Nelson, Timothy S. Thomas, and Lindiwe Majele Sibanda. Washington, DC: International Food Policy Research Institute.

Mather, Charles. 1996. "Towards Sustainable Agriculture in Post-Apartheid South Africa." *GeoJournal* 39 (1): 41–49.

McKeever, Matthew. 2008. "Regional Institutions and Social Development in Southern Africa." *Annual Review of Sociology* 34 (1): 453–473.

Neth, Mary. 1994. "Gender and the Family Labor System: Defining Work in the Rural Midwest." *Journal of Social History* 27 (3): 563–577.

Newsham, Andrew J. and David S.G. Thomas. 2011. "Knowing, Farming and Climate Change Adaptation in North-Central Namibia." *Global Environmental Change* 21 (2): 761–770.

North, Douglas. 1990. *Institutions, Institutional Change, and Economic Performance.* Cambridge: Cambridge University Press.

O'Laughlin, Bridget, Henry Bernstein, Ben Cousins, and Pauline E. Peters. 2013. "Introduction: Agrarian Change, Rural Poverty and Land Reform in South Africa since 1994." *Journal of Agrarian Change* 13 (1): 1–15.

Ransom, Elizabeth. 2011. "Botswana's Beef Global Commodity Chain: Explaining the Resistance to Change." *Journal of Rural Studies* 27 (4): 431–439.

Ransom, Elizabeth and Carmen Bain. 2011. "Gendering Agricultural Aid: An Analysis of whether International Development Assistance Targets Women and Gender." *Gender and Society* 25 (1): 48–74.

Sachs, Carolyn. 1996. *Gendered Fields: Rural Women, Agriculture, and Environment.* Boulder, CO: Westview.

SADC. 2008. "SADC Multi-country Agricultural Productivity Programme" (Ref: SADC/MAPP/2007/D). Gaborone, Botswana: Southern African Development Community. Retrieved April 26, 2014 (http://www.sadc.int/files/3913/5851/0000/SADC_MAPP_Programme_Document-_April_08.pdf).

Sadr, Karim. 2013. "A Short History of Early Herding in Southern Africa." Pp. 171–197 in *Pastoralism in Africa Past, Present and Future,* edited by Michael Bollig, Michael Schnegg, and Hans-Peter Wotzka. New York: Berghahn Books.

Schwalbach, L.M., I.B. Groenewald, and C.B. Marfo. 2001. "A Survey of Small-Scale Cattle Farming Systems in the North West Province of South Africa." *South African Journal of Animal Sciences* 31: 200–204.

Thwala, Maxwell. 2011. "Analyzing the Value Chain of the Family Poultry Sub Sector in the

Lower Usuthu Project Area in Swaziland." IFAD. Retrieved April 1, 2014 (http://www. fao.org/docrep/018/aq625e/aq625e.pdf).

UNICEF. 2009. "Eastern and Southern Africa: HIV and AIDS Overview." Retrieved April 16, 2014 (http://www.unicef.org/esaro/5482_HIV_AIDS.html).

Wily, Liz Alden. 2011. "'The Law is to Blame': The Vulnerable Status of Common Property Rights in Sub-Saharan Africa." *Development and Change* 42 (3): 733–757.

World Bank. 2013. "Lesotho Overview." Retrieved May 12, 2014 (http://www.worldbank. org/en/country/lesotho/overview).

World Bank. 2014. "Namibia Overview." Retrieved May 16, 2014 (http://www.worldbank. org/en/country/namibia/overview).

You, Liangzhi, Claudia Ringler, Gerald Nelson, Ulrike Wood-Sichra, Richard Robertson, Stanley Wood, Zhe Guo, Tingju Zhu, and Yan Sun. 2010. "What is the Irrigation Potential for Southern Africa? A Combined Biophysical and Socioeconomic Approach." IFPRI Discussion Paper 00993, June 2010. Washington, DC: International Food Policy Research Institute.

Zhou, Peter P., Tichakunda Simbini, Gorata Ramokgotlwane, Timothy S. Thomas, Sepo Hachigonta, and Lindiwe M. Sibanda. 2013. "Botswana." Pp. 41–70 in *Southern African Agriculture and Climate Change: A Comprehensive Analysis*, edited by Sepo Hachigonta, Gerald C. Nelson, Timothy S. Thomas, and Lindiwe M. Sibanda. Washington, DC: International Food Policy Research Institute.

## 2. "100% pure"? Private governance efforts to mitigate the effects of "dirty dairying"on New Zealand's environment
### Carmen Bain and Tamera Dandachi

## INTRODUCTION

"Clean and green" and pastoral farming are images synonymous with New Zealand. While long held as part of New Zealanders' (colloquially known as "kiwis") cultural identity these images have more recently been developed to create a niche for New Zealand commerce within the global marketplace. The government, together with business, has carefully crafted the identities of New Zealand's pastoral clean, green image, captured in the "100% pure" international brand and marketing campaign (see Figure 2.1). This brand is centered on the natural environment and the perceived cleanliness of the country, which is critical for the country's second biggest economic sector, tourism. For example, New Zealand was the location for the popular *Lord of the Rings* movie trilogy, which showed off the country's spectacular unspoilt national beauty and has brought in tens of millions of dollars as tourists flocked in to visit places such as Hobbiton. The clean, green image is also central for the identity and promotion of New Zealand's agricultural products, especially dairy and organics, as distinctive within the global market. The image projects an ideal where agriculture exists within an environment of clean water and air, pasture raised livestock, low use of agrichemicals, and a population density that is low (Meister and Beechey 2012). A quantitative report commissioned by the Ministry for the Environment in 2001 found that New Zealand's image as clean and green is a key economic driver in the international markets, worth "at least hundreds of millions, possibly billions of dollars" to the country's economy (Ministry for the Environment 2001:1).

For over a decade, the extent to which the veracity of these images stack up against reality have fueled an intense debate within New Zealand. For example, the majority of New Zealand's rivers are too unsafe to swim in due to pollution, and some studies have ranked New Zealand among the worst per capita in its efforts to preserve its native vegetation and habitat (Bradshaw et al. 2010; Reuters 2013). At the center of this debate is New Zealand's most important economic sector: dairy. Market liberalization

*Figure 2.1    International marketing campaign for 100% pure New Zealand*

together with strong export demand has led to a significant expansion and intensification of New Zealand dairy since the late 1990s. New Zealand is the number one global exporter in dairy products and accounts for a third of the world's trade in dairy (https://www.nzte.govt.nz/en/buy/our-sectors/food-and-beverage/dairy/). In 2013 the dairy sector contributed NZ$14.6 billion to the New Zealand economy, 30 percent of all New Zealand's export earnings (Statistics New Zealand 2014). Export volume is expected to continue rising. This expansion is both a reflection of a depreciated exchange rate but also the continued growth and intensification of an industry that has seen a growth in cow numbers and milk solid production per cow (Baskaran, Cullen, and Colombo 2009).

While the dairy industry makes an important social and economic contribution to New Zealand's society, there is widespread criticism that expansion and intensification of the sector is having significant effects on the environment, especially water quality. To highlight the effects that the intensification of dairy farming was having on New Zealand's natural environment, the environmental organization, Fish and Game New Zealand, launched its "dirty dairying" campaign in 2002. The organization argued that on-farm practices were negatively affecting water and habitat quality—claims supported by the scientific evidence (Blackett and Le Heron 2008). For example, streams in areas with dairy farms are rated as being in very poor condition (Blackett and Le Heron 2008). Fish and Game New Zealand argued that the dairy industry itself had to take primary responsibility for fixing the environmental problems, with "second order responsibility" lying with "central and regional government" (Deans and Hackwell 2008). In response to these criticisms, the government and dairy industry implemented the Dairying and Clean Streams Accord in 2003, which would see responsibility for mitigating dairy's impact on the environment shift from regional governing authorities to the dairy industry itself. The Accord expired in 2012 and was superseded in 2013 by the Sustainable Dairy: Water Accord.

In this chapter, we discuss the factors leading up to the implementation of these two Accords and assess the potential of voluntarist approaches to successfully regulate environmental impacts within a global market. We argue that embedded within these efforts lays an important dilemma confronting the dairy industry. While benefiting from New Zealand's positive environmental image abroad, lax environmental laws at home have played a critical role in facilitating the expansion of the industry and ensuring its competitiveness in international markets (Burton and Peoples 2014). However, New Zealand generally, and the dairy sector specifically, continues to be plagued with questions as to whether it is living up to its clean and green brand and whether the value of its exports attributable to this image is at risk.

It is important to note that these trends are not unique to New Zealand but are illustrative of some of the salient changes we find unfolding within the international global agrifood system. As national economies become more deeply embedded and interdependent within the global economy, a major challenge for nations is how to govern and regulate social goods, such as protecting the local environment. Within this context, one of the key trends of interest to political economy and agrifood scholars has been the shift towards private and voluntarist efforts to govern human impacts on the environment, which we turn to discuss next.

## ENVIRONMENTAL GOVERNANCE

In 1984 New Zealand became one of the first developed economies to institute sweeping neoliberal political and economic reforms. Since then, the country has been viewed as an ideal "laboratory" for studying neoliberal policies, especially its effects on agriculture (Sautet 2006 *cited in* Burton and Peoples 2014). Central to neoliberal theory is the idea that the market is the most efficient form of organization: superior at guiding human organization and behavior, setting prices and wages, and distributing resources, goods, and services (Allen and Guthman 2006).

With the deepening of neoliberal economic policies, together with the extension of global trade, scholars increasingly draw upon the concept of governance for understanding how agrifood systems are regulated (Gibbon and Ponte 2008). While governance is frequently contrasted with the idea of government, the line between governance and government can be overdrawn. New forms of governance do not represent the demise of state authority, but the blurring of regulatory boundaries between the state, market, and civil society (Higgins and Lawrence 2005; Smith and Mahutga 2008). There is no such thing as a "free market"; the state defines the formal rules of the market and even what we think of as private governance always takes place within these rules. Thus, neoliberalism does not eliminate either the state or state regulation; instead it involves changing the role of the state to one more focused on managing and making markets (Mansfield 2007). Rather than just the state, governing includes a wider array of economic and political agents, including businesses, civil society organizations, industry associations, and multi-stakeholder organizations (Busch and Bain 2004; Harvey 2005). Non-state actors emphasize the use of market approaches and economic incentives to govern, including for achieving environmental objectives. The goal is to encourage compliance with environmental objectives through the use of market signals rather than "command and control" state approaches. The idea is that individuals and businesses, including farmers, are motivated through self-interest to meet environmental goals and that market approaches provide them with more flexibility to do so (Mansfield 2007).

Below, we examine the example of the Dairying and Clean Streams Accord as an example of voluntarist environmental governance, whereby responsibility for mitigating dairy's impact on the environment was shifted from regional governing authorities to the dairy industry itself.

## THE DEVELOPMENT OF THE DAIRY INDUSTRY

With a relatively small population of just over 4 million people, the economic success of New Zealand has always depended on its export market. Throughout the entire history of the country, agricultural-based products have made up its most important exports. In 2013 the value of all agricultural exports was NZ$28.8 billion (Statistics New Zealand 2014), the highest in history. New Zealand's moderate climate and rich soils are conducive to a broad range of farming, including dairy, sheep, and beef as well as horticulture and viticulture (Meister and Beechey 2012). Almost half of the country's land mass—14.7 million hectares—is used for agriculture, supporting some 70,000 farms (Meister and Beechey 2012). Of this, some 83.5 percent of the agricultural land is used for livestock farming (Meister and Beechey 2012).

Implementation of neoliberal reforms in 1984 became synonymous with the removal of production subsidies from agriculture, especially for sheep farmers. Other changes included market deregulation, the phasing out of subsidies for fertilizers and weed eradication, and the rise in interest rates from the Rural Bank and Finance Corporation to market levels (Burton and Peoples 2014). At the same time, the New Zealand dollar was floated, which sent the currency skyrocketing, leading to a decline in export sales, soaring interest rates, and a 40 percent decline in land values (Arnold 2007; Burton and Peoples 2014).

Combined, these factors led to serious levels of indebtedness for farmers (Burton and Peoples 2014), with initial predictions that 10 percent of farms would be forced to declare bankruptcy. In protest, thousands of farmers marched on the capital in Wellington, letting loose sheep and flying overhead with crop dusters (Arnold 2007). In an effort to reduce the negative effect, farm leaders successfully negotiated with New Zealand banks to write down some farm debt, providing some relief to producers. In the end, about 1 percent of commercial farmers—approximately 800— lost their farms (Arnold 2007). As the most heavily subsidized sector, the sheep sector was hardest hit and, together with the beef sector, never fully recovered from this period of liberalization. While New Zealand's image remains one where "sheep outnumber humans" (Meister and Beechey 2012), the reality is quite different. To remain competitive in the wake of losing government supports, these sectors were forced to diversify, and today there are few specialized sheep or cattle producers (Burton and Peoples 2014). Sheep numbers peaked in 1982 with a total of around 70 million sheep and have since declined significantly to around 31 million in 2012.

In contrast, the dairy industry, which had previously received almost no direct subsidies, emerged from this period virtually unscathed and went on to become neoliberalism's most important success story (Burton and Peoples 2014). Of particular importance is the significant expansion and intensification that the sector has undergone since 1998 in response to high export prices (see Figure 2.2) (Greig 2012). To facilitate this growth, land used for dairying has expanded from traditional wetter parts of the country, primarily in the North Island, including Waikato, Taranaki, Northland, Manawatu, into areas not previously used for dairy production. This includes areas traditionally used for dry-stock pasture and exotic

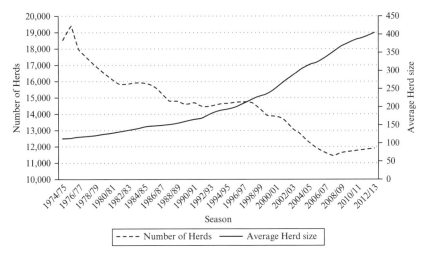

*Figure 2.2    Trend in the number of herds and average herd size 1974/1975–2012/2013*

forestry, including expanding into the South Island, which was traditionally used by sheep and cattle producers (Burton and Wilson 2012; Meister and Beechey 2012). At the same time, changes in milk and feed prices, increased volatility of milk prices, and increased land prices have encouraged existing dairy farms and production practices to become more intensive, and the number of cows milked, herd sizes, and productivity levels have all increased. Production rates from pastoral farming have increased due to more intensive farming practices and higher productivity per animal (Meister and Beechey 2012). For example, the number of cows increased 96 percent, from approximately 2.44 million in 1992 to 4.78 million in 2012 (DairyNZ 2013a), and dairy productivity increased 34 percent, from approximately 259 kilograms of milk solids (kg ms) per cow a season to 346 kg ms during this same period (DairyNZ 2013a). The country's major dairy export markets are the United States, China, and Japan.

In 2001 the giant dairy cooperative, Fonterra, was created from a merger between the New Zealand Dairy Board, which controlled the export and marketing of all New Zealand dairy products (New Zealand Dairy Board 1961), and two of the largest dairy cooperatives: New Zealand Dairy Group and Kiwi Co-operative Dairies (Burton and Peoples 2014). With more than 11,000 farmer members, Fonterra is by far the largest of New Zealand's three dairy companies, covering 96 percent of all milk production. The cooperative represents over 20 percent of total New Zealand merchandise exports, contributing 7 percent of the nation's GDP.

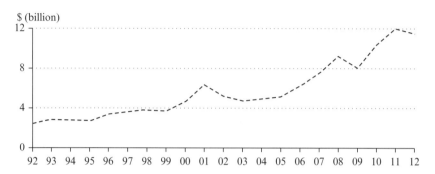

*Figure 2.3    Dairy export values to all countries 1992–2012*

As a result of this growth, New Zealand established itself as the number one global exporter in dairy products, including milk powder, butter, and cheese, and accounts for approximately 35 percent of the world trade in dairy products. Internationally, the dairy industry is New Zealand's biggest export earner, with exports exceeding NZ$13.7 billion and generating more than 26 percent of export revenue in 2012 (up from 14 percent in 1992). Export volume is expected to continue rising (see Figure 2.3).

Increases in productivity through sector expansion and input intensification is critical to maintaining international competitiveness. At the same time, New Zealand feels significant pressure to remain a low-cost producer since most of its exports and growth in demand are to "middle and low income countries" and developing economies, such as China (Baskaran et al. 2009:378). In addition, New Zealand feels disadvantaged by exclusionary trade practices, such as transnational mergers or export cartels in North American and European countries, that it perceives as having an anti-competitive effect against countries with liberal trade policies (Baskaran et al. 2009).

## THE DAIRY INDUSTRY AND THE ENVIRONMENT

New Zealand's natural environment has a long history of being remade to suit the needs of agriculture. Beginning in the 1700s, colonists transformed New Zealand's natural habitat into that of a neo-Europe (Crosby 2004). New Zealand's climate was ideal for European agriculture, and colonists were able to introduce their own flora, fauna, and livestock to displace indigenous vegetation (Crosby 2004). More recently, the expansion and intensification of pastoral dairy production has had a major impact on the natural environment, with a range of indicators suggesting a significant reduction in environmental quality, especially in rural areas (Burton and Peoples 2014). This shift has contributed to soil erosion problems in some areas as well as water quality problems due to sediment and nutrient run-off and discharge of agricultural wastes (Meister and Beechey 2012). Wetlands and lowlands have been destroyed and ecosystem services, such as clean air and water, have also been degraded (Baskaran et al. 2009). Mike Joy, an ecology and environmental sustainability scientist at Massey University argues that "because we've had a lack of regulation of farm waste for 20 years it's been a free for all, so farmers have done what they can to produce more milk—which is to put more cows on pastures" (Reuters 2013). Soil integrity has been significantly impacted by changes in dairy production. In addition to soil erosion problems in some areas, soil contamination and damage to soil structure are also prevalent as a result of more intensive dairying (Meister and Beechey 2012). Damage to soil integrity poses both immediate and long-term impacts for pastoral agriculture. Weight from livestock on both lowlands and hill areas can cause compression of the soil, which leads to issues with aeration and drainage (Mackay 2008). Even if there are not immediate visible signs of damage there is risk of soil degradation. Signs of such degraded soil quality include increased soil run-off and pooling of water on the surface of the soil (Mackay 2008).

Soil erosion together with nutrient run-off from increased inputs, such as fertilizer, and discharge of agricultural waste have all contributed to problems of water quality. Surface water and groundwater have been polluted and contaminated, and excess nutrients, particularly nitrogen and phosphorous from animal waste and fertilizer, have seeped into waterways (Baskaran et al. 2009). For example, the National Institute of Water and Atmospheric Research estimate that farming has polluted 90 percent of lowland rivers, either in the form of animal waste or fertilizer run-off (2009). This has caused the levels of nitrogen to be elevated above natural groundwater levels, and in some areas the amount of nitrogen exceeds the drinking water standard of 11.3 milligrams per liter (Baskaran et al. 2009). Additionally, there have been instances of insufficient water for irrigation during droughts and irrigation bans in some areas because of increasing water demands. As the dairy industry continues to expand and intensify production into traditionally drier areas, this could become a more frequent occurrence (Burton and Peoples 2014).

Air quality has also been impacted by the intensification and expansion of the dairy industry. Approximately half of all domestic greenhouse gas emissions come from the agriculture sector, with the dairy industry being the biggest contributor (Greenpeace 2009). During the period 1990–2009, greenhouse gas emissions increased by 15 percent (Greenpeace

2009), coinciding particularly with nitrous oxide and methane due to the increased use of nitrogenous fertilizers and emissions from livestock waste (Baskaran et al. 2009).

## ENVIRONMENTAL GOVERNANCE AND THE DAIRY SECTOR

Despite the "rhetoric of sustainability" with hints of environmentalism from the dairy sector, political concern for the environmental impact of the dairy industry seems to have been minimal (Burton and Peoples 2014:86). Some scholars argue that lax environmental laws have played a critical role in driving the expansion of the dairy industry and ensuring its economic success. For example, Baskaran et al. (2009:388) argue that New Zealand dairy products are relatively cheap because their prices do not "reflect the external costs of depleting environmental resources or causing environmental degradation." Requiring dairy farmers to meet and pay for more stringent environmental standards would result in a decline in dairy exports, economic value, and international competitiveness (Burton and Peoples 2014).

At the same time, the ability of the state to regulate the dairy industry is constrained by its paramount environmental law, the Resource Management Act (RMA), which emphasizes a neoliberal "hands-off" and flexible approach. The RMA was implemented in 1991 and its purpose is to "promote sustainable management" of New Zealand's "natural and physical resources," such as air, water, soil, and ecosystems, while allowing for their use and development (Meister and Beechey 2012:81). The RMA includes a number of other key statues, such as the Conservation Act (1987), the Hazardous Substances and New Organisms Act (1996), and the Local Government Act (2002). The RMA shifted environmental management away from a mandated set of prescriptive standards and technologies towards a neoliberal approach where actors are provided with flexibility to achieve environmental objectives (Meister and Beechey 2012). This approach is reflected in several core concepts including "intervening only where required and clearly justified," focusing "outcomes (targets) where intervention is justified," and using policy instruments that "achieve cost-effective solutions" (Meister and Beechey 2012:82).

Following neoliberal principles of devolution, the RMA shifts decision-making responsibility away from the national government "to regional councils, city authorities and unitary authorities" (Meister and Beechey 2012:82). That is, those communities most impacted by resource usage are responsible for implementing and enforcing the RMA (Meister and

Beechey 2012). This stands in contrast to most other Organisation for Economic Co-operation and Development (OECD) countries, where environmental management remains the responsibility of central government. For example, discharges to water and land are subject to the constraints of the RMA, and consent for a discharge to water or a discharge of effluent to land is the responsibility of regional councils (Cassels and Meister 2002). Regional councils also control the allocation of surface and groundwater for irrigation through a resource consent[1] process (Baskaran et al. 2009).

Local and regional councils often lack the resources or political will to monitor and enforce compliance by the dairy sector with the RMA due to insufficient funding from the national government, low revenues due to a small taxpayer base, and a "questionable commitment to environmental issues" (Barnett and Pauling 2005 *cited in* Burton and Wilson 2012). Additionally, given that responsibility lies on regional councils, there has been substantial variation in the implementation and enforcement of policies under the Act, with some councils choosing not to place any restrictions on water and land discharges at all (Burton and Wilson 2012). Because of the weak RMA and a lack of enforcement and use of penalties by the industry and regional councils, many farms are non-compliant with resource consent policies (Burton and Wilson 2012). At the same time, the national government has also stepped in to ensure that environmental actions by local governments are in line with neoliberal approaches (Burton and Peoples 2014). For example, an elected regional council (Environment Canterbury) was replaced with an unelected body when the council was perceived to be blocking irrigation development for dairy expansion (Burton and Peoples 2014).

### "Dirty Dairying" and the Dairying and Clean Streams Accord

Frustrated at ongoing violations by the dairy industry of the RMA and the lack of consequences for those who are committing infractions, Fish and Game New Zealand, an organization that has statutory responsibility for freshwater sport fishing and game bird hunting, launched its "dirty dairying" campaign in 2002. The "dirty dairying" campaign aimed to highlight the pollution of New Zealand's waterways as a result of the intensification of the dairy industry. The organization explains on its website (http://www.fishandgame.org.nz/dairy-farming-environment) that it was frustrated that the government was failing to act when numerous reports, including from government agencies, had identified that dairy farming was failing to comply with key sections of the RMA, including Section 17, "Every person has a duty to avoid, remedy or mitigate any adverse effect on the environment arising from an activity carried on by or on behalf of that person," and Section 15, "No person may discharge any Contaminant into water; or Contaminant onto or into land in circumstances which may result in that contaminant entering water." Fertilizer is defined in the Act as a contaminant.

Fish and Game New Zealand argued that failure to act will have broader economic ramifications. It explains that it is widely recognized that "New Zealand's unique point of difference, in terms of how it defines itself as a nation and differentiates its products in world markets, centres around its natural environment," and without its brand of "clean and green/100% Pure" the country "would have very little to command market status and an attractive international identity" (http://www.fishandgame.org.nz/dairy-farming-environment). To ensure the integrity of this brand, New Zealand must move towards environmentally sustainable agriculture.

The response to Fish and Game New Zealand's high-profile "dirty dairying" campaign was increased self-regulation in the dairy industry through the voluntary Dairying and Clean Streams Accord. Fonterra, the Minister for the Environment, the Minister for Primary Industries, and Local Government New Zealand on behalf of regional councils, agreed upon the Accord in 2003, which expired in 2012. The goal of the Accord is "on reducing the impacts of dairying on the quality of New Zealand streams, rivers, lakes, ground water and wetlands" (Ministry for the Environment 2003). It was to accomplish this through the following five performance targets in place for the dairy industry (Ministry for the Environment 2003):

- Dairy cattle excluded from access to streams, rivers, and lakes (50 percent by 2007; 90 percent by 2012).
- Regular crossing points have bridges or culverts (50 percent by 2007; 90 percent by 2012).
- Dairy farms effluent discharges comply with resource consents and regional plans (100 percent immediately).
- Dairy farms have systems in place to manage nutrient inputs and outputs (100 percent by 2007).
- Regionally significant wetlands to be fenced (50 percent by 2005; 90 percent by 2007).

While major farm organizations, such as Federated Farmers, initially opposed the Accord, the Accord has since become the key defense by the dairying industry to accusations that it is not doing anything to protect the environment (White 2007). From an environmental perspective, however, the effectiveness of the Accord remains in question. At the time the Accord

*Table 2.1    Progress toward Accord targets—2007/2008 to 2011/2012*

| Accord Target | | 2007/08 | 2008/09 | 2009/10 | 2010/11 | 2011/12 |
|---|---|---|---|---|---|---|
| Dairy cattle excluded from streams, rivers and lakes (Target: 90% by 2012) | | 78% | 80% | 85% | 84% | 87% |
| Regular crossing points have bridges or culverts (Target: 90% by 2012) | | 98% | 98% | 99% | 99% | 99% |
| Dairy farm effluent appropriately treated and discharged in compliance with regional council resource consent and/or permitted activity conditions (Target: 100% immediately) | | 64% | 60% | 65% | 69% | 73% |
| Farms have systems in place to manage nutrient inputs and outputs (Target: 100% by 2007) | Farms with a nutrient budget | 98% | 99% | 99% | 99% | 99% |
| | Farms with a nutrient management plan | | | 10% | 46% | 56% |

*Source:*    Adapted from *The Dairying and Clean Streams Accord: Snapshot of Progress 2011/2012* (Ministry for Primary Industries 2013).

was established in 2003, a third of farmers (33 percent) were not in full compliance with environmental regulations, such as meeting requirements for treating and discharging dairy effluent. By 2011/2012, over a quarter (27 percent) of farmers were still fully non-compliant (Burton and Peoples 2014).

The extent to which the Accord's targets were met was documented in annual Snapshot reports (Ministry for Primary Industries 2013). These annual reports provide a detailed explanation of which targets have or have not been met. Table 2.1 provides a look at the progress made between the Snapshot report of 2007/2008 through the Snapshot report from 2011/2012. The reports also break the targets down by region, which shows the variation across New Zealand and shows which regions have been the least successful in meeting Accord targets. These reports show that progress towards meeting the targets is on the rise.

There was progress made towards the target that all farm dairy effluent discharges should comply with their resource consents, but the target was not met. A standardized system was put in place to report compliance with regional plan and resource consent requirements in 2007/2008. The annual Snapshot report estimated that 16 to 24 percent of farms were in serious non-compliance in 2007/2008 (Ministry for Primary Industries 2009). This dropped to approximately 10 percent in 2011/2012 (Ministry for Primary Industries 2013). Although the overall levels of serious non-compliance dropped, some regions still had high levels of serious non-compliance in 2012, which was the final year of the Accord. For example, the Snapshot report states that Northland, Waikato, Bay of Plenty, and Southland had the highest levels of serious non-compliance, ranging from 12 to 27 percent (Ministry for Primary Industries 2013).

The Snapshot reports are intended to show the progress towards meeting Accord targets, but there are discrepancies with the way that the data is reported. Deans and Hackwell (2008) argue that "the Snapshot Report is inaccurate and doesn't represent the true levels of uptake of the Dairying and Clean Streams Accord's original target," and there has not been a consistent, positive change in water quality as an effect of the Accord.

Although the purpose of the Accord is to improve water quality, there is not a standard, consistent way in which water quality is measured to determine if the Accord has been effective in meeting its goals (Deans and Hackwell 2008). This means that regional councils are not all using the same criteria to measure water quality. Because of this inconsistency, accurate comparisons cannot be made between regions or across the country (Deans and Hackwell 2008). Changes in water quality over time in a region can be measured as long as the analysis was conducted in the same way. The same goes for measuring water quality between regions (Deans and Hackwell 2008). For example, water quality trends have been measured and are able to be compared in some regions. These regions include Waikato, Canterbury, Marlborough, and Taranaki. In each of these regions there is a trend of declining water quality over time. This casts doubt on the effectiveness of the Accord and the "best practices" that the Accord prescribes.

High levels of serious non-compliance have led to a number of prosecutions of farmers for this. Many farmers have been fined for discharging effluent to lands that could potentially reach water, because discharging effluent to land that could run-off into water sources is not in compliance with resource consent requirements. The fines range from NZ$300 to NZ$120,000, with the largest fine going to the biggest offender, Potae and van der Poel Limited, for "eight charges of unlawful effluent discharges and breaching abatement notices on three farms" (Sharpe 2012). The prosecutions from the years 2008 to 2012 include "151 prosecutions involving more than 300 charges against 198 companies," with fines totaling more than NZ$3,250,000 (Sharpe 2012). In addition to fines, community service sentences were also given out to those who violated the policies. While these numbers seem high, there was a decrease in prosecutions from 2008 to 2012, and Bruce Willis, the President of Federated Farmers, vows that the worst has already happened, and the industry will increase efforts to prosecute those who violate resource consent requirements (Sharpe 2012). The number of convictions dropped from 51 to 18, abatement notices fell from 537 to 329, and infringement notices fell from 500 to 330 (Sharpe 2012).

Since the end of the Dairying and Clean Streams Accord, another Accord to improve environmental quality in New Zealand has been introduced. The new Sustainable Dairy: Water Accord went into effect on August 1, 2013 and applies to all dairy companies. This new Accord is intended to be an update and succession to the previous Dairying and Clean Streams Accord. The new Accord covers five key areas (DairyNZ 2013b):

- Riparian management—requirements for excluding dairy cattle from significant waterways and drains (greater than 1 meter in width and deeper than 30 centimeters that permanently contain water) and significant wetlands (identified by regional councils) within a phased timeframe; development of riparian planting plans.
- Nutrient management—improving management of nitrogen and phosphorus loss from dairy farming systems through an industry-wide monitoring and support system.
- Effluent management—compliance with regional council effluent management rules and continued investment in fit for purpose systems.
- Water use management—improving water use efficiency in irrigation systems and around the cowshed.
- Conversions—comprehensive good practice standards for all new dairy farms.

The timeframes set forth include:

- Dairy cattle excluded from waterways: 90 percent by May 31, 2014; 100 percent by May 31, 2017.
- Dairy cattle excluded from wetlands: 100 percent by May 31, 2014.

The new Accord has already faced considerable critique. For example, Bryce Johnson (2014), Chief Executive of Fish and Game New Zealand, points out that the new Accord applies to fewer streams than the original Accord. He argues that "it has actually got worse. And let's not forget the previous Accord failed to meet key objectives, even after more than a decade of being in place." Johnson (2014) suggests that the government's dedication to environmental quality is lacking, and smarter farming is not only necessary, but what the majority of people in New Zealand want.

## DISCUSSION AND CONCLUSIONS

It is over a decade since Fish and Game New Zealand launched its "dirty dairying" campaign and the dairy industry implemented the Dairying and Clean Streams Accord. However, it appears that voluntarist efforts to mitigate dairy's impact on the environment have done little to quiet criticism across the spectrum—from the general public, to the media, to scientists—that the country's economic values and priorities are out of sync with its environmental values and priorities.

This tension was reflected in a survey of New Zealanders in early 2014.[2] Kiwis are renowned for their strong cultural affinity to the environment and here 9 out of 10 respondents said that they viewed their Kiwi identity and lifestyle as fundamentally linked to their natural environments (Halleron 2014). These same respondents expressed considerable concern about the effects of intensive dairy farming on the environment, especially regarding its quality. Approximately one-third of respondents said that the New Zealand economy is "too dependent on dairy farming (37%)" or that "the growth of intensive dairying has gone too far (31%)" (Halleron 2014). Two-thirds of respondents (70 percent) said that the dairy sector has worsened the quality of fresh water compared with 20 years ago, while only 6 percent thought it had improved (Halleron 2014).

New Zealand continues to face criticism within the international media, with accusations about potential political and economic "greenwashing" finding its way into the pages of *The New York Times*, the United States' *Huffington Post*, the United Kingdom's *The Guardian*, and China.org.cn among others. Headlines include: "New Zealand's Environment-Friendly Image Marred by Dairy Contamination" (Reuters 2013), "Report Highlights Toxic Effects on New Zealand Dairy Industry on Waterways" (Xinhua Agencies 2013), "New Zealand Was a Friend to Middle Earth, but it's No Friend of the Earth" (Pearce 2009), and "New Zealand's Green Tourism Push Clashes with Realities" (Anderson 2012). These articles reiterate that the majority of rivers and streams are too polluted to swim in (Anderson 2012; Reuters 2013) and native vegetation has become rare in some places, which would be a shock to many tourists who equate New Zealand with "Middle Earth" from the *Hobbit* and the *Lord of the Rings* trilogy (Anderson 2012). These articles highlight the tension that this contradiction presents for New Zealand's two key economic sectors: dairy and tourism. Tourists want to travel to the untouched, "100% pure" New Zealand that they compare to "Middle Earth," which has caused the country to continue to rely on its clean green image (Reuters 2013; Pearce 2009). The clean green image is also critical to promoting New Zealand's dairy industry because there is a market for produce from a country with a positive environmental image (Anderson 2012; Reuters 2013; Pearce 2009).

Some scholars argue that efforts by Fonterra and regional governments to promote voluntarist environmental management practices and policies have done little to halt the intensification of dairy production and the worsening of the environment in these areas (Baskaran et al. 2009). Part of the problem is that these approaches do not adequately ensure that all farmers are complying with the regulations. In response, Fish and Game New Zealand is calling for mandatory compliance. In addition, any improvements are offset by the environmental harm of converting farming systems that are less intensive, such as sheep and beef, with farming systems that are more intensive, such as dairy (Baskaran et al. 2009). This trend is unlikely to abate with the government's goal of doubling the value of agricultural exports by 2025.

These concerns were reinforced in 2013 when the Parliamentary Commissioner for the Environment released its report, "Water Quality in New Zealand: Land Use and Nutrient Pollution," that shows that "nitrogen stress" is increasing every year in almost every region. The report details how the shift away from sheep and beef to dairy has increased the levels of nitrogen and phosphorus in the country's waterways that, in turn, has produced excessive growth in weeds and algae that are choking these waterways. Using models for land use and nutrient run-off, the report "paints a grim picture of the future, predicting that loss of nitrogen and phosphorus into waterways will continue to increase—even under 'optimistic' assumptions" (Science Alert: Experts Respond 2013).

In response to the report, Dr. Mike Scarsbrook, Environment Policy Manager for DairyNZ, reiterated that "the days of unconstrained growth in dairy farming are over" but that mitigation efforts that go beyond industry best practices, such as improvements in fertilizer use and effluent management, can help the industry meet nutrient levels set by communities. On the other hand, Dr. Russell Death of the Institute of Agriculture and Environment at Massey University responded (Science Alert: Experts Respond 2013) that while he "would love to see [a] win-win for the economy and environment" the report:

> illustrates what many scientists and economists already know, if we continue with increasing dairy intensification, without some drastic changes in how we farm, the most likely outcome is lose-lose. Many of our waterways are already badly degraded, agriculture creates pollutants (nitrogen, phosphorous and sediment) and thus increasing agriculture even with the best mitigation practices (none of which are even close to perfect) will still result in more pollutants entering our waterways. More pollutants, lower water quality, it's not rocket science.

In sum, New Zealand finds itself in a difficult position and one where "business as usual" may no longer suffice. The success of the nation's economy is highly dependent on exports and within this context dairy has proved to be a star within a competitive international market. Yet, continued efforts to grow this industry have produced significant detrimental consequences for both the environment and the country's reputation nationally and internationally as an environmental leader. Voluntarist efforts, led by the dairy industry itself, to set performance targets have done little to abate scientific concerns about declining environmental indicators, especially for water quality. Significant political and economic challenges remain in determining how to reconcile these competing concerns and determine what sorts of governance approaches can best meet these challenges.

## NOTES

1. Resource consents are permissions given by a regional council to undertake activities that could cause harm to the environment. Examples of these activities include discharging effluent to land and damming or diverting water.
2. The survey was commissioned by Fish and Game New Zealand and conducted independently by Horizon Research Limited.

## REFERENCES

Allen, Patricia and Julie Guthman. 2006. "From 'Old School' to 'Farm-to-School': Neoliberalization from the Ground Up." *Agriculture and Human Values* 23:401–416.

Anderson, Charles. 2012. "New Zealand's Green Tourism Push Clashes with Realities." *The New York Times*. November 16.

Arnold, Wayne. 2007. "Surviving without Subsidies." *The New York Times*. C1 August 2.

Baskaran, Ramesh, Ross Cullen, and Sergio Colombo. 2009. "Estimating Values of Environmental Impacts of Dairy Farming in New Zealand." *New Zealand Journal of Agricultural Research* 52:377–389.

Blackett, Paula and Richard Le Heron. 2008. "Maintaining the 'Clean Green' Image: Governance of On-farm Environmental Practices in the New Zealand Dairy Industry." Pp. 75–88 in *Agri-food Commodity Chains and Globalising Networks*, edited by C. Stringer and R.B. Le Heron. Aldershot, UK: Ashgate Publishing Ltd.

Bradshaw, Corey, Xingli Giam, and Navjot S. Sodhi. 2010. "Evaluating the Relative Environmental Impact of Countries." *PLOS one* 5(5) e10440. Retrieved November 16, 2014 (http://www.plosone.org/article/fetchObject.action?uri=info%3Adoi%2F10.1371%2Fjournal.pone.0010440&representation=PDF).

Burton, Rob and Sue Peoples. 2014. "Market Liberalisation and Drought in New Zealand: A Case of 'Double Exposure' for Dryland Sheep Farmers?" *Journal of Rural Studies* 33:82–94.

Burton, Rob and Geoff A. Wilson. 2012. "The Rejuvenation of Productivist Agriculture: The Case for 'Cooperative Neo-productivism.'" *Research in Rural Sociology and Development* 18:51–72.

Busch, Lawrence and Carmen Bain. 2004. "New! Improved? The Transformation of the Global Agrifood System." *Rural Sociology* 69:321–346.

Cassells, Sue M. and Anton D. Meister. 2002. "Cost and Trade Impacts of Environmental Regulations: Effluent Control and the New Zealand Dairy Sector." *Australian Journal of Agricultural and Resource Economics* 45:257–274.

Crosby, Alfred W. 2004. *Ecological Imperialism: The Biological Expansion of Europe, 900–1900.* New York: Cambridge University Press.

DairyNZ. 2013a. "New Zealand Dairy Statistics 2012–13."

DairyNZ. 2013b. "Sustainable Dairying: Water Accord."

Deans, Neil and Kevin Hackwell. 2008. "Dairying and Declining Water Quality: Why Has the Dairying and Clean Streams Accord Not Delivered Cleaner Streams." Wellington: Fish and Game and Forest and Bird.

Gibbon, Peter and Stefano Ponte. 2008. "Global Value Chains: From Governance to Governmentality?" *Economy and Society* 37:365–392.

Greenpeace. 2009. "The Changing Face of NZ Farming: Why Boom and Bust is Not Working." Auckland: Greenpeace New Zealand Aotearoa.

Greig, Bruce. 2012. "Changing NZ Dairy Farm Systems." SIDE Conference June. Dunedin, New Zealand: South Island Dairying Event.

Halleron, Richard. 2014. "Brakes Could Be Put on Expansion of New Zealand Dairy Sector." *Agriland.* March 23. Retrieved November 16, 2014 (http://www.agriland.ie/news/brakes-put-expansion-new-zealand-dairy-sector/).

Harvey, David. 2005. *A Brief History of Neoliberalism.* Oxford: Oxford University Press.

Higgins, Vaughan and Geoffrey Lawrence. 2005. "Introduction: Globalization and Agricultural Governance." Pp. 1–15 in *Agricultural Governance: Globalization and the New Politics of Regulation*, vol. 10, edited by Vaughan Higgins and Geoffrey Lawrence. New York: Routledge.

Johnson, Bryce. 2014. "Time to Prosecute Those Who Milk Dirty Dairying." *NZFarmer. co.nz.* March 21.

Mackay, Alec D. 2008. "Impacts of Intensification of Pastoral Agriculture on Soils: Current and Emerging Challenges and Implications for Future Land Uses." *New Zealand Veterinary Journal* 56:281–288.

Mansfield, Becky. 2007. "Articulation between Neoliberal and State-Oriented Environmental Regulation: Fisheries Privatization and Endangered Species Protection." *Environment and Planning A* 39(8):1926–1942.

Meister, Anton and Nicole Beechey. "Decentralized, Outcome Oriented Management of Agricultural Environmental Issues in New Zealand." Pp. 79–96 in *The Economics of Regulation in Agriculture: Compliance and Public and Private Standards*, edited by F. Brouwer, G. Fox, and R. Jongeneel. Oxfordshire, UK: CAB International.

Ministry for Primary Industries. 2009. "The Dairying and Clean Streams Accord: Snapshot of Progress 2007/2008."

Ministry for Primary Industries. 2013. "The Dairying and Clean Streams Accord: Snapshot of Progress 2011/2012."

Ministry for the Environment. 2001. "Valuing New Zealand's Clean Green Image." *Sustainable Development*, August. Wellington: Ministry for the Environment. Retrieved June 12, 2014 (http://www.mfe.govt.nz/publications/sus-dev/clean-green-image-value-aug01/).

Ministry for the Environment. 2003. "Dairying and Clean Streams Accord."

New Zealand Dairy Board. 1961. "Dairy Board Act 1961."

Pearce, Fred. 2009. "New Zealand Was a Friend to Middle Earth, but It's No Friend of the Earth." *The Guardian.* March 5.

Reuters. 2013. "New Zealand's Environment-Friendly Image Marred by Dairy Contamination." *HuffPost Green.* August 5.

Science Alert: Experts Respond. 2013. "Shifts in Farming Put Pressure on Water Quality—Report." *Science Alert: Experts Respond*, November 21. Retrieved June 11, 2014 (http://www.sciencemediacentre.co.nz/2013/11/21/shifts-in-farming-put-pressure-on-water-quality-report/).

Sharpe, Marty. 2012. "Dirty Dairying Laid Bare." *The Dominion Post*. June 5.

Smith, David and Matthew Mahutga. 2008. "Trading up the Commodity Chain? The Impact of Extractive and Labor-Intensive Manufacturing Trade on World-System Inequalities." Pp. 63–82 in *Frontiers of Commodity Chain Research*, edited by J. Bair. Stanford, CA: Stanford University Press.

Statistics New Zealand. 2014. "Global New Zealand—International Trade, Investment, and Travel Profile: Year Ended December 2013." Wellington: Ministry of Foreign Affairs and Trade and Statistics New Zealand.

White, Mike. 2007. "Fat Cows and Filthy Streams." *North and South* 260:52–63.

Xinhua Agencies. 2013. "Report Highlights Toxic Effects of New Zealand Dairy Industry on Waterways." *Global Times*. November 21.

# 3. The political economy of agri-food in Mexico

*Francisco Martínez and Gilberto Aboites*

## INTRODUCTION

The objective of this chapter is to review salient characteristics of the current agri-food economic policy of Mexico that resulted in an increasingly polarized sector split between agri-firms and small family/peasant farms. This sector bears the consequences of the adoption of market-oriented policies that stress the enhancement of production and productivity and that have generated a negative balance of payment and increased economic and food dependency (Otero, Pechlaner and Gurcan 2013). While it boosted exports of fruits and vegetables, it fostered the restructuring of a sector that is now more globalized and more functional to the interests of transnational corporations (TNCs). Additionally, the chapter illustrates the emergence of social resistance to this globally oriented model and the contradictions that it entails. It discusses the delegitimation of state actions vis-à-vis the fragility of the adopted model.

This introduction is followed by three sections. The first is a brief summary of the structural reforms that took place from the 1940s to the early 1980s. It also discusses the characteristics of movements of social resistance that emerged during that period. The second section reviews the evolution of agri-food since the 1990s, stressing the consequences generated by the implementation of neoliberal measures and the emergence and strengthening of networks of production and consumption. These are networks that, while global, operate with great intensity at both sides of the border between Mexico and the United States. The significant role played by TNCs and their contributions to the growth of inequality and poverty are discussed. The chapter concludes with some reflections on the social impact of the structural reforms in agri-food in Mexico.

## THE EARLY AGRI-FOOD ECONOMIC POLICY IN MEXICO (1940–1982)

According to Gómez-Oliver (1994), three periods characterized the economic policy of Mexican agriculture up the early 1980s. The agricultural reform years of the Cárdenas Administration (1938–1940) is the first of these periods. It allowed the development of "the 1940–1958 agricultural growth era" that was followed by the 1958–1982 stabilizing development period. The agricultural growth era saw the end of the almost monopolistic power of the owners of large latifundia (*terratenientes*), the growth in political and economic importance of the ejidatarios (those participating in the ejido public land distribution program) and significant government investment in infrastructure and farm programs. These changes promoted a growth of production and productivity that was supported by the expansion of domestic demand. Coupled with the post-World War II growth of international demand, these items contributed to the establishment of what is known as the "Mexican Economic Miracle" (Reynolds 1973). Accordingly, between 1940 and 1958 agriculture grew at an annual average rate of 5.8 percent, and its contribution was equal to about one-fifth of the GDP.

The 1958–1982 stabilizing development period was characterized by the adoption of a model of development that identified urban industrialization as the engine of growth and subordinated agricultural policies to this goal. Through Fordist-style policies, agri-food prices were kept relatively stable, with the objective of fostering the creation of new employment, limiting inflation, increasing productivity and consumption, and in so doing expanding industrial development (Norton 1993). State intervention involved spending in research and extension services, credit support, distribution of agricultural inputs, and price support programs. These measures generated a pattern whereby lower commodity prices were compensated by increasing public investment and expenditures. Accordingly, between 1957 and 1981 the average public investment for agriculture grew at an annual rate of 10 percent while the overall state intervention accounted for 20 percent of the sector's GDP (Gómez-Oliver 1994).

This policy was consistent with the then popular modernization theory. Supporting pronouncements about the effectiveness of modernization, Johnston and Mellor (1962) noted that in this model agriculture impacts economic development in five ways. Agriculture impacts: (a) the expansion of the food supply; (b) the growth of agricultural exports; (c) the mobilization of labor; (d) the growth of manufacturing; and (e) the expansion of net cash income for the rural population. In Mexico, however, the contradictory aspects of this policy were strident. In particular, it was characterized by a sharp concentration of economic subsidies to large agri-firms and farms that engendered a marked structural dualism between a small group of large profitable firms and a large segment of small and peasant farms. Accordingly, in the early 1950s, half of all farm land was occupied by small and peasant holdings that contributed only 6 percent to the total production. Because of this type of state intervention, a decade later the contribution of small and peasant farms declined to 4 percent, and in 1970 it further fell to be just over 2 percent (Gómez-Oliver 1994; Gordillo 1979; Hewitt 1999; 2007).

To be sure, up to 1957 the ratio between corn prices and minimum wages was stable, and often corn prices remained above minimum wage levels. This situation contributed to the persistence of small and peasant farms as it discouraged farm family members from taking off-farm jobs. Subsequently, however, this ratio changed in favor of wages as corn prices dropped significantly. By 1973 they accounted for only 29 percent of the 1957 level. Firms responded by replacing corn with sorghum and other commodities, while small farm holders and peasants left the sector in search of better jobs. This migration, however, contributed not only to the depeasantization of Mexican farming but also to the increased presence of a significant stratum of a poor marginal labor force in large metropolitan areas such as Mexico City (Gómez-Oliver 1994:15).

**Resistance**

These conditions, and the overall development of the sector, engendered resistance. According to Poitras, Aboites and Otero (2014), the evolution of the period's rural resistance can be divided into two phases. In the first phase, which began in the late 1930s, corporatism dominated and the sector was regulated by a strict Institutional Revolutionary Party (PRI) structure under the control of the National Peasant Confederation (CNC). This system operated as a mechanism of political control of the peasantry, regulating access to land and housing and containing social dissatisfaction. It ultimately generated a context dominated by deep clientelist relations (Mackinlay 1996; Mackinlay and Otero 2006). It began to crumble in the late 1950s as peasant and rural workers' unions were able to free themselves from the control of the state. As unions increased their power, the difficult situation allowed the emergence of extremist armed revolutionary groups such as the Zapatista movement of Rubén Jaramillo (Padilla 2012).

In the second phase, there was the development of new movements and organizations that, while furthering the process of political independence from the corporatist Mexican state, directed their struggles to enhance workers' control of production processes. In the 1970s, organizations centered on specific crop productions and services developed. They first grew under the control of the CNC but soon gained full independence (Mackinlay 1996). Important was their opposition to the historical alliance between the agricultural bourgeoisie and the state, which dominated Mexican agri-food development in the 1950s and 1960s, and their struggle against the clientelist approach to state investment and redistributive policies (Gordillo and Andersson 2003; Hewitt 2007; Gordillo 1979; Bartra 2008; Rello 1997; Mackinlay and Otero 2006). During this period, other types of organizations emerged such as those that would eventually generate the Zapatista movement in Chiapas. Their new forms and objectives of struggle questioned the traditional strategies of modernization and found support in workers' movements that emerged in other sectors (Harvey 1996; Mackinlay 1996). They also searched for support among other groups such as intellectuals. In this respect, the connection that developed between these organizations and research initiatives in universities was important.

# GLOBAL POLITICAL ECONOMY: AGRI-FOOD IN MEXICO IN THE 1990s AND THE 21ST CENTURY

### Resistance in the 1990s and Beyond

From the late 1980s onward, rural resistance in Mexico centered on opposition to neoliberal globalization. It included struggles for the independence of the Mexican state from policies dictated by international institutions, such as the World Bank and the International Monetary Fund (IMF), and the United States. Anti-imperialist struggles were coupled with calls for food sovereignty, productive self-determination, alternative agriculture and the emancipation of subordinate and indigenous groups. The implementation of the North American Free Trade Agreement (NAFTA) in 1994 and the concomitant response of the Zapatista movement in Chiapas defined this type of resistance. Similarly, the emergence of Via Campesina and its global program of struggle based on indigenous agriculture and traditional agro-ecology constituted a proposal that achieved global recognition and following (Via Campesina 1999; Desmarais 2007). Since 1965, and up to this time, the indigenous community movement has been only formally included into the CNC (Mackinlay 1996). In the 1990s the prominence of the "campesino" movement allowed the development and success of an agenda that opposed the CNC and the clientelist and paternalist Mexican state (Bartra and Otero 2007; Acuña Rodarte 2003).

## The Current Conditions

This resistance continued into the new century as the consequences of neoliberal globalization become increasingly visible. In effect, the current situation in Mexico is a good example of the results of several decades of implementation of neoliberal measures on a less-developed agri-food sector (Otero et al. 2013; Martínez, Aboites and Constance 2013). These measures left rural Mexico with widespread poverty and inequality accompanied by the control of the economy and polity by a few large TNCs. The structural reforms that were implemented re-regulated the sector and allowed these agri-food TNCs to further their control on production processes through mechanisms featuring vertical and horizontal integration, mergers and acquisitions, increased foreign direct investment (FDI) and the creation of production and distribution networks first at the regional level and later at the national and international levels. In effect, this growth transcended the domestic and bi-nations (Mexico–United States) spaces as illustrated by the case of the poultry industry whereby TNCs positioned themselves as the primary actors in the construction and control of global value chains (Martínez et al. 2013; Constance, Martínez, Aboites and Bonanno 2012).

Along with the negative economic consequences, the growth of transnational agriculture has been associated with environmental degradation and the worsening of the overall health conditions in the country due to the adoption of the corporate diet. As far as the first aspect is concerned, it has been documented that the commodification of agricultural genes and the control and use of natural resources by TNCs has permanently affected the quality of water, soil and air, significantly decreased the rich genetic diversity of the region and accelerated the dangerous process of climate change (Esquinas-Alcázar, Frison and López 2011). For the second issue, it is argued that emergence of poor eating habits in urban but also rural areas is the consequence of patterns promoted by agri-food corporations that while enhancing their profit do very little to provide consumers with adequate food choices. In this contest, the astonishing growth of obesity has been interpreted as one of the most serious consequences of the corporatization of food. Acknowledging this difficult situation, the Mexican Government has estimated that 71.3 percent of the entire population is either overweight or obese. Moreover, the same sources stress that poor nutritional habits and weight excess have contributed to a host of illnesses that now affect local residents (SAGARPA 2013). Departing from views that address these problems as individual choices, it has been recognized that the corporate model tends to offer low-cost products that, while appear attractive to lower strata of the population, are nutritionally inadequate.

**Inequality and Rural Poverty**

The effect of the neoliberal structural reforms initiated in the 1980s and continuously implemented in the next three decades achieved harmful results for the majority of the population. The country's economic growth has been sluggish as GDP grew at an annual rate of 0.8 percent from 1980 to 2010. This is a sharp decline from the value of 3.15 percent recorded from 1940 to 1980 (Romero 2012). This poor economic performance is accompanied by equally dismal employment growth whereby unemployment and precarious employment (60 percent of all workers are employed in the informal economy) characterize the Mexican labor structure (INEGI 2014). Moreover,

> Mexico is second in income inequality and first in relative poverty among all OECD countries (one out of five Mexican residents is poor in comparison with the OECD average of one out of ten) and for half of the population it is difficult to live with their current levels of income. This is again a much higher level of economic difficulty than that recorded for the rest of the OECD countries. (OECD 2011:12)

The situation of rural Mexico is even worse as 64.9 percent of all rural residents are below the poverty line as opposed to 40.6 percent of urban residents (CONEVAL 2013:12).

The strengthening of the neoliberal project in Mexico, the restructuring of expenditures and the reorganization of political priorities marked the end of the social pact between the government and small farm holders and peasants and the increased vulnerability of the latter. Accordingly, thousands of these agriculturalists could not continue to live on their farms and had to migrate. Data for 2009 indicate that 2.4 million of daily wage workers were employed by agricultural firms that year. At least 20 percent of these workers defined themselves as migrant from some of the poorer farm states in the country. The majority of these workers migrated with their family, accepting poorly paid, harsh and flexible contract jobs, and received no social benefits. They were also fired at the total discretion of the employer. These poor working conditions are reproduced also because more than one-third of these workers are members of indigenous groups with limited or no knowledge of Spanish (Consejo de Derechos Humanos 2012).

Poverty and migration are also the consequences of neoliberal government policies that reduced and reoriented expenditures for agriculture and rural areas, creating a highly unequal wealth redistribution system (World Bank 2009; Scott 2010). In effect, 70 percent of all farm and peasant families receive an average of 500 Mexican pesos (38 USD) per month in subsidies. But 10 percent of families receive more than 3,000 pesos (World Bank 2009). The six poorer states receive only 7 percent of all state expenditures for agriculture despite the fact that 55 percent of the farm population is concentrated in these states. Similarly, 70 percent of all rural municipalities received only 6 percent of state expenditures, and less that 8 percent of all farm programs is devoted to small and peasant farms (Consejo de Derechos Humanos 2012). In essence, poverty and social inequality remain, with 64.9 percent of the total rural population living under the poverty line as opposed to 40.6 percent of the urban population (CONEVAL 2013:22).

**The Restructuring of Agriculture and Public Policies**

Available statistics indicate that between 1982 and 2008 the number of farms increased from 25.5 million to 53.2 million units. Among these farms, peasant farms decreased to 73 percent of all farms from 86.5 percent. Also the number of semi-peasant farms decreased, while large business-oriented farms increased significantly from a mere 1.9 percent to representing almost two-thirds of all farms (18.6 percent) (CEPAL 1982; SAGARPA/FAO 2013). In 2012 the tertiary sector accounted for 62.4 percent of the GDP while manufacturing and agriculture covered 34.5 percent and 3.1 percent respectively. However, in terms of employment, farming occupied 14.5 percent of all the employed population while manufacturing and the tertiary sector contributed 30.1 percent and 55.4 percent respectively. This situation indicates that agriculture employs more workers per each unit of value generated. Agricultural production also declined as a result of the implementation of neoliberal policies (Rodríguez 1979; 1980; 1983; Rodriguez and Ortiz 1983). During the 1960s and throughout the 1970s, Mexican agriculture grew at a faster rate than many other Latin America countries (Table 3.1). However, after market liberalization in the early 1980s, this trend reversed (Table 3.1) (Caballero, Hoberg, de Dinechin and McMahon 2005).

Within Mexico, between 1994 and 2010, agriculture, forestry and fisheries also grew at a lower rate than the overall economy. This trend was attributed to a number of factors including the inadequate development of productive and entrepreneurial technical skills; low levels of technological innovation; insufficient levels of productivity; limited access to markets for agricultural and fisheries products; insufficient funding for pertinent economic activities; unfavorable animal and health conditions and high levels of economic risk associated with farming and fishing (SAGARPA/FAO 2013:11). Despite this decline, however, the socio-economic impact of changes in agriculture remains relevant as indicated by the relatively higher decrease of the monetary income of households where at least one of their members works in the primary sector (Table 3.2).

*Table 3.1   Annual growth of the "total factor productivity" in Mexico and other Latin American countries*

| Countries | Crops | | Livestock | | Agriculture | | Average |
|---|---|---|---|---|---|---|---|
| Years | 1961/80 | 1980/01 | 1961/80 | 1980/01 | 1961/80 | 1980/01 | 1961/2001 |
| Argentina | 3.08 | 3.93 | 0.90 | 0.43 | 1.83 | 2.35 | 2.09 |
| Brazil | 0.38 | 3.00 | 0.71 | 3.61 | 0.49 | 3.22 | 1.86 |
| Chile | 1.08 | 2.22 | 0.24 | 1.87 | 0.69 | 2.05 | 1.37 |
| Colombia | 2.01 | 1.27 | 0.49 | 2.24 | 1.37 | 1.73 | 1.55 |
| Mexico | 1.53 | 1.43 | 3.02 | 1.63 | 2.26 | 1.51 | 1.89 |
| **LAC average** | **1.46** | **2.40** | **1.42** | **2.21** | **1.39** | **2.31** | **1.85** |

*Source:*   Authors' elaboration of data available in Avila and Evenson (2004).

*Table 3.2   Total monthly family income in Mexico, according to economic sectors of employment of family members 2012*

| Total Monthly income | Agriculture | Manufacturing | Tertiary | Ag. & Man. | Ag. & Ter. | Man. & Ter. | All sectors | Total Household Income |
|---|---|---|---|---|---|---|---|---|
| Number of Households | 3,135,756 | 4,258,894 | 13,604,852 | 765,168 | 1,764,887 | 4,538,305 | 552,776 | 31,559,379 |
| Average | 5,686 | 12,087 | 15,478 | 7,345 | 9,982 | 17,233 | 11,874 | 39,999 |
| Median | 4,158 | 7,983 | 10,850 | 5,704 | 7,411 | 12,762 | 9,118 | 26,751 |
| Mode | 3,067 | 5,869 | 17,044 | 6,702 | 15,342 | 22,941 | 12,363 | 51,134 |
| Minimum | 501 | 190 | 483 | 519 | 1,099 | 1,411 | 1,620 | 571 |
| Maximum | 138,196 | 264,298 | 255,453 | 123,515 | 131,097 | 257,299 | 51,898 | 792,894 |

*Note:*   Income reported in 2012 Mexican pesos. 1 USD 5 12.82 Mexican pesos.

*Source:*   Authors' elaboration on census data.

As stressed above, the adverse effects of neoliberal policy generated social discontent and resistance.

In order to prevent loss of legitimacy, the Mexican state enacted measures that attempted to address the claims of the lower classes. These programs included initiatives such as *Progreso-Oportunidades-Solidariedad* (Progress-Opportunities-Solidarity) and, for agriculture, the *Procampo* (For-Agriculture) scheme. These moves indicate that despite the neoliberal turn, the state remains a central actor in the economy and society given the lack of resources and its unwillingness and/or incapacity to devolve some of its powers. However, socio-economic stability remains a distant objective. Politically, and unlike the case of the Fordist era, the state has not been able to apply, and receive the support for, measures that were successful in the past (McMichael 1996a). Accordingly, it has resorted to arguments that speak of productivity and reliance on the market to a public that can hardly gain access to it. In this context, even programs for the development of agriculture became impracticable and delegitimizing (Bonanno 2004). With its emphasis on the expansion of productive, technological and market efficiency, the neoliberal model of growth not only has run counter to the expectations of the lower and middle classes but has prevented the creation of adequate forms of solidarity that could re-establish a workable social pact. Ultimately, this posture has provided a stagnant situation whereby the government has continued to repeat the application of similar plans but achieved no real significant change (Poitras, Otero and Aboites 2014).

The search for enhanced productivity through the implementation of "associative models (i.e., cluster) that would improve the productive capacity of small farms and integrate them into the productive chain" (SAGARPA 2013: 59) has represented a longstanding objective that has not been successful, neither in terms of the creation of a new organizational structure nor in terms of the growth of the socio-economic viability of small farms. In effect, in 1980 the Federal Government introduced the Agricultural Development Act (Ley de Fomento Agropecuario) that allowed the establishment of common productive units that contemplated the joining of ejidos farms with small farms. It generated the legal framework that could have fostered a new form of associationism. Years later, in 1994, with the amendment of Article 27 of the Constitution promoted by President Carlos Salinas de Gortari, the institutional conditions to allow small farms to obtain rural credit were generated. Despite these attempts, agri-food developed in different directions and was characterized by the growth of contract and corporate farming (Aboites and Martínez 2014). More recently, and in regard to seeds, again the government proposed the Sustainable Modernization of Traditional Agriculture (MasAgro) program for the development and distribution of seed varieties and hybrids at low cost to farmers. This current initiative wants to assist small producers in the planting of more varieties of corn and wheat and create greater competition in the seed producing sector of Mexico (SAGARPA/FAO 2013). Additionally, it is aimed at strengthening cooperation between the Department of Agriculture and the International Maize and Wheat Improvement Center. While the language used points to support for the small farm and peasant sector, the insistence on the growth of agricultural productivity through the application of economic and commercial rationality plays into the hands of TNCs given the existence of a quasi-monopolized seed market. In effect, over the last 15 years more than 80 percent of all improved seeds have been purchased either from Monsanto or Pioneer. In addition, the national institute responsible for generating new materials (INIFAP) has focused on the creation of hybrid corn rather than open-pollinated materials, making it difficult to generate any change that would favor small producers (Aboites 2012).

There is, thus, a mismatch between the government's continuous insistence in the promotion of a productivist economic policy and the perennial poverty and subordination of peasants and small producers. More importantly, there is a constant insistence on the idea of the inefficiency of the small farm and peasant sector. Missing, therefore, is consideration for the overall importance of this sector. A student of the topic observes:

> It is not to show that as producers of certain goods [small farmers and peasants] are as efficient as other producers. It is about demonstrating that in addition to commodities, they produce social, environmental and cultural products that are absolutely essential. Additionally, they are much more efficient than first world producers – particularly those in the U.S. – and their unsustainability. It seems, then, that the best strategic bet of small farmers and peasants is to enhance the plurality of their functions and structure their struggles comprehensively articulating strictly economic aspects with social, environmental, cultural and political dimensions. Because small farmers and peasants are good producers, and should be even better ones, their historical project does not rest on business efficiency. (Bartra 2002:54)

This is particularly important because the successful mass production of undifferentiated goods, such as corn and wheat, remains highly problematic given international competition and the historically constructed environment of the country. For example, in Mexico the states that record the highest production per hectare of corn are Sinaloa, Chihuahua and Guanajuato. They generate yields that vary from 8.8 to 9.5 metric tons per hectare. In Iowa the average yield is 10.4 metric tons per hectare. Simultaneously, cost per metric ton produced ranges from 1,899 pesos in Guanajuato to 2,140 pesos in Sinaloa. In Iowa it averages 1,366 pesos (Ochoa 2010).

In December 2013 the Mexican Federal Government introduced the

2013–2018 Agricultural Sector Development Program for Fisheries and Food, which highlighted the guidelines for the economic and social policy of agri-food (SAGARPA/FAO 2013). This document proposed an increase in productivity and the reduction of the rigidities that it was considered were affecting the productive structure and pertinent institutions. The overall objective was to achieve greater "resilience" for agri-food. The strategy for achieving better competitiveness for the sector was based on ten major points:

1. Increase the productivity of small farms through the implementation of a partnership model (cluster) and their integration of the productive chain.
2. Promote modernization, maximization and sustainable use of water resources, with emphasis on more efficient production through a more efficient water use.
3. Promote domestic production of strategic inputs, particularly fertilizers and improved seeds.
4. Promote innovation, technological development and applied technical assistance through a new form of extension service.
5. Improve the management and prevention of climatic and market risks.
6. Promote the production of healthy and safe food.
7. Promote timely and competitive financing.
8. Promote regional development along with strategic projects and agroparks.
9. Establish a planning system to balance supply and demand.
10. Establish a new organizational model for the Department of Agriculture based on the objective of being Innovative, Flexible, Agile and Transparent (IFAT).

While it is too early to assess the specific consequences of this policy, it is clear that this proposal continues the trends illustrated above. In essence, rather than exploring new avenues for growth, Mexican agri-food policy continues to propose the same types of solutions to chronically unsolved problems.

**Global Agri-food Network in Mexico and the United States**

The establishment of global networks of agri-food production finds in the connection between the United States and Mexico one of its more relevant dimensions. Among the reasons for this relevance is the growth in power of TNCs that dominate these networks by operating on both sides of the border.

Telling of the expansion of the network system is the growth of the volume of exchange between the two countries. Mexican exports to the United States grew by 75 percent from 1993 to 2012. Imports from the United States grew at an almost similar pace, increasing by 73 percent over the same time period (USDA 2012). Despite this balanced grow of imports and exports, the TNC controlled networks fostered a process of unequal exchange whereby the agricultural trade deficit of Mexico rose by 4,168 billion USD from 2002 and 2012 (SAGARPA 2013). FDI also grew further, indicating the expansion of the network system. Favored by the deregulation of norms limiting foreign investment, FDI in agri-food expanded from 210 million USD to 2.3 billion USD from 1983 to 1993 and from 30 billion USD in 1997 to 36 billion USD in 2011, increasing at an annual rate that fluctuated between 5 and 10 percent (USDA 2012). The increased hypermobility of capital became a characteristic of this process (Bonanno and Constance 2008; Harvey 2005). In the case of the grain–meat complex, FDI in grain mills and oilseed by US based firms increased from 278 million USD in 1999 to 2.5 billion USD in 2010 as a significant portion of FDI in agri-food was invested in this area (USDA 2012). Simultaneously, grains, oilseeds, meat and related products cover two-thirds of the Mexican exports to the United States, yet livestock production in Mexico depends to a significant extent on the import of grains and oilseeds from the United States (USDA 2012). The result is that in the case of basic food items, such as beef and chicken meat, the market is highly concentrated, with a few large TNCs, such as Tyson, Pilgrim Pride and Bachoco, controlling most of the production, with units operating both in Mexico and the United States (Constance et al. 2012; Martínez et al. 2013; Almanza 2013).

The liberalization of agri-food and the growth of networks of production are at the roots of the strong process of rural outmigration that has been affecting Mexico in the last three decades. A significant portion of these immigrants lost their peasant and/or wage workers status because of the agri-food restructuring described above. As the push factor is accompanied by increasingly stringent requirements to enter the United States, unauthorized migration remains the norm. Without the required status, these immigrants are exposed to overt economic and political exploitation that translates into extremely poor working conditions and pay but also high levels of productivity that propel corporate profit.

**The Transformation of the Nation-State**

As indicated above, the neoliberal project initiated in the 1980s broke the long-established social pact between the government and the small farm holders and peasants. This pact was established to address the claims and struggles of the Mexican peasantry that characterized the first portion of the 20th Century and that led to the creation of protectionist policies, a relatively large welfare state and import substitution developmental strategies (Mackinlay 1996; Mackinlay and Otero 2006; Mackinlay 2006; Teubal 2001). At the outset of the 1970s, the high rate of growth of the Mexican population mandated an equally large expansion of the demand for agri-food items. The solution to address this issue was identified in the adoption of measures that followed the so-called green revolution; that is, a model based on the increase of the use of chemicals, machines and highly productive plant varieties created through genetic improvement techniques. To this end, fundamental was the financial and technical support provided by international organizations that, under the auspices of the United States, intervened with the more than secondary geopolitical objective of countering the threat represented by socialist movements and struggles (McNamara 1981; Martínez 2003; Otero 2008; Teubal 2001).

The end of the 1970s signaled the crisis of this model, triggered by the high levels of surpluses of grain in the United States and the members of the European Union and the desire of these countries to dispose of the extra production through exports. Simultaneously, fiscal problems and the adoption of neoliberal postures promoted the reduction of international organizations' spending in agriculture (Teubal 2001). Similarly, the economic and technical intervention of the nation-state in the sector was reduced and increasingly seen as unnecessary and often damaging. The alternative was identified in measures that eliminated protectionism in favor of market-oriented strategies. In 1982 the inability of the Mexican Government to service its international debt, and the subsequent declaration of insolvency, promoted a broader fiscal crisis that was addressed through structural adjustment measures. This restructuring severely impacted agriculture, with the elimination of funds and institutions that once supported and regulated the sector. An instance of this process was the elimination in the 1990s of CONASUPO (National Company for Popular Subsistence), an organization that was pivotal in the regulation of grain prices and exports. However, and like similar cases, its elimination did not achieve the desired result of a much more efficient and equitable system. Instead, it contributed to the strengthening of those corporate-dominated networks of production discussed above. Ultimately, the privatization of institutions that provided technical and financial assistance to farmers and peasants has been an overall failure.

In the 1970s, state-sponsored institutions were able to satisfy more than 90 percent of the local demand through a policy of discounted and stable prices (Ruiz Funes 2013). Currently, more than 87 percent of domestic demand is addressed through imports whose prices have been steadily on the increase. According to SAGARPA (The Secretariat of Agriculture, Livestock, Rural Development, Fisheries and Food), this is the result of the fact that "the current market structure favors the existence of a few suppliers that sell agricultural inputs at quasi monopolistic prices" (SAGARPA 2013:2). The examples of the negative consequences of the introduction of neoliberal policies are seemingly endless. Through liberalization, the Mexican Government hoped that the opening of the market would allow more efficient production and availability of basic crops such as corn, wheat, rice, beans, sorgo and soya. Yet, not only have the international prices of these commodities constantly risen but also the volume of imports. Accordingly, and since 2000, imports covered at least 38 percent of the domestic demand for basic crops, with peaks of over 40 percent in a context in which the FAO (Food and Agriculture Organization of the United Nations) recommends that the maximum threshold for these types of imports should not be greater than 25 percent. Accordingly, Mexico is in a serious situation of import dependency, which is more dangerous given the fact that the government plans to maintain this level of imports at least up to 2018, and that it disproportionally affects the lower classes (SAGARPA 2013; Otero et al. 2013).

In this context, the government's design to establish competitive conditions for local producers appears anachronistic at best. In effect, only a small number of agri-food firms can take advantage of this policy, while the majority of farmers and the large stratum of peasants are increasingly condemned to poverty and migration. The lack of access to credit and the sharp decline in government support leave little room for hope for the survival of the small farm/peasant sector. Data indicate that only 9 percent of all farms have access to credit (FIRA 2014). And while the government contends that it intends to increase this percentage, the significant reduction of funds devoted to agriculture indicates a different trend. In effect, the total amount of agricultural subsidies declined by 50 percent since the mid-1990s. And the total support to agriculture does not exceed 0.7 percent of 2012 GDP. This is less that the average of the Organisation for Economic Co-operation and Development (OECD) countries (OECD 2012). Moreover, foreign producers have been able to sell at very low prices (dumping effect) given the fact that they could count on greater support from their governments and more efficient productive units. Under these conditions, the government rhetoric appears nothing more than a justification for the increased presence and control of local agriculture by TNCs and their practice of contracting and outsourcing (Rodrik 2006). Faced with these conditions, large segments of the agricultural sector oppose the government policy. Telling is a recent statement from the leader of the popular farmer movement El Barzón, Alfonso Ramírez Cuéllar, who "asked the government to eliminate the power that oligopolies have over agri-food; stop social and productive inequality in the sector and resume regulation of the market of production inputs" (Padilla Tanalís 2012:2).

## SOME FINAL OBSERVATIONS

The Mexican agri-food sector is characterized by a significant degree of socio-economic inequality. The neoliberal policies implemented since the 1980s and reinforced after the signing of NAFTA clearly contributed to its growth (CEPAL 2002; CEPAL 2010). The structural reforms carried out over the last three decades achieved results that stand opposite to the redistributive goal that often characterized government pronouncements. They placed the Mexican Government in a highly contradictory position. On the one hand, it is committed to market-oriented strategies to enhance the productivity and efficiency of agriculture. On the other, this posture engendered ineffective solutions to address the socio-economic issues facing the great majority of farmers and peasants. The government partially attempted to solve this contradiction through factually timid but rhetorically strong pronouncements about redistributive measures. Yet, the results have been a growing fiscal crisis of the state and the worsening of the socio-economic conditions in rural areas (OECD 2013).

This contradictory situation has been complemented by many important crises that have emerged since 2008: the energy crisis, the environmental and climate change crisis, the crisis of the price of corn and other commodities and, significantly, the financial crisis (Murphy, Burch and Clapp 2012; Wahl 2009; Wise 2013). The crises of the prices of corn and of the national staple food tortillas are emblematic of a combination of the negative consequences of the neoliberalization of the economy and politics and of the inability of the nation-state to address them through market-oriented measures. Moreover, the power of TNCs is as such that the situation is recognized even by established institutions such as the OECD. According to the OECD:

> Poor families spend more than one third of their incomes on goods that are sold in markets with limited or no competition. This is the result of lack of regulation by public institutions and the fact that they have been weaker than monopolies. The negative effects on prices, quality and variety of these goods and services is quite visible. (OECD 2013:4)

Neoliberalism as the dominant ideology of globalization facilitated the mobility of capital, commodities, labor and also ideas across national borders, through axes of power that are much more polycentric than the traditional imperialist North–South dichotomy (Margulis, McKeon and Borras 2013). This is certainly the case of Mexico, where the great majority of farmers now operate within global networks. In this context, the national territory is increasingly subject to a crisis of sovereignty and the domination of non-national authorities such as international organizations, TNCs and even non-governmental organizations (NGOs) (Sassen 2006; 2013). While the awareness of these conditions and their distortions has led to resistance, the lack of instruments to control the actions of these dominant actors makes the defense of the interests of farmers and peasants more problematic than ever (Prats 2005). Caught in this global evolution, the Mexican Government is the embodiment of this crisis, as the instruments that it mobilizes to address current problems often contribute to their growth rather than being part of the solution.

# REFERENCES

Aboites, Gilberto. 2012. *Semillas, Negocio y Propiedad Intelectual*. Mexico City, Mexico: Trillas and Universidad Autónoma de Coahuila.
Aboites, Gilberto and Francisco Martínez. 2014. "Labor Relations and Issues in the Poultry Sector in Mexico." Pp. 77–94 in Alessandro Bonanno and Josefa Salete Barbosa Cavalcanti (eds.) *Labor Relations in Globalized Food*. Bingley, UK: Emerald.
Acuña Rodarte, Olivia. 2003. "Toward an Equitable, Inclusive, and Sustainable Agriculture: Mexico's Basic Grains Producers Unite." Pp. 129–148 in Timothy A. Wise, Hilda Salazar and Laura Carlsen (eds.) *Confronting Globalization: Economic Integration and Popular Resistance in Mexico*. Bloomfield, CT: Kumarian.
Almanza, Jonathan. 2013. "Globalización y Restructuración Financiera en la Industria Avícola: El Caso de JBS/Piligrim's Pride." Baccalaureate Thesis in Agricultural Economics and Agribusiness. Department of Socio-Economic Sciences, Universidad Autónoma Agraria Antonio Narro, Saltillo Coahuila, Mexico.
Avila, Flavio and Robert E. Evenson. 2004. "Total Factor Productivity Growth in Agriculture: The Role of Technological Capital." Paper presented at the Yale Economic Growth Center and the Fondo Regional de Tecnología Agropecuaria (FONTAGRO) Annual Meeting, Lima, Peru, March; Quoted in José María Caballero, Yurie Tanimichi Hoberg, Frederic de Dinechin and Matthew McMahon 2005:255.
Bartra, Armando. 2002. "III y Ultima Un Campo que no Aguanta Más." *La Jornada*. December 16. Mexico City. Retrieved at http://www.jornada.unam.mx/2002/12/16/008a1pol.php on April 2, 2014.
Bartra, Armando. 2008. *El Hombre de Hierro. Los Límites Sociales y Naturales del Capital*. Mexico City: UACM-ITACA-UAM.
Bartra, Armando and Gerardo Otero. 2007. "Rebeldía Contra el Globalismo Neoliberal y el TLCAN en el México Rural: ¿Del Estado Corporativista a la Formación Político-Cultural del Campesinado?" *Textual* 50:1–34.
Bonanno, Alessandro. 2004. "La Globalización Agroalimentaria: sus Características y Perspectivas Futuras." *Sociologias* 5 (10):190–218.
Bonanno, Alessandro and Douglas H. Constance. 2008. *Stories of Globalization: Transnational Corporations, Resistance, and the State*. University Park, PA: Pennsylvania State University Press.
Caballero, José María, Yurie Tanimichi Hoberg, Frederic de Dinechin and Matthew McMahon. 2005. "Agriculture, Rural Development and Land Policies." Retrieved at http://siteresources.worldbank.org/INTMEXICOINSPANISH/Resources/capitulo-8.pdf on April 16, 2014.
CEPAL. 1982. *Economía campesina y agricultura empresarial*. Mexico City: Siglo XXI.
CEPAL. 2002. "Desigualdades y Asimetrías del Orden Mundial." Pp. 77–98 in CEPAL *Globalización y Desarrollo*. Santiago de Chile, Chile: CEPAL.
CEPAL. 2010. "La Hora de la Igualdad. Panorama de la Gestión Pública en América

Latina." Retrieved at http://www.eclac.cl/noticias/paginas/8/33638/101214_OITfinal.pdf on April 14, 2014.
CONEVAL (The National Council for the Evaluation of Social Development Policy). 2013. "Medición de la Pobreza en México y en las Entidades Federativas 2012." Retrieved at http://www.coneval.gob.mx/Medicion/Paginas/Medici%C3%B3n/Pobreza%202012/Resumen_ejecutivo.aspx on March 8, 2014.
Consejo de Derechos Humanos. 2012. "Informe del Relator Especial sobre el Derecho a la Alimentación." Retrieved at http://www.derechoalimentacion.org/gestioncontenidosKW DERECHO/imgsvr/publicaciones/doc/Misión%20del%20relator%20en%20la%20FAO.pdf on April 14, 2014.
Constance, Douglas H., Francisco Martínez, Gilberto Aboites and Alessandro Bonanno. 2012. "The Problems with Poultry Production and Processing." Pp. 155–175 in Harvey S. James, Jr. (ed.) *The Ethics and Economics of Agrifood Competition*. New York: Springer.
Desmarais, Annette A. 2007. *La Via Campesina: Globalization and the Power of Peasants*. Halifax, Canada: Fernwood Press.
Esquinas-Alcázar, José T., Christine Frison and Francisco López. 2011. "A Treaty to Fight Hunger – Past Negotiations, Present Situation." Pp. 1–27 in Christine Frison, Francisco López and José T. Esquinas-Alcázar (eds.) *Plant Genetic Resources and Food Security: Stakeholder Perspectives on the International Treaty on Plant Genetic Resources Food and Agriculture and Biodiversity*. New York: The Food and Agriculture Organization of the United Nations.
FIRA (Fideicomisos Instituidos en Relación con la Agricultura). 2014. "Programa Institucional 2012–2018 de los Fideicomisos Instituidos en Relación con la Agricultura." *Diario Oficial*. Mexico. Retrieved at http://www.fira.gob.mx/Nd/Programa_Institucional. PDF on May 27, 2014.
Gómez-Oliver, Luis. 1994. "El Papel de la Agricultura en el Desarrollo de México." Retrieved at http://r.search.yahoo.com/_ylt=AwrSbmBR1VpT9Q4ARHdzKRh.;_ylu=X3oDMT BzaTFycmVoBHNlYwNzcgRwb3MDMTgEY29sbwNncTEEdnRpZAM-/RV=2/RE =1398490577/RO=10/RU=http%3a%2f%2fwww.pa.gob.mx%2fpublica%2fcd_estudios %2fPaginas%2fautores%2fgomez%2520olivier%2520luis%2520el%2520papel%2520de%2 520la%2520agricultura.pdf/RK=0/RS=JdOEXKg6F_rozsTognV3hfya.HY- on April 24, 2014.
Gordillo, Gustavo. 1979. "Estado y Sistema Ejidal." *Cuadernos Políticos* 21:7–24.
Gordillo, Gustavo and Krister Andersson. 2003. "Globalization Desde El Desarrollo Local." Retrieved at http://www.grupochorlavi.org/php/doc/documentos/globalizaciondesloc.pdf on April 14, 2014.
Harvey, David. 2005. *A Brief History of Neoliberalism*. Oxford: Oxford University Press.
Harvey, Neil. 1996. "Nuevas Formas de Representación en el Campo Mexicano: La Unión Nacional de Organizaciones Regionales Campesinas Autónomas (UNORCA), 1985–1993." Pp. 239–283 in Hubert Carton de Grammont (ed.) *Neoliberalismo y Organización Social en el Campo Mexicano*. Mexico City: Plaza y Valdés/UNAM.
Hewitt de Alcántara, Cynthia. 1999. *La Modernización de la Agricultura Mexicana*. Mexico City: Siglo XXI.
Hewitt de Alcántara, Cynthia. 2007. "Ensayo Sobre los Obstáculos al Desarrollo Rural en México Retrospectiva y Prospectiva." *Desacatos* 25:79–100.
INEGI (The National Institute of Statistics and Geography). 2014. "Seis de Cada 10 Empleos Son Informales." Retrieved at http://www.elfinanciero.com.mx/economia/en-mexico-de-cada-10-empleos-son-informales.html on May 23, 2014.
Johnston, Bruce F. and John W. Mellor. 1962. "El papel de la Agrícultura en el Desarrollo Económico." *El Trimestre Económico* 22 (4):279–307.
Mackinlay, Horacio. 1996. "La CNC y el 'Nuevo Movimiento Campesino.'" Pp. 180–202 in Hubert Carton de Grammont (ed.) *Neoliberalismo y Organización Social en el Campo Mexicano*. Mexico City: Plaza y Valdés/UNAM.
Mackinlay, Horacio. 2006. "Agronegocios y globalización en México: 1992–2006." Paper

presented at the VII Congreso de la Asociación Latinoamericana de Sociología Rural. Quito, Ecuador.

Mackinlay, Horacio and Gerardo Otero. 2006. "Corporativismo estatal y organizaciones campesinas: hacia nuevos arreglos institucionales." Pp. 135–153 in Gerardo Otero (ed.) *México en Transición: Globalismo Neoliberal, Estado y Sociedad Civil.* Mexico City: Miguel Angel Porrúa.

Margulis, Matias E., Nora McKeon and Saturnino M. Borras, Jr. 2013. "Land Grabbing and Global Governance: Critical Perspectives." *Globalizations* 10 (1):1–23.

Martínez, Francisco. 2003. *La Globalización en la Agricultura: Las Negociaciones Internacionales en Torno al Germoplasma Agrícola.* Mexico City: Plaza y Valdés.

Martínez, Francisco, Gilberto Aboites and Douglas H. Constance. 2013. "Neoliberal Restructuring, Neoregulation and the Mexican Poultry Industry." *Agriculture and Human Values* 30 (4):495–510.

McMichael, Philip. 1996. "Globalization: Myths and Realities." *Rural Sociology* 61 (1):25–55.

McNamara, Robert S. 1981. *The McNamara Years at the World Bank 1968–1981.* Baltimore, MD: John Hopkins University Press.

Murphy, Sophia, David Burch and Jennifer Clapp. 2012. "Cereal Secrets: The World's Largest Grain Traders and Global Agriculture." Oxfam Report. August. Retrieved at http://www.grainsa.co.za/upload/report_files/rr-cereal-secrets-grain-traders-agriculture-30082012-en.pdf on May 22, 2013.

Norton, Roger. 1993. *Integración de la Política Agrícola y Alimentaria en el Ambito Macroeconómico en América Latina y el Caribe.* Rome: FAO, Estudio Económico y Social 111.

Ochoa, Neira Miguel Gerardo. 2010. "La Consultoría, Ante la Competitividad." Retrieved at http://eleconomista.com.mx/columnas/agro-negocios/2010/02/04/consultoria-ante-competitividad on April 1, 2014.

OECD. 2011. "Mexico. Indicadores Sociales. Resultados Clave." Retrieved at http://www.oecd.org/mexico/47573255.pdf on April 15, 2014.

OECD. 2012. "Agricultural Policy Monitoring and Evaluation." Retrieved at http://www.keepeek.com/Digital-Asset-Management/oecd/agriculture-and-food/agricultural-policy-monitoring-and-evaluation-2013/mexico_agr_pol-2013-19-en#page3 on April 14, 2014.

OECD. 2013. "Apertura del Foro México Políticas Públicas para un Desarrollo Incluyente." Palabras de Angel Gurria, Secretario General de la OECD. Retrieved at http://www.oecd.org/mexico/aperturadelforomexicopoliticaspublicasparaundesarrolloincluyente.htm on April 15, 2014.

Otero, Gerardo (ed.). 2008. *Food for Few: Neoliberal Globalism and Biotechnology in Latin America.* Austin, TX: University of Texas Press.

Otero, Gerardo, Gabriela Pechlaner and Efe Gurcan. 2013. "The Political Economy of 'Food Security' and Trade: Uneven and Combined Dependency." *Rural Sociology* 78 (3):1–45.

Padilla, Tanalís. 2012. "Rubén Jaramillo: a 50 años de su muerte." *La Jornada.* May 15, 2012. Retrieved at http://www.jornada.unam.mx/2012/05/15/politica/021a2pol on April 15, 2014.

Poitras, Manuel, Gerardo Otero and Gilberto Aboites. 2014. "Movimientos Sociales y Tecno-democracia: ¿Hacia el Rescate de los Recursos Fitogenéticos comunes?" In Gerardo Otero (ed.) *La Dieta Neoliberal.* Mexico City: Porrua.

Prats, Joan. 2005. "Políticas y Gestión Pública: El impacto de la Globalización." *Revista Gobernanza* 35:95–111.

Rello, Fernando. 1997. "Retos y Perspectivas del Campo Mexicano." *Estudios Agrarios* 6:12–24.

Reynolds, Klark W. 1973. *La Economía Mexicana: su Estructura y Crecimiento en el Siglo XX,* Mexico City: Fondo de Cultura Economica.

Rodríguez, Gonzalo. 1979. "El Comportamiento de los Precios Agropecuarios." *Economía Mexicana* 1 (2):15–26.

Rodríguez, Gonzalo. 1980. "Tendencias de la Producción Agropecuaria en las dos Ultimas Décadas." *Economía Mexicana* 2 (3):22–40.

Rodríguez, Gonzalo. 1983. "Campesinos, Productores Transicionales y Empresarios en la Crisis Agrícola (Conducta Productiva Diferencial en Siete de los Principales Cultivos)." *Economía Mexicana* 5 (1):54–72.

Rodríguez, Gonzalo and Mario Ortiz. 1983. "Expansión Ganadera y Crisis Agrícola: el Papel del Consumo y la Rentabilidad." *Economía Mexicana* 5 (3):33–47.

Rodrik, Dani. 2006. "Goodbye Washington Consensus, Hello Washington Confusion?" Retrieved at http://www.hks.harvard.edu/fs/drodrik/Research%20papers/Lessons%20 of%20the%201990s%20review%20_JEL_.pdf on May 23, 2013.

Romero, José. 2012. "Inversion Extranjera Directa y Crecimiento Económico en México 1940–2010." Retrieved at http://cee.colmex.mx/documentos/documentos-de-trabajo/2012/ dt201212.pdf on May 28, 2014.

Ruiz Funes, Mario. 2013. "Producción de Fertilizantes. No sólo es Gas Barato." Retrieved at http://beta.elfinanciero.com.mx/opinion/produccion-de-fertilizantes-no-solo.html on May 23, 2014.

SAGARPA. 2013. "Programa Sectorial de Desarrollo Agropecuario, Pesquero y Alimentario." Secretaria de Agricultura, Ganadería, Desarrollo Rural y Pesca. Official Records, December 13, 2013. Retrieved at http://www.sagarpa.gob.mx/quiene somos/introduccion/Documents/Programa%20Sectorial%20de%20Desarrollo%20Saskia Agropecuario,%20Pesquero%20%20y%20Alimentario%202013-2018.pdf on May 22, 2014.

SAGARPA/FAO. 2013. *Diagnóstico del Sector Rural y Pesquero: Identificación de la Problemática del Sector Agropecuario y Pesquero de México 2012.* Mexico City: SAGRAPA/FAO.

Sassen, Saskia. 2006. *Territory, Authority, Rights: From Medieval to Global Assemblages.* Princeton, NJ: Princeton University Press.

Sassen, Saskia. 2013. "When Territory Deborders Territoriality." *Territory, Politics, Governance* 1 (1):21–45.

Scott, John. 2010. "Agricultural Subsidies in Mexico: Who Gets What?" Pp. 67–118 in Jonathan Fox and Libby Haight (eds.) *Subsidizing Inequality: Mexican Corn Policy since NAFTA.* Washington, DC: Woodrow Wilson International Center for Scholars.

Teubal, Miguel. 2001. "Globalización y Nueva Ruralidad en América Latina." in *¿Una Nueva Ruralidad en América Latina.* Retrieved at http://168.96.200.17/ar/libros/rural/ teubal.pdf on April 24, 2014.

USDA. 2012. "Mexico Trade, Policy and FDI." Economic Research Service, United States Department of Agriculture. Retrieved at http://www.ers.usda.gov/topics/international-markets-trade/countries-regions/nafta,-canada-mexico/mexico-trade-fdi.aspx#.UzJg7q 15OIV on May 12, 2013.

Via Campesina. 1999. "Biodiversidad, Bioseguridad y Recursos Geneticos." Unpublished Paper. Mexico City: Via Campesina.

Wahl, Peter. 2009. "Food Speculation: The Main Factor of the Price Bubble in 2008." World Economy, Ecology and Development. Retrieved at http://www2.weed-online.org/uploads/ weed_food_speculation.pdf on April 20, 2013.

Wise, Timothy A. 2013. "The Damaging Links between Food, Fuel, and Finance: A Growing Threat to Food Security." Retrieved at http://triplecrisis.com/the-damaging-links-between-food-fuel-and-finance-a-growing-threat-to-food-security/?utm_source= GDAE+Subscribers&utm_campaign=e2ef6c118d-TCB_04_09_2013&utm_medium=em ail on May 23, 2014.

World Bank. 2009. "Mexico: Agriculture and Rural Development Public Expenditure Review." Report No. 51902-MX. Retrieved at (http://siteresources.worldbank.org/ INTMEXICO/Resources/EnglishPERDec16.pdf on May 26, 2014.

# 4. Argentina's agri-food transformations in the context of globalization: Changing ways of farming
## Clara Craviotti

## INTRODUCTION

When trying to understand the transformations of the Argentinean agri-food sector, the issue of globalization immediately positions itself as a relevant entry point. In the early 1990s, it became apparent that the food economy was increasingly driven by the global demand and the internationalization of the agri-food industry, with an increasing move towards private regulation (Watts and Goodman 1997). Studies also associated globalization with the growing control of strategic assets by a small number of transnational corporations, deep changes in the international division of labor and the emergence of a new "map" of winners and losers within the North and the South (Bonanno, Busch, Friedland, Gouveia and Mingione 1994).

As globalization of agri-food proceeded, these issues continued to grow, accompanied by others that began to gain salience in academic and public debates. The rising role played by financial institutions in reorganizing various stages of the agri-food supply chain (Burch and Lawrence 2009), the new *technical frontier* of plant and animal engineering and the new *profit frontier* of agrofuel production (Bernstein 2013), and the rise in land grabbing particularly in developing countries (Borras, Franco and Wang 2012) are particularly relevant processes because of their impact in shaping new phases of global capitalism. While general concerns are placed on the environmental, the territorial and social consequences of these changes, various areas of controversy still remain. These relate to the emergence of new farming models, the scope of alternative geographies of food production and consumption, and the importance of institutional mediations in shaping commodity chains.

Taking into account the overall objective of this volume, this chapter aims to contribute to some of these areas of inquiry by focusing on the impressive transformations undergone by Argentina, which has emerged as a fundamental supplier of the global food–feed–energy complex in the last two decades. Indeed, in the early twentieth century, the country was a major supplier of meat and grain to the world market, and Argentineans also mass consumed these commodities domestically. Subsequently, due to import-substitution policies, agriculture experienced a period of relative stagnation and local products lost international market shares. This stagnation was reversed in the 1990s as production and export growth resumed. In 2007 Argentina accounted for 3.11 percent of the world's agricultural trade, making it the twelfth largest exporter worldwide (Castro and Chirwa 2011). The agricultural export basket, however, was dominated by a few commodities – particularly soybean and its derivatives – that remained largely irrelevant in the consumption patterns of the local population.

It is my primary contention that the role presently played by Argentina in the international division of labor is associated with the emergence of a new farming model that is the outcome of the complex interplay of external and internal driving forces. Salient global trends play their part in the recent expansion of Argentina's agri-food sector, including the growth in demand for high-protein food in emerging countries (particularly China and India); the rise in oil prices and the implementation of alternative energy policies that bolster biofuel production (Puyana and Constantino 2013); and the shift of speculative funds to the commodities markets (Gudynas 2008). The significance of these global trends notwithstanding, the policies adopted by several Argentinean Administrations have affected the evolution of local agri-food, either by fostering certain developments or being permissive towards them. In the next sections I outline some of the primary features of these policies and the different perspectives on the social and environmental aspects of the processes of change experienced by Argentinean agriculture.

## CHANGES IN ARGENTINEAN AGRICULTURE IN THE PERIOD 1990–2010: AN OVERVIEW

In a context in which the globalization of agri-food has grown steadily since the 1970s and accelerated since the 1990s, it is important to recognize the multiple trajectories associated with agrarian internationalization and the continuous central role that the state continues to play in domestic restructuring (Watts and Goodman 1997). In the Argentinean case, and since 1976 after the end of the military dictatorship, the country became the theater of important changes that were strengthened by the Administration of President Carlos Menem (1989–1999). This period was characterized by the end of import-substitution policies and an emphasis on financial investment that resulted in loss of jobs and a sharp decline in wages (Arceo and González 2008). Enmeshed in a stage of deepening neoliberalization worldwide (Brenner, Peck and Theodore 2010), the most outstanding features of the policies adopted during the 1990s included deregulation, trade liberalization (the reduction of tariffs on imports and the removal of export taxes) and the privatization of public services and utilities (ports, roads and railways). With a 1991 governmental decree, the agencies that had regulated agriculture since the 1930s were eliminated, along with production quotas and price support programs for major crops. Undoubtedly the cornerstone of these policies was the Convertibility Plan introduced in 1991, which established the parity of the Argentinean peso with the US dollar.

Aided by the new regulatory conditions and the implementation of Mercosur in 1991, these policies fostered a wave of foreign investment that particularly affected the industrial segments of input provision, industrial processing and large-scale retail distribution (Bisang and Gutman 2005). In the case of agriculture, these policies exposed local producers to international price fluctuations, requiring them to enhance their levels of competitiveness and to have a greater amount of capital to be able to remain in production (Murmis 1998). Trade liberalization enabled the acquisition of imported machines and inputs that engendered increases in productivity but also provoked greater indebtedness.[1]

A combination of internal and external factors led to the country's most severe economic crisis by the end of 2001. The policies adopted by the government following the resignation of President Fernando de la Rúa included the default of the external debt, the abandonment of the Convertibility Plan and a sharp devaluation of the local currency. The social perception of the negative consequences of neoliberalism made possible a political reorientation (particularly during the Néstor and Cristina Kirchner Administrations) towards recovering the capacity of the state to regulate the economy, address social issues and promote economic growth.

The "pesification" of the pre-existing debt at a discounted rate of 1 USD = 1 peso benefited the agri-food sector by de facto generating a debt reduction. The depreciation of the peso meant also a substantial improvement of profit for the export-oriented sectors of the economy. In this context, the agri-food sector strengthened its importance as it provides most of the country's hard currency and contributes to offsetting the restrictions to international credit that have been in place since the debt default of 2002.[2] Simultaneously, the reintroduction of fees on major agricultural exports (which were eliminated in the 1990s) brought relief to the state coffers and significantly contributed to state spending.[3]

Recording varying rates of growth throughout this period, the agricultural GDP increased by about 70 percent between 1993 and 2010.

Exports of some traditional products grew along with products previously unknown in the country (e.g., blueberries). Consequently, the export share of the agri-food sector grew from 16 percent in 1993 to 36 percent in 2011 (Obschatko 2013). Although a number of products contribute to this expansion of agricultural exports, soybean and its derivatives have been the most exported commodities since the end of the 1990s. In 1999 the soybean complex generated sales of nearly 3.5 billion US dollars and accounted for 15 percent of all exports. In 2011 it totaled more than 20 billion US dollars and represented 25 percent of all exports (National Bureau of Statistics and Censuses, www.indec.gob.ar).[4] A globalized product *par excellence*, the growth of soybean production and the fact that over 90 percent of it is not consumed locally have been interpreted as symbols of the neoliberal agricultural model and its shift from food production for popular consumption to production of exportable commodities (Teubal, Domínguez and Sabatino 2005).

The development of soybean production in Argentina finds its roots in the crisis of the production of Peruvian anchovy in the 1970s, then a primary source for feed. This insertion in the livestock–feed complex at a global scale was later complemented by the demand of soybean oil for the production of biofuels (Reca 2006). In 2013, with over 20 million hectares devoted to this crop (totaling 55 percent of all farmed land) and with production at about 50 million metric tons per year, Argentina is part of the world's largest soybean producing area, which also includes all Mercosur countries and Bolivia. However, unlike its neighboring countries, Argentina has an important local soybean processing industry that is able to transform production into exportable flour and oil. Argentina leads the world in exports of both products and is the third largest supplier of soybean grain, with China and the European Union as major destinations.

The strengthening of the soybean complex is a result of the interplay of international factors, domestic policies and the early adoption of new technology such as genetically modified (GM) seeds, glyphosate and no tillage. The lower operating costs and the simplification of tasks that these practices entail were crucial factors when the first transgenic varieties were introduced in the mid-1990s. The policies implemented during this period led to the appreciation of the peso and increased local costs of production. In a context of declining international grain prices, this situation promoted the adoption of cost-saving strategies by local farmers (Craviotti 2002). Consequently, the area sown with herbicide-tolerant soybeans increased from less than 1 percent of the total soybean planted area in 1997 to more than 90 percent in 2002. This rate of adoption was higher than the one reached in the United States, which was the first country to introduce this technology (Trigo and Cap 2003). Based on this data, some analysts argued that Argentina – which had adopted the green revolution belatedly and imperfectly – had an early entry into the new, biotechnology-based, production "paradigm" (Bisang 2011).[5]

The use of GM crops was approved by a public body (The National Commission for Knowledge and Use of Biodiversity – CONABIA) formed by members of the state, the industry and the scientific community, yet failed to represent the incipient public debate on the issue. In the case of GM soybean seeds, their widespread adoption was facilitated by the existence of an intellectual property system that allowed the non-patentability of the gene and by the autogamic nature of the seed whose reproduction does not alter its initial characteristics (Bisang and Sztulwark 2007). The further use of GM seeds in other key crops followed,[6] while the associated technology of no tillage arrived to cover nearly 80 percent of grain and 90 percent of soybean planted areas (AAPRESID 2012).

These changes have been also driven by the high concentration and transnationalization of firms located in upstream and downstream sectors. Upstream, seeds distribution is controlled by a limited number of global companies that also provide chemical inputs, although particularly in the case of soybeans, local companies hold a relevant position. These companies hold retail outlets throughout the primary agricultural areas of the country, finance the use of inputs through popular schemes that use the harvest as collateral, and promote the diffusion of additional new technological packages (Gras and Hernández 2009). While tractors and harvesters are provided by a very small number of subsidiaries of multinationals, other types of machines, such as sowing machines and sprayers, are primarily supplied by local firms (Lavarello 2012).

Downstream, oilseed crushing is also highly concentrated, with 60 percent of the processing capacity in the hands of transnational companies (Trigo and Cap 2006; Bisang and Sztulwark 2007). These firms usually have full or partial stakes in freighting companies, shipping ports and traders (Barsky and Dávila 2008). Concentration in exports is more marked in soybean oil and meal than in non-processed grains, where it has somewhat diminished in recent years.[7]

Although data suggests an important participation of foreign capital in the grain production chain, its involvement in direct land ownership is not so relevant. In a context of greater public concern on the subject, legislation was enacted in 2011 establishing limits on foreign ownership and the creation of a national land registry. The latter showed that 6 percent of rural land is foreign owned, although 48 departments – some of them located in border regions – exceed the 15 percent limited by law (Registro Nacional de Tierras Rurales n/d).

From 1976 to 2013 the area used to cultivate grains and oilseeds increased from 19 million hectares to 36 million hectares, a process involving changes in the use of land formerly devoted to other crops or livestock production and the expansion of agriculture on previously not-farmed areas. Accordingly, grain production increased from 24 million metric tons to 105 million metric tons during the same period (SIIA 2013). In the cases of other commodities, trends were mixed. Those produced in lands suitable for soybean (such as dairy or meat) either stagnated and/ or declined (Rodríguez 2012). These developments are associated not only with the technical innovations mentioned above but also with organizational changes that will be discussed in the next section.

## THE EMERGING STRUCTURE OF AGRICULTURE

Since the 1990s, and increasingly in the 2000s, the Argentinean soybean and grain sectors have developed a flexible, network-based system of production that some analysts have compared to those characterizing the most dynamic manufacturing industries (Bisang, Anlló and Campi 2008). This form of production is exemplified by the case of sowing pools (*pools de siembra*). Although they differ in size and territorial extension, the most important ones operate nationwide, combining size with risk diversification. The firms that practice this form of organization do not necessarily own the land that they operate but, rather, lease it on a short-term basis under various contractual arrangements while outsourcing basic farm tasks through contracting. Consequently, these firms are asset-light companies with low investments in fixed capital and permanent labor. Their core assets consist of their access to funding sources to obtain operating capital and their management skills to coordinate and supervise activities.

Small sowing pools are mainly informal associations that can be compared with a modern and more equalitarian form of sharecropping, whereby participants provide different resources (land, machinery, inputs and technical assistance) and share returns according to the contribution of each party. In contrast, the most important pools – those that farm more than 100,000 hectares – employ more sophisticated *modus operandi* which includes the establishment of public limited companies and the creation of trust funds to raise capital.[8] In the last decade, some of these pools have established operations in neighboring countries such as Uruguay, Paraguay, Bolivia and Brazil. In order to do so, Argentinean companies have joined forces with partners of other countries and adapted their procedures to the varied local contexts (Bell and Scott 2010).

The firms that organize the most important sowing pools are not controlled by Argentina's traditional landowners, although they often come from farm families (Murmis and Murmis 2010). In spite of these roots, sowing pools can be considered a relatively *new farming model* with a specific rationale towards maximizing scale and short-term benefits. Current agricultural censuses are ill equipped to offer a real picture of their importance. Some estimates indicate that they cover between 6 percent and 10 percent of the area devoted to grains, while others provide more generous evaluations and point out that they involve 50 percent or even two-thirds of the land assigned to these crops. The latter, however, tend to draw a direct equivalence between land not worked directly by landowners and land operated by sowing pools, and thus may suggest the (erroneous) impression that these types of firms are the prevailing form of farming in the country.[9]

What must be highlighted, however, are the qualitative changes associated with this farming model. First, because of the large operating capital required and the mobilization of this capital through trust funds, hedge funds, pension funds and other types of financial instruments, pools can be seen as part of the process of financialization of agriculture. Second, these firms operate on a large scale and adopt an industrial type of production based on high levels of flexibility and use of modern technology (such as precision agriculture) and agrochemical input. Third, there are instances of the decoupling of farm ownership and farming.

Flexibility may be seen not only in these pools' organizational structure and interaction with other actors, but also in their primary mechanism to land access. Differing from similar instances recorded internationally – such as the case of the Canadian prairies whereby newly created farmland investment funds purchase land, lease it and generate profit from rent and land value appreciation (Sommerville 2013) – Argentinean sowing pools do not immobilize capital in land assets but, rather, invest to establish larger operations. This type of development shows a preference for the control of strategic resources without involving direct ownership.[10] Census data indicate that between 1988 and 2002 there has been a contraction of agricultural land property by 7.5 percent (approximately 12 million hectares) and a 33 percent increase in the area cultivated through different types of contracts. This area is equal to 6 million hectares. It should be pointed out, however, that the increase in leasing is not only driven by sowing pools but also by medium and large landowners who expanded their operations.

As a whole, the importance of leasing arrangements in the land tenure system shows the peculiarity of Argentinean agricultural development when compared with that of other countries. The flip side of this phenomenon is the emergence of a stratum of small-scale rentiers particularly in the Pampas region. Some of these former farmers have become machine contractors, taking advantage of the equipment that they own and their know-how (Craviotti and Gras 2006). A survey conducted in the province of Buenos Aires revealed that 68.7 percent of machine contractors were former farmers and 55 percent of them began working in the 1990s (Lódola 2008).

The changes described have led to a farming structure that includes a smaller number of producers and the strengthening of units based on hired wage workers. From 1988 to 2002, about 87,000 farms, or slightly more than 20 percent of all farms, ceased operation, while the size of those that remained increased. According to data from the Agricultural Census, 95 percent of the farms that went out of business had less than 500 hectares and 67 percent were located in the Pampas region.[11] Family agriculture also shows a trend towards social differentiation. Farmers developed more complex identities and social reproduction strategies. In the case of the Pampas region, while some farmers also began to work as machine contractors, others increasingly use this service and contract other farm activities.[12] The latter indicates a loss of centrality of the family workforce devoted to physical activities and the growing importance of managerial work (Craviotti 2000). It is also associated with farmers moving into small towns and cities. Some of these farmers have also been able to expand their operations by renting land. An innovative feature identified is the creation of partnerships with non-family members to increase their farmed area (Gras 2009).

A differentiation process that involves the transformation of family farmers into capitalist farmers is one possible path of development. Along with pluriactivity, other types of strategies have also been identified, such as increasing productive diversification, diminishing monetary costs, intensifying family labor and/or developing short marketing circuits (Craviotti and Palacios 2013). The latter sometimes gives rise to stable forms of reproduction indicating the emergence of new forms of connection with the sector and the territory. However, taking into account the broader picture of the recent development of the Argentinean agri-food sector, an issue open to question is whether or not these strategies give rise to *new models of family farming* that are able to grow and coexist with large-scale agriculture.

In regard to wage workers, census data show that their overall number declined but their relative share of the entire agricultural workforce grew.[13] While the expansion of the cultivated land of the country and the intensification of production may have increased labor demand, greater use of machinery and other technologies have worked in the opposite direction.[14] This process is particularly visible in grain production and in crops such as cotton and sugar cane, but it is less the case in fresh and counter-seasonal crops for export. A general trend, however, is the increase in temporary jobs, which engenders greater levels of precarious employment (Neiman 2012).

## THE PROCESSES OF AGRARIAN CHANGE AND THEIR CONSEQUENCES: CONTRASTING PERSPECTIVES

Analyses of recent transformations in the Argentinean agri-food sector have primarily focused on different aspects of grain production and its organizational structure. While since the 1990s different agri-food chains have undergone significant changes, the development of soybean production has taken primacy in the academic and public debates. In this context, the emergence of sowing pools has led to the viewpoint that two different farming models coexist in Argentinean agriculture. In the first model, farmers carry out all production activities, reap all gains, but also face all associated risks and losses. The second model, in contrast, is based on a network of actors – farmers, input and service providers, rentiers – linked by a multiplicity of contracts whereby risks and benefits are shared. Following arguments from the business literature,[15] this perspective argues that this model not only is expanding but involves a win-win situation since it fosters cooperation as everyone's income depends on collective performance. It also generates greater spillover effects than the other model in which the farmer carries out all the activities on the farm (Bisang et al. 2008).[16] This view emphasizes the innovative character of rural entrepreneurs and the inevitability that processes of change generate losers. It enjoys support among some academic circles, farmer unions and mass media, as well as the support of some state agencies, revealing that the network of actors that sustain this way of farming is broader than the agricultural sector itself.

The win-win approach is also applied to biotechnology in general and to the soybean technological package in particular. It is maintained that the coupling of no tillage with herbicide-tolerant soybeans represents a virtuous cycle of technological intensification. This is because it involves the recovery of soil fertility and the replacement of atrazine (an herbicide that has residual effects and negative impacts on the environment) with environmentally neutral glyphosate.[17] This line of interpretation continues to stress that the lion's share of the benefits of these technological improvements is reaped by farmers, and that soybean has been the crop selected by small farm holders to strengthen the sustainability of their operations

(Trigo and Cap 2006). The reduction of the area devoted to livestock and/ or other crops is not seen as a problem, because the increases in productivity countered any possible decline in production. Accordingly, the accomplishment of food security is not viewed as at risk (Barsky and Dávila 2008).[18] Over-reliance on a single commodity is not questioned, since the concentration on a single crop is not completely new in Argentinean agriculture (Reca 2006).

Despite these arguments, it should be noted that soybean expansion has gone hand in hand with a spatial reorganization that changed the traditional division of labor within the country, whereby the Pampean region was connected to global markets and extra-Pampas regions were basically engaged in productions oriented to the domestic market. In effect, census data show that between 1988 and 2002 cultivated land in the extra-Pampas provinces increased by 50 percent while the land devoted to soybeans grew by almost 200 percent. In contrast, in the Pampas region the increases were 9 percent and 77 percent respectively for the same period (Barsky and Fernández 2008). While in the Pampas it is estimated that 70 percent of the growth of land devoted to soybeans occurred at the expenses of pasture (Azcuy Ameghino and León 2005), in extra-Pampas regions it replaced land previously occupied by traditional crops and native ecosystems (Navarrete et al. 2007). Facilitated by the adoption of new technology, the growth of the cultivation of soybeans in these areas has affected biodiversity rich areas of the Yungas and Chaco forests. As the best land is converted into soybean fields, cattle is moved into lands previously unused (Gudynas 2008).

Optimistic readings of these changes emphasize that there is little objective information about their negative environmental impacts and that, at worst, they are limited to specific areas and/or have been compensated by the benefits accrued in other areas. It is argued that the expansion of agriculture is due to multiple reasons (including changes in the rainfall system) which were already underway prior to the explosion of soybean production. Eventually, it is contended that it is the state's responsibility to implement policy measures to encourage the cultivation of other crops and crop rotation and to implement land management policies (Trigo and Cap 2006; Barsky and Dávila 2008). It should be noted, however, that in 2007 Congress passed legislation that protects native forests, defines three categories of conservation areas, establishes the types of activities that could be carried out in each of them and decentralizes the responsibility to establish zoning to provinces. Yet this legislation was enacted after much of the deforestation was already completed[19] and, in some instances, procedures were resisted and the zoning requirements were not followed.[20]

From a social point of view, the impact of the growth of soybean production is most visible in the North of the country than in the Pampas region. In the case of the Northwest, the forms of production of local peasant and indigenous small farm holders clash with that of capitalist firms and sowing pools, most of them non-local (Reboratti 2010). In these areas, the existence of precarious land tenure situations – no legal titles in the hands of peasants – opens the door to different ways of gaining control of the land ranging from voluntary purchase to violent evictions of peasants who are unable to assert their consuetudinary rights.[21] These phenomena are accompanied by the contamination of soils and waterways and conflicts over the availability and use of common resources (Domínguez, Lapegna and Sabatino 2006). Some recent institutional innovations – such as the creation of a Secretary for Rural Development and Family Agriculture – seem not enough to reverse these processes. Following Harvey (2004), a number of studies carried out in the Northwest and Northeast of Argentina frame these situations as cases of *accumulation by disposses-sion* (Cáceres 2014; Goldfarb 2012; Percíncula, Jorge, Calvo, Mariotti, Domínguez, Estrada, Ciccolella, Barbetta, Sabatino and Astelarra 2011).

In the Pampas region the displacement of family farming is, however, less visible. High land prices[22] and access to land titles have enabled the development of a group of *rentiers* who have been able to retain their farm properties. As stated for other countries with a strong tradition in grain production (Sommerville 2013), these farmers may benefit from the rapid appreciation of land associated with the growth of the dynamic agricul-tural sector, but this simultaneously constrains their ability to expand their operations as local producers cannot compete with sowing pools in bidding for rented land. The importance of tenancy in the Argentinean land tenure system also explains an apparent paradox: the fact that concentration of land ownership is not as high as concentration of production.[23] However, the latter involves the strengthening of capitalist enterprises at the expense of family farmers and affects the intensity of land use as lease arrange-ments make conservationist practices more difficult.

Accordingly, those who support optimistic views of the situation min-imize the social and environmental costs of the position of Argentina in the current agri-food global system. Their response to criticisms rests on their emphasis on alternative factors such as the expansion of production and productivity. The opposing camp contends that the shift from a family-farm-based agriculture to a highly productive, locally disembedded capitalist agriculture has reached a point of crisis because of the lack of available land that can only be obtained through further destabilizing dispossession of the family farm holders (Sili and Soumoulu 2011).

To be sure, the power of these sweeping generalizations should be taken cautiously. Both views of the process are intrinsically dualistic and neglect a careful appreciation of the particularities of different production chains, regions and social actors. In effect, the evolution and characteristics of some important production chains cannot be simply equated to the soybean sector because they require investments in fixed assets, permanent labor at the farm level and have longer cycles of production that hinder the pursuit of short-term benefits (Craviotti 2014).

Moving beyond the debate on the agri-food sector, the role of Argentina in a renewed international division of labor is also being discussed from other perspectives such as political ecology. From this standpoint, the agricultural export model that prevailed from the late nineteenth century until the 1930s has been retaken and intensified by the post-neoliberal governments that ruled the country after the 2001 crisis. This view emphasizes that while a part of the revenue generated by taxes on agricultural exports is employed to service Argentina's external debt, another part is invested in domestic social programs to engender political support. This debate is also characterizing discussions in other Latin American countries and focuses on concepts such as neo-developmentalism (Grugel and Riggirozzi 2007), export-oriented populism (Richardson 2009) or, from a more critical insight, progressive neo-extractivism (Gudynas 2012). In this light, the internal contradictions of a model that introduces substantial changes regarding the neoliberal period (such as the recovery of state capacities and improvements in the conditions of popular classes) are highlighted. In the case of Argentina, these contradictions refer to the persistent vulnerability of the country to fluctuations of the global market and the absence of redistributive tax policies that would reduce inequality (Grugel and Riggirozzi 2007; Wylde 2010).

## FINAL REMARKS

Since the 1990s, and as the globalization of agri-food has evolved, Argentina has become a major supplier of the food–feed–energy complex at a global level, mainly through soybean and its derivatives: a *flex-crop* capable of multiple uses. To be sure, not all the phenomena discussed in the previous sections are due to the expansion of soybean production. The latter cannot be simply employed as a lens for understanding the whole set of transformations of the local agri-food sector. A good deal of heterogeneity still persists. However, the development of the soybean complex clearly illustrates some of the features that define the present globalization of agri-food: the shift to exportable commodities; the use of technological packages based on the centrality of private knowledge; the concentration and transnationalization of upstream and downstream sectors; and a greater penetration of finance in agriculture.

This insertion of the country in the global system has been framed in a clear division of labor that selectively excludes and simultaneously includes regions, forging a complementary relationship (Bonanno 2003). Although measures have been recently put into practice by the state to counteract part of the negative social and environmental effects generated by this process, on the whole, the different Administrations have contributed to tracing a specific path of agrarian development. A key aspect in this regard has been the early approval of the use of biotechnology products that turned the country into one of the early adopters of this technology worldwide. Institutional mediations have narrowed the scope for alternative geographies of food production and consumption capable of reaching important segments of the rural and urban population.

The singularities of the Argentinean path of agri-food development are associated with the growing importance of leasing arrangements in the land tenure system and of contractual arrangements within and beyond the farm sector. The latter support a flexible combination of resources and units operating at various stages of the labor process with relevant implications on the way agricultural activities are carried out. Although family farmers and labor have been affected by changes, particularly important is the growth of a new farming model represented by sowing pools. It has proven extremely effective in diminishing investments in fixed capital and permanent labor while maximizing the benefits associated with large-scale and geographical diversification. In this case, there is a separation between land ownership, work and control, making the "farm" no longer the center of decision making.

The relevant role of private local actors – some of farm origin – in these schemes does not conform to land grabbing processes experienced by other countries. Notwithstanding this, they set forth important questions related to the sustainability of traditional and more embedded ways of farming and communities. From another perspective, the expansion of the largest Argentinean sowing pools and other firms that provide inputs and services to the neighboring countries of the Mercosur illuminates the interrelated dimensions of globalization of the agri-food sector as well as the role of some leading companies of middle-income countries in shaping significant changes in their regions.

# NOTES

1. Between 1991 and 1999 bank credit for the agricultural sector as a whole grew significantly (242 percent), although 90 percent of this debt was denominated in dollars (Lódola 2008).
2. Considering both raw and processed products, the share of agriculture reached 58 percent of all exports in 2011.
3. Agricultural export tax covered between of 8 to 11 percent of the Kirchner governments' overall tax revenue (Richardson 2009) and reached 13 percent of the total revenue in 2008 (Sinnott 2009).
4. This growth was driven by increases in the demand and prices of soybeans at the international level. It was 98.5 percent in constant dollars for the period 1999–2011 (Puyana and Constantino 2013).
5. While the introduction of GM soybeans undoubtedly marked a breaking point, it is also important to stress that this technological change followed the massive mechanization of agriculture of the Pampas that began in the 1960s. Additionally, improved seeds in grain production (particularly wheat, corn, sorghum and sunflower) were introduced in the 1970s along with a greater use of agrochemicals in wheat and corn production (Barsky and Dávila 2008).
6. Currently, GM crops occupy 99 percent of the acreage devoted to soybeans, 83 percent of the acreage devoted to corn and 94 percent of the acreage devoted to cotton (Burachik 2010).
7. In 2005 six companies controlled 82 percent of all grain exports. In 2012 the same percentage of exports was controlled by ten companies. At the same time, Cargill's share fell from 23 percent to 15 percent, Bunge's from 17 percent to 9 percent, Dreyfus's from 12 percent to 10 percent and Nidera's from 9 percent to 6 percent. Conversely, the relative share of local cooperatives increased (Ámbito Financiero 2013).
8. In these instances, investors buy units proportionally to the capital invested. Trust funds have been enabled by Law 24,441 passed in 1995. In the case of financial trusts, the trustee is either a financial institution or a company specifically authorized by Argentina's National Securities Commission (Craviotti 2007).
9. According to media reports, and since mid-2012, there has been some shrinking of the largest sowing pools due to increases in local costs of production.
10. These firms use most of their profits for horizontal growth. To be sure, however, some of them also invest in vertical integration activities and, to some degree, in the acquisition of land property. The most important sowing pools have recently purchased tracts of land in connection with the introduction of international capital in their financial structure (Manciana, Trucco and Piñeiro 2009; Murmis and Murmis 2010).
11. In spite of these changes, according to the Inter-American Institute for Cooperation on Agriculture (IICA)–PROINDER study (Obschatko, Foti and Román 2006), family farmers who do not hire permanent workers represent 65.6 percent of all producers and employ 53 percent of all agricultural workers. They control only 13.5 percent of land and generate 19 percent of production.
12. According to the Ministry of Agriculture, in the case of grain production, machine contractors are in charge of 95 percent of harvest and 60 percent of sowing operations (Dirección Nacional de Contratistas Rurales e Insumos Agrícolas 2014).
13. According to the Population Census, from 1991 to 2001 the number of wage workers fell by 132,000 units or 21 percent. However, their relative share within the entire farming labor force rose from 45 percent to 55 percent during the same period (National Bureau of Statistics and Censuses 1991; 2001).
14. The decline in the number of workers in farming is partially offset by the increase in employment in related sectors. For instance, the number of permanent workers in the machine contractor sector in the province of Buenos Aires grew by 68 percent between 2001 and 2006 (Lódola 2008). This has been seen as evidence of the "spillover" effect of the development of agriculture. Some authors (e.g., Llach, Harriague and O'Connor

2004) estimate that the employment generated by agribusiness activities covers about 36 percent of the total employment in the sector (this calculation includes both direct and indirect employment). However, the methodology employed in the generation of this data has been questioned by others (e.g., Rodríguez 2005).

15. As stated by Dicken, Kelly, Olds and Wai-Chung Yeung (2001), the business and management literature provide a great number of contributions that view the new network paradigm as the recipe for business success.

16. The phenomenon of sowing pools could also be viewed as a process of network building that allows unequal processes of production and distribution of wealth and power (Busch and Juska 1997).

17. Regarding the latter, Viglizzo, Frank, Carren, Jobba, Pereyra, Clatt, Pince and Ricard (2011), in a study based on an analysis of 399 administrative departments for the period 1960–2005, maintain that, due to improved tillage practices and the application of less aggressive pesticides, erosion and pollution risks are lower today than in the mid-twentieth century.

18. For instance, in cattle production there has been a process of intensification that includes methods of cattle raising, such as feedlots, that are relatively new in Argentina. These methods were supported by government programs that paid for the cost of feeds. This intensification of livestock production has partially offset the negative impact of the reduced availability of land and the lower quality of the soils devoted to cattle production (Charvay 2012).

19. Data from the Native Forests Directorate indicate that, between 1998 and 2002, 767,000 hectares were cleared in seven Northern provinces alone.

20. A report referring to the province of Salta reveals that the rules regarding the clearing of certain areas have not been observed. Also, some restrictions (such as the moratorium of land clearing established by the National Supreme Court for four departments of this province between 2009 and 2011) were established after allegations from peasant and indigenous organizations that they were not respected (REDAF 2012).

21. The Argentinean Civil Code recognizes the possibility of acquiring land property rights by those who have lived on the same land for more than 20 years and made improvements on it. The acquisition of these rights requires a Prescription Trial, a procedure not always available to small farm holders and peasants. A recent study of the Ministry of Agriculture documented existing conflicts regarding land tenure (Bidaseca, Gigena, Gómez, Weinstock, Oyharzábal and Otal 2013) and indicated that almost 80 percent of them involve squatters (*poseedores*), namely people who have lived on, and worked, this land for decades but had never gained legal ownership.

22. The rise in land prices in the core area of the Pampas region has been extraordinary, reaching an average of 9,100 US dollars per hectare in 2007. This price is well above that recorded during the 1990s, when it averaged 3,200 US dollars per hectare. This change brought about a parallel rise in the price of land for lease (Arceo and González 2008). In the North of the country, prices remain substantially less expensive but have also increased.

23. Optimistic readings of these changes view the concentration of production as the continuation of established trends that characterized the Pampas region. This situation, it is argued, is compatible with processes experienced by other leading countries in grain farming such as Australia, Canada and the United States (Trigo and Cap 2006).

# REFERENCES

AAPRESID (Asociación Argentina de Productores en Siembra Directa). 2012. "Evolución de la Superficie en Siembra Directa en Argentina. Campañas 1977/78 a 2010/11."

Ámbito Financiero. 2013. "Según Agricultura, Aumentaron los Exportadores de

Cereales." Retrieved at http://www.agroeventos.net/index.php/ganaderia/79-agricultura/161-segun-agricultura-aumentaron-los-exportadores-de-cereales on July 3, 2014.

Arceo, Nicolás and Mariana González. 2008. "La Transformación del Modelo Rural." *Le Monde Diplomatique* 11–12: 1–2.

Azcuy Ameghino, Eduardo and Carlos Alberto León. 2005. "La Sojización: Contradicciones, Intereses y Debates." *Revista Interdisciplinaria de Estudios Agrarios* 23: 133–157.

Barsky, Osvaldo and Mabel Dávila. 2008. *La Rebelión del Campo. Historia del Conflicto Agrario argentino.* Buenos Aires: Editorial Sudamericana.

Barsky, Osvaldo and Leonardo Fernández. 2005. *Tendencias actuales de las economías extrapampeanas, con especial referencia a la situación del empleo rural.* Buenos Aires: SAGPyA-RIMISP.

Bell, David and Cintra Scott 2010. "Los Grobo: Farming's Future?" Harvard Business School General Management Unit Case Number 511088. Retrieved at http://papers.ssrn.com/sol3/papers.cfm?abstract_id=2004666 on July 21, 2014.

Bernstein, Henry. 2013. "Food Sovereignty: A skeptical view." Conference paper #1. International Conference, Yale University September 14–15. Retrieved at http://www.yale.edu/agrarianstudies/foodsovereignty/pprs/1_Bernstein_2013.pdf on July 3, 2014.

Bidaseca, Karina, Andrea Gigena, Fabiana Gómez, Ana Weinstock, Enrique Oyharzábal and Daniel Otal. 2013. *Relevamiento y Sistematización de Problemas de Tierra de los Agricultores Familiares en la Argentina.* Buenos Aires: Ministerio de Agricultura, Ganadería y Pesca de la Nación, PROINDER.

Bisang, Roberto. 2011. "Agro y Recursos Naturales en la Argentina: ¿Enfermedad Maldita o Desafío a la Inteligencia Colectiva?" *Boletín informativo Techint*: 63–83.

Bisang, Roberto, Guillermo Anlló and Mercedes Campi. 2008. "Una Revolución (no tan) Silenciosa. Claves para Repensar el Agro en Argentina." *Desarrollo Económico* 48 (190/191): 165–207.

Bisang, Roberto and Graciela Gutman. 2005. "The Accumulation Process and Agrofood Networks in Latin America." *Cepal Review* 87: 113–127.

Bisang, Roberto and Sebastián Sztulwark. 2007. "Tramas Productivas de Alta Tecnología. El caso de la Soja Transgénica en Argentina." Pp. 181–224 in *Estructura Productiva y Empleo. Un Enfoque Transversal.* Buenos Aires: Ministerio de Trabajo Empleo y Seguridad Social.

Bonanno, Alessandro. 2003. "La Globalización Agroalimentaria: sus Características y Perspectivas Futuras." *Sociologias* 5 (10): 190–218.

Bonanno, Alessandro, Lawrence Busch, William Friedland, Lourdes Gouveia and Enzo Mingione (eds.). 1994. *From Columbus to Conagra: The Globalization of Agriculture and Food.* Lawrence, KS: University Press of Kansas.

Borras, Saturnino, Jennifer Franco and Chunyu Wang. 2012. *Tendencias Políticas en Disputa para la Gobernanza Global del Acaparamiento de Tierras.* The Hague: Transnational Institute.

Brenner, Neil, Jamie Peck and Nik Theodore. 2010. "After Neoliberalization?" *Globalizations* 7 (3): 327–345.

Burachik, Moisés. 2010. "Experience from Use of GMOs in Argentinean Agriculture, Economy and the Environment." *New Biotechnology* 27 (5): 588–592.

Burch, David and Geoffrey Lawrence. 2009. "Towards a Third Food Regime: Behind the Transformation." *Agriculture and Human Values* 26: 267–279.

Busch, Lawrence and Arunas Jushka. 1997. "Beyond Political Economy: Actor Networks and the Globalization of Agriculture." *Review of International Political Economy* 4 (4): 688–708.

Cáceres, Daniel. 2014. "Accumulation by Dispossession and Socio-environmental Conflicts Caused by the Expansion of Agribusiness in Argentina." *Journal of Agrarian Change*, doi: 10.1111/joac.12057.

Castro, Lucio and Ephraim Chirwa. 2011. "A Tale of Extremes: The Political Economy of Agricultural Policies in Argentina and Malawi." Global Development Network Working Paper Series 45. Retrieved at http://www.egfar.org/es/content/tale-extremes-political-economy-agricultural-policies-argentina-and-malawi on July 21, 2014.

Charvay, Patricia. 2012. "Los Cambios en la Producción Ganadera en la Posconvertibilidad." *Voces en el Fénix* 12: 22–29.

Craviotti, Clara. 2000. "Los Procesos de Cambio en las Explotaciones Familiares Pampeanas: Tendencias en el Trabajo Agrario y Dinámicas Familiares," *Cuadernos de Desarrollo Rural* 45: 69–89.

Craviotti, Clara. 2002. "Pampas Family Farms and Technological Change: Strategies and Perspectives towards Genetically Modified Crops and No-Tillage Systems." *International Journal of the Sociology of Agriculture and Food* 10 (1): 23–30.

Craviotti, Clara. 2007. "Non-Sectorial Agents and Recent Changes in Argentina's Agricultural Sector." *Revista de la CEPAL* 92: 159–170.

Craviotti, Clara. 2014. "Agricultura Familiar-Agronegocios: Disputas, Interrelaciones y Proyectos." *Territorios* 30: 17–37.

Craviotti, Clara and Carla Gras. 2006. "De Desafiliaciones y Desligamientos: Trayectorias de Productores Familiares Expulsados de la Producción en la Región Pampeana Argentina." *Desarrollo Económico* 181: 117–134.

Craviotti, Clara and Paula Palacios. 2013. "Estrategias de Productores Familiares en Contextos Socio-Productivos Adversos: La Fruticultura Familiar en el Noreste de la Provincia de Buenos Aires, Argentina." *Trabajo y Sociedad* 20: 259–279.

Dicken, Peter, Phillip Kelly, Kris Olds and Henry Wai-Chung Yeung 2001. "Chains and Networks, Territories and Scales: Towards a Relational Framework for Analyzing the Global Economy." *Global Networks* 1–2: 89–112.

Dirección Nacional de Contratistas Rurales e Insumos Agrícolas. 2014. *Presentación Contratistas Rurales*. Buenos Aires: Ministerio de Agricultura, Ganadería y Pesca.

Domínguez, Diego, Pablo Lapegna and Pablo Sabatino. 2006. "Un Futuro Presente: Las Luchas Territoriales." *Nómadas* (24): 239–246.

Goldfarb, Lucia. 2012. "The Frontiers of Genetically Modified Soya in Argentina. Possession Rights and New Forms of Land Control and Governance." Paper presented at the International Conference on Global Land Grabbing II. Cornell University, Ithaca, NY. October 17–19.

Gras, Carla. 2009. "La Agricultura Familiar en el Agro Pampeano. Desplazamientos y Mutaciones." Pp. 17–40 in Talía Gutiérrez and Juan Manuel Cerdá (eds.) *Trabajo Agrícola. Experiencias y Resignificación de las Identidades en el Campo Argentino*. Buenos Aires: CICCUS.

Gras, Carla and Valeria Hernández. 2009. "El fenómeno Sojero en Perspectiva: Dimensiones Productivas, Sociales y Simbólicas de la Globalización Agrorrural en Argentina." Pp. 15–37 in Carla Gras and Vaeria Hernández (eds.) *La Argentina Rural. De la Agricultura Familiar a los Agronegocios*. Buenos Aires: Biblos.

Grugel, Jean and Pía Riggirozzi. 2007. "The Return of the State in Argentina." *International Affairs* 83 (1): 87–107.

Gudynas, Eduardo. 2008. "The New Bonfire of Vanities: Soybean Cultivation and Globalization in South America." *Development* 51 (4): 512–518.

Gudynas, Eduardo. 2012. "Estado Compensador y Nuevos Extractivismos. Las Ambivalencias del Progresismo Sudamericano." *Nueva Sociedad* 237: 128–147.

Harvey, David. 2004. "The New Imperialism: Accumulation by Dispossession." *Socialist Register* 40: 99–129.

Lavarello, Pablo 2012. "La Recuperación de la Producción de Maquinaria Agrícola." *Voces en el Fénix* 12: 42–50.

Llach, Juan, Marcela Harriague and Ernesto O'Connor. 2004. *La Generación de Empleo en las Cadenas Agroindustriales*. Buenos Aires: Fundación Producir Conservando.

Lódola, Agustín. 2008. *Contratistas, Cambios Tecnológicos y Organizacionales en el Agro Argentino*. Santiago de Chile: United Nations.

Manciana, Eduardo, Mario Trucco and Martín Piñeiro. 2009. *Large-Scale Acquisition of Land Rights for Agricultural or Natural Resource-Based Use: Argentina*. Buenos Aires: CEO.

Ministry of Agriculture. 2013. "Estimaciones Agrícolas." Retrieved at http://www.siia.gob.ar/sst_pcias/estima/estima.php on October 25, 2013.

Murmis, Miguel. 1998. "Agro Argentino: Algunos Problemas para su Análisis." Pp. 205–248 in Norma Giarracca and Silvia Cloquell (eds.) *Las agriculturas del Mercosur: el Papel de los Actores Sociales*. Buenos Aires: Editorial La Colmena.

Murmis, Miguel and María Rosa Murmis. 2010. "El caso de Argentina." Paper presented at the conference *Dinámicas en el Mercado de la Tierra en América Latina*. FAO: Santiago de Chile, Chile.

National Bureau of Statistics and Censuses. 1991. *Censo Nacional de Población y Viviendas*. Buenos Aires: Secretaría de Política Económica.

National Bureau of Statistics and Censuses. 2001. *Censo Nacional de Población y Viviendas*. Buenos Aires: Secretaría de Política Económica.

Navarrete, David, Gilberto C. Gallopín, Mariela Blanco, Martín Díaz-Zorita, Diego O. Ferraro, Hilda Herzer, Pedro Laterra, María R. Murmis, Guillermo P. Podestá, Jorge Rabinovich, Emilio H. Satorre, Filemón Torres and Ernesto F. Viglizzo. 2007. "Multi-causal and Integrated Assessment of Sustainability: The Case of Agriculturization in the Argentine Pampas." *Environment, Development and Sustainability* 11 (3): 612–638.

Neiman, Guillermo. 2012. "Acerca de la Estructura y Condiciones del Empleo en el Sector Agropecuario Argentino." *Voces en el Fénix* 12: 31–35.

Obschatko, Edith. 2013. "El Sector Agroalimentario Argentino Como Motor del Crecimiento." Pp. 76–90 in Cámara de Comercio Argentino-Holandesa (ed.) *Alimentar el Futuro. Argentina Proveedora de Alimentos para el Mundo*. Buenos Aires: Cámara de Comercio Argentino-Holandesa.

Obschatko, Edith, María del Pilar Foti and Marcela Román. 2006. *Los Pequeños Productores en la República Argentina. Importancia en la Producción Agropecuaria y en el Empleo en base al Censo Nacional Agropecuario 2002*. Buenos Aires: SAGPyA-IICA.

Percíncula, Analía, Andrés Jorge, Claudia Calvo, Daniela Mariotti, Diego Domínguez, María de Estrada, Mariana Ciccolella, Pablo Barbetta, Pablo Sabatino and Sofiá Astelarra. 2011. "La Violencia Rural en la Argentina de los Agronegocios. Crónicas Invisibles del Despojo." *Revista Nera* 19: 8–23.

Puyana, Alicia and Agostina Constantino. 2013. "Sojización y Enfermedad Holandesa en Argentina: ¿La Maldición Verde?" *Revista Problemas del Desarrollo* 175 (44): 81–100.

Reboratti, Carlos. 2010. "Un Mar de Soja: la Nueva Agricultura en Argentina y Sus Consecuencias." *Revista de Geografía Norte Grande* 45: 63–76.

Reca, Lucio. 2006. *Aspectos del Desarrollo Agropecuario Argentino 1875–2005*. Buenos Aires: Academia Nacional de Agronomía y Veterinaria.

REDAF (Red Agroforestal Chaco Argentina). 2012. *Bosque Nativo en Salta: Ley de Bosques, Análisis de Deforestación y Situación del Bosque Chaqueño en la Provincia*.

Registro Nacional de Tierras Rurales. n/d. *Departamentos que Superan el Límite del 15% Establecido por la Ley 26.737 a Septiembre 2013*. Buenos Aires: Ministerio de Justicia y Derechos Humanos.

Richardson, Neal. 2009. "Export-Oriented Populism: Commodities and Coalitions in Argentina." *Studies in Comparative International Development* 44 (3): 228–255.

Rodríguez, Javier. 2005. "Los Complejos Agroalimentarios y el Empleo: Una Controversia Teórica y Empírica." *Realidad Económica* 218: 107–135.

Rodríguez, Javier. 2012. "Los cambios en la producción agrícola pampeana." *Voces en el Fénix* 12: 15–21.

SIIA (Sistema Integrado de Información Agropecuaria). 2013. *Estimaciones Agrícolas*. Buenos Aires: Ministerio de Agricultura, Ganadería y Pesca.

Sili, Marcelo and Luciana Soumoulou. 2011. *La Problemática de la Tierra en Argentina. Conflictos y Dinámicas de Uso, Tenencia y Concentración*. Buenos Aires: IFAD.

Sinnott, Emily. 2009. *Commodity Prices and Fiscal Policy in Latin America and the Caribbean*. Retrieved at http://siteresources.worldbank.org/EXTLACOFFICEOFCE/Resources/870892-1253047679843/6438618-1254513204494/Sinnott2009.pdf on July 22, 2014.

Sommerville, Melanie. 2013. "Financializing Prairie Farmland: Farmland Investments Funds and the Restructuring of Family Farming Systems in Central Canada." Working

Paper 38. PLAS, Institute for Poverty, Land and Agrarian Studies. Retrieved at http://www.plaas.org.za/plaas-publication/ldpi-38 on July 22, 2014.

Teubal, Miguel, Diego Domínguez and Pablo Sabatino. 2005. "Transformaciones Agrarias en la Argentina. Agricultura Industrial y Sistema Agroalimentario." Pp. 37–78 in Norma Giarracca and Miguel Teubal (eds.) *El Campo Argentino en la Encrucijada. Estrategias y Resistencias Sociales y Ecos en la Ciudad.* Buenos Aires: Alianza Editorial.

Trigo, Eduardo and Eugenio Cap. 2003. "The Impact of the Introduction of Transgenic Crops in Argentinean Agriculture." *AgBioForum* 6 (3): 87–94.

Trigo, Eduardo and Eugenio Cap. 2006. *Diez Años de Cultivos Genéticamente Modificados en la Agricultura Argentina.* Buenos Aires: Consejo Argentino para la Información y el Desarrollo de la Biotecnología.

Viglizzo, Ernesto, Federico Frank, Lorena Carren, Esteban Jobba, Hernan Pereyra, Jonathan Clatt, Daniel Pince and M. Florencia Ricard. 2011. "Ecological and Environmental Footprint of 50 Years of Agricultural Expansion in Argentina." *Global Change Biology* 17: 959–973.

Watts, Michael and David Goodman. 1997. "Agrarian Questions: Global Appetite, Local Metabolism: Nature, Culture and Industry in Fin de Siècle Agro-Food Systems." Pp. 1–24 in David Goodman and Michael Watts (eds.) *Globalising Food: Agrarian Questions and Global Restructuring.* London: Routledge.

Wylde, Christopher. 2010. Argentina, Kirchnerismo and Neodesarrollismo: Argentine Political Economy under the Administration of Néstor Kirchner 2003–2007. Buenos Aires: FLACSO Argentina.

# 5. The political economy of agriculture in Colombia: An unfinished business

*Anouk Patel-Campillo and*
*María del Rosario Castro Bernardini*

## INTRODUCTION

In Colombia, the social relations and historical trajectory of land distribution are complex and multidimensional. Largely shaped by regional, socio-political, economic and cultural differences, as well as biophysical and climate conditions, the Colombian political economy of agriculture is a kaleidoscope of social relations entrenched in struggles over the (dis)possession of land embedded in the multiple layers of local, regional, national and global historical and economic processes. To this end, we apply Harvey's (2005) concept of accumulation through dispossession to partially explain how particular factors have shaped social relations in rural areas through the prism of land and its distribution. Here, we find that in contrast to the fluidity of social relations, land and its materiality is a useful means to analytically ground dynamic and complex social, political, economic and class relations with the objective to identify trends across time and space. We add to Harvey's conceptualization of accumulation by dispossession, which is largely focused on economic relations, by incorporating the socio-political aspects that accompany economic accumulation and the crisis of legitimacy. Taking Harvey's conceptualization as a point of departure, we analytically broaden it to include not only economic but also the socio-political relations that stem from the (dis)possession of power and legitimacy and variegated forms of accumulation sought after by dissimilar actors across time and space: colonos (and later campesinos), elites and counter-elites (guerrilla groups, drug traffickers and paramilitaries), and the state. In this chapter, our aim is not to provide an exhaustive analysis of the political economy of Colombian agriculture, but to analytically tease out some of the factors that account for such complexity.

While particular types of agricultural production co-exist across time, it is important to recognize that in addition to complex social relations associated with land and its (dis)possession, regional variation in the biophysical nature of the goods produced, and their intended markets, play a crucial role in forms of accumulation in the Colombian rural landscape.

For instance, unlike large sugar plantations located at the coast and in the low-lying and flat areas of the Valle del Cauca, which relied on slaves during the first period under study, and later "wage" labor, coffee production in mountainous areas was carried out by small growers in family farms. This contrasted with foreign agricultural enclaves characteristic of the first period monopolizing not only land but also the commercialization of products and infrastructure as in the case of the United Fruit Company (UFC), which controlled not only thousands of hectares of land but the commercial infrastructure of the Colombian banana industry (Fajardo 1983). Colombian agriculture, thus, is diverse in its composition and can be characterized by the presence of agricultural enclaves and large-scale commercial enterprises, as well as family farms producing for domestic and export markets.

Differentiated forms of production, however, did not occur naturally but were largely shaped by the domestic and foreign trade agricultural policies of a relatively weak central government seeking to affirm its power and influence over its "national" territory and sub-national socio-political dynamics while navigating its incorporation into the agricultural world-system. Here, two key factors are important to note. First is that differentiated production systems are associated with variegated yet often overlapping forms of accumulation requiring particular regulatory and institutional architectures for their reproduction. And second is that differentiated production systems are associated with particular forms of market incorporation that encourage variegation in economic and consumptive relations as well as social mobilization. These two factors are at the crux of the agrarian question in Colombia. In the sections that follow, we analyze the historical trajectory of the Colombian political economy of agriculture by focusing on three broad yet salient periods, from independence to the 1960s, the 1960s to the 1980s, and the 1990s to the mid-2000s, which were marked by important shifts in the regulatory regimes governing processes of land (dis)possession and associated processes of accumulation.

## COLONIAL LEGACIES: OLD PROCESSES IN NEW GUISES?

Following the early colonial political economy of Colombian agriculture, where territorial claims were made in the name of the Spanish crown, the dispossession of indigenous peoples' land and the establishment of new social relations through extraneous mechanisms of accumulation was epitomized by the formation of latifundia. With independence from Spain in 1819, the territorial process of nation-building required not only the continued expansion of the internal frontier encouraged by the government and realized by settler "colonos," but also the lengthening of the political reach of the central state to isolated rural areas. Reflecting this dynamic, Law 13 of 1821 declared all unoccupied land as property of the government, legitimizing the territorial authority of the central government through the appropriation of "vacant" land and by claiming the right to sell it. Because small agricultural producers played a vital role in supplying food for local markets, the land distribution policies of the central government favored producers who worked the land.

The government's objective to distribute land was reflected in the failed Law 200 of 1936 and Law 100 of 1944, which recognized the rights of small holders to own land and sought to break apart large and unproductive estates. Nonetheless, attracted by the opportunities to establish large-scale commercial enterprises while boosting their social status, elites[1] used land titling mechanisms to acquire land and accumulate capital resulting in the concentration of land ownership and expansion of commercial agriculture and less labor intensive yet productive cattle ranching. The inability to de-concentrate land was largely due to colono difficulties using the central government's mechanisms of land distribution to their advantage given their lack of resources, political leverage and their relative isolation (Legrand 1986). That is, for colonos and later peasants, the legal land acquisition and titling of vacant lands they settled was largely hindered by the government's requirement for them to travel to the capital, Bogotá, to register ownership. Instead, it was comparatively easier for wealthy entrepreneurs to acquire titles over large tracts of public land.

In addition to acquiring vast areas of land, the accumulation practices of elites entailed "enclosing" colonos and their lands with the purpose of extracting the labor necessary to make commercial agriculture viable and threatening them with eviction or expropriation (Legrand 1986:38–59). That is, while colonos settled in vacant land, elites specifically sought to legally acquire land occupied and made productive by settlers. This accumulation strategy increased social unrest and contestation deepening social conflict over land distribution. Because land utilization was a priority for the Colombian central government and expropriation an important enforcement mechanism, land entrepreneurs and elites responded to the threat of expropriation and redistribution of unproductive lands by engaging in cattle ranching. While the process of converting large lowland forests into pasture required large upfront financial investment, labor and risk (Van Ausdal 2009), once established, cattle ranching was comparatively a more effective means to legally acquire, control and manage large tracts of land while minimizing the social frictions that characterized labor-intensive commercial and plantation production activities.

In the aftermath of independence, the Colombian political economy of agriculture was shaped by the nation-building efforts of the Colombian government through the (dis)possession of vacant lands and their distribution, as well as the colonization of the internal frontier. While in the early twentieth century the use of land as a means of consolidating power continued, land and its (dis)possession played[2] a key role in legitimizing the authority of the central government and structuring class relations. For capitalized elites, profit accumulation strategies entailed partaking in production systems associated with large-scale agriculture and the extraction of labor through the enclosure of colono lands. Production systems associated with this form of accumulation by (dis)possession characterized large-scale commercial plantation agriculture and foreign agricultural enclaves utilizing coerced "wage" labor. Land concentration and the accumulation strategies of landed elites fueled social unrest and contestation, which took specific forms according to differences in the agricultural landscape as well as the nature of production.

In large-scale commercial agriculture, social unrest revolved primarily around labor conditions rather than land ownership, in contrast to small coffee growers and peasants for whom land titling served to secure their means of production. Legitimized by Act 83 of 1931, which allowed for the establishment of workers' unions (Fajardo 1983:47), the collective struggles over land tenure took many forms including land invasions and plantation worker conflict (Legrand 1986:99–108). Peasant struggles used government policy frameworks laid out with the objective of expanding the internal frontier, putting land to productive purposes and dealing with land concentration through redistribution, as exemplified in the 1936 "Ley de tierras" (Law 200). To this end, Law 200 recognized the land tenure rights of rural workers and colonos, and it facilitated the purchase of land by tenant farmers, whereas Law 100 of 1944 established the legal rights and obligations between landowners and their sharecroppers/tenants.

Within the global context, Colombia's reliance on export agriculture, and particularly large coffee surpluses, not only contributed to its tighter incorporation into world markets as an agricultural supplier, but also as a consumer. More precisely, Laws 30 and 74 of 1926 reduced import tariffs on foods, increasing food imports for the first three decades of the twentieth century and thus weakening the position of small agricultural producers in domestic markets, creating discontent among landowners (Fajardo 1983). At the same time, the expansion of roads and transportation systems in the 1920s facilitated the incorporation of formerly isolated local markets, encouraging what some scholars call a shift from an agricultural export-based economy to one geared toward the internal consumption of primary and industrial goods (Legrand 1986:91–92). In turn, domestic market expansion provided the upper class and land entrepreneurs with the incentive not only to diversify their economic interests but to intensify primary good production through the coercion of sharecroppers and tenant farmers, thus intensifying social conflict and provoking a response that was short of passive.

In sum, agricultural policy at this time was characterized by the support of small family farms and the efforts to rein in the speculative and accumulative practices of large latifundistas (Legrand 1986:96). Central to this strategy were regulatory frameworks that allowed the government to expropriate public lands claimed by large latifundistas and distribute them to settler families to be put to use. This strategy, however, was fraught with social strife amplified by national policy frameworks directed at the tightening of Colombia's agricultural system into global markets, the expansion of domestic markets and an emphasis on increased productivity of food production for domestic consumption. Often at odds, national policy frameworks thus contributed to the emergence of the so-called agrarian problem of the 1920s and early 1930s (Legrand 1986), giving way to La Violencia (1948–1964), a period in Colombian history marked by bipartisan civil war, which claimed the lives of nearly one million people and was particularly brutal in rural areas (Jaramillo 1998).

In 1950[3] expropriation as a means to achieve land redistribution came to an end with the first World Bank mission to Colombia. Within the context of increased industrialization and urbanization, the expansion of cattle ranching and commercial agriculture and ensuing food shortages, the Bank's recommendation to the Colombian government was to intensify the use of land through taxation rather than expropriation, to encourage the modernization of the agricultural sector through the development of infrastructure, targeted crop and tax subsidies, and technical assistance, among others. According to Legrand (1986:149), by the 1960s, government policies encouraging modernization irreparably ruptured the Colombian agricultural production landscape along class lines identifiable through their distinct geographic locations, political access, forms of production and commodities produced, and target markets.

More specifically, while large cattle ranching, commercial agricultural operations and non-traditional exports were often located in the best quality lands in the valleys and coastal planes, shrinking tenant and family farms operated in mountain areas with poor quality soils. And although, as Legrand (1986:149) points out, commercial agriculture did not compete with mountain producers, it did displace food-producing small holders. The social transformation of rural areas not only created an expanding labor dependent on purchased foods, but accentuated social dislocation and unrest manifested in La Violencia.

## RURAL UNREST (1960s–1990s): BETWEEN GUERRILLA WARFARE, PARAMILITARY VIOLENCE AND DRUG TRAFFICKING

In the aftermath of La Violencia, widespread rural poverty, displacement, unrest, the government's agricultural modernization strategies and the geopolitical and ideological struggles of the Cold War led to the emergence of guerrilla groups such as the National Liberation Army (ELN), a student-led group; the Fuerzas Armadas Revolucionarias de Colombia (FARC) with links to the Communist Party in alliance with self-defense peasant units, a radical wing of the Marxist–Leninist party; the Popular Liberation Army (EPL), a radical wing of the Marxist–Leninist party; and later the urban Movimiento 19 de abril (M-19) (Zamosc 1990:56). Within this context, the US Alliance for Progress provided a platform for the Colombian government to pass the 1961 agrarian reform law (Land Reform Act 135) that for the first time in history created an institutional body – the Instituto Colombiano de la Reforma Agraria[4] (INCORA) – to redistribute land to landless peasants, which ultimately failed in its mission. Equally important was the creation of the Asociación Nacional de Usuarios Campesinos (ANUC) by the Carlos Lleras government in an effort to promote the direct political participation of peasants. However, ANUC was subsequently repressed by the Misael Pastrana administration and weakened by internal ideological divisions (Albán 2011:348; Zamosc 1990:51).

According to Zamosc, while different in their approaches to sociopolitical and economic change and the inclusion of peasant political and economic interests, the activities of these counter-elite groups were a clear representation of a legitimacy crisis of what he calls the "país político" (political society) (1990:56). While initially the FARC sought to incorporate itself in the political life of the country through traditional electoral channels, government repression led to its radicalization and alienation. As a result, segments of the FARC as well as M-19 moved their operations to rural areas where they

> behaved as the state, imposing order and assuming political control over the population. In the Middle Magdalena valley, for example, where colonists competed for land with expanding cattle ranches, the guerrillas arbitrated disputes, offered guarantees of protection, and exacted cash contributions from the landowners, and demanded electoral support from the peasantry at large. (de Rementería 1986 as cited in Zamosc 1990:58)

Peasant struggles over land tenure were not only met with repression and violence by governing elites, land entrepreneurs and traditional landowners but also by vigilante groups hired to protect their properties from land occupations, a common practice used by peasants. The central government's endorsement of the use of assault weapons and the creation of self-defense units led to the emergence of paramilitary militia as landed elites sought to prevent or eradicate peasant land occupations and social unrest (Grajales 2011:775–778). Stigmatized as guerrilla sympathizers and troublemakers, paramilitary militias often assassinated peasant leaders and civilians with impunity. Guerrilla groups, on the other hand, often found peasants ideologically removed and failed to incorporate peasant interests into their political agendas. Added to this explosive mix, drug traffickers were active in rural areas accumulating vast tracts of land and cattle ranches (Richani 2012). For drug traffickers, land accumulation strategies served two main purposes, namely to launder the proceeds of illegal activity and to legitimize their social standing as rural elites (Grajales 2011).

While the socio-political and economic dynamics stemming from the violent convergence of the activities of the government and the military, landowners, hired vigilantes (and later paramilitary groups), guerrillas and drug traffickers are too complex to address in this chapter, what is important to note is that relative to these other groups, peasants lacked the political, economic and armed power to effectively advocate for their rights. Instead, they were caught in the middle – what Marx would characterize as "cannon fodder." Equally important is to point out that the activities of drug traffickers, paramilitary militia, guerrilla groups and the military in rural areas shifted the political attention away from the issues concerning peasants and rural workers to the multifaceted rural warfare.

Within this context, the (dis)possession of land took on a different meaning in the Colombian rural landscape. While still the epicenter of contentious social relations between landowners and the peasantry, land dis(possession) now revolved around the operations of the paramilitary, drug traffickers and, to a certain extent, guerrilla groups. Whereas land as a means to accumulate power, status and profit remained somewhat unaltered, in the hands of drug dealers and the paramilitary, land became a means of transforming fictitious capital into legal and real assets. According to Grajales (2011:771), far from being external to the government's political and bureaucratic machine, the use of violence and corruption to differentially (dis)possess and (dis)enfranchise resulted in the forced displacement of thousands of peasant families and the concentration of lands in the hands of the drug traffickers, paramilitaries and their associates. Here, the forced displacement of peasants facilitated money laundering and processes of accumulation and legitimation through land grabbing. From this perspective, the transformation of illicit capital into land holdings and their legal incorporation into formal land markets through the acquisition of titles served not only to concentrate land but also to facilitate the insertion of these "new" rural actors into the global economy through agricultural exports such as palm oil (Grajales 2011:772). Unsurprisingly, it is at this junction that the combined interests of drug traffickers, paramilitaries, governing elites and state converge.

Under the banner of "apertura," the 1991 presidency of César Gaviria officially launched aggressive and systematic efforts to liberalize the Colombian market, decentralize political responsibilities and transform the role of the national government by continuing to weaken social safety nets and corresponding government institutions while consolidating its reach over selected economic areas through (de)regulation including foreign direct investment, international trade, export-oriented policy, among others. Opting for market-based mechanisms instead of redistributive land reform, in 1992 the central government and the Council on Economic and Social Policy (CONPES) encouraged peasants to "negotiate" the purchase of land, which would then be subsidized by the government by up to 70 percent (Albán 2011; Franco and De los Ríos 2011; Jaramillo 1998:52).[5] Coordinated by INCORA, Law 160 of 1994 created the National System of Agrarian Reform and Peasant Rural Development (Sistema de Nacional de Reforma Agraria y Desarrollo Rural Campesino) and provided the means to subsidize the purchase of land to encourage rural worker and peasant access to land (Albán 2011:351–354; Thomson 2011). Unsurprisingly, lack of enforcement and intervention in land redistribution and, in this case, purchase for the purposes of redistribution prevented the realization of the government's stated objectives.

As part of the decentralization process, municipal governments were given powers to create agricultural technical units (or UMATAS) with the aim to support small and medium producers. According to Jaramillo (1998:139), the breadth and magnitude of the central government liberalization policies wreaked havoc in the countryside with the rapid inflow of agricultural imports and a sharp drop in real wages for rural workers. At the same time, during the 1990s the central government's export bias was evidenced by the decline in agricultural production of transitional crops for domestic consumption. During this decade, the agrarian sector's participation in the national GDP was the lowest in the twentieth century, dropping from 32 percent in 1960 to less than 15 percent in the late 1990s (Kalmanovitz and López 2004:6).

The government's neoliberal policies accelerated the restructuring of agricultural production. From 1991 to 2005, food imports significantly increased by 424 percent while agro-exports rose by 66 percent (Tobasura Acuña 2011:646–651). Similarly, there was a decline in the production area dedicated to transitional crops (i.e., barley, cotton, soybeans, wheat and corn, among others, for domestic consumption) compared to that of permanent crops (i.e., fruit, palm oil, sugar cane, among others, for export) (Kalmanovitz and López 2003; Pérez Correa and Pérez Martínez 2002; Tobasura Acuña 2011:652). In addition to deepening the insertion of Colombian agriculture into world markets as a supplier of commodity crops and a net food importer, the neoliberalization of the rural landscape raised food prices, affecting Colombian consumers and having adverse impacts on the livelihoods of small farmers engaged in the production of transitional crops (Tobasura Acuña 2011:651).

The neoliberalization of Colombian agriculture, however, did not affect all in the same way. For landed elites, whose socio-political status and power had long been consolidated through their historical control over land, the processes of apertura or economic liberalization offered renewed opportunities to reiterate elite centrality in the political and economic life of the country. Because at the heart of apertura was the tighter insertion of Colombia into world markets through export-oriented development, landed elites were well suited to fill this role through the strengthening of large-scale industrialized commercial agriculture. Thus, the neoliberalization of Colombian agriculture and a tighter insertion into world markets not only served landed elites' capital accumulation strategies but also secured the political leverage of those engaged in export-oriented activities (Patel-Campillo 2014). Moreover, exacting profit from export-oriented commercial agriculture is largely contingent on securing low labor costs and relies on a large pool of landless workers. Thus, in addition to relying on government support, the accumulation practices of landed elites in commercial agriculture depended on their control over large tracts of land and the disciplining of labor, often carried out by hired paramilitary groups.

For drug traffickers and paramilitary militias, territorial control constituted a means to legalize fictitious capital as well as to socially embed their activities by gaining local socio-political status and power. The increased regional presence and strength of paramilitary groups in the countryside, evidenced by the emergence of the Autodefensas Unidas de Colombia (AUC), a confederation of right-wing militia groups, intensified land grabbing accumulation strategies and accounted for a large portion of the forced displacement of peasants (Grajales 2011:782). Land (dis)possession and the accumulation strategies of landed elites as well as drug traffickers could not have been achieved without state facilitation. Whereas export-oriented activity was encouraged through market liberalization and government support and promotion, the (dis)possession of peasant lands by drug traffickers and paramilitary groups was facilitated when the "attempts" of INCORA to carry out land redistribution were redressed in 1991 and the lands previously given to peasants were declared to be vacant and transferred to new owners (Grajales 2011:784).

To summarize, within the context of apertura, the diverse interests of rural actors, drug trafficking, armed struggles among the military, guerrilla groups, paramilitary militias and elite extractive activities intensified violence in rural areas, reaching new heights. As a result, induced and massive rural outmigration characterized the apertura period, with an estimated one million rural displaced people between 1996 and 1999 (Pérez Correa and Pérez Martínez 2002:53).[6]

## UNDER THE VEIL OF A PARAMILITARY STATE: LEGITIMIZING LAND GRABBING IN THE 2000s AND BEYOND

Álvaro Uribe's administration put an end to INCORA (Decree 1300). Replaced by the Instituto Colombiano de Desarrollo Rural (INCORDER), the government's emphasis on export agriculture benefited the commercial interests of commercial landowners and agro-businesses. Based on neoliberal principles of market integration, specialization and increased competitiveness, Uribe's administration continued to deepen the entrenchment of landed elites and their economic activities. In this period, processes of accumulation through (dis)possession continued through the creation of regulatory and institutional frameworks and discourse dedicated to the entrenchment of neoliberal principles (Patel-Campillo 2014). Programs such as Agro Ingreso Seguro[7] and Apuesta Exportadora 2006–2020 (the export bet), not only exacerbated food insecurity but also used the neoliberal discourse to gouge the social significance of the peasantry by redefining them as "entrepreneurs." Peasants continued to be driven out of rural areas, with only a few of them becoming agricultural wage workers (Tobasura Acuña 2011:653) and many more joining the ranks of the urban poor.

Largely due to the accumulation strategies of drug traffickers, paramilitary groups and landed elites, millions of peasants and rural workers have faced relentless violence, coercion, mass killings and forced displacement. The (dis)possession of peasant lands and ownership concentration, or what in this period has been called land grabbing, has been legitimized, and to a certain extent encouraged, by the central government through the legalization of land titles (Grajales 2013; Thomson 2011). According to the Comisión Colombiana de Juristas (Colombian Commission of Jurists), the 2007 Estatuto de Desarrollo Rural (Statute of Rural Development) facilitated the land grabbing strategies of powerful actors by titling land after only five years regardless of whether ownership is in dispute (as cited in Grajales 2013:228). In March 2009, after sustained pressure from peasant and indigenous and Afro-Colombian communities, supported by national and international non-governmental organizations (NGOs), the Constitutional Court declared the Estatuto de Desarrollo Rural unconstitutional (Grajales 2013; Thomson 2011:346).

The central government's role in the concentration of land is exemplified by the use of its regulatory powers to selectively (dis)possess and (dis) place rural populations in favor of powerful economic actors engaged in state-supported, export-oriented and large-scale commercial agriculture. In 2005 Colombia was one of the world's top five suppliers of palm oil, an activity linked to the displacement of thousands of people, violent armed conflict and the land grabbing practices of producers (Albán 2011; Grajales 2013; Richani 2012; Thomson 2011). Keen on providing additional support to an already economically successful activity, and under Uribe's leadership, a succession of decrees (Decree 383 of 2007, Decree 2629 of 2010 and 2012) provided the political legitimacy and regulatory basis to expand the economic activities of the industry by establishing tax-free zones, creating a domestic market for palm oil and mandating the use of biodiesel in new cars and other motorized equipment (Grajales 2013:226).

With financing from USAID (United States Agency for International Development) through its Colombian Agribusiness Partnership Program (CAPP) (Grajales 2013:227; Thomson 2011:348), oil palm producers not only received economic support but gained political leverage to continue "business as usual." Although overtly linked to the dispossession, violence and displacement of rural communities, the Colombian central government, far from delegitimizing the economic activities of palm oil producers, instead utilizes its regulatory powers to concentrate land and public resources in the hands of elites and landed paramilitary at the expense of the rural populace. True to its extractive nature, the central government's actions clearly show its inadequacy as a means to achieve land reform and redistribution. Nominal efforts to demobilize paramilitary militia and restitute lands usurped from peasants during Uribe's administration included a reparation fund linked to Law 975 of 2005, or the so-called Justice and Peace Law. Nevertheless, as commonly practiced by the Colombian central government, lack of implementation and the obscure language in which the law was written prevented any significant land redistribution (Thomson 2011:346).

The neoliberalization of the Colombian rural landscape characterized by the twin processes of (dis)possession and accumulation is evidenced by the fact that less than 5 percent of the population owns over 70 percent of arable land (Instituto Geográfico Agustín Codazzi 2012:73). Coupled with the fact that currently Colombia ranks second in the world for the largest number of displaced people (Programa de las Naciones Unidas para el Desarrollo 2011:72), these numbers show the staggering inequality and social dislocation that characterize the Colombian rural landscape. However, what makes the neoliberalization of the Colombian rural landscape particularly brutal is the cost in human lives and livelihoods, increasing food insecurity and endemic rural unemployment that promises to continue under the auspices of an illegitimate and criminal state.

## NOTES

1.  It is important to note that Colombian elites had significant political clout, often holding public office, which enabled them to increase their land holdings and power. Thanks to the book editors for highlighting this point.
2.  Building on Marx's concept of primitive accumulation, the notion of accumulation by dispossession highlights not only the processes associated with capital accumulation at a global scale but also its role in easing the inherent crisis of the capitalist system by expanding markets and lowering prices. Thus, an important difference between the concept of primitive accumulation and processes of accumulation by dispossession centers on the role that accumulation plays in capitalism. That is, primitive accumulation magnifies class tensions within capitalism leading to crisis whereas processes of accumulation by dispossession eases these tensions and enables capitalism to adapt across time and space. From this perspective, the unevenness of capitalism or the variegated forms it takes relate to socially contingent and spatially embedded forms of accumulation.
3.  It is important to mention that Colombia experienced a substitution process of agricultural imports between 1950 and 1980 (Tobasura Acuña 2011). This model consisted of two phases, the first dedicated to the production of raw materials including cotton and grain, the second the production of export-oriented crops such as flowers (644–645).
4.  According to Benítez Vargas (2005), between 1960 and 2004 the INCORA distributed land in their main three programs: (i) land allocation, (ii) certification of vacant land and (iii) establishment and extension of indigenous reservations. Of the three programs, the third was the most active one, with 59.1 percent of participation, followed by certification of vacant land (37 percent) and land allocation (3.4 percent).
5.  It is important to note that although subsidies are contrary to neoliberal principals of government intervention, they are of lesser importance than upholding private property and integrating peasants into land markets.
6.  For instance, in 1996 "Operation Genesis" was carried out by the military to expel guerrillas in the Urabá region, and "tactics such as aerial bombardment, massacre, forced disappearance and torture caused approximately 17,000 people to flee the area" (Internal Displacement Monitoring Center 2007 as cited in Thomson 2011:346).
7.  See Albán 2011:352; Grajales 2013; Thomson 2011.

# REFERENCES

Albán, Álvaro. 2011. "Reforma y Contrarreforma Agraria en Colombia." *Revista de Economía Internacional* 13 (24):327–356.

Benítez Vargas, Regis Manuel. 2005. "La Reforma Agraria en Colombia Vigente y Por Hacer." *Economía Colombiana: Revista de la Controlaría General de la República* (309):45–55.

Fajardo, Darío M. 1983. *Haciendas, Campesinos y Políticas Agrarias en Colombia, 1920–1980*. Bogotá, Colombia: Fundación Friedrich Naumann.

Franco, Angélica and Ignacio De los Ríos. 2011. "Land Reform in Colombia: Historical Evolution of the Concept." *Cuadernos de Desarrollo Rural* 8 (67):93–119.

Grajales, Jacobo. 2011. "The Rifle and the Title: Paramilitary Violence, Land Grab and Land Control in Colombia." *Journal of Peasant Studies* 38 (4):711–792.

Grajales, Jacobo. 2013. "State Involvement, Land Grabbing and Counter-Insurgency in Colombia." *Development and Change* 44 (2):211–232.

Harvey, David. 2005. *The New Imperialism*. New York: Oxford University Press.

Instituto Geográfico Agustín Codazzi. 2012. *Atlas de la Distribución de la Propiedad Rural en Colombia*. Bogotá, Colombia: Instituto Geográfico Agustín Codazzi.

Jaramillo, Carlos Felipe. 1998. *Liberalization, Crisis, and Change in Colombian Agriculture*. Oxford: Westview Press.

Kalmanovitz, Salomón and Enrique López. 2003. "La Agricultura en Colombia entre 1950 y 2000." *Borradores de Economía* 255:1–45.

Kalmanovitz, Salomón and Enrique López. 2004. "Patrones de Desarrollo y Fuentes de Crecimiento de la Agricultura." *Borradores de Economía* 288:1–45.

Legrand, Catherine. 1986. *Frontier Expansion and Peasant Protest in Colombia, 1850–1936*. Albuquerque: University of New Mexico Press.

Patel-Campillo, Anouk. 2014. "For Competitiveness's Sake? Material Competition vs. Competitiveness as a National Project." Pp. 207–224 in *The Neoliberal Regime in the Agri-Food Sector: Crisis, Resilience, and Restructuring*, edited by S.A. Wolf and A. Bonanno, New York: Routledge.

Pérez Correa, Edelmira and Manuel Pérez Martínez. 2002. "El Sector Rural en Colombia y su Crisis Actual." *Cuadernos de Desarrollo Rural* 48:35–58.

Programa de las Naciones Unidas para el Desarrollo. 2011. *Informe Nacional de Desarrollo Humano 2011. Colombia Rural. Razones para la Esperanza. Resumen ejecutivo*. Bogotá, Colombia: Programa de las Naciones Unidas para el Desarrollo.

Richani, Nazih. 2012. "The Agrarian Rentier Political Economy: Land Concentration and Food Insecurity in Colombia." *Latin American Review* 47 (2):51–78.

Thomson, Frances. 2011. "The Agrarian Question and Violence in Colombia: Conflict and Development." *Journal of Agrarian Change* 11 (3):321–356.

Tobasura Acuña, Isaías. 2011. "De Campesinos a Empresarios: la Retórica Neoliberal de la Política Agraria en Colombia." *Espacio Abierto* 20 (4):641–657.

Van Ausdal, Shawn. 2009. "Pasture, Profit, and Power: An Environmental History of Cattle Ranching in Colombia, 1850–1950." *Geoforum* 40 (5):707–719.

Zamosc, Leon. 1990. "The Political Crisis and the Prospects for Rural Democracy in Colombia." *Journal of Development Studies* 26 (4):44–78.

# 6. Brazilian farmers, quality and markets
*Josefa Salete Barbosa Cavalcanti and*
*Evander Eloi Krone*

## INTRODUCTION

Studies of the development of agriculture in Brazil stress the nation's colonial past based on the role that geographical discoveries and the rule of Portugal played in the establishment of a system of production of goods for European markets. In the first few centuries of Brazil's economic and agricultural expansion, two key production systems were employed. The first consisted of sugar plantations on the fertile coastal wetlands, and the second was the extensive livestock operations on large tracts of land in the interior of the country (Andrade 1973; Garcia 1975). In the *Sertão* of the Northeast,[1] ownership was defined through land grants called *capitanias hereditárias*, or hereditary captaincies, and their partitions "sesmarias." These were lands granted to representative segments of the power structure of the colony, called "sesmeiros" or grantees, who became the actors of a hierarchical structure characterized by a powerful landowning class that prevails to this day (Faoro 1958; Bruno 2009).

The Land Law of 1850 (Law No. 601 of September 18, 1850) was the legal instrument that defined the rules for the formalization of occupancy and land use. The use of slave labor, the lack of protection of family farming, and the little or no attention paid to food production, were important (Andrade 1973). In sugarcane plantations and animal husbandry, those dispossessed of land worked under the rule of local landowners. The sugar cycle was succeeded by others: coffee, cotton, rubber (in the Amazon) and, more recently, soybeans. The production of sugarcane and cattle continued during these cycles, supported by market policies and demand.

The country's colonization policy consisted of the settling of the Southern and Southeastern regions through the immigration of European settlers, mainly Italians and Germans in the second half of the nineteenth century and Asians, mainly Japanese, in the coffee plantations of São Paulo in the early twentieth century. These waves of immigrants and the introduction of new social actors became part of a process of "modernization and whitening" of society. In agriculture, State programs awarded

German settlers 80 hectares of land while Italians, who arrived later, received smaller plots (Roche 1969).

## FROM POLICIES OF LAND PROPERTY VALUATION TO A CONSERVATIVE MODERNIZATION OF AGRICULTURE

Although this implantation of family farms was associated with food production, the latter remained inadequate and involved only relatively small portions of available land. In effect, land concentration remained high in the hands of large landowners who increased their wealth through production for export. Accordingly, as early as the first half of the twentieth century, the role and status of family farms versus that of large plantations began to emerge as a both a social and an economic issue. Despite calls for the modernization of family farming, this remained a difficult process. Most of these farms were managed by new immigrants and their families and ex-slaves, who were emancipated after legislation ending slavery was enacted in 1888. And while this labor force contributed to the strengthening of agriculture through increases in production, profits, and farm size, there were limited margins for the actual improvement of these farms (Neves and Silva 2008; Neves 2009; Welch et al. 2009; Forman 1975).

The concentration of land and the resulting power structure were challenged by a number of movements including the "runaway slaves," the peasant leagues,[2] and in recent years the "Sem Terra" (landless) movement.[3] Other forms of resistance also regularly emerged (Carter 2010; Martins 1986; Medeiros 1989; Paulilo 1996; Scott 1979; Stédile 2005). Their number was accompanied by their relatively limited power and effectiveness. In fact, for the entire first half of the twentieth century, these movements were contained by the power of dominant groups (Foweraker 1982). It was only after the momentum generated by the social movements of the 1960s, the protest against the military dictatorship in the 1980s, and the actions of more recent movements, that this opposition acquired visibility at the national level. Opposing land concentration, labor exploitation, and labor control, these movements directed claims against agribusiness and processes of exclusion based on ethnicity, class, and gender (Fernandes, Medeiros, and Paulilo 2009; Godoi, Menezes, and Marin 2009a; 2009b).

Responses to these struggles have been strong and permitted the continuous exploitation of human and natural resources. Importantly, these responses involved the mobilization of new discourses based on the creation of new identities for dominant groups. It has been argued that the ruling class in agri-food reinvented itself, riding on the neoliberal claim that the search for profit is the most desirable outcome for the entire society and a universal right. Bruno (2009:116) states, "Unlike previous times, it is openly assumed the profit is the most important goal of agribusiness and society." Wilkinson adds that in a context in which profit is the driving force of society, ownership of large segments of land is proposed as a fundamental right (Wilkinson 2008:205).

Wilkinson further stresses that the existing conflict between agribusiness and farmers has recently coalesced on the reactions to policies implemented by the Ministry of Agriculture, Livestock and Supply (MAPA) as well as actions of other ministries, particularly the Ministry of Agrarian Development (MDA). In effect, the Brazilian government has recently moved in support of family farms, reversing a policy that has characterized its actions for decades. The government has espoused the view that movements that favor alternative agriculture and that stress family farming represent the engine for creation of new patterns of development, based on the promotion of traditional and quality food, new spaces of sociability, and the renewed centrality of locality and community (Carneiro 2012; Almeida 1999). According to Almeida (1999:33):

> The new propositions and collective actions by a different agriculture rely heavily on critical notions of modernity and modernization, outlining the contours of another modernization, which relies on the notions of "collective" and "community/local". Beside the attempts to build a socio-cultural identity, it is actually another modernization that these groups claim, that can address the precariousness and the deficit of the current modernity.

This proposal involves new emancipatory territorial policies, such as the "Territories of Citizenship"[4] by the MDA and other ministries, supported by the demands of social movements, which include indigenous communities, quilombola (African-Brazilian) communities, rural settlements, and the Movement of Landless Rural Workers (MST). For Wilkinson (2008:202) the new territorial approach promotes the coexistence of farming with off-farm income and employment that ultimately allows the vital reproduction of family farming.

There is, however, some convergence in the duality of agribusiness family farms. This is primarily represented by the expansion of quality agri-food production which sees both agribusiness and family farms involved in the creation of global production networks controlled by corporate retailers. In this context, global supermarket chains emerge as promoters of goods and commercial messages that are part of the domain of family farms. In particular, supermarkets have recently championed "organic, traditional, fair trade and handmade" products that are predominantly associated with family farming (Wilkinson 2008).

# INSTRUMENTS OF AGRICULTURAL POLICIES

The evolution of agri-food since colonial times had crucially depended on State intervention. Influenced by colonial political views first and by modernization theory later, State actions almost always supported agribusiness. In recent years, though, worsening conditions of labor, unmet economic and social promises, environmental degradation, and challenges by various social movements, made this State posture increasingly untenable and in need of reversal. In this context, a number of new policies were recently implemented. Among them, emblematic of this new course is the National Program to Strengthen Family Agriculture (PRONAF), which provides enhanced credit opportunities to family farms (Goodman and Redclift 1981). Wilkinson (2008:201–202) points out:

> Since the New Republic,[5] distinct currents and movements converged in iden-
> tifying family farming as the axis of both the struggle against landlordism
> (symbolized by the movement for the agrarian reform supported by the New
> Republic) and against "conservative modernization" seen as another example
> of the "green revolution." In this sense, it is relevant to stress the existence of
> polyculture family farming as opposed to monoculture agribusiness, and the
> role of family farming as a supplier of basic food as opposed to the exportation
> bias of agribusiness.

### From the Second Half of the Twentieth Century to the Present

Worldwide, the changes that took place after World War II promoted the intensification of agricultural production justified by calls to address the growing global demand for food (Friedmann 2005). These changes generated a new paradigm that centered on the modernization of agriculture and resulted in the introduction of new technologies and inputs, the improvement of crop quality and yields, and the alteration of traditional diets (Friedmann 2005; Mazoyer and Roudart 2010). Brazil, like other Latin American societies, experienced processes of industrialization and urbanization that engendered "supply problems and high prices that retarded industrial growth" (Medeiros 1989:17; Bielschowsky 1998). It is at this juncture that, according to Medeiros (1989), intellectuals and political forces consensually agreed that Brazilian agriculture was a backward sector featuring an archaic agrarian structure and, as such, represented an obstacle to the industrialization of the country.

Over the course of the 1950s and 1960s, two main proposals emerged. The first argued for an increase in food production to be carried out through land reform. The second advocated the modernization of agriculture but without changing the established agrarian structure. This second option gained strength after the advent of the military dictatorship in 1964 and eventually became what Guimarães (1977) calls "conservative modernization." This strategy, unlike the social movement supporting agrarian reform, intended to modernize agriculture through increases in production and productivity, intending to establish a presence in export markets and the adoption of new technologies, but without altering the process of land concentration that had been in place since Brazil's colonial period. Following this view, the developmental model implemented in Brazil since the 1960s was legitimized by the ideas that farming was a backward sector and that small farm holders and their way of life should disappear because they represent an irrational form of social organization and obsolete lifestyles. Their presence, it was argued in pertinent literature, represent the real obstacle to the development of capitalism in agriculture (Leite Lopes 1981).

Economist Graziano da Silva (1996) indicates that the project of modernization of agriculture called for the transformation of the productive structure through the adoption of technological packages that involved the enhanced use of machines and fertilizers, and the availability of technical assistance. This process, he continues, was supported by the intervention of the State, which enacted policies that promoted the then dominant "Green Revolution" project and contributed to the creation of agro-industrial complexes. Changes in the definition of the physical and economic spaces of production ultimately favored the development of cash crops over local consumption needs.

It was in this context that the National System of Rural Credit (SNCR) was established in 1965. Institutionalized by Law No. 4829 (Brasil 1965), it represented a tool to stimulate modernization. SNCR's goal was to make ample and inexpensive credit available to farmers, and in particular medium and small farms, in order for these operations to mechanize and, in general, adopt new technology. Yet, this credit system worked in favor of large producers in the export sector. According to Redin and Fialho, "the ability that the large producers had to access credit was so large that many used such credit to acquire more land or urban properties" (2010:5). Small and medium farmers were largely left out and forced to enter the specialized export market in order to get access to credit. Additionally, the military government promoted a price support program, the Guaranteed Minimum Price Program, or PGPM, in 1966. This control of prices shifted important resources toward large operations that could generate more volume of production and disadvantaged small producers, local food needs, and self-consumption. In effect, the promotion of export-oriented production created a dual system of food availability that excluded poor segments of the working population in urban and rural areas alike.

*Table 6.1  Brazilian agricultural production from 1961 to 1981*

| Crop | 1961 | 1981 | Percentage change |
|------|------|------|------|
| | Production (metric tons) | Production (metric tons) | |
| Soy | 271,488 | 15,007,367 | 5427.82 |
| Oranges | 1,761,768 | 11,393,332 | 546.70 |
| Wheat | 544,858 | 2,209,631 | 305.54 |
| Sugarcane | 59,377,392 | 155,924,112 | 162.60 |
| Corn | 9,036,237 | 21,116,912 | 133.69 |
| Milk | 5,227,380 | 11,675,010 | 123.34 |
| Beef | 1,266,056 | 2,994,435 | 119.20 |
| Pork | 534,021 | 979,989 | 83.51 |
| Potatoes | 1,080,310 | 1,912,169 | 77.00 |
| Rice | 5,392,477 | 8,228,326 | 52.59 |

*Source:*  FAO (2014) 1961–1981.

By the early 1970s, the military government created the Brazilian Agricultural Research Corporation, or EMBRAPA, and the Brazilian Agency for Technical Assistance and Rural Extension, or EMBRATER, as tools to enhance modernization. EMBRAPA was in charge of agricultural research while EMBRATER covered extension and in particular the adoption of new technology (Redin and Fialho 2010). During the 1960s and 1970s the Brazilian government organized an institutional apparatus that supported agricultural modernization, subsidized rural credit and guaranteed minimum prices and provided improved research, development, and extension. Among the declared objectives associated with this model, the State wished to establish ways to generate a "trade surplus . . . adopting patterns that had already been implemented in other countries, especially in the United States" (Matos and Pessôa 2011:294). The results of this campaign matched production expectations (see Table 6.1). As the sector output expanded, the country's trade balance improved as well. At the level of production between 1961 and 1981 – the peak period of the agricultural modernization process – the output for most Brazilian commodities more than doubled, wheat production nearly tripled, while the production of oranges increased by more than 500 percent (Graziano da Silva 1996). However, soybean production was the most impressive in this period. Negligible in the early 1960s, soybean production increased over 5,000 percent in 20 years, becoming the leading commodity in Brazil.

According to Graziano da Silva (1996), the first phase of the modernization of agriculture in Brazil consisted of the transformation of the technical and productive base, followed by the industrialization of rural production with the development of the agricultural machine industry and the food industry, followed by the integration of agriculture and industry, and finally, under the control of finance capital, the integration of agricultural capital, industrial capital, and the banking system. This promoted the agribusiness sector and those commercial farmers who specialized in the production of commodities and that were supported by the State. Yet, it also contributed to the marginalization of small farmers, who experienced difficulties in adapting to the new technical-productive requirements. Very few alternatives were proposed for this group of farmers and migration emerged as the most practiced option. Between 1960 and 1990, a significant portion of rural labor was replaced by mechanization, with virtually no alternative employment created as small farm holders lost their farms to large modernized firms.

According to the Brazilian Institute of Geography and Statistics (IBGE), in 1960 the farm population accounted for 54.6 percent of the total population, but three decades later this percentage dropped to 24.5 percent. Between 1960 and 1991, about 38 million people abandoned the sector (Brasil 1960; 1991). The reduction of farm/rural residents as part of the growth of industrialization is common. However, the Brazilian rural exodus turned into the exponential and uncontrolled growth of large Brazilian cities and was not accompanied with the necessary development of urban employment. Accordingly, the expansion of these urban areas featured the growth of "slums" – the infamous favelas – characterized by housing problems, unemployment, and escalating violence (Furtado 1961). In effect, between the late 1960s and early 1970s, Brazil benefited from a favorable international context; its GDP grew at a rate of about 10 percent[6] (Bresser 1997). Yet, as the country's GDP grew, poverty and misery increased at a comparable pace, making rural folks the most visible victims of this exclusionary development. According to 2012 data (see Figure 6.1), in 1960 the Gini economic equality index for Brazil was 0.535. It rose during the following three decades, reaching 0.607 in 1990, indicating that the country was among the world's worst in income distribution. Only in 2001 did Brazil begin to reverse nearly four decades of deepening socioeconomic inequality, reaching the lowest level of social inequality in its history in 2011.

With the global oil crisis of the 1970s, the Brazilian economic growth stalled and high inflation, economic recession, and high foreign debt characterized the following decades. While the crisis had a severe negative impact throughout the lower and middle classes, it also delegitimized the military rule, prompted the growth of social movements in the 1980s, and eventually led to the processes of political opening and transition to

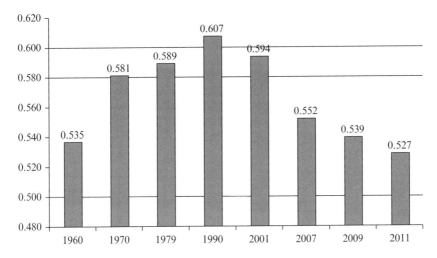

*Source:* Elaboration on data from IPEA (2012).

*Figure 6.1* *Historical evolution of the Gini coefficient in Brazil*

democracy. Yet, the 1980s also signified the adoption of neoliberalism worldwide and the associated radical change in agricultural policies that in Brazil took place after 1985 (Harvey 2007). This neoliberal turn included the reduction of State intervention, the elimination of credit subsidies, as well as the disruption of rural extension services.

**Neoliberal Policies**

In 1985, José Sarney[7] was elected to lead the first civilian government after the military dictatorship. During this period, various economic plans were implemented with the objective of stabilizing the national economy. Pressed by the fiscal crisis, a national plan for an agrarian reform was drawn but never implemented. Additionally, subsidies to credit were eliminated and the overall lending requirements were drastically tightened, pushing all agricultural activities to be managed according to neoliberal requirements (Coelho 2001). In the 1990s, during the government of President Fernando Collor,[8] State intervention was further reduced and EMBRATER, the Brazilian Coffee Institute (IBC), and the National Bank of Cooperative Credit were closed. The required membership in free trade agreement programs, such as the General Agreement on Tariffs and Trade (GATT) and the World Trade Organization (WTO), also played a fundamental role in the economic liberalization of agriculture.

*Table 6.2    Brazilian agricultural production 1989–1991*

| Crops | 1989 | 1991 | Percentage change |
|---|---|---|---|
| | Production (metric tons) | Production (metric tons) | |
| Beef | 4,198,531 | 5,506,824 | 7.34 |
| Oranges | 17,773,580 | 18,936,344 | 6.54 |
| Potatoes | 2,129,334 | 2,267,035 | 6.47 |
| Sugarcane | 252,290,000 | 260,887,888 | 3.41 |
| Corn | 26,589,870 | 23,624,340 | −11.15 |
| Rice | 11,029,800 | 9,488,007 | −13.97 |
| Soy | 24,051,670 | 14,937,806 | −37.89 |
| Wheat | 5,555,184 | 2,916,823 | −47.49 |

*Source:*    FAO (2014) 1989–1991.

It was at this point that funding opportunities and supply and demand of agricultural products were virtually deregulated and left at the mercy of the functioning of the free market (Redin and Fialho 2010). With the elimination of credit subsidies, it is the PGPM[9] that emerged as one of the primary makers of agricultural national policies engendering negative consequences for the development of the sector (Coelho 2001).

According to Massuquetti, Souza, and Beroldt (2010), already in the 1989/1990 harvest the agricultural GDP decreased by 4.4 percent. There was also a similar decrease in the sales of machines and inputs and a reduction in the yields of some crops. Between 1989 and 1991 the production of some commodities remained stable while others experienced small growth, but a number of agricultural productions showed considerable decreases. For example, soybean production declined by 37.89 percent, and in the case of wheat the situation was even worse with a decrease of 47.49 percent (see Table 6.2).

The high inflation of the early 1990s further contributed to the crisis of the sector, and this combined set of negative events, along with the abovementioned reduction of production, engendered the risk of food shortages. Faced with a supply crisis, the Collor government operated to reverse its agricultural policy and drafted the Agricultural Plan and the National Agricultural Plan in 1991. These plans were followed by the Reconstruction Plan of Agriculture in 1992. In June of 1994, the Federal Government launched the Real Plan[10] that consisted of the introduction of a new currency, the Real, exchanging at parity with the US dollar. Anti-inflationary measures featuring high interest rates were also implemented to reduce domestic consumption and the opening up of the domestic market to foreign competitors implemented primarily through the elimination and/or reduction of tariffs on imports.

Melo (1999) pointed out that trade liberalization reduced production costs, particularly of fertilizers and pesticides. In parallel, there was an increase in the international prices of some commodities. Also according to Melo (1999), between 1992 and 1997 there was an increase of 46.6 percent in the index of international commodity prices – a situation that benefited products with export potential, including commodities such as soybeans, orange juice, cotton, sugarcane, and coffee. However, the new economic policy also favored the import of agricultural products. According to Lucena and Souza (2001:194), in 1998 Brazil became the world's largest importer of wheat (5.9 million metric tons). In the same year, it imported 2 million tons of corn and 1.7 million tons of rice, among other food products. In 1995, as a renewed attempt to address the crisis in the rural sector, the State began implementing new agricultural policy instruments and reshaping the rural credit policy. In this context, in 1999 the MDA was created with one of its primary objectives being to manage the promotion of sustainable rural development.

## THE REINVENTION OF FAMILY FARMING AND THE EMERGENCE OF QUALITY MARKETS

In step with the appreciation of family agriculture in global contexts (Veiga 1991), in 1996 the Federal Government created PRONAF, institutionalizing the support for family farming. Because of its objective of strengthening family-based agriculture and sustainable rural development, PRONAF became a landmark of Brazilian agricultural policies and offered growth opportunities, access to credit, agricultural insurance, and technical assistance to limited-resource farmers. Although family farming was not a new analytical category in the field of agricultural development in the 1990s, PRONAF promoted and renewed it as a legitimized sector of Brazilian agriculture (Wanderley 2001). This interest in family farming was supported by the claims and struggles of rural workers, the pressure of rural social movements, their strength gained under the recent governments of Lula da Silva[11] and Dilma Rousseff[12], the growth in importance of the MDA, and the expansion of State programs like PRONAF.

Census data indicate that there were 43,567,902 family farms in 2006 in Brazil, representing 88 percent of all farms in the country.[13] However, despite the fact that they represented the absolute majority of farms, family farms made up only 24.3 percent of agricultural business and received only 28.9 percent of all agricultural credit but produced 38 percent of the

*Table 6.3    Percentage of production by family farms*

| Crops | Family farming % of total production |
|-------|--------------------------------------|
| Cassava | 87 |
| Beans | 70 |
| Pork | 59 |
| Milk | 58 |
| Poultry | 50 |
| Corn | 46 |
| Coffee | 38 |
| Rice | 34 |

*Source:*    Elaboration of data from França et al. (2009).

*Table 6.4    Brazilian agricultural production from 2002 to 2012*

| Crops | 2002 | 2012 | Percentage change |
|-------|------|------|-------------------|
| | Production (metric tons) | Production (metric tons) | |
| Sugarcane | 364,391,008 | 721,077,287 | 97.89 |
| Corn | 35,933,000 | 71,072,810 | 97.79 |
| Poultry | 7,058,490 | 11,588,139 | 64.17 |
| Soy | 42,769,000 | 65,848,857 | 53.96 |
| Milk | 22,314,700 | 32,304,421 | 44.77 |
| Beef | 7,130,832 | 9,399,963 | 31.82 |
| Pork | 2,798,154 | 3,465,216 | 23.84 |

*Source:*    FAO (2014) 2002–2012.

agricultural production value (França, Grossi, and Marques 2009). In the second decade of the twenty-first century, family farming remains a major supplier of basic foods for the Brazilian population, as shown in Table 6.3.

Notwithstanding this recent recognition of the importance and contribution of family farming, agribusiness firms continue to enjoy the majority of State investment and are viewed as the primary vehicles for the enhancement of the sector's international competitiveness. Thus, during Lula da Silva's and Dilma Rousseff's governments, the budget devoted to agribusiness jumped from 21.7 billion Reals in 2002 to 156 billion Reals in 2014 (68 billion USD) (Brasil 2002; 2014a). Following the patterns established in the past, there was an increase in production of some major Brazilian commodities (Table 6.4).

There was also a significant increase in credit for family farms. The

Harvest Plan of 2014/2015 budgeted a record amount of 24.1 billion Reals (10.4 billion USD) for PRONAF, which means a 14.7 percent increase from the 2013/2014 harvest season. The total rural credit currently available for family farms through PRONAF represents an increase of 947 percent in the volume of resources compared with the 2002/2003 harvest season when the PRONAF budget was only 2.3 billion Reals (Brasil 2014b).

One of the strategies to promote family farming adopted by the governments of Lula da Silva and Dilma Rousseff was the strengthening of food procurement programs such as the Food Acquisition Program (PAA) and the National School Meals Program (PNAE). The PAA[14] was created by Article 19 of Law No. 10.696 of July 2, 2003 (Brasil 2003) in order to purchase food produced by family farmers without bidding. The program is intended to provide food for people in situations of food and nutritional insecurity. This food is also destined to serve as a support to social assistance organizations, such as low cost restaurants, community kitchens, food banks and charities, and the creation of public food depositories. PAA is funded through the Ministry of Social Development (MDS) and MDA, but it is the National Supply Company (CONAB) that administers the program in partnership with states and municipalities. According to data presented by the MDS, in 10 years the program has invested 5.3 billion Reals (2.3 billion USD) and bought 4 metric tons of food from approximately 388,000 farmers (Brasil 2014c).

PNAE is managed by the National Fund for Education Development (FNDE), which ensures the transfer of financial resources to states and municipalities in order to facilitate the feeding of students enrolled in all public basic education schools. It was determined that at least 30 percent of the funds allocated to municipalities and states by FNDE were spent on food produced by family farmers (Brasil 2014d). It should also be noted that since 2004 alternative mechanisms have been developed to ensure the inclusion of family agriculture in "quality" markets such as organic[15], ethnic, and designation of origin production.

## QUALITY PRODUCTION, ITS ACTORS AND CONTRADICTIONS

The emergence of these new food quality markets is defined through processes of certification and quality labels such as geographical designation: a green stamp that indicates that this food is produced according to the requirements of new agro-ecological sensitivities (Bowen 2011). Morgan, Marsden, and Murdock (2008) illustrate the actors, places, ways, and powers established in this construction of the new "Worlds of Food." This is a context in which the relations among places of production, networks of distribution and consumption, conventions and the building of productive regions represent lenses for the study of the evolution and social relations in agri-food. And Brazil has emerged as key theater in this process with the contraposition of the growing presence of agri-food production and distribution corporations and a politically important family farm sector (Silva, Menezes, and Ribeiro 2014).

**Supermarkets**

The increased consumption of quality food counted on the role of supermarkets that increased the sales of these products as an economic expansion strategy. They operate to capture a growing share of this expanding market through product differentiation and the convenience offered to consumers. Belik (2004) analyzes the process of expansion of supermarkets in Brazil. Based on studies by Furtuoso (1985) and Farina and Reardon (2002), his argument is that in 1970 Brazilian supermarkets were responsible for the sale of 29.3 percent of all food while accounting for only 2.2 percent of commercial sites. Three decades later, food sales in supermarkets account for 86.8 percent of all sales and represent 17 percent of commercial sites. Belik (2004) further shows that by 1995 Brazil had only one global supermarket chain,[16] but between 1995 and 2000, a number of supermarkets such as Sonae, Jerónimo Martins, Casino, Royal Ahold, and Wal-Mart established themselves in the country. Guivant (2003) also points out that the 1990s witnessed a process of concentration in the retail sector, promoted by the participation of a growing amount of financial capital. Based on data from ABRAS (Brazilian Association of Supermarkets), Guivant indicates that in 2001 the largest supermarket chains controlled 75 percent of industry sales, and the participation of financial capital grew from 16 percent in 1994 to 57 percent in 2001.

Accordingly, since the 1990s the supermarket sector in Brazil has been undergoing a process of concentration, with a larger presence of foreign capital. To Belik (2004), this is a phenomenon that occurred on a global scale and reflects the search for markets with growth potential and low competition. However, he adds that the entry of new competitors caused changes in the relationship between suppliers and customers, especially in the case of the supply of fruits and vegetables. Thus, according to Belik (2004:11):

> Supermarket chains have sought to establish forms of coordination with small producers that can address the need for standardization of quality and also guarantee regularity and a steady supply for each point of sale. Studies of European networks show that the perception of quality by consumers is

directly linked to the degree of integration between producers and retailers. This has led supermarkets to intensify their efforts to create their own brands and control suppliers of these products, which increasingly weigh more in terms of sales volume and profit margins.

## Family Farming and Quality Markets

Wilkinson (2003) shows that new approaches to rural development are based on territorial dynamics. Such approaches "recognize that even traditions are being redefined based on new knowledge, values, regulations and levels of demand." Flores adds that "the economic dynamics of territorial development is based on the success of new territorial resources upon which processes of innovation are promoted and new relationships with consumers established" (2006:9). Accordingly, tradition becomes an item that can be reinvented (Hobsbawm and Ranger 1983). Traditional products are no longer perceived as remnants of the past, doomed to disappear by the growth of modernity, but emerge as items in demand according to the valuation of tastes, cultures, and practices, that energize local economies (Appadurai 1999).

These new uses of the territory materialize through the certification of local products, geographical indications of origin, and seals of quality that legitimize the new agri-food goods. According to Caldas (2004), the system of geographical indications already features an important institutionalized legal framework and is regulated in many countries. In this context, some international agreements and laws assume particular importance, such as the cases of the "Madrid Agreement," in which Brazil and another 12 signatories established protection against fake origin indications, and the Lisbon Agreement that determines a specific system of protection for geographical identifications. In Brazil the Intellectual Property Law No. 9.279 of May 14, 1996 outlines the rules of geographical indications in articles 176–183 (Brasil 1996). Article 176 defines two distinct species of geographical indications: the Identification of Origin (IP) and the Protected Designation of Origin (DO).[17] Both of them represent recent measures adopted in the country. The first Brazilian geographical indication dates only from 2002 and refers to a wine produced in the "Valley of the Vineyards" in Southern Brazil. However, in the last decade the number of geographical indications, both IPs and DOs, grew significantly. According to the National Industrial Property Institute (INPI 2013), by the end of 2013 the country had 21 recognized geographical indications of which products such as wine, cheese, rum, candy, coffee, and rice stand out.

Dullius, Froehlich, and Vendruscolo show that geographical indications are an instrument that generates added value and protects "products developed by traditional social groups, such indigenous and quilombola communities, through an emphasis on their identities modeled on territoriality, knowledge and specific ways of life and production" (2008:8). However, the current policy about geographical indications also tends to subordinate small local farmers to the power of transnational actors as it takes tradition and uses it in corporate controlled global value chains (Medaets 2006). Employing a case study of geographical indication, Bowen (2011:327) analyzes the interactions that take place between markets, global supply chains, producers, and territories. She concludes by illustrating the ways in which "actors actively operate to embed supply chains in specific localities as the globalizing processes increasingly remakes and alters the dynamics of the supply chain." In this sense, works such as those by Krone and Menasche (2010) and Cruz (2012) – that study the case of Serrano Cheese in the region of Campos de Cima da Serra in the state of Rio Grande do Sul – demonstrate the difficulties faced by small producers to conform to strict production standards associated with geographical indications. The application of standards, it is argued, allows the inclusion of only "a minority of producers in the formal market because it excludes a large number of them for not meeting the strict conditions of production mandates by these standards" (Krone and Menasche 2010:8). Accordingly, the "change in the scale and pace of demand for these products" (Wilkinson 2003:64) becomes an insurmountable barrier for many small farmers.

Additional barriers involve issues related to health. According to Cruz (2007), Brazilian regulation was influenced by international standards for food production and measures of the Food and Drug Administration of the United States (FDA)[18] and the Codex Alimentarius Commission[19]. As in those situations mentioned above, only a small group of large producers can meet standards and gain approval, leaving a great number of farmers outside the formal system. Receiving virtually no institutional support to conform, small producers are forced to operate in the informal market, such as in the case of most producers of Serrano Cheese studied by Krone and Menasche (2010) and Cruz (2012).

To be sure, there are governmental policies that aim at the building and strengthening of locality and local production. Yet, and as mentioned above, they also move in the direction of inserting local production into global agri-food networks. Justified as safe ways to increase exports, create employment, acquire foreign currency, and pay for existing debts, these policies resulted in the reproduction of the North/South domination and labor and natural resources exploitation.

The San Francisco Valley in the state of Pernambuco is a case in point. The construction of the Sobradinho Dam transformed this semi-arid region into one of the most productive global areas (Silva 2001; Marsden, Cavalcanti, and Ferreira Irmão 1996; Cavalcanti 1999). However, this process also multiplied local socioeconomic contradictions such as the worsening of the conditions of labor (Brasil 1987; 2000b). Currently, over 150,000 workers work in the area. In the primary fruit export cultivations of grapes and mangoes, counting both permanent and temporary laborers, there are about 60,000 workers. Most of them are women who have a temporary and seasonal job (Silva 2012; Bonanno and Cavalcanti 2012). Additionally, this labor is largely made up of immigrants from adjacent states who are employed because they do not have the same level of unionization and class consciousness as local workers (Bonanno and Cavalcanti 2011). Firms have been also able to promote part-time, flexible female employment as "convenient" for women. Reproducing sexist discourses, they argue that part-time labor allows women to fulfill their "natural" roles of mothers and wives while holding a job. In reality, this is part of a broader process of exploitation of labor that, in the absence of State programs that protect workers, is left to permissive free market mechanisms and the significant power that they allow to firms (Bonanno and Cavalcanti 2014).

## CONCLUSIONS

Agri-food in Brazil evolved upon the relationship between large estates and family farms. The colonial process of concentration of land continued as modernization was pursued. However, the unsustainable contradictions of this model eventually delegitimized it and opened up new opportunities for family farming and subordinate groups. The democratization of the Brazilian society and political system along with the associated wealth redistribution policies gave new life to family agriculture and offered new forms of understanding of rural development. Insistence on productivist strategies, however, never lifted the sector out of its relative poverty and structural deficiencies.

The neoliberal era arrived with promises of fast development and new opportunities. Brazilian agri-food rapidly joined global networks of production and became part of a system that directly connects producers, retailers, and consumers in circuits dominated by highly controlled quality products. But it was this system of certification and control that, though enabled some producers to access global markets, excluded many. The current Brazilian political leadership recognizes the contradictions of neoliberal globalization. State sponsored programs that address these contradictions and buffer their unwanted consequences have been implemented with some results. Yet, there is an incompatibility between market-based strategies and social-oriented goals that Brazil is called on to address in agri-food and also in other areas of its social and economic life. It is this challenge that will define not only the future of Brazil, but that of all those countries and world regions that are prepared to counter neoliberalism with neo-Fordist State intervention.

## NOTES

1. The *Sertão* of the Northeast is a region comprising the interior of Brazil's Northeast states. This region is characterized by a semi-arid climate.
2. The peasant leagues were social organizations made up of landless, sharecroppers and rural workers groups that emerged in Northeastern Brazil during the 1950s and 1960s. They represent an important milestone in the establishment of a rural worker movement and their actions had a significant impact nationally. Ultimately, they became the symbol of the fight for land reform.
3. The Movement of "Sem Terra" is a social movement that arose in Brazil in the early 1980s, advocating a broad policy of land reform and expropriation of unproductive land. Presently, it continues its struggle with an updated agenda.
4. This is a Federal Program created in 2008 with the objective of promoting economic development through a strategy of sustainable territorial development in areas with low human development indicators.
5. New Republic is the name of the period of Brazil's history that followed the end of the military dictatorship in 1985.
6. This historical period of high GDP growth is commonly referred to as the "Brazilian Economic Miracle."
7. José Sarney served as President of Brazil from 1985 to 1990.
8. Fernando Collor de Mello was the first Brazilian president elected by direct vote after the end of military dictatorship. He remained in power between 1990 and 1992. He was ousted by impeachment proceedings after allegations of corruption.
9. According to Massuquetti, Souza, and Beroldt (2010), in this period about 70 percent of public resources for agriculture were employed for the PGPM.
10. The Real Plan was launched in June 1994 by the government of President Itamar Franco (1992–1994). Fernando Henrique Cardoso, Finance Minister of the Franco government, led the economic team that implemented this plan. The success of the Real Plan was essential for Fernando Henrique Cardoso to win the election for president in the first round in 1994. It is worth noting that Fernando Henrique Cardoso was re-elected in 1998, remaining in power until 2002.
11. Luiz Inácio Lula da Silva served as the president of Brazil between 2003 and 2010. He was the leader of the Workers' Party (Partido dos Trabalhadores), or PT.
12. In 2012 Dilma Rousseff became the first woman elected President of Brazil. She is a member of the Brazilian PT.
13. Between 1996 and 2006 there was a 9.9 percent increase in the number of family farms.
14. It is worth noting that the PAA consists of one of the actions of the "Brazil without Poverty" program launched in 2011 by President Dilma Rousseff. This program aims to reduce extreme poverty by promoting the productive and social inclusion of people with monthly income below 70.00 Reals or 30 USD.
15. Data from the 2006 Agricultural Census show that Brazil had at the time of the census 90,497 farms that used 4.93 million hectares for the cultivation of agro-ecological products. According to a document of the Institute for the Promotion of Development (IPD) (2011), in Brazil the sales value of organic products reached 1.3 billion Reals in

2006. According to the IPD (2011), the organic market grew at the rate of 20 percent annually.

16. According to Belik (2004), Carrefour established its first supermarket in the city of São Paulo in 1975 and for the next 20 years remained the only foreign supermarket chain in the country.

17. The term "Identification of Origin" contemplates the right to use a geographical name due to the reputation that that particular region has acquired as a place of production of a specific agricultural product. The term "Protected Designation of Origin" is more restrictive as it includes additional specifications above the reputation and fame of a regional product, including natural soil factors, climate, environment and human know-how, tradition, customs, history and culture.

18. The FDA is an agency that regulates and standardizes the laws on medicines and food production in the United States.

19. Created by the Food and Agriculture Organization of the United Nations (FAO) in partnership with the World Health Organization (WHO), the Codex Alimentarius Commission is a committee formed by members from various countries whose goal is to establish international standards both to determine the maximum acceptable and/or recommended intake of any food additive and to determine the microbiological parameters and risks of traditional/regional foods. However, Cruz (2012) points out that most members of the Codex Alimentarius are actually Americans and that, in addition, there are representatives of industries participating in scientific committees. Thus, according to the author, some approaches are privileged over others.

# REFERENCES

Almeida, Jalcione. 1999. *A Construção Social de Uma Nova Agricultura: Tecnologia Agrícola e Movimentos Sociais no Sul do Brasil*. Porto Alegre: Editora da UFRGS.

Andrade, Manuel Correia de. 1973. *A Terra e o Homem no Nordeste*. São Paulo: Brasiliense.

Appadurai, Arjun (ed.). 1999. *The Social Life of Things*. Cambridge: Cambridge University Press.

Belik, Walter. 2004. "Supermercados e produtores: limites, possibilidades e desafios." Pp. 1–12 in *XLII Congresso Brasileiro de Economia e Sociologia Rural*.

Bielschowsky, Ricardo. 1998. *Cinquenta anos de pensamento na CEPAL*. Rio de Janeiro: Record.

Bonanno, Alessandro and Josefa Salete Barbosa Cavalcanti. 2011. *Globalization and the Time–Space Reorganization: Capital Mobility in Agriculture and Food in the Americas*. Bingley, UK: Emerald.

Bonanno, Alessandro and Josefa Salete Barbosa Cavalcanti. 2012. "Globalization, Food Quality and Labor: The Case of Grape Production in Northeastern Brazil." *International Journal of Sociology of Agriculture and Food* 19(1):37–55.

Bonanno, Alessandro and Josefa Salete Barbosa Cavalcanti. 2014. *Labor Relations in Globalized Food: Research in Rural Sociology and Development*. Bingley, UK: Emerald.

Bowen, Sarah. 2011. "The Importance of Place: Re-territorializing Embeddedness." *Sociologia Ruralis* 4:325–348.

Brasil. 1960. "Censo Demográfico de 1960." Fundação IBGE. Departamento de Estatísticas de População.

Brasil. 1965. "Lei n. 4829 – Sistema Nacional de Crédito Rural." Retrieved on August 15, 2014 at http://www.planalto.gov.br/ccivil_03/leis/L4829.htm.

Brasil. 1987. *PLANVASF – Plano Diretor para o Desenvolvimento do Vale do São* Francisco: programas e projetos industriais e agroindustriais. Brasília: Brasil.

Brasil. 1991. "Censo Demográfico de 1991." Fundação IBGE. Departamento de Estatísticas de População.

Brasil. 1996. "Lei n. 9.279 – Lei da Propriedade Industrial." Retrieved on August 15, 2014 at http://www.planalto.gov.br/ccivil_03/leis/l9279.htm.

Brasil. 2000b. *PLANVASF – Plano Diretor para o Desenvolvimento do Vale do São Francisco: projeções demográficas preliminares para a Região PLANVASF até o ano 2000*. Brasília: Brasil.

Brasil. 2003. "Lei n. 10.696 – Programa de Aquisição de Alimentos." Retrieved on August 15, 2014 at http://www.planalto.gov.br/ccivil_03/leis/2003/l10.696.htm.

Brasil. 2002. "Plano Agrícola e Pecuário 2002/2003." Retrieved on August 15, 2014 at http://www.agricultura.gov.br/arq_editor/file/Ministerio/planos%20e%20programas/pap%20 2002%202003.pdf.

Brasil. 2014a. "Plano Agrícola e Pecuário 2013/2014." Retrieved on August 15, 2014 at http://www.agricultura.gov.br/arq_editor/file/acs/PAP20132014-web.pdf.

Brasil. 2014b. "Plano Safra da Agricultura Familiar 2014/2015." Retrieved on August 15, 2014 at http://www.fetraf.org.br/sistema/ck/files/Plano%20Safra%202014-2015.pdf.

Brasil. 2014c. "Em dez anos, Programa de Aquisição de Alimentos investiu R$ 5,3 bilhões." Retrieved on August 15, 2014 at http://www.mds.gov.br/saladeimprensa/noticias/2014/ fevereiro/em dez-anos-programa-de-aquisicao-de-alimentos-investiu-r-5-3-bilhoes.

Brasil. 2014d. "Programa Nacional de Alimentação Escolar." Retrieved on August 15, 2014 at http://www.fnde.gov.br/programas/alimentacao-escolar.

Bresser, Luiz Carlos. 1997. *Economia brasileira: uma introdução critica*. São Paulo: Editora 34.

Bruno, Regina. 2009. *Um Brasil ambivalente: agronegócio, ruralismo e relações de poder*. Rio de Janeiro: Mauad.

Caldas, Alcides dos Santos. 2004. "Novos usos do território: as indicações geográficas protegidas como unidades de desenvolvimento regional." *Bahia Análise and Dados* 14:593–602.

Carneiro, Maria José. 2012. *Ruralidades Contemporâneas: modos de viver e pensar o rural na sociedade brasileira*. Rio de Janeiro: Mauad.

Carter, Miguel (ed.). 2010. *Combatendo a desigualdade social: o MST e a reforma agrária no Brasil*. São Paulo: UNESP.

Cavalcanti, Josefa Salete Barbosa. 1999. "Desigualdades sociais e identidades em construção na agricultura de exportação." *Revista Latinoamericana de Estudios Del Trabajo* 5(9):155–171.

Coelho, Carlos Nayro. 2001. "70 Anos de Política Agrícola no Brasil (1931–2001)." *Revista de Política Agrícola* 3:3–58.

Cruz, Fabiana Thomé da. 2007. "Qualidade e boas práticas de fabricação em um contexto de agroindústrias de pequeno porte." Dissertação, Programa de Pós-Graduação em Agroecossistemas, Universidade Federal de Santa Catarina, Florianópolis.

Cruz, Fabiana Thomé da. 2012. "Produtores, consumidores e valorização de produtos tradicionais: um estudo sobre qualidade de alimentos a partir do caso do Queijo Serrano dos Campos de Cima da Serra – RS." Doutorado, Programa de Pós-Graduação em Desenvolvimento Rural, Universidade Federal do Rio Grande do Sul, Porto Alegre.

Dullius, Paulo Roberto, José Marcos Froehlich, and Rafaela Vendruscolo. 2008. "Identidade e Desenvolvimento Territorial – estudo das experiências de Indicações Geográficas no estado do RS." Pp. 1–21 in *XLVI Congresso da Sociedade Brasileira de Economia, Administração e Sociologia Rural*.

FAO. 2014. "Food and Agricultural Commodities Production (1961–1981; 1989–1991; 2002–2012." Retrieved on August 15, 2014 at http://faostat.fao.org/site/339/default.aspx.

Faoro, Raymundo. 1958. *Os donos do poder: formação do patronato político brasileiro*. Porto Alegre: Editora Globo.

Farina, Elizabeth M.M.Q. and Thomas Reardon. 2002. "Consolidation, Multinationalisation, and Competition in Brazil: Impacts on Horticulture and Dairy Products Systems." *Development Policy Review* 20(4):441–458.

Fernandes, Bernardo Mançano, Leonilde Servolo de Medeiros, and Maria Ignez Paulilo (eds.). 2009. *Lutas camponesas contemporâneas: condições, dilemas e conquistas: O campesinato como sujeito político nas décadas de 1950 a 1980*. Vol. 1. São Paulo: Editora UNESP and Brasília: NEAD.

Flores, Murilo. 2006. "A identidade cultural do território como base de estratégias de desenvolvimento: uma visão do estado da arte." *InterCambios* 64:1–30.

França, Caio Galvão de, Mauro Eduardo Del Grossi, and Vicente P.M. de Azevedo Marques. 2009. *O censo agropecuário 2006 e a agricultura familiar no Brasil*. Brasília: MDA.

Friedmann, Harriet. 2005. "From Colonialism to Green Capitalism: Social Movements and Emergence of Food Regimes." *New Directions in the Sociology of Global Development* 11:227–264.

Forman, Shepard. 1975. *The Brazilian Peasantry*. New York: Columbia University.

Foweraker, Joe. 1982. *A Luta pela Terra: a economia política da fronteira pioneira no Brasil de 1930 aos dias atuais*. Rio de Janeiro: Zahar Editores.

Furtado, Celso. 1961. *Desenvolvimento e subdesenvolvimento*. Rio de Janeiro: Fundo de Cultura.

Furtuoso, Maria Cristina O. 1985. "O Desempenho do Auto-Serviço no Brasil." *Conj. Alimentos* 7(1):39–42. São Paulo: SAA.

Garcia, Jr., Afrânio. 1975. *Terra de trabalho familiar de pequenos produtores*. Rio de Janeiro: Editora Paz e Terra.

Godoi, Emília Pietrafesa de, Marilda Aparecida de Menezes, and Rosa Acevedo Marin (eds.). 2009a. *Diversidade do campesinato: expressões e categorias. Construções identitárias e sociabilidades*. Vol.1. São Paulo: UNESP and Brasília: NEAD.

Godoi, Emília Pietrafesa de, Marilda Aparecida de Menezes, and Rosa Acevedo Marin (eds.). 2009b. *Diversidade do campesinato: expressões e categorias. Estratégias de reprodução social*. Vol. 2. São Paulo: UNESP and Brasília: NEAD.

Goodman, David and Michael Redclift. 1981. *From Peasant to Proletarian: Capitalist Development and Agrarian Transitions*. Oxford: Blackwell.

Graziano da Silva, José. 1996. *A nova dinâmica da agricultura brasileira*. Campinas: UNICAMP.

Guimarães, Alberto Passos. 1977. *Quatro séculos de latifúndio*. Rio de Janeiro: Paz e Terra.

Guivant, Julia S. 2003. "Os supermercados na oferta de alimentos orgânicos: apelando ao estilo de vida ego-trip." *Ambiente and Sociedade* 2:63–81.

Harvey, David. 2007. *A Brief History of Neoliberalism*. New York: Oxford University Press.

Hobsbawn, Eric and Terence Ranger (eds.). 1983. *The Invention of Tradition*. New York: Columbia University Press.

INPI. 2013. "Indicação Geográfica – IG." Retrieved on August 15, 2014 at http://www.agri cultura.gov.br/desenvolvimento-sustentavel/indicacao-geografica.

IPD. 2011. "Pesquisa – O mercado brasileiro de produtos orgânicos." Retrieved on August 15, 2014 at http://www.ipd.org.br/upload/tiny_mce/Pesquisa_de_Mercado_Interno_de_ Produtos_Organicos.pdf.

IPEA. 2012. "A década inclusiva (2001–2011): desigualdade, pobreza e políticas de renda." Retrieved on August 15, 2014 at http://www.ipea.gov.br/agencia/images/stories/PDFs/ comunicado/120925_comunicadodoipea155_v5.pdf.

Krone, Evander Eloi and Renata Menasche. 2010. "Políticas públicas para produtos com identidade cultural: uma reflexão a partir do caso do Queijo Artesanal Serrano do Sul do Brasil." Pp. 1–14 in *VIII Congreso Latinoamericano de Sociología Rural*.

Leite Lopes, José Sérgio. 1981. "O 'Tradicionalismo Camponês' segundo a Antropologia da Tradição." *Comunicação* PPGAS 6:41–53.

Lucena, Romina Batista and Nali de Jesus de Souza. 2001. "Políticas agrícolas e desempenho da agricultura brasileira: 1950–00." *FEE* 29:180–200.

Marsden, Terry K., Josefa Salete Barbosa Cavalcanti, and José Ferreira Irmão. 1996. "Globalisation, Regionalisation and Quality: The Socio-economic Reconstitution of Food in the San Francisco Valley, Brazil." *International Journal of Sociology and Food* 5:85–114.

Martins, José de Souza. 1986. *Os camponeses e a política no Brasil: as lutas sociais no campo e seu lugar no processo político*. Petrópolis: Vozes.

Massuquetti, Angelica, O.T. Souza, and L. Beroldt. 2010. "Intrumentos de política agrícola e mudanças institucionais." Pp. 1–20 in *48º Congresso Brasileiro de Economia e Sociologia Rural*.

Matos, Patrícia Francisca and Vera Lúcia Salazer Pessôa. 2011. "A modernização da agri-cultura no Brasil e os novos usos do território." *Geo UERJ* 22:290–322.

Mazoyer, Marcel and Laurence Roudart. 2010. *História das agriculturas no mundo: Do neolítico à crise contemporânea*. São Paulo: Editora UNESP and Brasília: NEAD.

Medaets, Jean Pierre. 2006. "Políticas de qualidade para produtos agrícola e alimentares: sistema de garantia da qualidade." Pp. 109–145 in *Valorização de produtos com diferencial de qualidade e identidade: indicações geográficas e certificações para a competitividade nos negócios*, edited by Léa Lagares, Vinícius Lages, and Christiano Braga. Brasília: Sebrae.

Medeiros, Leonilde Servolo de. 1989. *História dos movimentos sociais no campo*. Rio de Janeiro: FASE.

Melo, Fernando B.H. 1999. "O Plano real e a agricultura brasileira: perspectivas." *Revista de Economia Política* 19:146–155.

Morgan, Kevin, Terry K. Marsden, and Jonathan Murdoch (eds.). 2008. *Worlds of Food: Place, Power, and Provenance in the Food Chain*. New York: Oxford University Press.

Neves, Delma Pessanha (ed.). 2009. *Processos de constituição e reprodução do campesinato no Brasil. Formas dirigidas de constituição do campesinato*. Vol. 2. São Paulo: Editora UNESP and Brasília: NEAD.

Neves, Delma Pessanha and Maria Aparecida de Moraes Silva (eds.). 2008. *Processos de constituição e reprodução do campesinato no Brasil. Formas tuteladas de condição camponesa*. Vol. 1. São Paulo: Editora UNESP and Brasília: NEAD.

Paulilo, Maria Inês. 1996. *Terra à vista e ao longe*. Florianópolis: Editora da Universidade Federal de Santa Catarina.

Redin, Ezequiel and Marco Antônio Verardi Fialho. 2010. "Política Agrícola Brasileira: uma análise histórica da inserção da Agricultura familiar." Pp. 1–19 in *48º Congresso Brasileiro de Economia e Sociologia Rural*.

Roche, Jean. 1969. *A colonização alemã e o Rio Grande do Sul*. Porto Alegre: Globo.

Scott, James C. 1979. *The Moral Economy of the Peasant: Rebellion and Subsistence in Southeast Asia*. New Haven: Yale University.

Silva, Maria Aparecida de Moraes, Marilda Aparecida de Menezes, and Jadir Damião Ribeiro. 2014. "State and Regulation of Labor Relations in the Sugarcane Fields of Brazil." Pp. 167–191 in *Labor Relations in Globalized Food: Research in Rural Sociology and Development*, edited by Alessandro Bonanno and Josefa Salete Barbosa Cavalcanti. Bingley, UK: Emerald.

Silva, Pedro Carlos Gama. 2001. "Articulação dos interesses públicos e privados no polo Petrolina-PE/Juazeiro-BA: Em busca de espaço no mercado globalizado de frutas frescas." Doutorado, Programa de Pós-Graduação em Economia, Universidade Estadual de Campinas, São Paulo.

Silva, Pedro Carlos Gama. 2012. "Caso de Brasil." Pp. 85–141 in *Empleo y condiciones de trabajo de mujeres temporeras agrícolas*, coordinado por Boquero, Fernando Soto y Klein, Emilio. Tomo I: CEAPAL, OIT, FAO.

Stédile, João Pedro (ed.). 2005. *A questão agrária no Brasil: o debate tradicional – 1500–1960*. São Paulo: Expressão Popular.

Veiga, José Eli da. 1991. *O desenvolvimento agrícola: uma visão histórica*. São Paulo: Hucitec, Edusp.

Wanderley, Nazaré. 2001. "Raízes históricas do campesinato brasileiro." Pp. 23–65 in *Agricultura familiar: realidades e perspectivas*, organizado por Tedesco J.C. Passo Fundo: UPF.

Welch, Clifford A., Edgard Malagodi, Josefa S.B. Cavalcanti, and Maria de Nazareth B. Wanderley. 2009. *Camponeses Brasileiros. Leituras e Interpretações Clássicas*. Vol. 1. São Paulo: Editora UNESP and Brasília: NEAD.

Wilkinson, John. 2003. "A agricultura familiar ante o novo padrão de competitividade do sistema alimentar na América Latina." *Estudos Sociedade e Agricultura* 21:62–87.

Wilkinson, John. 2008. *Mercados, Redes e Valores: O novo mundo da agricultura familiar*. Porto Alegre: Editora da UFRGS.

# 7. The political economy of agriculture and food in North America: Toward convergence or divergence?
### Gabriela Pechlaner and Gerardo Otero

## INTRODUCTION

Much like the Chinese curse about living in "interesting times," agriculture and food have become profoundly interesting. The level of "interest" is a product of the seemingly limitless contradictory dynamics that are buffeting both the production and consumption of food—the bulk of which are, in turn, driven by various economic imperatives—and the bland fact of our persistent dependence on it. On the production side, we have been immersed since the late 1980s into a slow and inequity-laden liberalization of agricultural trade, with its associated industrialization of developing-country agricultures and concomitant urbanization of formerly peasant and agrarian societies. A significant part of this trade liberalization/agro-industrialization package has been the state-facilitated entrenchment of agribusiness multinationals (ABMs) as central organizers and beneficiaries of the evolving international division of labor in agricultural production (McMichael 2009a; Pechlaner and Otero 2010; Appendini 2014). Transgenic crops are another key component of agro-industrialization and they play a significant role in the global accumulation strategies of these ABMs, while simultaneously weakening the invisibility with which they operate (Pechlaner 2012a).

The above dynamics are only going to become increasingly "interesting." Population increases will continue to put pressure on increasing production, while new challenges—everything from "peak oil" to climate change and land scarcity—threaten to decrease it. Each of these pressures fosters new forms of economic and power jockeying, as we can already see in recent land grabs (see, for example, Borras, Hall, Scoones, White, and Wolford 2011). Further, consumption has its own myriad dynamics, heavily interlinked with those of production. Culturally, citizens are increasingly estranged from food production, and meals are increasingly less often cooked, so much as assembled according to package instructions. This process is in accordance with the globalization of what we call the neoliberal diet, manifested in high calorie, low nutritional value, processed foods (Otero, Pechlaner, and Gürcan, forthcoming). At the same time, international inequities in agricultural production are being replicated within nations, with diverging consumption patterns between the wealthy, specialty-foods consumers (Johnston and Bauman 2010) and the poorer recipients of mass-produced prepared foods (Friedmann 2005; Dixon 2009; Guthman 2011; Winson 2013).

All these production and consumption dynamics have certainly been subjected to counter-pressures from a wide array of opponents: organic, fair trade, pro-peasant, environmental, anti-genetically modified organisms (GMOs), and various health and lifestyle movements, to name a few. While this opposition has, as yet, fallen far short of altering the dynamics of what we call the neoliberal food regime (Pechlaner and Otero 2010), they have created small clouds on the horizon of ABMs' accumulation strategies. Some have significant potential for disruption, such as the persistent local and state level efforts to ban or label genetically modified ingredients in the United States (Pechlaner 2012b; Walsh-Dilley 2009), or the social movement pressures that led Mexico's judges to halt Monsanto's commercialization of transgenic maize in Mexico (Wise 2014).

In sum, the multiplicity and complexity of forces affecting the production and dissemination of food make it extremely difficult to predict the food production current. While obviously not all of the above processes are the result of globalization, it has played an undeniable role in many of them, particularly in the neoliberal character of liberalized trade and its accompanying neoregulation, or the new forms in which states intervene to abet this process. Our goal here is to focus on a key world region of these globalization-and-neoliberalism-related dynamics—represented by Canada, Mexico, and the United States, the three countries of the North American Free Trade Agreement (NAFTA). This is a key region in the global political economy of agrifood as both Canada and the United States have long been agro-exporting power houses in the world economy, and the United States is the dominant producer of agricultural technologies and a key proponent of trade liberalization, through which the country's dietary patterns are being globally disseminated. For its part, Mexico may be an example of the most radical adoption of the neoliberal doctrine, of which trade liberalization is a key component, particularly in agriculture. Thus, while increasing agricultural trade is a global phenomenon to varying degrees and depths, the 1994 NAFTA provides a good illustration of the changes that occur as a result of neoliberal globalization and its contrasting impacts on countries of differing levels of socioeconomic development and state power.

In this chapter, we argue that, rather than an all-out convergence in agricultural trade, diets, and development outcomes, what has resulted in the NAFTA region is a process of "differentiated convergence." For one, agricultural trade has increased between the three nations but not symmetrically, with clear patterns showing the United States as the dominant player. Consumption patterns also show differentiated convergence, with meat consumption increasing in all three countries, particularly chicken meat, whereas beef consumption is increasing in Mexico while decreasing in Canada and the United States.

In the first section, we will first briefly outline the neoregulatory stance in the NAFTA region, contextualizing it in food regime literature. We will then present key trade patterns, using macro data from the Food and Agriculture Organization (FAO), contrasting the experiences of the three NAFTA countries. We will subsequently describe changing consumption patterns in these countries that are occurring in conjunction with the globalization of agriculture and food production. Last we will discuss this data with respect to convergence and divergence in agriculture and development in the NAFTA region.

## NAFTA AS A REGIONAL FOOD REGIME

In NAFTA's early days, proponents touted its benefits for ALL three nations. United States Trade Representative, Mickey Kantor, for example, stated that "the whole idea of NAFTA is to make all of North America more competitive and that will create jobs" (Fagan 1994). This perspective was not just touted by American interests. Mexican Trade Secretary, Jaime Serra Puche, for example, is reported to have insisted "that new access for Mexican companies to Canada and the United States will accelerate Mexican economic growth in all parts of the country" (Fagan 1994). Indeed, neoclassical economic theory would expect that enhanced trade among nations will lead toward their complementarity and convergence. The actual experience of economic integration of the three NAFTA partners, however, has led toward divergence in socioeconomic-development outcomes between Mexico and its two wealthier neighbors.

NAFTA's explicit economic goals—increased trade and foreign investment—have been met in a differentiated way: trade has increased beyond expectations, but foreign direct investment has increased much more in the two wealthier nations than in Mexico. Furthermore, socioeconomic-development goals in Mexico have fallen quite short: increased numbers and proportion of poor people and deeper inequality (Acosta Córdova 2014). In regard to agriculture, even the most enthusiastic neoliberal cheerleaders have to acknowledge the significant negative impacts in Mexico. Neoliberalism's impacts were far more pronounced in Mexico given that it had the largest number of people dependent on agriculture and that the United States continued to support its farm sector through hefty subsidies. Consequently, we see evidence of divergence in an agricultural industrialization that has led to significant social consequences while increasing the Mexican peoples' food vulnerability (González 2013; Otero 2011). This trade liberalization has not resulted in consistent divergence, however. Most significantly, convergence is evidenced in dietary patterns, specifically through the globalization of the American diet, which we will discuss presently. Before we look at these dynamics through trade and consumption data, we will first briefly contextualize NAFTA in food regime literature.

The food regime perspective developed by Harriet Friedmann and Philip McMichael (see, for example, Friedmann 1992; 2005; Friedmann and McMichael 1989; McMichael 1992; 2005; 2009a; 2009b) is a multifaceted approach (geographical, historical, and political) for understanding international relations in the production and dissemination of agriculture and food. Its greatest analytical strength is its ability to draw together these facets to articulate distinct "regimes," or periods of stability in global agriculture and food relations. Thus the period between 1870 and 1914 (the "Settler-Colonial" regime) characterizes a period of nation building in settler states and industrial metropoles and articulates food-provisioning relationships formed around those dynamics. In contrast, the 1945–1973 "Surplus" regime characterized a period of U.S. hegemony, national agricultures (subsidized and outside of trade rules), and grain surpluses laying the groundwork for developing-country dependencies on imports from the United States.

We have argued elsewhere that the food regime perspective is more effective in its historical analysis than in its predictive ability (Pechlaner and Otero 2008; 2010; Otera 2013; Otero, Pechlaner, and Gürcan 2013). Its founders do articulate how periods of crisis between regimes are opportunities for myriad influences to shape the new regime. Consequently, assessments of the nature of the third food regime are necessarily rooted in the differential weighting of these influences. The key features that are consistently acknowledged in the food regime emerging after the 1980s, however, are its neoregulatory dynamics. These reduce trade restrictions on various environmental or food security grounds, strengthen intellectual property rights, and promote the central role of ABMs in the global production and distribution of food, and overall deepen trade liberalization. The further entrenchment of ABMs has occurred to such an extent that McMichael characterizes the new regime as a "Corporate" regime (2009a). Because the state has continued to be a key facilitator of this entrenchment, however, we have named this the *neoliberal* food regime. Its chief regulatory characteristic is not deregulation, as McMichael would have it, but what we have called neoregulation. Richard Snyder (2001) captured this specific content in state regulation in Mexico and called it "reregulation," but his term implies that regulation went back to some prior existence. It did not; the state has intervened in a new way to facilitate the rise to prominence of different economic actors in agriculture, namely agrarian capitalists and ABMs, while abandoning peasant producers and dismantling state institutions that supported both agricultural incomes and consumer prices (Appendini 2014).

While many of the characteristics of food regimes are as much the result of unwritten geopolitical dynamics, technological advances, and economic actualities, trade policy has played a highly significant role. Thus the post-World War II food regime was dominated by the United States, and its practices of protectionism and subsidies set the tone for global agricultural trade relations, with clear differentiation between countries that could afford these practices and those that could not, and whose commodities were forced to compete against these lower-priced goods. Agriculture thus remained a persistent exception to the trade liberalization ideology and a significant bone of contention in broader trade liberalization negotiations.

After the second food regime, there was an important opportunity for policy to drive the shape of the third regime. In 1987 a new round of negotiations began on the General Agreement on Tariffs and Trade (GATT), which had been in effect since 1948. The result of this round (the Uruguay Round) was the 1995 establishment of the World Trade Organization (WTO), an institution with far greater stability and much wider scope, including the addition of new areas of regulation, such as over intellectual property rights. The latter is fundamental for the advancement of agricultural biotechnologies, which are a central component of accumulation strategies in agriculture in the United States (Pechlaner 2012a). While the WTO has been successful in facilitating various aspects of international trade, and even made some advancement into reducing trade distortions in agriculture in its Agreement on Agriculture, it has nonetheless fallen far short of trade liberalization proponents' wishes for the sector. The 2001 Doha Round of negotiations, for example, which was intended to finally make inroads on this front, failed in the face of developing countries' resistance to developed countries' subsidies and protectionism. What has not been accomplished in agriculture at the WTO, however, was more effectively put in place in the 1994 NAFTA. While agricultural trade between Canada, Mexico, and the Unites States is not completely restriction free, NAFTA oversees significant agricultural trade liberalization between the countries.

In sum, while significant shifts have occurred at the global level and are well entrenched in the characteristics of a neoliberal food regime, the full manifestation of neoregulation in agriculture has not yet reached its ultimate expression. NAFTA, however, provides an important regional manifestation of the ultimate neoliberal food regime. An important remaining question is what these changes in the neoliberal food regime have meant for diets, specifically in the NAFTA region. To what extent does the neoliberal food regime dictate a particular dietary regime?

Anthony Winson (2013) has made some effort to tackle this question. He argues that dietary regimes are complementary yet differentiated from food regimes, as they have "their own emphases and temporal demarcations" (Winson 2013: 18). The first dietary regime does have some overlap with the first food regime, although Winson characterizes it as lasting nearly 30 years longer. Notably it resulted from significant technological developments, such as canning and flour milling. These allowed for the development of a range of new (increasingly processed) products. These products were launched with significant mass marketing, which has become a central feature of the long process of transitioning people from "whole foods," with many essential nutrients, to highly processed "industrial foods" which lack them (2013: 131).

Another similarity we can see between food regimes and dietary regimes is that the characteristics of one regime lay the groundwork for succeeding ones. Processing, mass marketing, and degraded diets are key features of succeeding regimes. In fact, their consistency is part of the distinction that Winson makes between food regimes and dietary regimes, arguing that the second food regime does not correlate with a transformation of diets; rather it corresponds to more of an intensification of the diet that had been given form in the previous regime. This diet is one that perpetuated the nutritional degradation of food. It is composed of highly processed, high fat, high sugar "energy dense" food with low nutritional value (Drewnowski and Specter 2004). We call this diet the neoliberal diet (Otero, Pechlaner, and Gürcan, forthcoming) and note that an important feature of it is its notable class differentiation (see, for example, Darmon and Drewnowski 2008; Dixon 2009; Lee 2011).

Winson argues that a third industrial dietary regime emerged post-1980. Its most distinguishing characteristic is the global expansion of the American diet, such that it entails a "dramatic qualitative change in eating experiences, and subsequent health outcomes, of whole new populations across the globe" (2013: 35). In fact, it is so extensive that in the late 1990s it was coined a "nutrition transition," and its advance has been highly facilitated by a rise in cheap vegetable oils, the use of which is ubiquitous in the processing and fast-food industries. Even in Asian countries like China and Japan, where the consumption of animal fats was never as high as that of vegetable oils, consumption increased dramatically, particularly since the late 1970s. China's average per capita daily consumption of vegetable oils went from 64 kilocalories in 1979 to a peak of 216 kilocalories in 2009, while Japan's figures went from 226 to 361 kilocalories in the same period; an increase of 238 percent and 60 percent, respectively (calculated with data from FAOSTAT).

There is already significant evidence that with the globalization of the neoliberal diet there has been an associated export of its negative health consequences already so common in the United States. Mexico's adult obesity rate (at 32.8 percent), for example, is now even higher than that of the United States (at 31.8 percent) (Althaus 2013). Further, there is every reason to believe that the dietary inequities that are evident within the United States will also be replicated in its exported manifestation— although the class demarcation is more complex in developing countries, where many of these cheap processed goods will nonetheless be prohibitively expensive for the lowest economic classes. The most at risk in these countries are likely the middle-income classes. We discuss class and diet further in the following section.

## DIET AND TRADE IN THE NAFTA REGION: CONVERGENCE AND DIVERGENCE

If the only goals of NAFTA were to increase trade and foreign investments, then it succeeded, although modestly in the latter for Mexico. There is no dispute that Mexico's overall trade increased dramatically: by 2012, total import and export flows were 5.3 times more than those in 1994. Exports were multiplied by 6.1 and imports by 4.7, which increased Mexico's export power and provides many Mexicans—but not the majority—with access to higher quality products and services at a better price. This is not the case for basic goods including food, clothing, and public services, however (Acosta Córdova 2014: 17). Mexico's total trade with the United States grew 4.4 times during the same period, with exports growing 5.6 times and imports 3.4. Much of this increased Mexican exporting ability directly benefits the United States. The U.S. Trade Representative who negotiated NAFTA, Carla Hills, reported that "for each dollar Mexico gains in exports, it spends 50 cents in U.S. products" (cited in Acosta Córdova 2014: 20).

Economic development measurements are made regarding both the size of gross domestic product (GDP) and GDP per capita for each nation. From 1994 to 2012, Canada declined in world economic (GDP size) rank from 7th to 11th, as Mexico did from 10th to 14th, while the United States

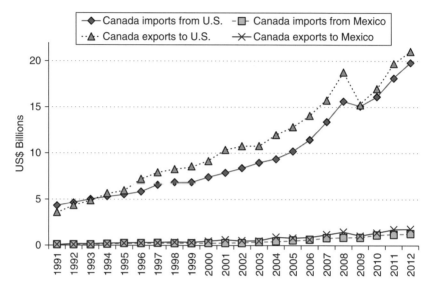

*Source:*    Constructed with data on domestic food supply from FAOSTAT, available at: http://faostat.fao.org/site/609/DesktopDefault.aspx?PageID=609#ancor (retrieved January 4, 2014).

*Figure 7.1    Canada–NAFTA agricultural trade*

retained the first place. The picture is different in terms of per capita income in each country during the same period, with Canada showing the best outcome: it went from 21st in world rank to 9th in per capita income, while Mexico dropped from 53rd to 61st and the United States dropped slightly from 9th to 10th.

Specific to agriculture, we have seen both imports and exports increase in all three countries, but the patterns of trade among each pair are considerably differentiated. The United States has developed very strong mutual agricultural trade relations with each of its two neighbors. Trade between Canada and Mexico is comparatively minor, however (see Figures 7.1 and 7.2), although we can see that Mexico's imports from Canada are slowly increasing. Mexico's main agricultural trade relation is clearly with the United States, displaying an agricultural trade deficit since the early 1990s—except for a dip after the 1994 peso devaluation crisis, which forced Mexico to decrease all its imports. Interestingly, the global food crisis of 2007–2008 was not reflected in declining U.S. imports from Mexico, but prompted a huge dip in Mexico's imports from the United States. These differentiated trends likely have to do with two distinct but combined issues. First, Mexico's imports from the United States are primarily basic

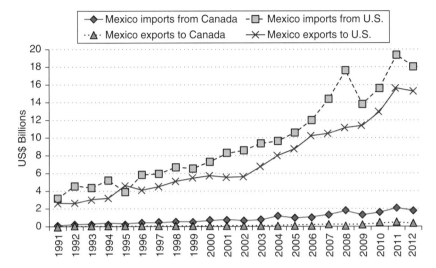

*Source:* Constructed with data on domestic food supply from FAOSTAT, available at: http://faostat.fao.org/site/609/DesktopDefault.aspx?PageID=609#ancor (retrieved January 4, 2014).

*Figure 7.2 Mexico–NAFTA agricultural trade*

foods (see below), which both make up a large proportion of total caloric intake (>25 percent) and disproportionally impact the lower-income population. Second, the United States' imports from Mexico are primarily fruits and vegetables, which both make up a meager portion of total caloric intake (about 2 percent) and are consumed chiefly by middle- and upper-income people. Sharp differences in inequality in each of these neighboring countries compound the effects of these combined issues: the official poverty rate, which by definition involves food insecurity, is less than 15 percent in the United States while Mexico's is 45.5 percent. Food insecurity means, in this context, that for each 1 percent rise in food prices there will be a 0.75 percent decrease in food expenditures (Von Braun 2007).

The agricultural trade relation between Canada and the United States has also strengthened after NAFTA. In contrast to the U.S. relation with Mexico, however, Canada's relationship marginally shifted from deficit in the early 1990s to one of surplus (see Figure 7.1). This trade relationship replicates the type that the United States has with Mexico: the United States exports luxury foods to Canada and imports basic foods from it. Consequently, another interesting contrast is that U.S. imports from

Canada sharply declined during the 2007–2008 food crisis, indicating that these contained primarily basic foods, but Canada's imports from the United States were hardly disrupted because these constitute primarily fruits and vegetables geared to higher-income groups. By this criterion, Canada appears to have benefited the most from NAFTA. This benefit is supported by world ranking of per capita income data: Canada's rank rose from 21st to 9th from 1994 to 2012, while Mexico slipped from 53rd to 61st, and the United States slipped from 9th to 10th (Acosta Córdova 2014).

If we look at the nature of agricultural imports and exports in these countries more generally (not limited to NAFTA trade), we again find that, by dollar value, the top agrifood imports in the United States were still largely luxury goods; in this case, alcoholic beverages, beef and veal meat, coffee, and crude or raw materials (for processing). In Canada the pattern was similar, with top agrifood imports by dollar value captured by alcoholic beverages, crude materials, chocolate preparations, and pet food (Pechlaner and Otero 2010). In Mexico, however, the greatest increase in food-import dependency has been in what we designate as basic foods, including grains and cereals (Otero, Pechlaner, and Gürcan 2013). But Mexico has also developed dependency in the import of some luxury foods like meats, especially chicken meat and wine, as will be seen below.

Import dependency in the context of food security pushes the importing country to internalize the world price for a commodity. For countries with a longstanding tradition of agricultural exports like Canada and the United States, this issue by itself does not cause major concerns in their domestic prices for two chief reasons. First, these nations have long been articulated to agricultural world markets, and they have exercised protectionist or other support policies for their farm sectors (e.g., sugar in the United States and the dairy sector in Canada); second, they also tend to be price fixers rather than takers. But new food-import dependence for countries such as Mexico, which had long protected its consumers and producers from volatile world prices, can and has introduced considerable food vulnerability for its population by subjecting it to world prices. When this dependence is on a basic food item, the impacts can be profound on those with the lowest income, who necessarily spend a greater proportion of their income on food. In our NAFTA region, this population is disproportionately in Mexico.

We propose that imports over 20 percent of domestic production in any food product represent import dependency status. We have investigated the top five food sources for each country and assessed their dependence levels before and after the neoliberal turn by comparing 1985 and 2007 (Otero, Pechlaner, and Gürcan 2013). In Table 7.1 we refine our analysis,

*Table 7.1   Dependency levels in top 80 percent food supply (kcal/capital/day) (quantity imports/domestic supply)*

| COUNTRY | 1985 | | 2007 | |
|---|---|---|---|---|
| | TOP FOODS* | IMPORTS >20% | TOP FOODS* | IMPORTS >20% |
| CANADA | **Wheat; Milk – Excluding Butter + (Total); Rape and Mustard Oil; Fats, Animals, Raw; Pigmeat; Potatoes; Bovine** Meat; Beer; Poultry Meat; Soyabean Oil; Butter, Ghee; Vegetables, Other; Eggs + (Total); Rice (Milled Equivalent); Groundnuts (Shelled Eq); Maize Germ Oil; Apples; Cream; Oranges, Mandarines; Maize; Treenuts + (Total); Fruits, Other; Bananas; Grapes; Oats; Sweeteners, Other; Tomatoes; Beverages, Fermented | Treenuts + (Total) – (104%); Sweeteners, Other (102%); Rice (Milled Equivalent) – (100%); Groundnuts (Shelled Eq) – (100%); Oranges, Mandarines (100%); Bananas (100%); Fruits, Other (81%); Grapes (79%); Vegetables, Other (47%); Apples (40%); Maize Germ Oil (34%); Tomatoes (33%) | **Wheat; Rape and Mustard Oil; Milk – Excluding Butter + (Total); Poultry Meat; Fats, Animals, Raw; Pigmeat; Soyabean Oil; Maize;** Potatoes; Bovine Meat; Rice (Milled Equivalent); Sweeteners, Other; Beer; Vegetables, Other; Butter, Ghee; Pulses, Other; Cream; Eggs + (Total); Groundnuts (Shelled Eq); Maize Germ Oil; Fruits, Other; Treenuts + (Total); Olive Oil; Apples; Bananas | Rice (Milled Equivalent) – (141%); Groundnuts (Shelled Eq) – (120%); Treenuts + (Total) – (104%); Olive Oil (103%); Fruits, Other (102%); Sweeteners, Other (100%); Bananas (100%); Vegetables, Other (68%); Apples (53%); Maize Germ Oil (40%); **Soyabean Oil (35%);** Rape and Mustard Oil (25%); Bovine Meat (21%); **Maize (20%)** |

*141*

*Table 7.1* (continued)

| COUNTRY | 1985 | | 2007 | |
|---|---|---|---|---|
| | TOP FOODS* | IMPORTS >20% | TOP FOODS* | IMPORTS >20% |
| MEXICO | **Maize; Sugar (Raw Equivalent); Wheat; Milk – Excluding Butter + (Total);** Pigmeat; Beans; Sunflowerseed Oil; Soyabean Oil | Milk – Excluding Butter + (Total) – (24%) Sunflowerseed Oil (21%) | **Maize; Sugar (Raw Equivalent); Wheat;** Milk – Excluding Butter + (Total); Pigmeat; Soyabean Oil, Poultry Meat; Beans, Eggs + (Total); Rice (Milled Equivalent), Bovine Meat; Palm Oil | Palm Oil (86%); Rice (Milled Equivalent) – (76%), **Wheat (58%)** Soyabean Oil (33%); Pigmeat (29%) **Maize (28%);** Milk – Excluding Butter + (Total) – (22%) |
| UNITED STATES | **Wheat; Soyabean Oil; Milk – Excluding Butter + (Total); Sugar (Raw Equivalent);** Sweeteners, Other; Bovine Meat; Pigmeat; Poultry Meat; Beer; Fats, Animals, Raw; Potatoes; Maize | **Sugar (Raw Equivalent) – (36%)** | **Wheat; Soyabean Oil; Milk – Excluding Butter + (Total); Sugar (Raw Equivalent); Sweeteners, Other;** Poultry Meat; Pigmeat; Bovine Meat; Beer; Maize; Potatoes; Rice (Milled Equivalent); Fats, Animals, Raw | Rice (Milled Equivalent) – (25%) **Sugar (Raw Equivalent) – (22%)** |

*Note:*  *Ordered by ranking in each country. The data in bold includes food sources that account for 48–50 percent of the total food supply.

*Source:*  Constructed with data on "food balance" for each nation from FAOSTAT for 1985 and 2007. Retrieved March 12, 2013 (http://faostat.fao.org/site/368/default.aspx#ancor).

showing changing import dependencies based on the crops that make up 80 percent of each nation's diet. The smaller number of crops highlighted in bold indicate those crops that make up 50 percent of a nation's diet, starting with the highest caloric contributor.

The first thing we can notice in Table 7.1 is the incredible diversity of the Canadian diet as compared to that in Mexico and the United States. While this diversity decreased marginally between 1985 and 2007, it was still significant. We can also see at a glance that dependence did not increase significantly in Canada in terms of the number of crops, although there is a fair amount of dependence in both periods. Of those crops that made up 80 percent of Canada's food supply, the country was import dependent on 12 in 1985 and 14 in 2007.[1] The majority of these crops were not highly significant to the Canadian diet, however, although they were more so in 2007 than in 1985. In 1985 none of the foods in which the country was dependent accounted for even 2 percent of total food supply, and many were far below that. By 2007 we do see slightly greater import dependence in more important foods, but even then only three of these contribute more than 3 percent of the total food supply (maize at 3.32 percent, rape and mustard oil at 9.75 percent, and soybean oil at 3.34 percent). If we calculate what percentage of the food supply is made up by all the foods in which the country is dependent we see some change between 1985 and 2007. Canada had >20 percent import dependence in 10.99 percent of the country's food supply in 1985 and 31.9 percent import dependence in 2007, a noticeable increase of 20.91 percentage points.

Diets in the United States have been consistently much less diverse, with a far smaller amount of crops accounting for 50 percent and even 80 percent of the U.S. diet than in Canada. The country has increased its dependency between these time periods by one crop. While it remained consistently dependent in sugar, in 2007 the country was also dependent in rice (importing 25 percent). Again, looking at the overall change in dependence on imports for total food supply as a whole, we see that the United States was >20 percent dependent for 8.5 percent of the food supply in 1985 (for sugar) and this had increased to 11.2 percent by 2007 with the addition of rice—an import dependence increase of only 2.7 percentage points. It should be clarified that sugar has been an imported item in industrial nations for centuries, and this particular crop is one that undergoes further processing in these nations. Sugar thus fits the traditional pattern of a primary good exported by a developing country with the developed country industrializing it. Although sugar has come to constitute a significant share of caloric intake, given its relative abundance in world markets, one can hardly think of sugar as anything other than a luxury food (Mintz 1985), the import dependence on which can hardly threaten low-income people's nutrition.[2]

Mexico has an even less diverse diet than the United States, although we can see that diversity in the diet has actually increased since NAFTA, more consistent with expectations about trade liberalization in agriculture than what we see in the United States. Mexico's food-import dependency increased notably compared to the other two countries, however. For example, in 1985 it was dependent in only two of the crops that made up 80 percent of its food supply, whereas by 2007 it was dependent in seven of them. This increase in dependency is notable, and the country's profound descent into food dependence is highlighted when looking at summary statistics for dependence in the food supply as a whole. The two crops in which Mexico had import dependency in 1985 comprised only 8.49 percent of the country's total food supply. In contrast, by 2007 the seven foods in which it was dependent comprised a whopping 56.29 percent of the country's average daily diet (see Table 7.1). We can thus see that the impact of trade liberalization has had a marginal to modest impact on Canada and the United States, but has had a profound impact on Mexico's food dependence. Given the greater impact that food price inflation has on lower-income populations, we can clearly see that this dependence on world food prices will have a disproportionately negative effect on this developing country, particularly on its poorest people.

## THE NEOLIBERAL DIET IN THE NAFTA REGION

The following data analysis shows how the neoliberal diet has evolved in the three member countries of NAFTA. While our assumption is that the neoliberal diet emanates primarily from the United States and became hegemonic in the neoliberal era, our goal here is to determine how it has been expressed in the three NAFTA countries. We start with a basic assessment of per capita food consumption in these regions, using "food supply" (i.e., pre-existing stocks, plus domestic production, plus imports, minus exports) as a proxy for consumption.

The first major point to be shown is that the least developed country in this association, Mexico, experienced the greatest increase in per capita food consumption *prior* to joining NAFTA. In fact, by the late 1970s and early 1980s, Mexico's per capita food intake was greater than Canada's, almost reaching the level of the United States. After the neoliberal turn in Mexico, however, food consumption declined or flattened in this country (see Figure 7.3), while its developed neighbors experienced substantial further average per capita increases in food consumption.

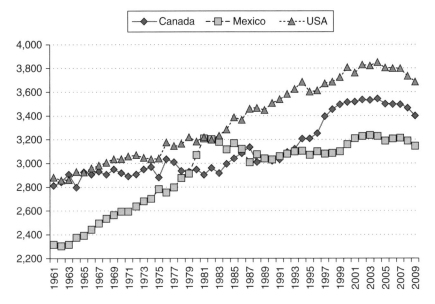

*Source:* Constructed with data on domestic food supply from FAOSTAT, available at: http://faostat.fao.org/site/609/DesktopDefault.aspx?PageID=609#ancor (retrieved January 4, 2014).

*Figure 7.3   NAFTA total food supply (kcal/capita/day)*

Figure 7.4 shows how the increase or decrease in per capita food con-sumption has evolved in different periods between 1961 and 2009. We divided this long period in order to differentiate the era prior to the start of the neoliberal turn (1961–1981) from the time after that. The earlier era was marked by the fact that food production was based primarily on the domestic market with very little agricultural trade. In contrast, food trade became very important in the later times, particularly after the start of NAFTA in 1994. In the calculation of the food-consumption data below, we must take into account that Mexico's per capita caloric intake was much lower at the start of the period in 1961, so the overall increase in food consumption between 1961 and 2009 was relatively larger than increases in its two neighboring countries. But the main point here is that the greatest gains were achieved prior to the neoliberal turn (mid-1980s) and NAFTA (1994). We show this in Figure 7.4 simply by calculating the ratios of food-intake increase in the specified periods, by dividing the later year's average per capita daily food intake by that of the earlier year. The resulting ratio indicates how much food consumption grew from one period to the other. After 1981, Mexico's caloric intake actually decreased

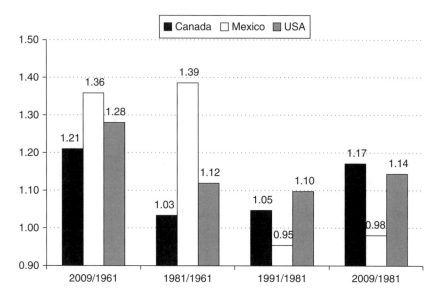

*Source:* Constructed with data on domestic food supply from FAOSTAT, available at: http://faostat.fao.org/site/609/DesktopDefault.aspx?PageID=609#ancor (retrieved January 4, 2014).

*Figure 7.4    NAFTA total food supply ratios, 1961–2009*

in the two periods compared (1991/1981 and 2009/1981), while those for Canada and the United States increased.

Per capita food consumption is only one aspect of the neoliberal diet, however. Another is the increasing role of meat, and the somewhat more complex role of fruits and vegetables, which is complicated both by the industrialization of diets and the increasing class dynamics of consuming fresh produce. Indeed, we find that the components of the neoliberal diet change differentially, depending on which economic classes have the primary access to any particular food type. Changes in consumption patterns of "luxury" foods such as meat, fresh fruit, and wine, for example, will differ from changes in the patterns of "basic" food consumption, such as grains. Beef provides an illustration.

A general trend in both Canada and the United States is that the per capita consumption of beef meat has declined, especially after the crisis of Fordism in the late 1970s. One interpretation of this trend is that, while middle- and perhaps lower-income people used to have access to beef prior to the crisis in these countries, lower-income people had greater difficulties buying it after 1976. Further, at around the same time health

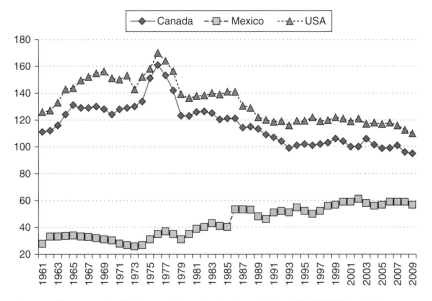

*Source:* Constructed with data on domestic food supply from FAOSTAT, available at: http://faostat.fao.org/site/609/DesktopDefault.aspx?PageID=609#ancor (retrieved January 4, 2014).

*Figure 7.5   NAFTA bovine meat supply (kcal/capita/day)*

concerns made the consumption of red meat less desirable in these countries, so many people switched to chicken instead—also a cheaper meat. In Mexico, however, the middle-to-upper-income classes were the primary adopters of the U.S. milk, meat, and wheat based diet (Pechlaner and Otero 2008). Therefore, as Figure 7.5 indicates, both Canada and the United States experienced increasing consumption of beef prior to 1976, after which there was mostly decline. Mexico started from a considerably lower base than its two northern neighbors, but has experienced substantial increases in beef meat consumption since 1961 with a few blips, such as in the early 1970s. Its absolute levels of per capita consumption are still well below the averages of its more developed neighbors, likely indicating that beef is consumed primarily by middle- to upper-income classes. By 2009, Mexico's average per capita caloric intake from beef was just 57 kilocalories per day, while Canada's was 95 and the United States' was 110. Considering Mexico's deeper class inequalities, however, and the fact that primarily middle- and upper-income classes have steady access to beef, their per capita levels of consumption likely equal or surpass those of equivalent classes in Canada or the United States.

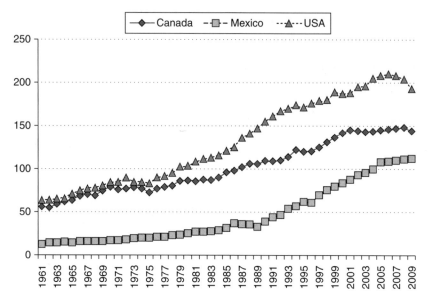

*Source:*   Constructed with data on domestic food supply from FAOSTAT, available at: http://faostat.fao.org/site/609/DesktopDefault.aspx?PageID=609#ancor (retrieved January 4, 2014).

*Figure 7.6    NAFTA total chicken meat supply (kcal/capita/day)*

Many people in NAFTA countries have turned to chicken meat, which appears in a growing number of industrialized food preparations like chicken nuggets. As Michael Pollan (2006) puts it, chicken piles corn upon corn, the United States' main subsidized crop. Since the 1970s the dramatic increase in chicken production has been largely based in the United States. Production has also been increasing in Mexico since the 1990s, although it is still far below that of the United States. As noted, in addition to cost concerns, by the 1980s, health concerns with red meat in the United States further facilitated the chicken revolution. This change of diet has taken place, as Winson notes, in spite of the fact that poultry raised in the confined animal feeding system has sufficient saturated fat to cast doubt on this "purportedly healthier meat" (Winson 2013: 145). Still, as Figure 7.6 illustrates, all NAFTA countries have experienced substantial per capita increases in the consumption of chicken meat, but to a greater extent in the more developed countries given the larger purchasing power of their working and middle classes.

As also evident from Figure 7.6, despite its lower price, per capita chicken consumption nonetheless declined in Canada and the United States after the 2007–2008 food inflation crisis, although it continued to grow slightly in Mexico. Our class interpretation of these trends is that chicken consumption had been widely adopted by lower-to-middle-income working classes in Canada and the United States, who had to reduce their consumption with the crisis. Conversely, in Mexico it was mostly middle-to-upper-income people that experienced increased access to chicken meat, and they did not have the economic need to reduce their intake as food expenditures for these classes is a relatively smaller proportion of their family budgets. By the time of the crisis, in fact, Mexico's supply of chicken meat had increased substantially both via imports from the United States and domestic production using imported U.S. corn as feed (Schwartzman 2013; Martinez, Aboites, and Constance 2013). In contrast to beef, one could say that chicken has become the main neoliberal meat, given that its consumption has increased throughout the period since 1961, but most dramatically after 1990. Mexico's rate of growth in chicken consumption has been faster, but it started from a much lower basis. By 2009 average-daily-per-capita caloric intake from chicken meat was as follows: United States, 193; Canada, 144; and Mexico, 110.

Another frequently articulated aspect of the changing international division of labor in agriculture has been the production and export of fresh fruits and vegetables by developing countries for wealthy consumers in developed countries. Nagatada (2006), for example, conducted an extensive investigation of global trade flows in fruits and vegetables to conclude that their trade has indeed expanded to form the "most significant part of the global agro-food systems under the third food regime" (2006: 38). At the same time, however, he argues that North–South differentiation is actually more nuanced and could even be characterized as multi-polarized as economic growth in developing countries, for example, fuels their importation of fresh fruit and vegetables. Nonetheless, he documents a significant amount of reciprocal "NAFTA flow" of vegetables between our three countries (39).

Somewhat surprisingly, average per capita fresh vegetable consumption in Mexico has been increasing since the 1970s, and particularly since NAFTA, as we can see from Figure 7.7. There have only been modest changes in the United States and Canada, but always with a much higher starting point. Measured as a percentage of total caloric intake, Mexico's intake from vegetable consumption started at just above 0.50 percent in 1961 and moved to about 1.3 percent of total food intake in 2009. In contrast, the figures for its northern neighbors were around 2 percent throughout the period, with Canada surpassing the United States in 1972.

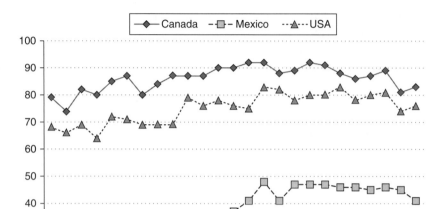

*Source:*    Constructed with data on domestic food supply from FAOSTAT, available at: http://faostat.fao.org/site/609/DesktopDefault.aspx?PageID=609#ancor (retrieved January 4, 2014).

*Figure 7.7    NAFTA vegetables supply (kcal/capita/day)*

While converging upwards, therefore, Mexico remains far below the other two in vegetable consumption.

In Figure 7.8, we see that in the mid-1960s, 1971, and early 1980s, Mexico's per capita fruit consumption was almost as large as that of Canada, whose consumption was highest through most of the period, especially in the early and later years. By the latter part of the long period analyzed here (1961–2009), however, it was only Canada that was able to sustain a high caloric consumption from fruit, some of it imported from Mexico. By contrast, Mexico's average fruit consumption experienced huge fluctuations and rarely went much above the pre-NAFTA high mark achieved in 1984, barely surpassing it in 2004. We suspect that Mexico's modest increases in fruit consumption in the latter part of the period analyzed are due primarily to the purchasing power of higher-income groups. In fact, Humberto González (2013) has shown that increased export of fruits and vegetables from Mexico has made them more expensive in the domestic market, thus reducing their earlier affordability. We can surmise that the increased consumption we see in Figure 7.8 is thus indicative of increased consumption by the wealthier classes.

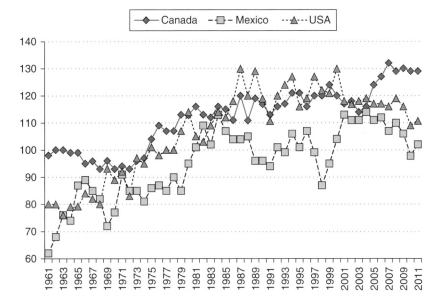

*Source:* Constructed with data on domestic food supply from FAOSTAT, available at: http://faostat.fao.org/site/609/DesktopDefault.aspx?PageID=609#ancor (retrieved January 4, 2014).

*Figure 7.8    NAFTA fruits (kcal/capita/day)*

## CONCLUSION

As a result of NAFTA, we indeed have seen growth of agricultural trade in all three of our countries, as a predicted result of trade liberalization. But there is also a marked divergence in the nature of agricultural trade between NAFTA countries, most notably from the perspective of import dependence of the least developed partner. The social consequences of this dependence are profound when prices rise, as was clearly evidenced by the 2007–2008 world food price crisis. All indications are that this vulnerability will have increasingly dramatic consequences in the future as extreme weather, population pressures, and land shortages consistently push food prices upwards in our very "interesting" times. Already we see that since 2011 the world food price index of the FAO has not dipped below what it was during the crisis; indeed, for many years it has been considerably higher (229.9 for 2011; 213.3 for 2012; 209.8 for 2013; versus 201.4 in the 2008 crisis (FAO n.d.)). Thus while we have seen the predicted convergence with respect to trade flows and dietary patterns in all three countries, if we consider this trade from the perspective of human well-being, there has been significant divergence in the experience of Mexico and its wealthier neighbors. Such divergence is class differentiated too.

With regard to dietary content, we see a convergence toward U.S. dietary patterns. While there are still significant differences between NAFTA countries—predictable, given the development differences between Mexico and the other two—there is also evidence of increasing class-differentiated convergence, most notably with respect to meat and fruit consumption. In short, while NAFTA has largely produced divergence in socioeconomic-development indicators, it has also facilitated dietary, if class-differentiated, convergence. Given that this socioeconomic divergence has negative consequences on social inequality and food security, and that dietary convergence has negative impacts on health, our case study strongly suggests that less-developed countries may experience a double-barreled impact from trade liberalization.

NAFTA has certainly had its detractors. Indeed, much friction between and within the countries has led to its being "somewhat controversial in all three nations" (Charlene Barshefsky, then U.S. Trade Representative, as cited in Morton 1999). Nonetheless, neoregulation in general, and trade liberalization in particular, remain hegemonic ideals. According to Canada's International Trade Minister, Ed Fast, for example, "free and open trade is one of the best job creators and is critical to Canada's long-term prosperity" (Fekete 2011). To the extent that NAFTA replicates dynamics on a global scale, our reading of the NAFTA region suggests that this divergence-and-class-differentiated convergence dynamic presents a significant challenge to the benefits of trade liberalization in agriculture for less-developed countries. Consequently, it offers a significant counter-point to neoregulatory policy imperatives, particularly those which regard trade liberalization in agriculture. As proposed by grassroots movements in Mexico, a food-sovereignty program that supports smallholder peasants and middle-sized entrepreneurial farmers seems warranted from our analysis.

## NOTES

1.  Note that imported raw sugar plays a very particular role in Canada, which processes and refines it, and thus it has been excluded from our list of food sources on which the country is dependent for exports (Otero, Pechlaner, and Gürcan 2013).
2.  Sugar does not play the same trade or manufacturing role in Canada and the United States: unlike Canada, which has eliminated some protectionism that allowed for the production of sugar beet in some provinces, the United States continues to heavily protect its sugar industry located in Louisiana, Florida, and Hawaii, while also indirectly

making it feasible for the Mid-West to produce sugar beet. The same protectionist policy made it economically feasible to start producing high-fructose corn syrup in the late 1970s. Still, sugar is not cheap in the United States; it is cheaper in both Canada and Mexico, to the point that some confectionary firms relocated to Canada in the early 2000s (Otero and Flora 2009).

# REFERENCES

Acosta Córdova, Carlos. 2014. "La Tierra Prometida que Nunca se Alcanzó." *Proceso*. No. 1940, January 5, 2014.

Althaus, Dudly. 2013. "Mexico Takes Title of 'Most Obese' from America." *Global Post*. CBS News. Retrieved July 10, 2013 (http://www.cbsnews.com/8301-202_162-57592714/mexico-takes-title-of-most-obese-from-america/).

Appendini, Kirsten. 2014. "Reconstructing the Maize Market in Rural Mexico." *Journal of Agrarian Change* 14(1): 1–25.

Borras, Saturnino M., Jr., Ruth Hall, Ian Scoones, Ben White, and Wendy Wolford. 2011. "Towards a Better Understanding of Global Land Grabbing: An Editorial Introduction." *Journal of Peasant Studies* 38(1): 209–216.

Darmon, Nicole and Adam Drewnowski. 2008. "Does Social Class Predict Diet Quality?" *American Journal of Clinical Nutrition* 87(5): 1107–1117.

Dixon, Jane. 2009. "From the Imperial to the Empty Calorie: How Nutrition Relations Underpin Food Regime Transitions." *Agriculture and Human Values* 26: 321–333.

Drewnowski, Adam and S.E. Specter. 2004. "Poverty and Obesity: The Role of Energy Density and Energy Costs." *American Journal of Clinical Nutrition* 79: 6–16.

Fagan, Drew. 1994. "Ministers Cite NAFTA Benefits Pact 'Will Create Jobs,' Kantor says in Mexico City." *The Globe and Mail*. January 15. Retrieved May 8, 2014 (http://search.proquest.com.proxy.lib.sfu.ca/docview/385184918?accountid=13800).

Fekete, Jason. 2011. "Free-Trade Frenzy." *National Post*. December 27. Retrieved May 8, 2014 (http://search.proquest.com.proxy.lib.sfu.ca/docview/913019954?accountid=13800).

Food and Agriculture Organization of the United Nations (FAO). n.d. "World Food Situation: FAO Food Price Index." Retrieved May 13, 2014 (http://www.fao.org/worldfoodsituation/foodpricesindex/en/).

Friedmann, Harriet. 1992. "Distance and Durability: Shaky Foundations of the World Food Economy." *Third World Quarterly* 13(2): 371–383.

Friedmann, Harriet. 2005. "From Colonialism to Green Capitalism: Social Movements and Emergence of Food Regimes." *Research in Rural Sociology and Development* 11: 227–264.

Friedmann, Harriet and Philip McMichael. 1989. "Agriculture and the State System: The Rise and Decline of National Agricultures, 1870 to the Present." *Sociologia Ruralis* 29(2): 93–117.

González, Humberto. 2013. "Especialización Productiva y Vulnerabilidad Agroalimentaria en México." *Comercio Exterior* 63(2): 21–36. Retrieved May 17, 2014 (http://revistacomercioexterior.com/rce/magazines/153/6/especializacion_productiva.pdf).

Guthman, Julie. 2011. *Weighing In: Obesity, Food Justice, and the Limits of Capitalism*. Berkeley, CA: University of California Press.

Lee, Hedwig. 2011. "Inequality as an Explanation for Obesity in the United States." *Sociology Compass* 5(3): 215–232.

Johnston, Joseé and Shyon Baumann. 2010. *Foodies: Democracy and Distinction in Gourmet Foodscape*. New York: Routledge.

Martinez, Francisco, Gilberto Aboites, and Douglas H. Constance. 2013. "Neoliberal Restructuring, Neoregulation, and the Mexican Poultry Industry." *Agriculture and Human Values* 30(4): 495–510.

McMichael, Philip. 1992. "Tensions between National and International Control of the

World Food Order: Contours of a New Food Regime." *Sociological Perspectives* 35(2): 343–365.

McMichael, Philip. 2005. "Global Development and the Corporate Food Regime." *Research in Rural Sociology and Development* 11: 269–303. Retrieved January 18, 2006 (http://www.agribusinessaccountability.org/pdfs/297_Global%20Development%20and%20the%20Corporate%20Food%20Regime.pdf).

McMichael, Philip. 2009a. "A Food Regime Analysis of the 'World Food Crisis.'" *Agriculture and Human Values* 26(4): 281–295.

McMichael, Philip. 2009b. "A Food Regime Genealogy." *Journal of Peasant Studies* 36(1): 139–169.

Mintz, Sidney. 1985. *Sweetness and Power: The Place of Sugar in Modern History.* New York: Penguin.

Morton, P. 1999. "Polishing the NAFTA Image Five-Year-Old Pact; Despite Growth in Trade, Misgivings Remain." *National Post.* April 22. Retrieved May 8, 2014 (http://search.proquest.com.proxy.lib.sfu.ca/docview/329472617?accountid=13800).

Nagatada, Takanayagi. 2006. "Global Flows of Fruit and Vegetables in the Third Food Regime." *Journal of Rural Community Studies* 102: 25–41.

Gerardo Otero. 2011. "Neoliberal Globalization, NAFTA and Migration: Mexico's Loss of Food and Labor Sovereignty." *Journal of Poverty* 15(4): 384–402.

Otero, Gerardo. 2013. "The Neoliberal Food Regime and Its Crises: State, Agribusiness Transnational Corporations and Biotechnology." Pp. 225–244 in Stephen A. Wolf and Alessandro Bonanno (eds.) *The Neoliberal Regime in the Agri-Food Sector: Crisis, Resilience, and Restructuring.* London and New York: Earthscan from Routledge.

Otero, Gerardo and Cornelia Butler Flora. 2009. "Sweet Protectionism: State Policy and Employment in the Sugar Industries of the NAFTA Countries." Pp. 63–88 in Juan M. Rivera, Scott Whiteford, and Manuel Chávez (eds.) *NAFTA and the Campesinos: The Impact of NAFTA on Small-Scale Agricultural Producers in Mexico and the Prospects for Change.* Scranton, PA and London: University of Scranton Press.

Otero, Gerardo, Gabriela Pechlaner, and Efe Can Gürcan. 2013. "The Political Economy of 'Food Security' and Trade: Uneven and Combined Dependency." *Rural Sociology* 78(3): 263–289.

Otero, Gerardo, Gabriela Pechlaner, and Efe Can Gürcan. Forthcoming. "The Neoliberal Diet: Fattening Profits and People." In Stephen Haymes, Maria Vidal de Haymes, and Reuben Miller (eds.) *Routledge Handbook of Poverty and the United States.* Routledge.

Pechlaner, Gabriela. 2012a. *Corporate Crops: Biotechnology, Agriculture, and the Struggle for Control.* Austin, TX: University of Texas Press.

Pechlaner, Gabriela. 2012b. "GMO Free America? Mendocino County and the Impact of Local Level Resistance to the Agricultural Biotechnology Paradigm." *International Journal of the Sociology of Agriculture and Food* 19(3): 445–464.

Pechlaner, Gabriela and Gerardo Otero. 2008. "The Third Food Regime: Neoliberal Globalism and Agricultural Biotechnology in North America." *Sociologia Ruralis* 48(4): 351–371.

Pechlaner, Gabriela and Gerardo Otero. 2010. "Neoliberal Globalism and the Third Food Regime: Neoregulation and the New Division of Labor in North America." *Rural Sociology* 75(2): 179–208.

Pollan, Michael. 2006. *The Omnivore's Dilemma: A Natural History of Four Meals.* New York: Penguin.

Schwartzman, Kathleen. 2013. *The Chicken Trail: Following Workers, Migrants, and Corporations across the Americas.* Ithaca, NY: Cornell University Press.

Snyder, Richard. 2001. *Politics after Neoliberalism: Reregulation in Mexico.* New York: Cambridge University Press.

Von Braun, Joachim. 2007. *The World Food Situation: New Driving Forces and Required Actions.* Washington, DC: International Food Policy Research Institute.

Walsh-Dilley, Marygold. 2009. "Localizing Control: Mendocino County and the Ban on GMOs." *Agriculture and Human Values* 26: 95–105.

Winson, Anthony. 2013. *The Industrial Diet: The Degradation of Food and the Struggle for Healthy Eating.* Vancouver: UBC Press.

Wise, Timothy A. 2014. "Monsanto Meets it Match in the Birthplace of Maize." *Triple Crisis: Global Perspectives on Finance, Development and Environment.* May 12. Retrieved May 12, 2014 (http://triplecrisis.com/monsanto-meets-its-match-in-the-birthplace-of-maize?utm_source=GDAE+Subscribers&utm_campaign=591b2a7943-TW_Monsanto_5_12_2014&utm_medium=email&utm_term=0_72d4918ff9-591b2a7943-46746905).

# 8. Transition of agriculture and agricultural policies in Japan: From postwar to the neoliberal era
*Kae Sekine*

## INTRODUCTION

In the second half of the twentieth century Japan experienced unprecedented economic growth and became the second largest economy after the United States.[1] Behind this economic expansion, less recognized is that the agricultural sector played an essential role for the country's recovery from the Second World War and the following Rapid Economic Growth. When Japan, in turn, entered the Low Economic Growth period in the early 1970s and introduced neoliberal policies in the 1980s, the agricultural sector started to suffer from the negative consequences of globalization. As a result the agricultural sector in Japan is experiencing a crisis that features: (1) one of the lowest levels of food self-sufficiency ratio (39 percent of daily needed calories) among the Organisation for Economic Co-operation and Development (OECD) countries,[2] (2) the quite rapid aging of the sector in which the average age of a farmer is 65.8 due to the lack of farming heirs and (3) more than 10 percent of total arable farmland abandoned (MAFF 2011a). Moreover, in 2011 a significant portion of the country's rural areas already suffering from this prolonged crisis were hit by the Great Eastern Japan Earthquake and subsequent tsunamis as well as radioactive contamination caused by explosions at the Fukushima Daiichi nuclear power plant. This incident exposed the vulnerability and contradictions of the agricultural sector and rural society and led to controversy over reconstruction of agriculture and agricultural policies. While the government continued to adopt neoliberal policies to address the disasters, local residents and alternative movements mobilized to oppose government policies.

Contextualized in this complex crisis, this chapter has a threefold objective: (1) to illustrate the transition of Japanese agriculture from the immediate post-Second World War years to the recent neoliberal era, (2) to review the transition of agricultural policies in the context of economic growth and globalization and (3) to analyze the impact of the Great Eastern Japan Earthquake on agricultural policy and the contradictions between neoliberal agricultural policy and local needs. The first section illustrates the transition of agriculture and agricultural policy from the postwar recovery period (1945–51) to the Rapid Economic Growth period (1951–73). The second section reviews the transition from the period of Low Economic Growth (1973–85) to the neoliberal globalization era (1985–2010). The third section focuses on the consequences of the 2011 Great Eastern Japan Earthquake and its impact on agricultural policy as well as local resistance. Finally, the declining role and status of agriculture and the negative consequences and contradictions of neoliberal agricultural policies on the wellbeing of rural communities and the rest of society are discussed.

# POSTWAR AND RAPID ECONOMIC GROWTH

### Postwar Recovery Period (1945–51)

Throughout the evolution of capitalism in Japan, the agricultural sector and rural communities provided vital resources and assets such as food, labor, safe and abundant water and air, energy (many of the power plants are located in rural areas), beautiful landscape and culture. These endowments were fundamental to the country's postwar socio-economic growth and created the base for development in subsequent years.

During the postwar military occupation by the Allied Forces (1945–51), Japan experienced a number of reforms that altered its militaristic and semi-feudal social and economic structure (Allinson 2004; Bailey 1996; Dower 1999). While policies aimed at the demilitarization and democratization of the country characterized the first portion of this period (1945–48), the second portion (1948–51) featured efforts to expand Japan's economy. In the context of the emerging Cold War, Japan's economic growth was not only relevant for the country's domestic stability, but it was also central to the US anti-communist campaign. In this context, American led reforms were implemented in three areas: (1) dissolution of Japanese monopolies – known as *zaibatsu* – that dominated the economy in the prewar decades, (2) pro-labor reforms to stabilize labor relations and provide social inclusion for workers and (3) the Land Reform Program for the elimination of the semi-feudal system of landlords and tenant farmers.

The improvement of agricultural productivity and increases in food production were crucial to the land reform. As tenant farmers constituted 70 percent of all agricultural households, worked in harsh conditions, paid high rents to landlords, generated very low productivity and remained poor with dismal hopes to own a farm, the Land Reform Program was pivotal for the improvement of their conditions and those of agriculture as a whole (Teruoka 2008). Ultimately, it resulted in the improvement of agricultural production and the release of the abundant surplus agricultural labor for urban employment in the developing industrial sector.

This reform decreased the portion of land occupied by tenants from 46.2 percent (1941) to 13.1 percent (1949). Simultaneously, more than six million landless agricultural workers gained land property rights (Teruoka 2008). After the reform, the economic conditions of farmers as well as social and education levels improved significantly. These improvements stabilized social relations and transformed rural areas into reservoirs of moderate conservative voters that supported the long administration of the Liberal Democratic Party (LDP). This also allowed for the reintegration of 6.5 million Second World War veterans and repatriates from the former colonies (Tashiro 2003). With better education and economic prospects, many rural unemployed and underemployed migrated to better paid and stable jobs in urban areas, further stabilizing conditions in rural areas. Ultimately, this rural to urban migration was fundamental to economic expansion during the Rapid Economic Growth years (1950s–60s) (Endo 1966).

**High Fordism and Rapid Economic Growth (1951–73)**

In North America and Europe, the 1950s–60s represented two decades of significant economic expansion and social stability. The combination of state intervention and economic planning, the success of the management-labor accord, and expanding markets and economic opportunities appeared to offer an endless path to development. This period represented the time when the Fordism regime reached its highest levels of stability and efficiency (Antonio and Bonanno 2000). Japan also followed this pathway but with some specific features: (1) a restricted level of wages due to the limited power of trade unions, (2) a significant wage gap between the labor force in large-sized and small- and medium-sized corporations and (3) weak redistributive measures (absence of a welfare state) which were covered through shared solidarity at the levels of family, community and corporation.[3] Despite these differences, Japan was part of this process and the 1951 signing of the Peace Treaty and the Treaty of Mutual Cooperation and Security with the United States signaled the beginning of its High Fordist era. Similar to the case of North America and Europe, the 1973 Oil Crisis and the collapse of the Bretton Woods accord brought Japan's Rapid Economic Growth period to an end. These years can be divided into three sub-periods: the takeoff period (1951–55), the first Rapid Economic Growth (1955–65) and finally the second Rapid

Economic Growth (1965–73) (Teruoka 2008). Each of these three sub-periods featured different policies and patterns of development for the agricultural sector.

The first period (1951–55) was characterized by a strong intervention-ist position of the state. The Japanese state stimulated private economic activities but also intervened through direct investment and ownership of businesses. This State Monopoly Capitalism Policy was intended to propel Japan to a position of economic self-reliance and maintain social stability (Moriya 1971; Teshima 1966). By allowing foreign direct invest-ment, technology and equipment, the industrial structure of Japan was redirected away from traditional light industries into the development of heavy mechanical and chemical production. Japan's membership in the International Monetary Fund (IMF) in 1952 and the General Agreement on Tariffs and Trade (GATT) in 1955 provided further impetus to the country's rapid industrialization process. In this sub-period, the country's agricultural policy was directed toward the twofold objective of increasing production and improving the low food self-sufficiency ratio. The 1952 Agricultural Land Law and the 1950 Carl S. Shoup Tax Reform provided the instruments to expand the production and productivity of family farms and reduce the burden of the tax system (Shimamoto 2011). The augmentation of farms' efficiency and output involved primarily the pro-duction of rice, the country's staple food. Rice production was controlled through price support programs aiming to keep low consumption prices. Also targeted was the upgrading of infrastructure that included reclama-tion of farmland, irrigation and drainage projects and the consolidation of paddy fields. Improved infrastructure allowed increased use of farm equipment and chemicals whose availability was expanded through the growth of cooperatives. Along with economic growth and improvement of agricultural productivity, farmers sought employment in the expand-ing off-farm labor market and the growth of part-time farming. While off-farm employment contributed to the improved socio-economic condi-tions of rural communities, it translated into a decline in community soli-darity (Jussaume 1991). Efforts to increase agricultural production and the food self-sufficiency ratio were, however, revised when Japan began participation in the US Food Aid Program in 1954. This program resulted in increased grain imports from the United States and reduced local pro-duction (Mikuni 2000).

During the second sub-period (1955–65), the country's fast economic growth propelled Japan into the ranks of the major industrialized econo-mies in the world (Allinson 2004; Endo 1966; Teruoka 2008). Growth in the automotive, home appliance, electronic and petrochemical sectors accom-panied early development in the steel, electric and shipbuilding sectors.

Japan's membership in the OECD in 1964 cemented the integration of the country into the growing world economy. These changes created a pattern in which Japan's economic development centered on its newly acquired world prominence in the production of industrial goods. The export of industrial products was accompanied by significant imports of agri-food commodities such as wheat and grains, resulting in a positive balance of trade but also in the decrease in food self-sufficiency. Throughout these years, the *zaibatsu* companies recovered from the postwar break-ups and formed new business organizations such as *Keidanren* (Federation of Economic Organizations). This renewed power was successfully employed to direct government policies to favor corporate economic interests and the creation of a "corporate state" featuring a strong state–corporation partnership (Moriya 1971).

Rapid industrialization further fueled rural to urban migration and contributed to the improvement of the economic conditions of rural families (Misawa 1969). It also facilitated the mechanization and modernization of farms and the resulting increase in crop and labor productivity (Teruoka 2008; Tsuchiya 1969). Simultaneously, outmigration generated rural population losses and a significant decrease in the number of full-time farmers and farms. Despite this decrease, farmland consolidation did not take place and the size of Japanese agricultural operations remained small. Part-time farming and expectations of very lucrative farmland prices offered by urban developers motivated farmers to keep their land. Improved economic conditions resulted in changes in the local diet and the end of rice shortages. High quality rice, dairy and meat products, fresh fruits and vegetables and processed food became part of the everyday food consumption. This Westernization of food consumption led to higher agri-food imports while the income gap between farmers and industrial workers grew larger. Facing overall socio-economic growth but also expanding inequality between urban and rural areas and industrial and agricultural workers, the government was under pressure to intervene.

The elimination of this gap between rural farmers and urban industrial workers was the objective of the Agricultural Basic Law (Mulgan 2006). Enacted in 1961, this fundamental legislation guided the evolution of agriculture until 1999, when a New Agricultural Basic Law was introduced following Japan's membership in the World Trade Organization (WTO). Agricultural policy makers of the period contemplated the expansion of production and productivity through an increase of the size of farms and the elimination of small and inefficient operations. At the time, two-thirds of all farms were less than 1 hectare in size, while only 4 percent exceeded 2 hectares (except in Hokkaido). Embracing GATT directives that suggested a more market oriented approach, the Japanese authorities gradually reduced import tariffs on a number of products. Simultaneously, they endorsed "selective" state intervention directed to the support of some commodities including dairy, meat products, fresh fruits and vegetables.

The third sub-period (1965–73) began with Japan's most serious postwar recession (Teruoka 2008). Deficit spending and the availability of credit promoted by the government, along with the economic benefits resulting from US involvement in the Vietnam War, engendered a rapid recovery. The ensuing growth known as the second Rapid Economic Growth was sustained and propelled Japan into the position of the second largest world economy after the United States. The power of large corporations increased and the burgeoning trade surplus created trade frictions with the United States and other countries. Japan's export oriented economy and its restrictive import policy in agri-food were the subjects of negotiations and trade "retaliations" (Hayami 1988). Ultimately, US requests to open the Japanese market to American agri-food exports and domestic corporate designs to provide cheap food for industrial workers motivated the Japanese government to reduce state intervention (Sekishita 1987). Japan's industrial growth continued but its food self-sufficiency ratio further declined.

Behind continuing economic growth, emerging social problems including pollution prompted the Japanese population to organize pro-environment movements and vote for reformist local governments throughout the country (Shimizu 1995). There was mounting dissatisfaction with mass production and consumption which creates environmental devastation and risks to human health. These concerns encouraged farmers and consumers to organize a scheme of direct partnerships, known as *Teikei* (Community Supported Agriculture) (Jordan and Hisano 2011). At the beginning of 1968, increases in rice productivity and declining consumption resulted in surpluses that encouraged the government to alter price support programs and introduce production adjustment measures. These policy changes prompted a decrease in farm income that was compensated by off-farm employment. The growth of part-time employment also contributed to the decrease of the gap between farm and industrial income that characterized the period.

## LOW ECONOMIC GROWTH AND THE GLOBALIZATION ERA

### Crisis of High Fordism and Low Economic Growth Period (1973–85)

The conditions that permitted the existence of the Fordist regime came to an end in the early 1970s. The ideology of modernization and its promises of constant economic growth, emancipation of subordinate groups and reduction of global inequality were delegitimized. The inability of developed nation-states to maintain high levels of domestic social spending and economic intervention engendered a fiscal crisis that negatively impacted corporate requests for state support and subordinate classes' calls for expanded and efficient welfare programs. The world Oil Crises (in 1973 and 1979), stagflation, rising unemployment and social instability ushered the end of the fixed exchange rates and Keynesian economic policies (Antonio and Bonanno 2000; Harvey 1989). By the beginning of the 1980s, neoliberalism established itself as the new dominant political ideology. The rise to power of Margaret Thatcher in Great Britain, Ronald Reagan in the United States and Yasuhito Nakasone in Japan marked this transition. As uncertainty and concerns about damaging economic downturns characterized the mood of the country during these years, Japan was able to extend its trade surplus. Technology innovations, labor restructuring measures and cost reduction moves that offset the appreciation of the yen explain this outcome. Toyota's "Just-in-Time" system, the world acclaimed business model of the time, symbolized Japan's success. Behind the glittering façade of corporate success and economic gains, workers' conditions deteriorated as the cost of living increased, wages stagnated and stable jobs were replaced with precarious, part-time and low-paying employment (Allinson 2004; Bailey 1996).

Despite the worsening conditions of urban employment, agricultural workers continued to abandon farming. Mechanization and structural changes generated excess farm labor and the total number of farms decreased. Indexed at 100 in 1965, farm labor stood at 60 in 1980. A group of larger farms emerged and the Japanese agricultural structure became polarized following similar trends in major advanced industrial countries of the time (Bonanno 1987). Part-time farming grew further (Teruoka 2008). Price support levels for rice were decreased by 1978 and land set aside and crop substitution programs were introduced. Farmers were encouraged to convert rice production into soybeans, wheat and feed crops. The further diffusion of the Western diet, however, kept these measures from being effective and rice overproduction became the norm. Because Japan's economic development policies required an emphasis on industrial exports, the adoption of price supports for agriculture became less feasible. Accordingly, agricultural policies focused on structural improvements and the deregulation of farmland. As urban and industrial uses of land increased, the price and pressure to make more land available also increased. As the 1980s unfolded, it was clear that the proclaimed objectives of the Agricultural Basic Law were far from being achieved (Teruoka 2008). To be sure, in comparison with the immediate postwar years, the economic conditions of rural residents had significantly improved and severe rural poverty was de facto eliminated. However, rural income growth was largely the result of increased off-farm work, and farmers' part-time jobs generated low wages and unstable employment.

**Neoliberal Globalization Era (1985–2010)**

The neoliberal reforms introduced since the late 1970s gave impetus to the globalization of social and economic relations including agri-food (Bonanno, Busch, Friedland, Gouveia and Mingione 1994; Bonanno and Constance 2008). The Plaza Agreement in 1985 and the related GATT Uruguay Round (1986–93) and establishment of the WTO represented some of the salient policy steps taken under the new regime. As a result of these policy agreements, Japan was asked to allow a significant appreciation of its currency and further liberalization of the agri-food market. Promoted by US plans to contain international competition, restore American companies' market share and dispose of US agricultural surpluses, these requests resulted in the elimination of the 1961 Agricultural Basic Law and its replacement with the New Agricultural Basic Law in 1999. This new policy for agriculture fully embraced neoliberal ideology and practices that inspired globalization oriented reforms. These conditions also led to the growth of Japan's "bubble economy" of the late 1980s and its eventual collapse in the early 1990s.

In response to the changed conditions, Japanese corporations introduced technological innovations and, more importantly, began to relocate production facilities to other countries. In this context, two important events oriented the Japanese agri-food policy in the neoliberal era (Okada 1998; Mulgan 2006; Teruoka 2008). First, following the report of the United States–Japan Advisory Commission in 1984 and under international pressure, Japan further deregulated its agri-food sector. In particular, in 1991 it removed barriers to beef and citrus fruit imports, ending their support initiated with the Agricultural Basic Law. Second, in 1986 the so-called Maekawa Report was adopted as a guiding principle for the development of agri-food. This report called for Japan to commit to the emerging neoliberal ideology by strengthening deregulations and adopting a low-interest monetary policy. Moreover, the report invited Japan to reverse its export oriented economic strategy and "protectionist" agri-food policies and called for the further modernization of farms to meet global market competition.

While the United States recovered from the economic downturns of the 1980s and entered the "roaring 1990s" (Stiglitz 2003), Japan experienced a period of prolonged stagnation. Known as the "lost decade,"[4] the 1990s revealed the dire consequences of the financialization-induced end of the bubble economy (Ikeda 2004). The prices of stocks, land and housing entered a downward spiral, bankruptcies and financial instability became constant features of the Japanese economy. Traditional measures of economic policy were ineffective. The introduction of very low interest rates did not translate into growth, and the deficits of national and local governments increased. The high appreciation of the yen reduced the trade surplus,[5] made exports difficult, curbed domestic production and employment and prompted local corporate elites to introduce drastic restructuring measures. Labor was the primary target of this process. In this context, the unemployment rate more than doubled over the decade. Despite these negative consequences, the increasingly less popular ruling LDP continued to pursue its pro-globalization neoliberal agenda and governed the country with only a brief interruption from 2009 to 2012.

Throughout the 1990s and the 2000s, the Japanese government strongly deregulated the economy, and postwar Fordist agri-food policies were revised and/or eliminated (Teruoka 2008). The measures that replaced them positioned the agri-food sector to follow free-market ideology inspired policies. The results were a further decrease in production, the number of farms, the number of full-time farmers and the amount of cultivated land.[6] Additionally, the aging of the population and the worsening of the socio-economic situation of farmers and rural communities completed the image of a sector in crisis. To be sure, the introduction of mechanical and chemical innovations prompted a sharp increase in productivity. But this growth was insufficient to make Japanese agriculture adequately competitive in the world market. In 1990 the number of farms stood at 3.8 million, down from 6 million in 1955 (MIC 2008).[7] This number further declined to 2.5 million in 2010, indicating the serious economic, but also social, problems affecting the sector (MAFF 2011a). About two-thirds of the remaining farmers were part-time. The reduction in cultivated land brought it to a total of 3.4 million hectares in 2010, down from 5.2 million hectares in 1955. As the total number of farms declined, those considered larger farms (5 hectares or greater, except in Hokkaido) increased in number between 2005 and 2010. Dissatisfied with the declining farm income, but also with the farm lifestyle, younger rural residents showed decreasing interest in agriculture. The resulting aging of the farm population emerged as one of the most significant problems of Japanese agriculture. Farmers' average age rose to 65.8 years in 2010 from 56.7 in 1990, while the number of farmers aged 65 and older stood at 61.6 percent of all farmers in 2010. Agricultural income peaked in 1975 at 2 million yen (20,000 USD) per year per household. But, it decreased to 1 million yen by 1999 (Teruoka 2008). Part-time farmers' off-farm income also declined and pensions covered a greater portion of the total farm household income. The reduced presence of farmers on the land contributed to the deterioration of environmental conditions, damages to the ecosystem and the unchecked growth of wildlife (Yorimitsu 2011). To revitalize the rural economy and support the agricultural sector, the government employed a set of policies that promoted corporations' investments in the agricultural production sector as a centerpiece of reform in agriculture (Sekine and Hisano 2009; Sekine and Bonanno 2015).

Neoliberal globalization was resisted and opposition movements emerged. In agri-food a number of initiatives sought to create alternative systems of food production and consumption and promote the balanced growth of rural areas. Programs such as green tourism and locally based developmental schemes, agro-ecology, organic farming and safe foods, farmer to consumer cooperation and Community Supported Agriculture emerged. Consumer cooperatives continued to pursue their objective of enhancing food safety through the creation of direct links with farmer groups and production cooperatives. However, they also faced difficulties under neoliberal globalization as they experienced strong competition from corporate supermarkets (Takizawa and Hosokawa 2000). Despite opposition, the Japanese administration kept its neoliberal policy and further liberalized agri-food through establishing bilateral and multilateral agreements, such as the Free Trade Agreement (FTA) and the Economic Partnership Agreement (EPA), and the Trans-Pacific Partnership (TPP).

# THE GREAT EASTERN JAPAN EARTHQUAKE, NEOLIBERAL PRESCRIPTIONS AND RESISTANCES

## The Great Eastern Japan Earthquake and Its Consequences

The Great Eastern Japan Earthquake of March 11, 2011 had a heavy impact on Japanese society and economy, as well as the agricultural sector and rural communities. Mistakenly viewed as the consequences of the inclemency of nature and/or the unpredictability of accidents, disasters overwhelmingly affect the weakest components of society and uncover its contradictory structure (Lundahl 2013; Jones and Murphy 2009; Okada 2012). Additionally, reconstructions are accompanied by conflict between corporate groups seeking to foster their business interests, fractions of the nation-state that often – albeit not always – side with big business, and members of the working and middle classes that frequently offer voices of dissent and resistance.

The Great Eastern Japan Earthquake hit the Tohoku Region,

Northeastern Japan, and created tsunamis and a meltdown at the Fukushima Daiichi nuclear power plant. The earthquake damaged a broad area of 24 prefectures with a magnitude of 9 (MS) (FDMA 2013; Japan Meteorological Agency 2011). The tsunami was measured at 16.7 meters (55 feet). It was one of the most severe earthquakes in the world and the fourth largest on record in the last 50 years. Eighteen thousand people were reported killed; an additional 2,700 people missing (FDMA 2013). Agricultural production processes were also severely damaged, with losses totaling more than 2.4 trillion yen (24 billion USD), including 40,000 farms covering 24,000 hectares (52,800 acres) (MAFF 2011b; 2012). Seawater contamination of farmland and debris generated by the tsunami damaged 21,500 hectares (47,300 acres) of the 24,000 hectares of farmland affected in the three most damaged prefectures of Iwate, Miyagi and Fukushima. Radioactivity continued to persist and contaminated land was taken out of production indefinitely. The complex nature of this triple disaster created significant recovery and reconstruction problems.

More than three years after the quake, the overall conditions of the local economy remained in jeopardy. One year after the disasters, there were 626 firms under bankruptcy procedures and 340,000 people who could not return to their homes. As the effects of the disasters unfolded, migration from these areas escalated and the shrinking of the local economy continued. Okada (2012) pointed out that this region's economy was already suffering from the negative consequences of globalization and the strengthening of the neoliberal posture of the Japanese government over the last two decades. The earthquake, tsunami, radioactivity and the ensuing social problems hastened the devastating economic fallout from globalization and neoliberal policies. Agriculture was the most affected sector under the neoliberal regime.

**Neoliberal Prescriptions toward Reconstruction**

Despite questionable neoliberal measures, the Japanese administration continued pursuing neoliberal policies in the phase of reconstruction. Below, is highlighted the creation of a "Special Zones for Reconstruction" (SZR) program, which became a symbol of reconstruction policy for agriculture. A new Act for the SZR was passed in December 2011. This Act promoted a set of pro-corporate deregulations that established tax abatements and incentives, state subsidies and convenient credit to promote corporate investment targeting reconstruction. The creation of the SZR followed the same rationale employed in the creation of Special Economic Zones (SEZs) in recent years. A move common to neoliberal restructuring, the creation of SEZs is based on the principle and practices that allow corporations a wide range of rights and advantages through the formation of areas that offer special concessions (Sassen 1998).

The SZR program aimed to support the 227 municipalities of 11 prefectures damaged by the disasters. As of April 2013, more than 60 areas requested and received SEZ status by the Reconstruction Agency (Reconstruction Agency 2013). While the adoption of SEZs was not new in Japan, the creation of the SZR program represented a milestone in the process of the neoliberalization of agriculture. For a number of years, corporate business circles vigorously pushed for the opening of farmland markets to publicly traded corporations. It was argued that corporate plans could represent the needed solutions to the economic decline experienced by farming regions in the wake of market deregulation. Following this posture, the SZR contemplated the deregulation of the Agricultural Land Act.[8] In addition, the construction of agricultural plant factories[9] emerged as a new trajectory for reconstruction. These factories rely on technology that is made possible through the IT monitoring of environmental components, such as temperature, humidity, light, concentration of carbon dioxide, nutrients and water supply, and the automatic collection of additional pertinent data. IT corporations, such as Fujitsu, NEC, Hitachi, Toshiba and IBM Japan, have been actively investing in this sector. The rationale behind this proposal rested on the premise that conventional agricultural production was not possible on contaminated land. The corporate proposal was supported by the government, and in the three most affected prefectures a number of plant factories were erected with reconstruction subsidies.

As the SZR program was approved, a number of corporations rushed to invest in agriculture. The introduction of the SZR program represented a moment in which corporations could not only benefit from deregulation, but also enjoy the support of state intervention that they so vocally opposed. The mobilization of taxpayer-generated funds for the promotion of corporate designs is an example of the immanent contradiction of the reconstruction process in Japan. Not surprisingly, behind the introduction of the SZRs there were vigorous requests from major business circles such as *Keidanren* and corporate funded think-tanks. The enactment of the SZR Act represents the most advanced point of the current push for the neoliberalization of disaster reconstruction.

**Resistance and Seeking Alternatives**

As recovery and reconstruction efforts were underway, their directions were debated. Pertinent discussions pointed to two primary alternatives. The "reconstruction for humans" approach stressed the importance of re-establishing social relations and environments in ways that bolstered residents' quality of life. This concept was opposed by the "reconstruction for business" view that identified economic growth as the condition for the development of all other facets of social life (Okada 2012). The latter received support from the government and corporate circles and was employed – albeit not exclusively – in reconstruction efforts.

Local governments chose different solutions. Among the three most affected prefectures, the government of the Prefecture of Miyagi sided with the national government and enacted policies that promoted the reconstruction of corporate supply chains, the creation of SZRs and the assignment of rebuilding contracts to large general contractors. Conversely, the government of the Prefecture of Iwate promoted projects that assisted the reconstruction of small- and medium-size businesses in the area. In this context, reconstruction plans for agriculture became the subject of controversy. As the administration associated reconstruction with neoliberal moves, others opted to resist these directions. Below are some instances of resistance to neoliberal reconstruction policies of the agri-food system.

Two years after the disaster, farmers were still struggling to clean their farmland from physical debris, salt brought by the tsunami and radioactive materials. Despite the assistance of volunteers, land reclamation evolved at a very slow pace. In Fukushima and adjacent areas, the issue of nuclear contamination of farmland and agricultural products remained over-whelming. As farmers proceeded to reorganize their lives and activities, grassroots efforts that favored alternative reconstruction plans emerged. In the city of Soma, in coastal area of the Prefecture of Fukushima, the farmer organization, Japan Family Farmers Movement, or *Nouminren*, a member of *Via Campesina*, established the not-for-profit organization *Nomado*. Its objectives were to create direct sales of agricultural products and processed foods along with the establishment of a community café to serve as a location for community support (Noumin Newspaper 2013). Additionally, local farmers joined forces with farmers across the country to protest against government plans to participate in the TPP. The TPP was viewed as a new step toward the further liberalization of agricultural markets and the reduction of farmers' protection against market fluc-tuations and downturns. This opposition consisted of gatherings, street demonstrations and the support of candidates at the national political election who opposed TPP (Daily Tohoku 2012). Overall, however, these oppositional efforts did not deter the government and likeminded business circles from supporting the SZR programs and the construction of plant factories. Additionally, farmers remained split as some groups of large farm owners joined forces with the government to support established reconstruction plans. In Sendai City, Miyagi, the authorities established SZRs and supported the creation of plant factories. This reconstruction program was supported by local large-scale farmers and large corporations including transnational corporations such as Kagome and IBM Japan (Nikkei Newspaper 2012). As local farmers encountered difficulties in their opposition to the government neoliberal reconstruction program, their resistance continued and took additional forms such as the refusal to participate in reconstruction projects (Sekine and Bonanno 2015).

## CONCLUSION

While manufacturing was the engine of the astonishing growth of the Japanese economy in the second half of the twentieth century, the roles of reservoir of labor for urban and industrial expansion, supplier of food and raw materials for industries and cities, market for chemical and mechanical products and a diplomacy trump card for international negotiations made agriculture a fundamental component of the Japanese economy and society. Despite the fact that economic expansion accompanying the relative decline of the agricultural sector is widely observed in advanced industrial societies, what makes Japan's current status outstanding is the seriousness of the crisis that the Japanese agricultural sector and rural communities face. This situation signifies, on the one hand, the existence of a powerful political shift toward further neoliberalization and, on the other hand, a lack of comparable power of alternative movements in the sector. However, it does not immediately mean the success or consensus of neoliberal policies in agri-food sector. Conversely, further adoptions of neoliberal prescriptions for reconstruction following the disasters are questioned by not only farmers in disaster areas but also by many of the country's residents. Their resistance stresses that neoliberal restructuring efforts offer limited assurance that they could generate sustainable development, socio-economic growth of the sectors, an appropriate national land conservation program, enhanced food sovereignty and the overall wellbeing of the local economy and communities' social relations.

## NOTES

1. Japan enjoyed this position from 1968 until 2010, when it was replaced by China.
2. To compare, the food self-sufficiency ratios of major counties (needed calories) were: the United States (130 percent), Canada (223 percent), Australia (189 percent), France (121 percent), Germany (93 percent) in 2009 (MAFF 2014).
3. Boyer called Fordism in Japan "Hybrid Fordism" (Boyer 1990).

4. Economic downturn in Japan continued in the 2000s.
5. For the first time in 2005, profit from trade exceeded profit from investment and this posture became the norm of the Japanese Current Account Balance.
6. The total size of the cultivated farmland decreased due to urban development that involved the construction of homes, plants, resorts and roads and the end of farming activities in less favorable regions such as mountain areas.
7. These data include commercial and subsistence farmers.
8. Corporations do not have the right to own land even in the SZRs. However, some regulations on conversion of farmland were weakened for the purposes of reconstruction.
9. Plant factories refer to a production system that has become widespread recently in Japan whereby fresh fruits and vegetables are produced in a closed growing environment that often operates without soil and through the systematic control of all components of the growth process (Lindhout 2010).

# REFERENCES

Allinson, Gary D. 2004. *Japan's Postwar History*. Second Edition. New York: Cornell University Press.
Antonio, Robert J. and Alessandro, Bonanno. 2000. "A New Global Capitalism? From Americanism and Fordism to Americanization-Globalization." *American Studies* 41 (2/3):33–77.
Bailey, Paul J. 1996. *Postwar Japan: 1945 to the Present*. Oxford: Blackwell Publishers.
Bonanno, Alessandro. 1987. *Small Farms: Persistence with Legitimation*. Boulder, CO: Westview Press.
Bonanno, Alessandro, Lawrence Busch, William H. Friedland, Lourdes Gouveia and Enzo Mingione (eds.). 1994. *From Columbus to Conagra: The Globalization of Agriculture and Food*. Lawrence, KS: University Press of Kansas.
Bonanno, Alessandro and Douglas H. Constance. 2008. *Stories of Globalization: Transnational Corporations, Resistance, and the State*. University Park, PA: Pennsylvania State University Press.
Boyer, Robert. 1990. *L'Introduction à la Régulation*. Tokyo: Fujiwara Shoten (in Japanese).
Daily Tohoku. 2012. "3 Organizations of Agriculture, Forestry and Fishery Collaborate in Recommendation for Anti-TPP." *Daily Tohoku*. November 27 (in Japanese).
Dower, John W. 1999. *Embracing Defeat: Japan in the Wake of World War II*. New York: W.W. Norton & Company.
Endo, Shokichi. 1966. *Postwar Japanese Economy and Society*. Tokyo: Chikuma Shobo (in Japanese).
FDMA (Fire and Disaster Management Agency). 2013. "Report on the Great East Japan Earthquake." FDMA (in Japanese).
Harvey, David. 1989. *The Condition of Postmodernity*. Oxford: Basil Blackwell.
Hayami, Yujiro. 1988. *Japanese Agriculture under Siege: The Political Economy of Agricultural Policies*. Hampshire: Palgrave Macmillan.
Ikeda, Satoshi. 2004. "Japan and the Changing Regime of Accumulation: A World-System Study of Japan's Trajectory from Miracle to Debacle." *Journal of World-Systems Research* 10(2):363–394.
Japan Meteorological Agency. 2011. "Portal Site on the Great East Japan Earthquake." Japan Meteorological Agency. Retrieved on May 8, 2013 at http://www.jma.go.jp/jma/menu/jishin-portal.html (in Japanese).
Jones, Eric C. and Arthur D. Murphy (eds.). 2009. *The Political Economy of Hazards and Disasters*. Lanham, MD: AltaMira Press.
Jordan, Sangeeta and Shuji Hisano. 2011. "A Comparison of the Conventionalisation Process in the Organic Sector in Japan and Australia." *Agricultural Marketing Journal of Japan* 20(1):15–26 (in Japanese).

Jussaume, Raymond, Jr. 1991. *Japanese Part-Time Farming: Evolution and Impacts.* Ames, IA: Iowa State University Press.

Lindhout, Gerard. 2010. "Japan Reconstituting Plant Factory Concept." Retrieved on May 25, 2013 at http://www.freshplaza.com/news_detail.asp?id=61481.

Lundahl, Mats. 2013. *The Political Economy of Disaster: Destitution, Plunder and Earthquake in Haiti.* New York: Routledge.

Mikuni, Hidemi. 2000. *Development Process of Food Distribution Problems.* Tokyo: Tsukubashobo (in Japanese).

MAFF (Ministry of Agriculture, Forestry and Fisheries). 2011a. "Summary of Results of 2010 World Census of Agriculture and Forestry in Japan." MAFF. Retrieved February 20, 2013 at http://www.maff.go.jp/j/tokei/census/afc/about/pdf/kakutei_zentai.pdf (in Japanese).

MAFF (Ministry of Agriculture, Forestry and Fisheries). 2011b. "Press Release on the Great East Japan Earthquake." MAFF. Retrieved on May 9, 2013 at http://www.maff.go.jp/j/press/keiei/saigai/111125.html (in Japanese).

MAFF (Ministry of Agriculture, Forestry and Fisheries). 2012. "Recovery and Reconstruction of Agriculture and Fishery from the Great East Japan Earthquake." MAFF (in Japanese).

MAFF (Ministry of Agriculture, Forestry and Fisheries). 2014. "Food Balance Sheets in 2012." MAFF. February 21, 2014 (in Japanese).

MIC (Ministry of Internal Affairs and Communications). 2008. "Report on Results of Past Census of Agriculture and Forestry in Japan." Retrieved March 26, 2013 at http://www.e-stat.go.jp/SG1/estat/List.do?bid=000001012037&cycode=0/ (in Japanese).

Misawa, Takeo. 1969. "An Analysis of Part-time Farming in the Postwar Period." Pp. 250–269 in K. Ohkawa, B.F. Johnston, and H. Kaneda (eds.) *Agriculture and Economic Growth: Japan's Experience.* Tokyo: University of Tokyo Press.

Moriya, Fumio. 1971. *Postwar Japanese Capitalism.* Tokyo: Aoki Shoten (in Japanese).

Mulgan, Aurelia G. 2006. *Japan's Agricultural Policy Regime.* London: Routledge.

Nikkei Newspaper. 2012. "Eco-town in Disaster Area Using Natural Energy. IBM Japan and Kagome Establish Plant Factories in Sendai City." *Nikkei Newspaper.* September 1 (in Japanese).

Noumin Newspaper. 2013. "Nomado as Base of Reconstruction in Fukushima." *Noumin.* January 7 (in Japanese).

Okada, Tomohiro. 1998. "Conversion of Japanese Agri-food Policy and Agribusinesses." Pp. 195–209 in I. Nakano (ed.) *Agribusinesses.* Tokyo: Yuhikaku (in Japanese).

Okada, Tomohiro. 2012. *Regeneration of Regions from Earthquake Disasters: Recovery of Human Beings or "Structural Reform" Under Shock Doctrine?* Shin Nihon Press (in Japanese).

Reconstruction Agency. 2013. "Certified Programs for Promotion of Reconstruction." Reconstruction Agency. April 26 (in Japanese).

Sassen, Saskia. 1998. *Globalization and its Discontents.* New York: The New Press.

Sekine, Kae and Alessandro Bonanno. 2015. *The Contradictions of Neoliberalism in Agri-food: Corporations, Resistance and Natural Disasters in Japan.* Morgantown, WV: West Virginia University Press.

Sekine, Kae and Shuji Hisano. 2009. "Agribusiness Involvement in Local Agriculture as a 'White Knight'? A Case Study of Dole Japan's Fresh Vegetable Business." *International Journal of Sociology of Agriculture and Food* 16(2):70–89.

Sekishita, Minoru. 1987. *Trade Friction between Japan and the U.S. and Food Trade.* Tokyo: Dobunkan Shuppan (in Japanese).

Shimamoto, Tomio. 2011. "Postwar Farmland System and its Revision and Effects." Pp. 8–36 in S. Harada (ed.) *Regeneration of Local Agriculture and Farmland Systems.* Tokyo: Nobunkyo (in Japanese).

Shimizu, Miyuki. 1995. *History of the Anti-Pollution Movement in the Modernization of Japan.* Tokyo: Nihon Keizai Hyoron Sha (in Japanese).

Stiglitz, Joseph E. 2003. *The Roaring Nineties.* New York: W.W. Norton & Company.

Takizawa, Akiyoshi and Hosokawa Masashi (eds.). 2000. *Distribution Reorganization and Agri-food Market*. Tokyo: Tsukuba Shobo (in Japanese).

Tashiro, Yoichi. 2003. *An Introduction to Agricultural Issues*. Tokyo: Otsuki Shoten (in Japanese).

Teruoka, Shuzo (ed.). 2008. *Agriculture in the Modernization of Japan (1850–2000)*. New Delhi: Manohar.

Teshima, Masaki. 1966. *Japanese State Monopoly Capitalism*. Tokyo: Yuhikaku (in Japanese).

Tsuchiya, Keizo. 1969. "Economics of Mechanization in Small-Scale Agriculture." Pp. 155–171 in K. Ohkawa, B.F. Johnston and H. Kaneda (eds.) *Agriculture and Economic Growth: Japan's Experience*. Tokyo: University of Tokyo Press.

Yorimitsu, Ryozo (ed.). 2011. *Deers and Forest in Japan*. Tokyo: Tsukiji Shokan (in Japanese).

# 9. The European Common Agricultural Policy: A tale of slow adjustment to neoliberal globalization
*Manuel Belo Moreira*

## INTRODUCTION

Trying to give a synthetic appraisal of the history of the Common Agricultural Policy (CAP) from a political economic perspective requires an understanding of the inner logic of the process. One must look at the changing of the ideological and political views underlying the continuous negotiation process conducted through numerous fora and involving a great number of institutions, often with conflicting views not only at the European Union (EU) level,[1] but also inside each member state. Obviously, all these complex relations are also greatly influenced by the profound world changes within the political, economic and social realms.

To identify the driving forces behind the construction of the CAP, one must consider the following: (1) the characteristics of the dominant ideology and its influence on policy changes, starting at a period of undisputed Keynesian oriented policies, passing on to the emergence in the 1970s of the neoliberal ideology which explored the incapacity of prior policies to efficiently tackle the stagflation period, up to the highly reinforced neoliberal hegemony of the 1980s following the implosion of the Soviet Union;[2] (2) the changing balance of power, between those who consider agriculture to be a declining sector and the CAP to be an inefficient and costly policy and others who consider that agriculture and rural development need a strong common policy (these competing views are not only present within each member state, but are widespread at both the European and global level; for example, there are competing views concerning the General Agreement on Tariffs and Trade (GATT)/World Trade Organization (WTO) trade negotiations); and finally, (3) the inner logic and dynamics of the technological evolution that by conditioning and being conditioned by the effectiveness of each particular policy, imposes limits, for example, on the degree of freedom in the functioning of the technological treadmill.

The chapter considers four periods. The first is the long period between 1962 to 1992, when the EU was enlarged first from six to nine and then to twelve countries and the determinants of the policy were principally driven by internal EU decisions. This period was characterized by the prevalence of strong protectionism under the common market preference principle. In the 1980s forces exterior to the EU became influential in contesting this policy, namely at the GATT Uruguay Round negotiations when the common market preference principle came formally under attack. The second is the period from 1992 to 2003, starting with the MacSharry reform when EU membership was increased by three more countries and when compliance with trade liberalization resulting from GATT/ WTO negotiations started to be enforced. The third period describes the implementation of the 2003 CAP that saw the number of member states increased to 28 countries and the adjustment to liberalization that led to further developments. The fourth period consists of an appraisal of the recently approved guidelines for the period after 2014. Finally, some concluding remarks will be made.


## THE CAP: AN AGRICULTURAL AND SECTORIAL POLICY

At the Stresa Conference in 1958, the six founding countries (Belgium, France, Italy, Netherlands, Luxembourg and West Germany) agreed to implement the CAP that started in 1962, following the guidelines defined in Article 39 of the Treaty of Rome that established the European Economic Community (EEC) (which preceded the EU designation):

> 1. The objectives of the common agricultural policy shall be: (a) to increase agricultural productivity by promoting technical progress and by ensuring the rational development of agricultural production and the optimum utilisation of the factors of production, in particular labour; (b) thus to ensure a fair standard of living for the agricultural community, in particular by increasing the individual earnings of persons engaged in agriculture; (c) to stabilise markets; (d) to assure the availability of supplies; (e) to ensure that supplies reach consumers at reasonable prices.
>
> 2. In working out the common agricultural policy and the special methods for its application, account shall be taken of: (a) the particular nature of agricultural activity, which results from the social structure of agriculture and from structural and natural disparities between the various agricultural regions; (b) the need to effect the appropriate adjustments by degrees; (c) the fact that in the Member States agriculture constitutes a sector closely linked with the economy as a whole.

This group of countries, while still recovering from the destruction of World War II, was already living a period of economic expansion, namely through the development of industry and services. The post-World War II European Recovery Program, known as the Marshall Plan, was having positive results and the leitmotif of the agricultural policy was *moderniza-tion*. It was a moment when ideologically and politically the "commitment to productionism" (Lang, Barling and Caraher 2009) dominated and the idea of giving agriculture the protection equivalent to that of an infant industry was widely accepted. However, the CAP design in that matter did not show full policy autonomy, since it involved negotiations with the United States that established limits to EU protectionism. For example, cereals were protected but not oilseeds.

It was a period when the hegemonic political forces in Europe, Christian Democrats and Social Democrats, agreed on the protection of the family farm as a strong ideological line of defense against the idea of collectivism. This ideological choice gave farmers and the rural population a dispropor-tionately high electoral power and, therefore, contributed to the consoli-dation of a political discourse which was unfavorable not only to collective farms but also suspicious of the corporate type of capitalist farms that were emerging as the driving force of international agricultural markets.

The CAP more or less followed what the member states were already putting into practice by themselves and was essentially designed to increase agricultural productivity to assure food supply and to liberate the labor force for other sectors. That is, it was essentially a solely agricultural (at that point in time the CAP did not contemplate rural development) and sectorial policy, favoring almost exclusively the most important products of the northern founding countries, mainly dairy products, bovine meat, cereals and sugar beet (Mediterranean products of southern France and Italy had nothing like the same protection).

To achieve these goals, under the ideological stance prevailing at that time, it was unthinkable to give free rein to market forces. Instead, a complex design of interventionist policies was implemented. The general idea was to design a carefully balanced policy that, while guaranteeing the growth of food production at reasonable prices to consumers, could assure that family farmers, a privileged political constituency of the domi-nant political forces in those countries, were protected from the full conse-quences of the dynamics of capitalism.

Supporting and modernizing an agricultural sector based on the family farm requires broad policy support, since it is particularly difficult when farm dimensions are relatively small thus hampering most of the potential economic gains of scale. In fact, to modernize agriculture under the pre-ferred commitment to productionism requires modern means of produc-tion capital, which implies granting subsidies and assuring easy access to credit to facilitate acquisitions.

The resulting increasing family indebtedness appears to have been the main drive of the dynamics of modernization. However, to convince farmers to become credit dependent, it was necessary to protect them from commercial risks, such as price volatility, and to assure them that they would have no problems selling all their products at prices high enough to keep most of the family farms in business.[3]

Furthermore, it was necessary to modernize and increase agricultural productivity innovation. Scientific knowledge was made accessible to the family farm through a number of services available to farmers, and family farmers' skills were improved through training efforts. This required essentially state-led extension partnerships, which were very effective at the local level without incurring additional costs for farmers.

That is, during this period the CAP consisted of a mixed policy. On the one hand it restrained much of the capitalist dynamics using the protectionist price regime and by introducing measures seen as precursors to rural development.[4] On the other hand, market forces internal to the EU were free enough to allow the functioning of the technological treadmill, to which other agricultural and land structure policies jointly contributed by slowly pushing out of business the less productive farmers.

The CAP was based on a number of principles: (1) *market unity*, that is, free trade among member countries, with equal institutional prices, defined at each Common Market Organization (CMO), created for the more important agricultural products of the founding member states;[5] (2) *common market preference*, meaning imposing tariffs on imports, which contributed to balancing the CAP budget; (3) *financial solidarity*, that is, a common budget to support CAP costs managed by the European Agricultural Guidance and Guarantee Fund (EAGGF).

The main instruments of the CAP consisted of: (1) a negotiated price system supported by the CAP budget that used to define the price regime for each single CMO; (2) the intervention regime regulating the withdrawals of surpluses and assuring a minimum guaranteed price; (3) the aids regime of either direct price subsidies or deficiency payments aimed at complementing farmers income; and (4) the trade regime regulating the trade outside the EU space and export refunds.

To ensure the desired *price stabilization* at levels considered favorable enough to keep most family farmers in business, the CMOs annually defined a target price, an intervention price that was a minimum guaranteed price, and a border limit price that was the protectionist threshold price. These mechanisms exempted farmers from most market risks, particularly by ensuring that *market withdrawals and export subsidies* would be used when necessary in the case of eventual surpluses.

During the first years of this period the CAP was seen as a tremendous success. Labor productivity and agricultural production grew substantially, and while not attaining the promised income parity with other sectors, farmers nevertheless enjoyed stable prices and did not have to fear lack of demand for their products. Consumers had enough products at reasonable prices and the CAP budget was under control, being fueled by import taxes.

However, it soon became evident that in spite of this success the CAP path would not be sustainable while the most protected productions continuously exceeded EEC consumers' capacity to consume, since agricultural production was growing at a higher pace than the population. The problems of *production surpluses* were crystal clear:[6] guaranteed prices and modernization stimuli created the continuous growth of agricultural output of the most protected products, making the common market less and less dependent on imports and increasingly dependent on exports. This lead to recurrent budget crises due to fewer tariffs being captured from imports and the increasing of export subsidies (euphemistically called restitutions) since EU prices, annually fixed through a negotiation process among the members, largely exceeded world prices.

In 1968 Sicco Mansholt, the European Commissioner for Agriculture, prepared a plan to tackle the problem, which was not adopted in the face of strong criticism from farmers' organizations and farmers' massive and violent street manifestations.

During this first CAP period the negotiation process had been able to achieve annual consensus for the continuity of the above-mentioned mixed policy. Relatively minor changes were introduced to tackle the main causes of unsustainability, such as the introduction of the Monetary Compensatory Amounts to address the problems caused by a common price in a common market with different currencies and the clause of *co-responsibility* as a first major measure of a *supply management policy*. This clause imposed the process of self-restraining production on the agriculture sector by the application of penalties when production exceeded the manageable level of the quotas accorded at the annual negotiations that limit the maximum volumes guaranteed at the common price (a regime of planting vineyards rights was introduced in 1976, a milk quota was established in 1984 and the sugar sector was also operating under quotas).

Nevertheless, budgetary problems and the issues involved with membership enlargements made the annual negotiations more complex and difficult each year, while increasing criticism from different groups of interests and opinion makers along with internal and external liberalization forces, eventually forced a major reform.

# DETERMINANTS OF THE MACSHARRY REFORM OF 1992

The most important reasons for a major reform were:

1. the opposition to EU protectionism and to export subsidies from the traditional exporting countries, namely the Cairns group at the GATT negotiations during the Uruguay Round and subsequently at the WTO. This opposition along with selective retaliations and the threat of even higher levels of retaliation was, probably, the most effective driving force for the reform;
2. the growing opposition by mainstream economists, describing the CAP as a rent-seeking device, mainly aimed at favoring some vested interests that hamper market development, cause market distortions and influence negatively resource allocation;
3. the fading attractiveness of the idea of productionism, since the emphasis on production and productivity growth no long seemed able to deliver its promises, particularly because of the persistence and visibility of famines all over the world (Lang et al. 2009);
4. the environmentalist movement opposing CAP modernization, which was based on the so-called industrialization of production that simplified productive systems and provoked air and groundwater pollution due to the uncontrolled use of chemicals. The episodes of acid rain, eutrophication of rivers and lakes and diminishing biodiversity were a powerful argument;
5. the emergence of grassroots movements influential in the richest markets; the consumers' movement influenced by the advice of nutritionists who were increasingly concerned with food safety and nutrition quality; groups concerned with animal welfare that shared some concerns with the environmentalists, namely the problems relating to the meat-feed industrial complex and the industrialization of production (pollution, bad odors, ethical concerns about the way animals are raised, etc.);
6. and finally the criticism of the agricultural sectors that could not count on identical price support systems and therefore became more susceptible to the capitalist dynamics, sharing the concerns of other sectors of the economy with regard to the most protected farmers' favored treatment. In fact, it was more and more difficult to accept the concession of subsidies and assurances that the other agents were not entitled to. It was particularly difficult to rationally explain why the CAP should have to give subsidies to farmers to produce more and more, knowing that it would require increasing subsidies and costs to get rid of these policy induced surpluses.

These criticisms were highlighted by the media, particularly at the time of the annual negotiations or when particular cases of agricultural surpluses needed to be addressed by exporting with subsidies, donations, or by withdrawing them from the market through denaturation for animal feed. Therefore public opinion became much more sensitive to the argument that the CAP was entitling farmers with unjustifiable privileges and a full reform was required.

On the other hand, the successive enlargement from six to nine countries and then to the southern European countries (Greece in 1981, Portugal and Spain in 1986), made the CAP negotiation process much more difficult and complex. However, probably the most important force driving reform was the recently achieved hegemony of neoliberal globalization/financialization.

In fact as soon as the neoliberal ideology became hegemonic in the Anglo-Saxon world, the neoliberal economic program based on what has been described as the movement to deregulate,[7] liberalize and privatize, started to be put into practice, initially during the Carter period and with much more vigor under Margaret Thatcher in the United Kingdom and Ronald Reagan in the United States, to become slowly, but progressively spread around the globe. The European Community started the adjustment to these new ideas and politics with the signature of the Single European Act in 1986 and later with the Maastricht Treaty in 1992, which, among other things, imposed tight budgetary constraints.

Even before the 1992 reform the CAP had already started adjusting to the changing ideological/political mood through a number of measures: the privatization of the functions performed by state-led partnerships used to control the market of important products, such as UK Marketing Boards or French Offices and their equivalents in other countries; the privatization of their infrastructures, such as the cereal elevators, that were taken over by large world operators such as Cargill, Continental and Louis Dreyfus; and the move to outsourcing through the privatization of research and development units as well as extension services. Similarly, a more corporate friendly stance was observed, due to the strategies of supply chain management, the tripartite standard regime,[8] and the movement that saw private regulation substituting state-led regulation (Morgan, Marsden and Murdoch 2008).

Nevertheless, this changing ideological mood did not produce a unidirectional path, since with the 1988 Structural Funds reform the European Commission acquired the ability to launch its own socio-economic development programs (Community Initiatives), and local and rural development, such as the Leader project, has emerged as an important element in EU structural policy (Ray 1997).

If the push toward neoliberal regulation and privatization followed a slow but continuous pace without raising too much opposition, the same cannot be said about liberalization. In fact, during the 1980s, most EU governments were far from sharing the Anglo-Saxon liberalizing stance and, furthermore, any attempt to liberalize trade and reduce farm subsidies received fierce opposition from farmers' organizations which, as it has already been mentioned, for historical reasons were one of the most important supporters of EU continental governments and therefore able to influence the national positions at every EU negotiating table.

However, it soon became clear that agriculture trade liberalization was an issue to be dealt with at the EU level and had to count on a strong reaction from non-EU countries. In fact, the EU has been forced to get rid of their agricultural surpluses through an increasingly subsidized export effort, therefore conflicting with the interests of traditional export countries. The United States, which saw their preferential markets suffering from EU competition, took the lead, placing at the negotiation table the menace of trade retaliations.

Furthermore, the strong push for global trade liberalization was also in the interest of other EU economic sectors. The EU aligned with the United States on the preparation of the 1986 GATT Uruguay Round that paved the way to the agreements that led to the building of the liberalizing WTO. This meant that at the EU level, agricultural interests increasingly conflicted with the industry and services sectors of the most powerful exporting countries, forcing the 1992 MacSharry reform.

In short, the aim of the reform was to address the above-mentioned criticisms, changing the CAP from an almost exclusively agricultural and sectorial policy to a more complex policy that, while trying to cope with the WTO requirements, would also address environmental and animal welfare concerns and give increased importance to rural development issues. But it was only after the 1996 Cork Conference and the 1997 approval of the Agenda 2000[9] that rural development started to be considered as the second pillar of the CAP.

## THE MACSHARRY REFORM

Under the above-mentioned circumstances, the CAP reached a new level of adjustment to a neoliberal globalized world. Within the EU, it coincided with the Maastricht Treaty and the implementation of the European Single Market as agreed by the 1987 Single European Act that constituted the first major revision of the Treaty of Rome.

While attempting to adjust to globalization, it must be stressed that the resulting trade regime was a long way from being completely liberalized, and the subsidies granted to agriculture, while substantially transformed to adjust to the GATT/WTO requirements, were far from being abolished.

Nevertheless, while keeping the bulk of financial transfers to agriculture, the wind was blowing toward an increasingly liberal orientation that brought about growing competition in the EU agricultural single market. This opened up new opportunities for the functioning of the technological treadmill and its structural effects: the expected outcome of the capitalist dynamics.

> The MacSharry reform started the shift from product support (through subsidies and prices supported by consumers) to producer support (through direct payments supported by CAP budget). The reform aimed to improve the competitiveness of EU agriculture, stabilise the agricultural markets, diversify the production and protect the environment, as well as stabilise the EU budget expenditure. Direct payments were introduced in order to compensate for the decrease of the price support (cereal guaranteed prices were lowered by 35%, and beef prices by 15%). Compulsory set-aside and other accompanying measures (agri-environment programmes, afforestation, early retirement, diversification) were also introduced. (EU 2013)

The reform consisted primarily of a substantial reduction in supported prices for cereals, along with less important reductions in other supported prices. In an attempt to appease farmers' organizations, at least on a temporary basis, those reductions on price support were compensated by granting direct payment to farmers based on the historic productivity of each region.

The reform also attempted to address many other above-mentioned criticisms, namely through the recognition of the *multifunctional* character of agriculture that was introducing new policy goals, such as rural development, diversification, environmental and natural resources protection and the preservation of natural spaces.[10] This multifunctional character was considered a defining element of the "European Model of Agriculture" in the official discourse.

The rationale was clear: the priorities were the reduction of price support, seen as a prudent compliance with WTO requirements, and the reduction of pressure over the CAP budget through a more market friendly way of price determination, therefore further liberating the structural effects of the technological treadmill, which affected primarily the smallest farmers. However, to achieve such important transformations, while assuring a peaceful and smooth transition, this shift needed to be balanced with maintaining the European Model of Agriculture. This meant maintaining the support measures but using direct compensatory payments to comply with WTO requirements; early retirement subsidies;

and other accompanying measures (as they were called). These measures essentially addressed the new policy goals covered by the concept of agriculture multifunctionality that was intended to countervail the hegemony of the productionism by supporting a more environmentally friendly transformation of agricultural activity (namely through agri-environmental measures such as compulsory set aside, extensification and afforestation).

Finally, the reform introduced a new look at the functions of agriculture, not only showing new concerns about food production and commercialization (including legislation about organic farming) but also considering agriculture as an essential activity for rural development and for the preservation of natural and manmade landscapes (the idea of farming as the stewardship of nature), therefore incorporating the sustainable development message of the Rio Earth Summit.

The proposals to implement the *eco-conditionality* and the facultative modulation of the subsidies were other relevant CAP outcomes of the MacSharry reform. Lately, the Agenda 2000 further deepened this orientation, dividing the CAP into two pillars: the first pillar (pillar 1) concerning production support, still keeping the largest share of the CAP budget, and a second pillar (pillar 2) of rural development, which gained new emphasis.

Another attempt to address the criticism concerning CAP productionism bias consisted of a proposal to make the agri-environment schemes compulsory and further incentivize diversification by introducing the compulsory set aside, an example of a cross-compliance mechanism generalized by the 2003 reform.

It was also in 2000 that the EU White Paper on Food Safety addressed the food fears that have been highly exacerbated by the evidence found in 1996 that bovine spongiform encephalopathy (BSE) was transmissible to humans.

Finally, the reform had to consider the EU enlargement, introducing into the negotiation processes some objective criteria of funds repartition among member states.

Nevertheless, the criticism about the CAP did not fade away. In fact, the cost reductions obtained by the 1992 reform were obfuscated by its new visibility, since they became entirely supported by the CAP budget instead of by consumers and import taxes.

Furthermore, the gap between the announced objectives for agricultural and rural development and the ways in which the instruments and costs were actually prioritized made clear the lack of coherence and efficiency of the CAP (Cordovil et al. 2004). In spite of Commissioner Franz Fischler's recognized concerns toward rural development (at the 1996

Cork Conference), it was considered that the Commission insufficiently addressed those issues.

In short, the different critical perspectives about the CAP still had many arguments to press the negotiation process toward a new reform.

## THE 2003 REFORM

This reform, following the proposals of Agenda 2000, came at a moment when the CAP was committed to two very important issues: it had to consider the negotiations involving the new enlargement to come (eight eastern countries and two Mediterranean islands in 2004 followed by Bulgaria and Romania in 2007, which would amount to a doubling of the EU farming population), and it was under both internal and external pressure to introduce instruments toward a more liberalizing regime in line with the WTO agreements.

The reform generalized the implementation of a number of requirements promoted by Agenda 2000 concerning public, animal and plant health; animal welfare; the maintenance of all agricultural land in Good Agricultural and Environmental Conditions and the 19 Statutory Management Requirements to be implemented through directives and regulations in successive years.[11]

To further implement the idea of eco-conditionality, cross-compliance became generalized as was promised following Agenda 2000, meaning that in the case of non-respect of legal requirements, direct payments would be reduced in proportion to the risk or damage concerned.

The reform was based on the principle of *flexibility* and *decentralization* (Cunha 2004), meaning that, for the first time, the CAP could be implemented in a way that gave member states room to apply the policy differently according to the regions and productive systems.

The reform also intended to address the criticism of mainstream economists and the liberalizing position of the EU negotiators at the WTO who wanted the EU to gain the initiative at the negotiation table instead of being constantly on a defensive position due to the CAP constraints.

In fact, radical changes on agricultural protectionism were implemented, the *decoupling* principle and the *single payment scheme*, meaning that aids should be decoupled from production and be given through a single payment per farm. This change was to be adopted by a single CMO that substituted the existing CMOs, though not uniformly, since some cases got a transitional period of adaptation that would end in 2013, and derogations were granted to new member states.[12]

Furthermore, in the mid-2000s, under the "everything but arms" agreement the EU has given free market access to all less developed countries, making it the largest importer of agricultural products from developing countries. This strengthened the position of the EU at WTO negotiations (EU 2013).

Another interesting issue concerns the *modulation* of the aids, intended to give member states an instrument to address a recurrent complaint about the equity of the aids, since the bulk of transfers went to a minority of big farms and/or corporations (in 2001 about 50 percent of the aids went to 5 percent of the beneficiaries, and almost 27 percent to 1.5 percent of them). This instrument was first proposed by MacSharry in 1991 but rejected by the Council before being finally accepted, but only on an optional basis, by Agenda 2000 and then by the 2003 reform (Alvarez-Coque 2006).

Finally, financial discipline mechanisms were reinforced in order to keep the CAP budget under control.

A quotation from an Overseas Development Institute publication summarizes the most remarkable achievements of the reforms of the past two decades:

> The CAP is funded from the EU (European Commission (EC)) budget and accounts for roughly 40% of total EU budgetary expenditure). Pillar 1 support includes both direct payments to farmers and market management measures. Pillar 2 support focuses on improving the structural and environmental performance of agriculture and on promoting local/rural development. Pillar 2 also requires Member State co-financing . . .
>
> These reforms have led to some major changes in practice. While the CAP budget has remained at around €50 billion over the past 15 years, it decreased as a percentage of the EU budget from 70% in 1985 to around 40% in 2009. The wider estimate of agricultural support used by the Organisation for Economic Co-operation and Development (OECD), the total support estimate (TSE), was around €100 billion per annum over the period 1986–2009; the producer support estimate (PSE) decreased as a percentage of agricultural output from 40% in 1986 to 25% in 2009. Coupled direct payments decreased from 77% of total CAP payments in 2004 to 15% in 2008; decoupled payments grew from 3% to 68% and rural payments from 15% to 18%. (Cantore, Kennan and Page 2011, p. v)

Looking at these results one can easily conclude that the transition from the commitment to productionism to the neoliberal rule, far from being complete, has, notwithstanding, been gradually gaining speed since 1992 and particularly since the 2003 reform,[13] showing that the political power of farmers and the rural population has, notoriously, decreased.

However, it should be noticed that this move is not unidirectional. Even if the result of the negotiation system points to a deepening of the neoliberal driven adjustment, other forces are present and able to prevent the complete surrender to this trend, as is exemplified by the new role of the European Parliament as co-legislator, which is supporting an increase in market regulation. In short, it has been possible to build new lines of policy that are present, for instance, in the new rural paradigm or in the idea of continuity and change mentioned by Goodman (2004).

Along with this complex game of disparate and sometime conflicting forces, a slow move to a renationalization of agricultural policies has been under way and deserves to be emphasized. Renationalization not only results from the greater flexibility given to countries and regions to comply with the CAP regulations enforced in 2003, but is also due to the diminishing share for agriculture in the EU budget while keeping pillar 2 of the CAP subject to national co-financing, thus making rural development issues highly dependent on the national budgets.

This renationalization, namely the increasing of the share of the budget requiring co-financing, is a powerful device which increases inequality among member states, since it allows rich countries without budgetary problems to direct funds to pillar 2 while the poorest countries have much more difficulty in doing the same as for them it is always more difficult to divert national budgets to rural development. This has been a particularly sensitive problem for eastern and southern European countries, or for the countries that due to the current crisis are forced to have austerity based programs that consist primarily of cutting government expenditures on social purposes and on cutting investment in public goods.

## PERSPECTIVES FOR THE FUTURE

In December 2013 the Official Journal published guidelines for the future, that is, the four basic regulations and transition rules, after approval by the European Parliament. These legislative texts reflect the agreement of the negotiations inside the Commission and between the Commission and the member states at the Council of Agriculture Ministers and, finally, the European Parliament, which has recently gained powers on such matters.

The four basic regulations concern rural development (Reg. 1305/2013); "horizontal" issues such as funding and controls, farm advisory, cross-compliance, management and control systems and clearance accounts (Reg. 1306/2013); direct payments (Reg. 1307/2013); and common organization of the markets (Reg. 1308/2013); and, to assure a smooth transition, Reg. 1310/2013 lays down transitional provisions.

According to the Commission, the main objectives of these regulations are: (1) tightening finance discipline and diminishing budgetary costs: "a series of tools (e.g., internal and external convergence thresholds, degressivity of payments, the so-called redistributive payment, and the small farmers scheme) will ensure that direct payments will be distributed in a fairer way between Member States, between regions and between farmers, with a further shift away from 'historical references'" (EU 2014a); and (2) simplifying the CAP by diminishing bureaucracy and facilitating internal and foreign trade; for instance, a single CMO replaced the 21 existing CMOs, "for imports, licence requirements were reduced from 500 to 65 and for exports, only 45 licence requirements remain" and "it repealed specific marketing standards for 26 types of fruit and vegetables" (EU 2014b).

In terms of the CAP budget, the regulations are intended to achieve a limited redistribution, using a formula based on a percentage of the average value of payments per hectare at the EU level, among member states and internal to each state. Another objective concerns the possibility of budget transfers between pillars 1 and 2, but in both directions, leaving the possibility to reinforce one or the other option in each member state.

A new model of direct payments by layers was introduced. The compulsory elements are the "basic payment scheme" and the "greening" and "young farmers" payments; and the optional elements are the payments for the "less favored areas" (now defined as areas with natural and other specific constraints) and the "payments coupled to production," since the derogations of the 2003 reform are allowed to be maintained.

A relevant option given to member states is the idea of redistributive payments, meaning the payment of higher amounts per hectare for the first hectares of a farm holding up to a certain limit, and lower amounts per hectare above that limit.

Greening payments are aimed at reaching 30 percent of the total envelope of direct payments. The greening rhetoric has been reinforced but the final decision still allows several derogations.

An interesting aspect of this concerns the single CMO that, besides simplifying procedures, reframed the level of acceptable liberalization: it became possible in the dairy sector to have practices of collective price negotiation by producers' organizations up to certain production thresholds; powers were granted to the producers' organizations to effectively manage supply (including the decision for market withdrawals) in the case of crisis; and a new system to control wine plantations up to 2030 was introduced. Nevertheless, a compromise was achieved to put an end to export subsidies, and they could only be reactivated if a specific market crisis exists.

With regard to rural development, and recognizing that the structural funds are more difficult to control, the reform introduced a joint framework with other EU Directorate-Generals (DGs) to avoid double financing and to give more coherence to the implementation of several existing instruments at the regional level (regional funds, cohesion funds, rural development, etc.) that are managed by different DGs (DG AGRI, DG REGIO, DG EMPL, etc.).

The new flexibility opened up by the reform, and the budgetary restrictions linked to pillar 2 expenses, namely when national co-financing[14] is required, provides an extra incentive toward renationalization, meaning that if this move is to be enforced then the CAP risks becoming solely an agricultural policy again, at least for the poorest member states.

In short, the result of the Commission proposals, as well as the outcome of the subsequent negotiation process, points essentially toward adjustments of the 2003 reform rather than to the radical changes sustained by those that propose a CAP constituting only pillar 2, by suspending pillar 1 support, or the most radical proposals suggesting that pillar 2 should be entirely renationalized (Bureau and Mahé 2008).

## CONCLUDING REMARKS

CAP history shows a continuous negotiation process that from the beginning of the 1980s started to be highly influenced by the ideological hegemony of neoliberalism.

However, far from being a quick and straightforward process, the neoliberal adjustment had to come to terms with opposition, particularly during the crucial moments of the preparation of the successive reforms, in order to build winning coalitions (Swinnen 2008). Among the most important factors, the following should be noted: the shift in the balance of power related to the number of agents involved (from 6 to 28 member states) and particularly to the voting procedures (from required unanimity to qualified majority due to changes in the EU treaties); the influence of internal and external liberalizing forces, namely at the GATT/WTO; the trend to increasingly renationalize important features of the CAP; the role of organized and looser grassroots movements that are involved in several issues, such as the environment, animal health and fears of genetically modified organisms (GMOs) as well as other food safety issues; the leadership and ability of the Commission and Commissioners (namely agriculture and trade) when negotiating among themselves and with member states; and, last but not least, the lobbying of farmers and agri-businesses. Finally, it is interesting to note that since the 2003 reform the European Parliament has gained influence and, in accordance with Commissioner Dacian Cioloş, has pushed toward more market regulation, such as the implementation of the dairy package of the CMO. However, the European

Parliament's and even the Commission's influence have been highly restrained by successive neoliberal treaties and by the ultimate power that rests with the Council, the Ecofin, where neoliberal ideology reigns.

This argument is exemplified by the fact that the initial CAP principles of market unity, common market preference and financial solidarity have been highly subverted. The rhetoric about the European Model of Agriculture and other measures that support the idea of a European exception can be seen as an attempt to appease criticisms, particularly as financial solidarity among member states is increasingly fading away and because cutting budgets is nothing more than putting into practice the strategy of starving the beast that is hampering the effectiveness of market regulation.

Furthermore, even if the CAP can exhibit only a slow move toward liberalism, in many aspects the Commission kept the neoliberal stance against all the odds, such as supporting the use of GMOs, and the intention to further liberalize trade by signing the Transatlantic Partnership Agreement that, if signed, will come along with overall rules that are able to supersede particular regulations.

In a nutshell, the trend toward an increasing compliance with neoliberal views that gained hegemony among policy deciders all over the world has been tempered during these successive negotiation processes. This shows the pragmatism of the neoliberal ideological collective, which does not have any problem in forgetting its ideological purity in particular issues providing that the trend to its ultimate goals can be reinforced (Mirowski 2013). That is, from the neoliberal point of view, the strategy has been to ensure that the powers that be at the EU do not abandon the neoliberal orientation, since the major EU treaties are able to successfully overcome particular episodes of each country's political majority. Therefore sectorial policies such as the CAP can use a step-by-step approach, with improvements and retreats, but maintain a dynamic toward the ultimate neoliberal goal of increasing the realm of market relations.

## NOTES

1. The European Commission and its different Directorate-Generals; the European Parliament and its commissions; and the CoAM (Council of Ministers of Agriculture), ultimately obeying the guidelines of the ECOFIN (Economic and Financial Affairs Council) and of the European Council (which consists of the heads of state or government). In fact as Daugbjerg and Swinbank (2007) put it, the 1992 reform was made by the CoAM while the Agenda 2000 was made by the European Council.
2. Neoliberal ideology characterized by strong pragmatism in using the state apparatus to enforce policies that by re-regulating facilitate the ultimate goals of privatization and liberalization (Mirowski 2013).

3. CAP policy rhetoric publicized that farmers should be in income parity with the other sector workers.
4. Such as the Council Directive about the less favored areas (LFA) measures concerning mountain and hill farming and other disadvantaged areas aimed at ensuring the continuation of farming, maintaining a minimum population level and/or conserving the countryside. The LFA measures, with successive amendments, are still operating now.
5. This led to a difference of treatment benefiting northern products: in 1993 the share of the typical northern products benefiting from the Guarantee Fund was 42.5 percent, while the typical Mediterranean products only got 11.4 percent (Varela 1996). This has been a source of complaint since the first EU enlargement.
6. For instance, in 1986 the EU stocks attained the following volumes: butter 1.5 million tons; bovine meat 600,000 tons; cereals 15 million tons; powder milk 850,000 tons and alcohol from wine distillations 10,556 million hectoliters (Varela 1996).
7. Deregulation, would be better designated as re-regulation (Bonanno et al. 1994) or neoregulation (Otero and Pechlaner 2010). In fact, it seems that the primary goal of neoliberalism is not to promote a generalized deregulation, but instead to promote the changes of state-led regulations that are necessary to facilitate the ultimate goals of liberalization and privatization (Mirowski 2013).
8. Consisting of standards, certifications and accreditations, with the involvement of state and private institutions (Busch 2010).
9. An action program approved in 1997 aimed at reforming the CAP and the EU Regional Policy considering the future enlargement to eastern countries.
10. Agricultural multifunctionality, a so-called non-trade concern at WTO negotiations, "is still best apprehended as a highly politicised, essentially discursive and deeply contested policy idea. Within an unfolding 'geography of multifunctionality' many different constructions are possible depending on spatial scale and politico-institutional context. Some of these are undoubtedly part of a movement of resistance to the neoliberalisation of agriculture but others are in the process of being integrated into the 'norm complex' that defines what neoliberalism is as a political project" (Potter and Tilzey 2007).
11. "A revised Council Regulation on rural development has introduced cross compliance concept into most of the 'Axis 2' measures as from 2007" (Jaffrelot n/d). "In addition to the SMRs there are a set of Good Agricultural and Environmental Conditions (GAEC), that do not (as yet) have a legislative basis and focus mainly on issues that are seen as crucial but fall outside existing legislation, such as soil quality" (Juntii 2012).
12. A detailed account can be found in OECD (2004).
13. As it is expressed by the discourses of Agricultural Commissioners and EU concerned persons (Erjavec and Erjavec 2009).
14. Only for the post-2013 period, a initiative from the European Parliament successfully diminished the share of co-financing due from the countries under financial assistance from the EU.

# REFERENCES

Alvarez-Coque, J.M.G. 2006. *La Reforma de la Política Agraria Común*. Madrid, EUMEDIA e Ministerio de Agricultura, Pesca y Alimentación.
Bonnano, A., W. Friedland, L. Llambí, T. Marsden, M. Moreira and R. Schaeffer. 1994. "Global Post-Fordism and Concepts of the State." *International Journal of Sociology of Agriculture and Food* IV:11–29.
Bureau, J.C. and P. Mahé. 2008. "CAP Reform beyond 2013: An Idea for a Longer View." Retrieved November 16, 2014 (http://www.notre-europe.eu/media/etude64-cap-propositions-en_01.pdf?pdf=ok).
Busch, L. 2010. "Can Fairy Tales Come True? The Surprising Story of Neoliberalism and World Agriculture." *Sociologia Ruralis* 50 (4):331–351.

Cantore, N., J. Kennan and S. Page. 2011. "CAP Reform and Development: Introduction, Reform Options and Suggestions for Further Research." London, Overseas Development Institute. Retrieved November 16, 2014 (http://www.odi.org.uk/sites/odi.org.uk/files/odi-assets/publications-opinion-files/7245.pdf).

Cordovil, F. et al. 2004. *A Política Agrícola e Rural Comum e a União Europeia*. Cascais, Principia.

Cunha, A. 2004. *A Política Agrícola Comum na Era da Globalização*. Coimbra. Almedina.

Daugbjerg, C. and A. Swinbank. 2007. "The Politics of CAP Reform: Trade Negotiations, Institutional Settings and Blame Avoidance." *Journal of Common Market Studies* 45 (1):1–22.

Erjavec, K. and E. Erjavec. 2009. "Changing EU Agricultural Policy Discourses? The Discourse Analysis of Commissioner's Speeches 2000–2007." *Food Policy* 34:218–226.

EU. 2013. "50 Years of CAP." Retrieved November 16, 2014 (http://ec.europa.eu/agriculture/cap-history/1992-reform/index_en.htm).

EU. 2014a. "Commission Publishes Annual Report on Direct Aids to Farmers in 2012." Retrieved November 16, 2014 (http://ec.europa.eu/agriculture/newsroom/158_en.htm).

EU. 2014b. "Simplification of the CAP." Retrieved November 16, 2014 (http://ec.europa.eu/agriculture/simplification/index_en.htm).

Goodman, D. 2004. "Rural Europe Redux? Reflections on Alternative Agro-Food Networks and Paradigm Change." *Sociologia Ruralis* 44 (1):3–16.

Jaffrelot, J.-J. n/d. "CAP Reform: Implementing Cross Compliance." Directorate-General for Agriculture and Rural Development. European Commission. Retrieved November 16, 2014 (http://www.ecaf.org/docs/ecaf/cap.pdf).

Juntti, M. 2012. "Implementing Cross Compliance for Agriculture in the EU: Relational Agency, Power and Action in Different Socio-material Contexts." *Sociologia Ruralis* 52 (3):294–310.

Lang, T., D. Barling and M. Caraher. 2009. *Food Policy: Integrating Health, Environment and Society*. Oxford, Oxford University Press.

Morgan, K., T. Marsden and J. Murdoch. 2008. *Worlds of Food: Place, Power, and Provenance in the Food Chain*. Oxford: Oxford University Press.

Mirowski, P. 2013. *Never Let a Serious Crisis Go to Waste: How Neoliberalism Survived the Financial Meltdown*. London: Verso.

OECD. 2004. "Analysis of the 2003 CAP Reform." Retrieved November 16, 2014 (http://www.oecd.org/agriculture/agricultural-policies/32039793.pdf).

Otero, G. and G. Pechlaner. 2010. "The Neoliberal Food Regime: Neoregulation and the New Division of Labor in North America." *Rural Sociology* 75 (2):179–208.

Potter, C. and M. Tilzey. 2007. "Agricultural Multifunctionality, Environmental Sustainability and the WTO: Resistance or Accommodation to the Neoliberal Project for Agriculture?" *Geoforum* 38:1290–1303.

Ray, C. 1997. "Towards a Theory of the Dialectic of Local Rural Development within the European Union." *Sociologia Ruralis* 37 (3):345–362.

Swinnen, J. (ed.). 2008. *The Perfect Storm: The Political Economy of the Fischler Reforms of the Common Agricultural Policy*. Brussels: Centre for European Policy Studies.

Varela, J.A. Santos. 1996. *A Política Agrícola Comum. Os Princípios, as Reformas Actuais, a Futura Europa Verde*. Lisboa: Dom Quixote.

# 10. An overview of Spanish agriculture in the 21st century
## Miren Etxezarreta, Jordi Rosell and Lourdes Viladomiu

## INTRODUCTION

In order to understand the changes that have taken place in Spanish agriculture, as with any other economic sector, it is important to consider two aspects beforehand: the objectives towards which it is directed and the perspective adopted by the analyst. The evolution of the agricultural sector can be analyzed from several perspectives and with different objectives in mind: from a business perspective (obtaining a profit for those who have invested their capital); from an economic perspective (obtaining a food supply that enables the sector to match the rest of the economy); or from a social perspective (an active, dynamic, and sustainable rural sector with a population that enjoys a decent standard of living). According to conventional economic theory, all of these objectives would be achieved by market forces automatically and simultaneously. However, it is well known that this is not the case and that these objectives may even be contradictory, hence the importance of knowing the specific objectives behind this process of evolution. It is also necessary to be clear about the perspective adopted by the analyst. It is not valid to argue that agriculture, the rural sector, and the economy constitute homogeneous entities; in all economic sectors there are several groups with conflicting interests which must be taken into account and in respect of which a position must be adopted. The current economic situation is the result of the dynamics of the global capitalist system, whose objective consists of making an adequate profit for the owners of the capital, which leads to the concentration and internationalization of both the capital and the production units. Transnational corporations (TNCs) and financial institutions are the main active agents of these dynamics. Although the agricultural sector has some specific characteristics, in order to understand its behavior it must also be placed in this context. Agricultural and food markets, modern technology, and public regulations (whether national or supranational, such as those of the European Union) are interacting elements that condition the development of the agricultural sector in specific territories, conform the structure of agricultural enterprises and farms (determining their micro-economic decisions to a large extent), and shape the social classes that in the agricultural sector are expressed in complex and varied ways.

This chapter does not aim to provide an exhaustive analysis of all the components that make up the Spanish agricultural system but rather is a review of the most significant aspects of the recent development of Spanish agriculture, considering its principal elements.[1] This approach assumes that the farming sector must provide the economy and country in question with an adequate supply of agricultural products and food while at the same time ensuring a sustainable environment, all of which must be compatible with the existence of rural populations with satisfactory standards of living for those who are its direct agents.

## FROM TRADITIONAL AGRICULTURE TO THE MODERNIZATION OF THE SECTOR

In the early 1960s the Spanish agricultural sector[2] was a highly traditional and closed production system, consisting of latifundia (large estates), family farms, peasant farmers, and agricultural day laborers, which employed almost half of the Spanish working population. This period marked the start of an intense process of growth, modernization, and opening up of the Spanish economy, which started a rapid industrialization and urban

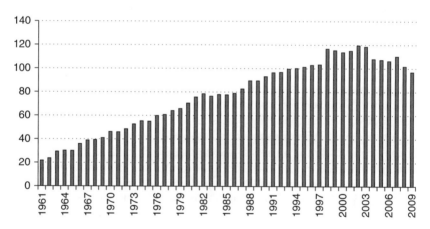

*Source:*   FAOSTAT (2014).

*Figure 10.1   Meat consumption per capita in Spain, 1961–2009 (kg/
            capita/year)*

development as half of the population moved to a different municipality in the space of 15 years. In addition to seeing an increase in spending power, the population underwent a rapid process of Westernization in terms of lifestyle and eating habits (Cussó and Garrabou 2009). There was a growing demand for animal protein, which required and facilitated a profound transformation of the agricultural sector.[3]

Since then, the sector has undergone an extremely rapid transformation, falling into line with Western practices and becoming integrated into the general process of capital accumulation. As such, agriculture has increasingly mirrored other sectors, becoming incorporated into the general dynamic of the economic process. The penetration of foreign capital has increased at every stage of the agro-food chain. Agriculture has gradually lost its singularity and autonomy, becoming increasingly integrated into the agro-industrial system (agro-food chains, integration contracts, advanced technology, significant investment and debt, mass production, etc.). Meanwhile, different types of integration contracts between farmers and industrial corporations have emerged.[4] One highly illustrative example of this development is the finishing pig production sector, where 80 percent of production is currently carried out under contract (Soldevila 2008). All of these changes facilitated a significant increase in production and productivity along with a reduction in costs.

The agricultural sector has become a large consumer of industrial inputs such as fertilizers and machinery (intermediate consumption now constitutes half the value of agricultural production). With the onset of intensive, specialized agriculture and the adoption of the technology package transferred from the agro-industrial sector, which is controlled to a large extent by multinational companies, agricultural production has gradually turned into the mass production of raw materials for the food industry. This allows the production of cheap food for global urban markets. Production is first split into various units and the end product is then put together by the food industry, "made in the world." Meanwhile, the intense restructuring and reduction of farms occurred, with the consequent reduction in the amount of labor that could be supported by agriculture. The latifundia became mass production farms while smallholdings became commercial family farms run by highly professional farmers. Many other farmers left their farms and moved to cities or emigrated abroad. Although in quantitative terms most agricultural produce is still consumed in places close to where it is produced, from a qualitative standpoint the agricultural approach is now global in nature. Spanish agriculture is competing with the rest of the world and even the most remote sectors are affected. The professionalization of farms is a process that occurred in parallel with their increase in size and concentration. This greatly strengthened the historical dual structure of farms. The concentration of agricultural production is achieved with fewer farms and a very small permanent workforce and, as such, does not ensure the existence of a sufficient rural population to maintain the land.

## THE AGRICULTURAL SECTOR AND THE SPANISH RURAL WORLD: THE BIG NUMBERS

### The Territory

Spain occupies a large and varied surface area of 504,645 km$^2$. It is one of the most mountainous countries in Europe with an average altitude of 650 m. It is one of the largest countries in the European Union (EU) in terms of agricultural surface area, with a utilized agricultural area (UAA) of 23,752,690 hectares. The practice of leaving land fallow is widespread in dry areas. There is also a significant presence of permanent crops, of which the two most important are olive groves (2,483,000 hectares) and vineyards (1,135,200 hectares). Meanwhile, irrigated land accounts for 3,818,101 hectares. The natural conditions of Spanish land vary widely, with an agricultural potential that differs greatly. Some areas are highly productive, with good soils and water provision, while other large areas have very poor soil quality, significant topographical difficulties, and low, irregular rainfall. Agriculture remains the main economic activity in these latter regions, while industry and services are underdeveloped. These differences were accentuated by the process of agricultural modernization and intensification.

Water availability has always been an important concern in the country. The Spanish rainfall regime is very irregular and non-irrigated crops have an inconsistent success rate. This is evidenced by their fluctuating annual production. Irrigation is the way to obtain higher and more stable production and, therefore, is a fundamental driving force of Spanish agricultural production. Irrigated land accounts for 16 percent of the UAA and produces 60 percent of final agricultural production (without livestock), accounting for 36 percent of agricultural GDP. Around 75–80 percent of water resources are channeled into the agricultural sector, creating conflicts with other uses. Conservation and environmental groups staunchly oppose the development of new irrigation areas. The ecosystems found in most Spanish regions are remarkably fragile, at high risk of natural hazards (erosion, fires, desertification, strong storms, flooding, very dry periods, frost, snowfall, etc.), so much so that a crop and weather insurance system was developed with the support of public funds. The disappearance of agricultural activity has a negative effect on a large number of these ecosystems. Land abandonment is a concern in some regions of Spain.

The modernization of the agricultural sector also increased the burden on natural resources and had a significant negative impact on the environment. In some areas, intensification led to serious erosion. Intensive livestock farming has contributed to the nitrate pollution of aquifers, while irrigation has led to the overexploitation and salinization of underground water. Over half of Spain's surface area is included in conservation programs of some kind. For example, the Natura 2000 network encompasses 27 percent of the country's surface area, as opposed to just 12.5 percent in France and 17 percent in the EU as a whole. These differences lead to a varied combination of both extensive and intensive farming systems.

Among the first one (i.e., extensive farming), of traditional nature and dry land, the following systems can be found: *traditional extensive systems*, in which land is devoted to herbaceous crops (cereals, sunflowers, and fallow); *Mediterranean crop systems*, devoted to vineyards, olive groves, and almond trees; the *Dehesa system*, a multifunctional agro-sylvo-pastoral system with a mixture of crops, cattle, and trees; and *extensive livestock systems*, predominantly in mountain or hill areas, with sheep, goats, and cattle. With the exception of the first two categories, in which large companies may be involved and returns may be acceptable, these systems present low productivity, poor returns, and scarce labor, leading to abandonment being the main concern of these regions. However, they are considered to be of high natural value in terms of bird populations in the herbaceous crop areas, landscape and sustainability in the high complementary *dehesa* lands, among other factors.

Irrigated land is dedicated to horticulture (vegetable and fruit crops) and other crops such as sugar beet, alfalfa, cereals, tobacco, and cotton. The bulk of agricultural production, labor use, and returns, comes from intensive agriculture, mainly on irrigated land and in intensive livestock systems. Water pollution and the overexploitation of aquifers are challenges to these systems. Spain has sparsely populated rural areas and the population is unevenly distributed; there are extensive mountain areas in nearly every region, along with large areas at risk of desertification and depopulation which present very low densities of population.

At the same time, peri-urban areas have expanded greatly and much of the best agricultural land is subjected to strong competition from alternative uses. Furthermore, the development model of the Spanish economy in the last few decades of the 20th century and at the turn of the 21st century gave clear priority to the building and real estate sector. Although land prices have not increased very much in terms of constant prices, there has

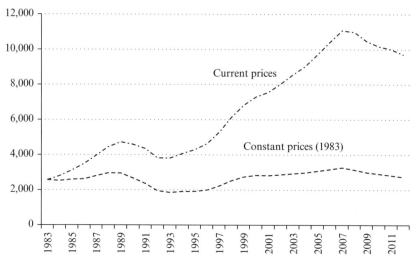

*Source:*   MAGRAMA (2014b).

*Figure 10.2    Evolution of agricultural land prices in Spain (1983–2011)*

been a significant variation between them according to location and quite a high degree of money illusion (i.e., the tendency of people to think of currency in nominal, rather than real, terms), which generates strong pressure that affects the dynamic of farms. The best agricultural land has been devoted to other uses that are more profitable in the short term. Offers of agricultural land in Spain, whether for purchase or rental, are very limited, making it very difficult for new farmers to set up business. A lot of land has been farmed on an unofficial basis; that is, without the existence of a signed contract between the landowner and the local farmers.

An appropriate word for describing the Spanish agricultural sector is *diverse*. In addition to the aforementioned differences in natural conditions, the idiosyncrasies of the country's socio-political organization have led to the establishment of a wide variety of farming models.

The *heterogeneity* of Spanish political organization has frequently been mentioned as the biggest non-weather-related element facing farmers, farm managers, and policy makers. The new Spanish constitution of 1978 recognized 17 regions and established the same number of regional governments (autonomous communities, ACs) with a high degree of political autonomy and responsibility for the implementation of agricultural policy. This was despite the fact that only the Madrid-based central Spanish government negotiates at the EU level. This high degree of regional autonomy makes it very hard to reach agreements on a common national position.

History has also played an important role in forming Spain's agricultural structure with vast latifundia in the south, minifundia and family farms in the north. The work involved on the different types of farms varies greatly. Farms devoted to the production of cereals, olive oil, wine, or citrus fruits are larger and require very little work on the part of their managers/owners, who together with limited use of salaried workers often hire the services of third-party companies or cooperatives to carry out their agricultural activity, which they also combine with their own external employment. Conversely, most livestock farms, in particular dairy farms, are labor intensive and the family is often an important part of the workforce. Meanwhile, on vegetable and fruit farms the employment of seasonal workers is the norm (Gómez et al. 1997).

**Production**

Although Spain has historically been an agricultural country, agriculture is currently of little importance in the Spanish economy. The agricultural sector accounted for 2.1 percent of Spain's GDP in 2012, slightly above the EU-28 average (1.7 percent) but half the figure recorded in 1994 (4.2 percent). In the last decade the agricultural sector has lost 23 percent of its revenue, falling from €26.324 billion in 2003 to €24.337 billion in 2013, although in the last few years it has recovered somewhat from the €21.101 billion recorded in 2009.

Employment in the agricultural sector continues to fall year after year. In 2013 it represented a mere 4.4 percent of total employment, compared to 7.4 percent in 1995. This reduction has occurred in conjunction with a rise in wage-earning employment: 35 percent in 1995 and 58 percent in 2013. Conversely, Spain has a strong food and beverage industry. Agro-food activity as a whole (agriculture and food industry) constituted 5.6 percent of GDP in 2013 and 16 percent of exports (MAGRAMA 2014a). It is currently one of the main industrial sectors in respect of employment (in 2000 it employed 10.6 percent of the working population and in 2012 7 percent). The Spanish agro-food sector is a major player in the EU (ranked fifth in importance among the EU-15), generating 11 percent of the EU total. The agro-food sector constitutes a significant percentage of the foreign trade of goods (see the section entitled "The Internationalizational of Agriculture").

An important livestock sector exists. Livestock production accounts for 40 percent of final agricultural production. It consists of two highly distinct systems: the *extensive livestock system* and the *intensive livestock system*. The *extensive livestock system is* predominantly based in mountain or hilly areas, with herds of sheep (18 million animals), goats, and cattle. The *intensive livestock system* has been developed more recently, in tandem with the modernization of agriculture, with pigs (23 million), milk cows, poultry, rabbits, and calves, which are reared in intensive livestock facilities located close to the cities. During Franco's dictatorship (1939–1975), the main objectives of agricultural policy were self-sufficiency and low food prices. The development of an intensive livestock system for pork and poultry was a way of meeting growing demand for protein products, enabling the production of a cheap supply of them thanks to the large-scale import of feed grain (corn and soybeans). The economic boom of the 1960s led to a dramatic increase in livestock products such as eggs, milk, and meat.

Spain has very high levels of consumption of meat per capita (97 kg/capita/year), in particular pork and poultry. Pork and poultry farms are operated under integration contracts with feed companies. Beef production was developed as a result of major funding through the Common Agricultural Policy (CAP), via intervention prices and direct payments. Extensive production systems were supplemented by intensive cattle farms. Presently, intensive livestock production is concentrated in large farms by Spanish standards. Constituting 15 percent of total EU pork production, the Spanish pork sector is the second largest producer in the Union, ranked only below Germany. Spain is also the third largest poultry producer. This system is largely concentrated in nitrate vulnerable areas, generating well-known social and environmental problems. Labor productivity in Spanish agriculture is well below that of the main countries of our context in Europe (24.326 Euros per Annual Working Unit (AWU) in Spain compared with 36.894 in France, 38.728 in Belgium, and similar figures for other developed countries, even if the average labor productivity for the EU has diminished to 14.967 after the entrance of the Eastern countries).

**The Internationalization of Agriculture**

The internationalization of Spanish agriculture is one of the most visible changes to have affected the sector. In recent years, the international exchange of agricultural products has grown at a much faster rate than agricultural production. As a result, the degree of openness (the ratio of the sum of exports and imports to production) has doubled in the last 20 years.

This internationalization has led to the increased specialization of Spanish agricultural production (Table 10.1). It has strengthened its

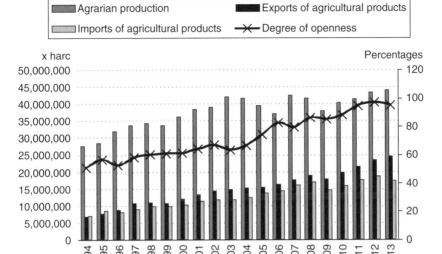

*Source:* Own elaboration with data from MAGRAMA (2014a).

*Figure 10.3   Degree of openness, 1994–2013*

*Table 10.1   Composition of Spanish agricultural production (averages for period)*

|                      | 1990–1994 (%) | 2008–2012 (%) |
|----------------------|---------------|---------------|
| Vegetables           | 16.9          | 19.1          |
| Fresh fruit          | 14.1          | 16.9          |
| Pork                 | 10.1          | 13.1          |
| Poultry              | 3.9           | 5.3           |
| Olive oil            | 4.1           | 4.8           |
| Wine                 | 2.2           | 2.6           |
| Other meat and eggs  | 16.5          | 11.7          |
| Cereals              | 11.4          | 10.4          |
| Milk                 | 7.1           | 6.6           |
| Others               | 13.7          | 9.5           |
| Total                | 100.0         | 100.0         |

*Source:*   MAGRAMA (2014a).

profile as a producer and exporter of fruit, olive oil, wine, and meat (mostly pork and chicken) while imports of vegetable oils, cereals, and dairy products, among others, have continued to grow.

The agro-food sector also presents interesting figures for external trade. In 2000 agricultural exports constituted 14.8 percent of the country's total exports, while agricultural imports accounted for 11.1 percent of total imports. In 2013 agricultural exports represented 16 percent of total exports, with Spain ranked as the seventh largest agricultural exporter in the world. The EU is the destination of 80 percent of Spain's agricultural products and the source of 50 percent of its imports (MAGRAMA 2014b). Given the impact on the evolution of the agricultural sector of agro-food companies in Spain, with capital from other European countries, it may be concluded that the Spanish agro-food system is a single branch of a European agro-food system.

**Farms: A Heterogeneous Structure of Farms and Organizational Models**

According to the data of the Agricultural Census, there are approximately one million farms in Spain (1,043,910) (INE 2009).[5] However, only 910,499 receive CAP subsidies and the farmers' unions (COAG and UPA) consider there to be only 300,000 active farming professionals. There is considerable disagreement over what constitutes a farm in terms of it operating as a significant productive unit. The reduction in the number of farms is a phenomenon that began with the onset of modernization and has continued ever since. According to data obtained from the agricultural censuses, there were 2 million farms in the 1960s, 1.3 million by the turn of the 21st century, and fewer than 1 million today. In the last six years the number of farms in Spain has fallen by almost 40 percent. This reduction has occurred in tandem with an increase in the average size of farms, growing from 22 to 38 hectares. However, over half the farms in the census occupy fewer than 5 hectares and their importance in terms of production is low except for those producing horticultural goods. Meanwhile, farms with over 100 hectares represent 5 percent of the total and have been growing in recent decades, leading to a distinctly dual structure of farms. Most farms operate on owned land, although 36 percent of farms of between 50 and 100 hectares operate on rented land.

The reduction in the number of farms and the jobs that they provide means that the relationship between agricultural production and the rural population is being steadily eroded. Rural life can no longer be based on agriculture. Agricultural modernization and economic development have set the Spanish rural environment on three different paths: some land is being abandoned; in other areas agricultural production has intensified thanks to irrigation, greenhouses, and intensive farms; and, finally, some areas are becoming peri-urban in nature with significant industrial, logistic, and tourism activity. This has placed the spotlight on what has been called rural development.

**Aging Farm Owners and Changing Work Systems**

More than half of farm managers are over 55 years old, while those under the age of 35 constitute just 5 percent. One out of every five farm managers is a woman, often due to the fact that spouses are wage earners off the farm, and so these women have formal ownership of the farms. Moreover, as explained above, work requirements and organizational models vary significantly according to the type of production. Part-time farming plays a very important role in the permanent crop sector. Agricultural service firms (for both cooperatives and farmers) are highly developed and take care of most tasks on farms devoted to cereals and permanent crops. The employment of temporary immigrant workers during peak periods is increasingly widespread.

Transformations in production and modern technology have changed the nature of the work of family farm owners, the owner often being the main (or indeed only) worker on the farm. The multipurpose worker, with a demanding load of physical work but a high degree of autonomy in immediate decision making, has now become the manager of a small company whose decisions are largely determined by three things: the demands of the buyer (in the case of agro-food chains and integration contracts), the advanced technology used on the farm (the large amount of capital invested in machinery and facilities demands their intensive use), and the need to manage the temporary workforce that is increasingly required.

**Restructuring under the Aegis of Private Capital**

National agricultural systems with strong public regulation started to weaken in the 1970s and the governance of the agricultural sector is now in the hands of the markets and large global agro-food corporations. The competition has become tougher for farms all over the world and only the strongest producers can keep up with the intensification of the use of capital now demanded by agricultural activity, which is bringing about a kind of "agricultural Darwinism." However, despite the prevailing neo-liberalism, the richest countries do not hesitate to prop up their agricultural systems with public funding. The regulations governing agricultural activity, put in place for health-related, ecological, or other reasons, are constantly multiplying. It might be argued that the sector is being simultaneously deregulated and bureaucratized.

## THE COMMON AGRICULTURAL POLICY (CAP)

The dynamic of Spanish agriculture since the country joined the EU in 1986 has been strongly conditioned by the Common Agricultural Policy (CAP), which in order to establish a common market for agricultural products, was introduced in 1962. The policy was very protective of the main products of Central Europe. When Spain joined the European Economic Community (EEC), the CAP was geared towards supporting prices under different sector-based schemes (Common Market Organizations). Integration into the European market was seen as an incentive to increase the production and yields of products whose intervention prices were higher than Spanish prices, such as milk, sugar, certain cereals, cotton, tobacco, and beef. The CAP was also designed to foster the modernization of farms through investment and opportunities for farming improvement. The production subsidy system encouraged the increase in the size of farms, leading to their transformation and the growth of their production, as well as facilitating the continued existence of a wide variety of farms.

Nevertheless, since the 1980s the CAP has been reformed to prevent any increase in the production of products with surpluses at the European level, through the imposition of quotas and other penalties. In the 1990s the process began by shifting CAP support from prices to direct payments to land, while keeping in place supply control tools. In most sectors direct or indirect restrictions were gradually imposed on supply, while many subsidies have been aimed at halting production growth, subsidizing the least productive agriculture. For Spanish agriculture, the continuous CAP reforms have simultaneously limited the increase of production and served as an important source of revenue. Spain received €5.83 billion in 2013, of which €4.532 billion was direct payments and almost €800 million was for rural development.

The impact of the CAP has been varied. While milk production has remained stable at the Spanish quota level (between 5 and 6 million metric tons per year), significant incentives were introduced in order to push out small producers from milk production, effective to such an extent that the number of milk producers has fallen by 85 percent, from 141,679 in 1994 to 21,101 in 2013 (MAGRAMA 2014a). Nevertheless, for the last 30 years Spain has had a continuous milk deficit. Milk imports are substantial and French firms currently control the Spanish milk industry. As regards grain, Spain's dependency has been significant since the 1960s. Soybeans and corn imports mainly came from the USA, and a special agreement to maintain these imports was signed when Spain joined the EEC. Today, grain deficits are still very significant and global grain companies such as Cargill and Bunge operate important logistics centers in Spain.

The sugar beet industry was dismantled and production was transferred to the more productive European countries, under the control of a small number of global firms. Spain has needed to import sugar for the last five years. Tobacco production was abandoned, and a small production of cotton is maintained due to a special clause included in the integration agreements of Greece and Spain. In respect of Mediterranean products, the impact of the CAP has been different. In the 1980s (during the nego- tiation process to join the European Community and over the first few years after joining), olive oil and wine production were discouraged and subsidies were provided for the uprooting of trees and vines, and for the abandonment of these crops. However, in the 1990s, increasing global demand for olive oil and the CAP support price system encouraged the development of new intensive and mechanized olive groves. Spain is the world's leading olive oil producer. Average production over the last five years has been 1.5 million tons, triple what it was when Spain joined the EEC. Exports have also tripled, rising from 260,000–270,000 tons in 1986– 1990 to 800,000–850,000 tons in the last few years. Cooperatives play a very important role at the first stage of oil production. However, bottling and distribution is in the hands of just a few companies. Disputes between companies to control the sector, and changes of ownership, are constant. In 2014 the main company was taken over by a British investment fund, while the second largest company is owned by a Portuguese group.

Spain has the largest vineyard area in the world. Traditionally, yields were very low and quality was very uneven. In the last two decades, new irrigated vineyards have been established, producing very good results in terms of both quality and quantity. Meanwhile, Spanish consumption is decreasing very sharply and exports are increasing, although the export price per liter is one of the lowest in the world. CAP measures for wine were mainly aimed at increasing wine quality and supporting the distilla- tion of low quality wine. Spain has been the main beneficiary of distilla- tion subsidies for a long time. Most wineries belong to Spanish companies, with few exceptions (Viladomiu and Rosell 2007). The concentration of the sector with large and multiregional companies took place in tandem with the start-up of new large-scale wine cellars producing very good quality wines. As a result, wine quality has greatly improved and Spain is now producing a wide variety of excellent wines. A strong regional labeling policy (*denominación de origen* – designation of origin) has been developed in recent years, and today there are 69 regional labels.

Since the turn of the 20th century, Spain has been an important supplier of fruit and vegetables to European markets. In recent decades, the production of vegetables under plastic and in greenhouses has increased greatly. New technologies make it possible to produce out of season and to supply the market before the arrival of their own home products. Spain has become increasingly specialized in vegetables (lettuces, cucumbers, artichokes, peppers, among others) and fruit (citrus fruits, peaches, pears). Certain areas, such as Almeria, have become year-round European fruit and vegetable suppliers as a result of highly intensive production systems and a temporary immigrant workforce. At the same time, some Spanish companies have taken the more labor intensive vegetable production (green beans, cherry tomatoes) abroad to North Africa and South America in order to guarantee an out-of-season fruit and vegetable supply. CAP support for fruit and vegetables is based on tariffs and quotas in order to limit imports from outside European countries.

The 1992 reform introduced direct payments to farmers decoupled from prices, and the CAP reform of 2003 decoupled direct payments from production. Today, farm production is no longer a requirement for receiving these payments. For Spain, the shift from price support to a decoupled subsidy system created significant confusion in terms of farm and farm union strategies, and has favored large landowners. The 2014 CAP reform is aimed at addressing some of the more notorious inconsistencies and at recovering the lost legitimacy of the CAP, limiting the payments to non-active farmers, and capping the total amount per beneficiary. The ultimate effects of these changes remain to be seen.

The existence of the CAP led to the abandonment of a national agricultural policy. This means that the only agricultural policy to have been implemented in Spain in the last 30 years is the CAP. In each round of negotiations, the Spanish government, through the agricultural authorities, pushes for measures to maximize Spain's slice of the European CAP budget, without pursuing any long-term strategy of its own for Spanish agriculture and Spanish rural areas.

## TOWARDS THE FUTURE: PENDING ISSUES

The Spanish agricultural sector today follows the model of modern Western agricultural systems but with the special characteristics of Mediterranean crops and wide-ranging conditions in terms of geography and social organization. Its various subsectors have extremely varied production conditions and markets, which explains the existence of such a diverse variety of business models and farms. In many subsectors, the model of concentrated production and large, dominant companies is still going strong and looks set to do so for the foreseeable future. It would appear that large production units devoted to intensive mass production, strongly integrated within agro-food systems and geared towards the world market, will be the main agents of the future dynamics. Nevertheless, this evolution may be slower in practice due to a series of elements which may produce somewhat different scenarios, such as: the resistance of family farms going out of business through important investments, their collective struggle to achieve a favorable agricultural policy, and the existence of specific market niches (as the peripheries of large cities), as well as increasing support received from population groups outside agriculture (ecological aspects, development of the territory, etc.).

However, it does not seem that these resistances are strong enough to countervail the main (concentration) trend because European countries have few advantages to outperform the most powerful agricultural countries under the intensive production model and the process may entail constant conflicts for Europe. On the one hand, it has already been explained above that agricultural modernization generates significant land-use conflicts in respect to the expansion of metropolitan and peri-urban areas devoted to residential and leisure uses. Furthermore, the reforms of the CAP have led to very important changes in terms of the instruments of intervention, but the intended objectives have remained in place and have even increased in number. The traditional objectives of food safety, price stability, and farm income improvement have been joined by food security, natural resource conservation, and climate change mitigation, among others. This long list of objectives has no hierarchical structure and the aforementioned intervention suffers from growing contradictions.

On the other hand, it should be pointed out that the model has negative environmental effects which society is finding more and more difficult to accept. European society is becoming increasingly urban in nature and many urban and environmental groups are voicing their opposition to assuming the environmental costs of intensive agrarian production models in their areas. Meanwhile, there are collectives exerting pressure in favor of powerful rural development while the reduction of the permanent workforce demanded by this production model is having a negative effect on large swathes of rural land in Europe that offer few possibilities of alternative activities. The intensive model is not conducive to maintaining a "living" rural environment in Europe.

In this context, the debate on the future of the European agricultural sector is open, and it is not proving easy to find the answers that European society needs to the big questions.

### How Much Agriculture?

This involves making a decision about self-sufficiency and European food sovereignty. Food needs must be met through imports and production must be defended as a strategic element; and decisions about this rest upon setting out the priorities of production systems, the relations between producers, agro-food companies and consumers, and the work absorption capacity of these systems in order to sustain a dynamic rural environment.

### What Type of Agriculture?

This involves determining what agricultural model and rural environment are desired, and analyzing whether the market niches detected today can form the basis of future agricultural development. That is, deciding whether the model can be based on local, organic, genetically modified organism-free (GMO-free) and regionally identified production, or whether it is necessary to press ahead with intensive production and the reduction in costs and prices that this entails.

### What Kind of Rural Environment is Desired?

A "living" rural environment requires economic and social activity. And the alternatives to farming for them are limited. The loss of agricultural activity and its knock-on effects have led to the depopulation of large areas. Diffuse industrialization and tourism have proved a fillip for growth in many regions, but there are huge areas in Spain and Europe that are hardly apt for this kind of development.

However, despite their importance in the dynamism of rural areas; farming and farming policies must not be burdened with the sole responsibility for these areas. Regional policy with the goal of regional balance will acquire much greater importance in the future. This policy should focus on the diversification of production and the improvement of quality of life, which will promote a higher level of public services in the rural environment. Agricultural development policy is geared towards a rural development model whose features vary significantly from those of agricultural policy.

### Who Should Assume the Costs of an Adequate Agricultural Model?

The CAP has been a permanent sign of Europe's willingness to support its agricultural sector, with a budget that remains very large despite the cutbacks implemented through reforms. Nonetheless, from the agreements reached at the various stages of the reform it is difficult to determine what agricultural model Europe really wants for the future. In fact, in the agreements reached to date much greater importance has been given to determining the distribution of the budget among member states than to establishing a road map for the future. The first two questions remain unanswered and the budget is now split according to acquired rights, constituting a source of rent for landowners.

In the future it will be necessary to consider the extent to which agriculture and rural development need broader financial support from the rest of society, given that it seems unlikely that the market will be sufficient to sustain farming, a dynamic rural environment, and the collective goods necessary for this purpose. How can investment be justified for a socially adequate rural environment that encompasses a very small percentage of the population? There can be no doubt that the wide-ranging social needs of a modern rural society will compete to achieve the necessary public support and that the arguments for safeguarding farming and the rural environment will have to be watertight in such a competitive scenario.

**Who Will Be the Active Agents of This Transformation?**

The social composition of rural society has altered substantially in the last few decades. The number of farmers is falling while the material basis is expanding, giving rise to mostly service-based activities (and to a lesser extent diffuse industrialization). The number of people using rural areas exclusively for residence purposes has risen and income from outside (wages, subsidies, pensions, public assets) is growing all the time. If agricultural and rural development is a social option and is partially supported by public funds, who will make the key social decisions? The inhabitants of these rural environments or the rest of society, which makes a significant contribution to supporting them? Without doubt, the farmers and inhabitants of rural areas must take center stage in this process, but it must also involve the rest of society. It is likely that only the share of the national and EU budgets will not be enough to cover these demands and, as such, it seems that in the future new ways will have to be considered of making collective (and therefore political) decisions in order for societies to meet the many requirements on the horizon.

## CONCLUSION

A modern, economically efficient and socially satisfactory agricultural model cannot be the spontaneous result of market forces; it must be generated by an economic, social, and political framework. The question of the survival of agricultural systems and the rural environment in the future must be addressed not only through market power but also through national and global political organizations (both agricultural and general). Only a positive response to these issues will lead to an agricultural model that provides a food supply for the entire population, provides a decent quality of living for all participants (farmers and farm workers), and enables the efficient and harmonious use of its components (natural resources, especially land, means of production and investment), and safeguards the environment and landscape. At the same time, only by incorporating these considerations into the framework of a transformed global agricultural system will it be possible to cooperate and strive towards achieving a fairer and more efficient agricultural model for everyone all over the world.

## NOTES

1. For a more exhaustive analysis of the evolution of Spanish agriculture in recent decades, see the works listed in the references.
2. This includes both agricultural and livestock farming.
3. In the 1960s and 1970s the debate on modernization was intense in academic circles. Good references that describe this process are found in Naredo (1971) and Leal et al. (1975).
4. The integration of Spanish agriculture into the agro-industrial system has been analyzed by Clar (2009), Fenollar (1978), Soldevila (2008), and Viladomiu (1985).
5. There is widespread acceptance that the census greatly overestimates the number of farms, constituting a cadastre (register of land ownership) rather than a register of productive companies. The strong discrepancy between the figures of the census and those of the farmers' unions corroborate this view.

## REFERENCES

Clar, E. 2009. "La Soberanía del Productor: Industrias del Complejo Pienso-Ganadero e Implantación del Modelo de Consumo Fordista en España: 1960–1975." Pp. 99–141 in L. German, R. Hernández, and J. Moreno (eds.) *Economía Alimentaria en España Durante el Siglo XX*. Madrid: Ministerio de Medio Ambiente y Medio Rural y Marino.
Cussó, X. and R. Garrabou. 2009. "Dieta Mediterránea y Transición Nutricional en España." Pp. 25–62 in L. German, R. Hernández, and J. Moreno (eds.) *Economía Alimentaria en España Durante el Siglo XX*. Madrid: Ministerio de Medio Ambiente y Medio Rural y Marino.
FAOSTAT. 2014. FAOSTAT Database (http://faostat3.fao.org/home/E).
Fenollar, J. 1978. *La Formación de la Agroindustria en España, 1960–1970: Una Aproximación Aausal y Regional*. Madrid: Servicio de Publicaciones Agrarias, Ministerio de Agricultura.
Gómez, C., C. González, and J. Jesús. 1997. *Agricultura y Sociedad en la España Contemporánea*. Madrid: Centro de Investigaciones Sociológicas.
INE (Instituto Nacional de Estadística). 2009. *Censo Agrario*. Madrid: INE.

Leal, J.L., J. Leguina, J.M. Naredo, and L. Tarrafeta. 1975. *La Agricultura en el Desarrollo Capitalista Español (1940–1970)*. Madrid: Siglo XXI.

MAGRAMA (Ministerio de Agricultura, Alimentación y Medio Ambiente). 2014a. *Cuentas Económicas de la Agricultura. Resultados Nacionales (serie histórica 1990–2013)*. Enero. Madrid: MAGRAMA.

MAGRAMA (Ministerio de Agricultura, Alimentación y Medio Ambiente). 2014b. *El Comercio Exterior Agroalimentario y Pesquero: Marzo 2014*. Análisis del Comercio Exterior. Mayo. Madrid: MAGRAMA.

Naredo, J.M. 1971. *La Evolución de la Agricultura en España. Desarrollo Capitalista y Crisis de las Formas de Producción Tradicionales*. Barcelona: Estela.

Soldevila, M.V. 2008. "El Impacto de los Costes Medioambientales en la Cadena de Porcino. El Caso de Catalunya." Unpublished doctoral thesis. University of Barcelona. Barcelona, Spain.

Viladomiu, L. 1985. *La Insercion de España en el Complejo Soja-Mundial*. Madrid: Servicio de Publicaciones Agrarias, Ministerio de Agricultura.

Viladomiu, L. and J. Rosell. 2007. "La Internacionalización en el Sector Vitivinícola." Pp. 25–62 in M. Etxezarreta (ed.) *La Globalización en los Sectores Agroalimentarios Españoles*. Madrid: Ministerio de Agricultura, Pesca y Alimentación.

# PART II

# SELECTED THEMES OF THE INTERNATIONAL POLITICAL ECONOMY OF AGRICULTURE AND FOOD

# 11. The political economy of agri-food: Supermarkets
*Geoffrey Lawrence and Jane Dixon*

## INTRODUCTION: THE RISE AND RISE OF SUPERMARKETS[1]

Since antiquity, food has been traded through bartering and money-based exchanges, with village marketplaces providing the mechanism for interactions and physical transactions. Industrialization, colonization and – more recently – agricultural "modernization" and globalization have changed relations between food providers and food consumers. These social forces have, importantly, resulted in the movement of people from the land to the cities and with it, the need to support burgeoning urban-based populations with farm-based goods including vegetables, milk, bread and meat. Whether it was in the industrializing cities of Paris or London, the 1850s' goldfields of California or Australia, or the twentieth century back-street slums of colonized nations like India, Kenya or Colombia, small grocery stores proliferated to meet consumer demand. In general terms, such stores were owner-operated and were reliant, for their economic reproduction, on the purchase of fresh produce, along with an array of simply manufactured food products (cheeses, preserved meats, canned vegetables) which were then on-sold to consumers at a higher cost than the original purchase.

In Europe, the UK, US, Canada, Australia, New Zealand, South Africa and a host of other nations, family-owned-and-operated grocery stores (known as "mom and pop" stores in the US) provided a regular supply of foods for urban dwellers. In the typical grocery store of the mid-1850s to the 1920s most food was stored as bulk items and the counter stood between customers and the products they wished to purchase. The grocers had very little influence over the ways goods on their shelves were produced, transported and packaged (Konefal, Bain, Mascarenhas and Busch 2007), and their role, behind the counter, was to act as both the purveyor and cashier. This model was soon to change. In 1916 Clarence Saunders introduced self-service in his "Piggly Wiggly" store in Memphis, Tennessee. Customers were able to walk through the store, rather than line up at a counter, allowing them to inspect the goods they wished to purchase. They then moved to a point of exit – the now familiar "checkout" – where they made payment (Shaw, Curth and Alexander 2004).

The first "supermarket" followed soon after. In 1930 in Queens, New York, Michael Cullen opened the first of many King Kullen stores. The principle (and indeed the firm's slogan) was "pile it high: sell it low" – making profits from moving large volumes, but at relatively thin margins (King Kullen 2006; Rodale Institute 2005). Mass merchandising combined with self-service as the two basic ingredients for supermarket expansion but, following the Second World War, additional stimulus was provided by suburbanization, increased motor-vehicle ownership and growing consumer affluence (Lawrence and Burch 2007). Public popularity engendered economic success and the supermarket model was quickly adopted in most countries throughout the developed world. Supermarkets began to exhibit a number of characteristics, including high-volume through-put at relatively low prices; branded, individually packaged, products, often in the tens of thousands per store; self-service; and ownership by large, national (and now international) corporations – the so-called food "chains" (Konefal et al. 2007:271; Lawrence and Burch 2007:3).

This became a recipe for success and, by the 1950s, some 35 percent of all food sales in the US were secured by the supermarket sector, jumping to 70 percent by 1960. In the same decade the number of stores doubled from 14,000 to 33,000 (Progressive Grocer 2012). But these were small stores in comparison with their equivalents today – where a supermarket outlet is defined as a store earning more than US$2 million in annual sales. There are currently some 37,000 stores in the US earning over and above this amount, with supermarket expansion having been at the expense of the smaller independent retailers. The UK witnessed the same trend where, from 1961–1997, some 116,000 independent retailers dropped to 21,000 (Blythman 2005:4, 6). In 1960 the small independent retailers in the UK held a 60 percent share of the food retail market but by 2000 that had fallen to 6 percent, with the supermarket share having grown to 88 percent (Corporate Watch 2014).

In recent times, it has been the global expansion of the supermarket sector that has been of great significance. The supermarket share of retail sales in regions such as central Europe, South America and Asia (excluding China) grew from around 10 percent in the 1990s to between 30 and 50 percent a decade later (McCullough, Pingali and Stamoulis 2008:13). The entry of supermarket chains in Asia is said to be "cannibalizing" local retail outlets, while supermarket growth in China is set to burgeon as both domestic and foreign firms grow in number and compete for customers (Gardner 2013; Young 2012). The rapid supermarket penetration of "traditional" food markets throughout Asia and Latin America has resulted in the widespread displacement of small retailers, wet-market traders and small-scale wholesalers – most finding it difficult to establish new livelihood options (Timmer 2008).

In 2013, the world's top five supermarket chains were:

- Wal-Mart Stores – US headquarters, global reach, 10,851 stores, US$469 billion sales
- Tesco – UK headquarters, global reach, 6,989 stores, US$103 billion sales
- Carrefour – French headquarters, global reach, 10,380 stores, US$99 billion sales
- Costco – US headquarters, global reach, 608 stores, US$97 billion sales
- Kroger Company – US headquarters, US only, 3,566 stores, US$96 billion sales (Supermarket News 2014).

Like most large corporations, all the major supermarket chains (except Kroger) have "global reach," with stores in locations as varied as Australia, Bulgaria, China, Columbia, Egypt, Malawi, Thailand, Turkey and Vietnam. The growth of Wal-Mart, which commenced operations in the early 1960s, has been spectacular. Wal-Mart captured its dominant global position by introducing innovations along the supply chain, including moving responsibilities (and costs) to other actors. It has, for example, provided its suppliers with sales information and, in turn, requires them to be responsible for guaranteeing product arrival on a just-in-time basis to its stores. In this way products spend shorter periods in warehouses, thus reducing costs (Konefal et al. 2007:274). Global expansion and scale of operation has also provided opportunities for the sourcing of cheaper consumer items. As profits for the larger chains grew, so competitors were forced to consolidate their activities or remain uncompetitive and eventually leave the industry.

This economic concentration continues apace. The sum of the market share of the top four or five companies in any industry is called the "concentration ratio." If 20 percent of the market is held by the top four or five companies the market is said to be concentrated, at 40 percent it is highly concentrated and at 60 percent or above it is significantly distorted (Carolan 2013:102). Yet, throughout the world, the top five supermarkets in most countries exhibit extraordinarily high levels of concentration. In Australia they control some 99 percent of sales, while in Sweden it is 91 percent, Ireland 83 percent, France 71 percent, the UK 71 percent and the US 60 percent (Carolan 2013:112). Importantly, there are often only one or two supermarkets operating in villages and towns, creating local dependence at the same time as stifling competition (Rees 2011). There is also evidence that the food-based supermarkets are, themselves, coming under pressure from the big box stores like Wal-Mart and Costco. These so-called hypermarkets ("superstores" combining a supermarket and department store under one roof) have even greater purchasing power than the supermarkets and, in the case of Wal-Mart, vociferously fight attempts at unionization as a means of containing wages. Their continuing attraction, however, is that they provide customers with the convenience of shopping in a single location (Rodale Institute 2005). It must be stated that there is not one "model" for supermarket success. While many super-market chains adopt the high-volume/low-margin approach, a firm like Costco pays its staff well and provides a different customer experience. Part of Costco's success has been to create a "treasure-hunt"-style experience for its customers: the stores rarely advertise and have a constantly changing inventory (including items as varied as diamond rings and caskets) which helps to create a "discount-chic allure," inducing people to actually spend more than they had intended (CNBC 2014).

With economic concentration comes the power to dictate the rules of engagement and, as will be discussed below, supermarkets have used their power to transform relations with producers, suppliers and consumers.

## SUPERMARKET POWER IN AGRI-FOOD SUPPLY CHAINS

In an effort to secure increased profits, supermarkets have restructured agri-food supply chains. This has occurred in a number of ways. While they once sourced products through a number of brokers, who engaged with a variety of clients, they now appoint just one broker and/or source the products themselves (Konefal et al. 2007). Furthermore, their size allows them to purchase large volumes and they usually do so by negotiating with increasingly large suppliers, which provides economies of scale for both parties. Through such bulk purchasing practices, lower per unit prices can be achieved, leading to more competitively priced goods which, in turn, can help to increase sales. It is a practice in the industry for the supermarkets to seek even lower prices in subsequent negotiations with suppliers – a manifestation of so-called oligopsony power where there are few buyers but many sellers (Fuchs, Kalfagianni and Arentsen 2009). Companies like Kroger and Wal-Mart completely avoid dealing with the wholesale sector and negotiate directly with processing firms, using their considerable power to obtain the lowest prices. The processing firms, in turn, squeeze the farmers, opening up a considerable gap between what farmers are paid and the price of food in the supermarket (Carolan 2013). Such tactics can and do deliver "cheap" food to western customers even if, as noted earlier, the smaller farmers and suppliers are marginalized or driven out of business (Competition Commission 2000; McMichael and Friedmann 2007; Young 2012).

Another sourcing strategy is to seek cheaper products from overseas locations. Such global sourcing – particularly of fresh fruit and vegetables – does provide opportunities for farmers in developing countries to enter global circuits of capital and thereby to obtain prices higher than they might have achieved in the domestic market (Vorley, Fearne and Ray 2007). For the supermarket, the purchase of out-of-season food is a major draw-card for consumers. However, in relation to some food products (such as canned fruits and vegetables), overseas sourcing is not about providing out-of-season foods. It is about undercutting domestic suppliers, which can mean local growers will have their income reduced, become increasingly indebted to banks, or be forced from the industry, with local rural communities suffering accordingly (Dixon and Isaacs 2013; Richards, Bjorkhaug, Lawrence and Hickman 2013). The exploitation of migrant farmworkers is a significant component of the cheap sourcing of fresh fruits and vegetables. According to Holmes (2013), Mexican migrant farmworkers in the US are treated inhumanely, dealing on a day-to-day basis not only with backbreaking work, but also with racism, pesticide poisoning, work insecurity and an accident-prone environment. Similarly, Gertel and Sippel (2014) document the exploitation of farmworkers in the Mediterranean. They argue that insecure seasonal labor conditions are a prerequisite for profit-making in industrial agriculture and that to supply the supermarkets of Europe with fresh fruit and vegetables (especially out-of-season), migrant workers experience emotional deprivation together with fear, stress, loneliness and economic servitude. The book provides compelling evidence that while "eating fresh" might be a goal for a more healthy society – with supermarkets being the vehicles delivering an array of nutritious, fresh foods to grateful customers – a more nuanced examination of the spatio-temporal dynamics of agri-food globalization reveals an underside of considerable social disadvantage for migrant farmworkers (Gertel and Sippel 2014).

Own branding or "private labeling" has been another means of strengthening the position of supermarkets over other food suppliers. Supermarkets have traditionally stocked the easily recognized products of the food processing "giants" – Nestlé, Heinz, Nabisco, Campbell's, Unilever and so forth. Since the mid-1990s, however, firms in the retail sector recognized that profits could be made from packaging products under their own brands. Initially, own brands were designed to provide customers with cheaper alternatives to the more-recognized branded items (Fox and Vorley 2004). They were generally considered to be "generic" products, inferior in quality to the branded products available on the supermarket shelves (Lawrence and Burch 2007). This is no longer the case. It is the supermarkets which own shelf space and can decide on what products they offer to consumers and where those products are placed on the shelf. They also have enormous bargaining power in sourcing processed goods. Supermarkets began negotiating with processors to develop high-quality grocery items, stocking own brand products that not only competed on price, but also on quality (Busch and Bain 2004; Konefal et al. 2007). They also began to distinguish their private label products on the basis of attributes desired by consumers – "healthy," "natural" and "organic" (Konefal et al. 2007:278). Clearly, if consumers want to purchase own brand products they must enter the supermarket that sells them – something that can help to engender consumer loyalty.

The emergence of private standards has accompanied the growth in own brand, private, labels. Several decades ago most western governments were heavily involved in regulating food safety. Government rules and laws dictated the acceptable standards for foods and various state departments employed inspectors to police those standards. Since that time, and in the context of neoliberal policies which have sought to limit state control of private enterprise, supermarkets have been developing and imposing their own standards which are often higher than those enforced by the state. The supermarkets do this for two main reasons: first, to help to ensure that their products are of the highest quality for consumers and, second, to gain increased control over the governance of the food chain (Burch, Dixon and Lawrence 2013; Clapp and Fuchs 2009; Davey and Richards 2013). Davey and Richards (2013) highlight the spread of "audit cultures" accompanying private standards, creating additional economic burdens for suppliers. According to Thompson and Lockie (2013), private standards are best understood as a "technology of power," providing a system of discipline for suppliers. The operationalization of private standards on the farm is similar to Foucault's "panopticon" – in this case enforcing a supermarket-inspired regime of self-discipline, even at times when the farmer is not undergoing an audit. Busch (2014:42) describes the "explosion" of private standards as a new form of food governance – with individual supermarkets, groups of supermarkets, industry associations and non-governmental organizations (NGOs) all creating standards for actors along agri-food chains. Importantly, he observes that these standards are often in tension with one another, are confusing to producers and consumers alike, and are developed and enacted with only limited reference to democratic processes (Busch 2014:42). For Burch, Dixon and Lawrence (2013:219):

the dominant position of the supermarkets combined with the private nature of auditing, means that the retailers are in a virtually unassailable position to impose their will on the suppliers. And this "forced compliance" is one driving the food industry towards a structure of few retailers dealing with increasingly fewer (compliant) suppliers.

Supermarkets have also employed a variety of other tactics to defray costs and improve profits including forcing suppliers to pay for the right to stock the supermarket's shelves; demanding compensation from suppliers if profits from the sales of items is less than anticipated; requiring suppliers to re-purchase any unsold items; compelling suppliers to pay for product promotions; delaying payments to suppliers; and over ordering items at a discounted "promotional" price and then later selling them at a higher retail price (Lawrence and Burch 2007; Towill 2005). Their position of power elicits often begrudging conformity and acceptance from those with whom they deal.

## SUPERMARKETS – THE NEW FOOD AUTHORITIES

Over the past 80 years, supermarkets have been mobilizing the attributes which fulfill the sociological notion of an authority, that is a social actor which "is always a superior of some kind, to be obeyed in some cases, in others to be followed, consulted, attended to, deferred to, or conformed to" (Watt 1982:7). For Weber (1947), there were three bases for becoming an authority. Traditional authorities occupied social status positions (often inherited), where the nature of command was based in unquestioned ethical superiority. Rational-legal authorities arose to enact socially agreed-upon or sanctioned rules and laws, which could be enforced through physical force. Charismatic authorities were individuals perceived to possess rare qualities which others admired.

From the outset, the major supermarket chains were headed by charismatic individuals (for example, F.W. Woolworth and John Sainsbury). They were early adopters of public relations techniques and used mass media channels to create and communicate an excitement about the new retail format. However, persuading householders that their approach to food provisioning was superior entailed having them abandon the traditional authority of family heads as food provisioners and to embrace a mode of shopping suited to the modernizing times where people were becoming freed from tightly bound cultural norms and assumptions about a singular and correct way to provide food for the household. Such was their success in forging trust relations with the public, as Friedberg (2007) has noted, government-auspiced self-regulation processes came to afford supermarkets the status of de facto policymakers within the food system. Through the usurpation of particular forms of traditional authority and the practice of rational-legal authority, supermarket retail chains were able to consolidate their position as greatly valued modern social institutions (Dixon 2007).

With the more recent advent of a highly concentrated supermarket sector throughout the world, along with fierce competition between firms, each chain has had to work diligently to build loyalty to its particular "brand." Numerous devices have been employed: two-for-one specials; taking a loss on popular products (the "loss leader" approach); shopper docket schemes; tailoring a product range to reflect an ethnic neighborhood or the passage of a significant event (Jewish Passover); cross-promotional alliances with medically aligned authorities, like dieticians; the sale of specialist prepared meals for dieters and the time-poor; and, as suggested earlier, the evolution of "own brand" products.

In addition to their in-store loyalty strategies, supermarkets have been reaching out to support community services and facilities in the rural and suburban areas where they are located. In this regard they operate as key local organizations providing small sums of money to junior athletics, hosting sausage-sizzle fundraisers for service clubs and offering a community noticeboard. The symbolic forging of partnerships is essentially a public relations exercise. In large part, it has arisen because of a widespread consumer backlash towards supermarket-sourcing of imported produce as well as exploitative supply chain arrangements (see, for example, Isaacs and Dixon in press).

## THE POLITICAL ECONOMY OF SUPERMARKET EXPANSION

The current phase of capitalist development is one firmly embracing processes of globalization, neoliberalism and financialization – all of which are affecting the manner in which food is grown, distributed and sold (Bonanno 2014; Burch and Lawrence 2013; Fairbairn this volume). As an ideology, neoliberalism lauds the freedom of the individual and embraces entrepreneurship. It proposes that free markets and minimal intervention by the state in economic matters will create a better world for all (Iba and Sakamoto 2014). Yet, in its globalized form, neoliberalism is viewed as having curbed democratic processes, supported the economic and political agendas of the rich and super-rich, concentrated and centralized capital, and promoted individualistic and largely ineffectual "self-help" solutions to a wide range of structural problems (Bonanno 2014). Importantly, the role of the state has been, first, to remove regulation deemed to be standing in the way of expanded capital accumulation and, second, to re-regulate in a manner favorable to transnational capital (the so-called "rolling back" of regulations since the 1980s and the subsequent "rolling out" of pro-corporate regulations and legislation from the 1990s [Peck and Tickell 2002]).

Food regime theorists have proposed that there have been two regimes governing capitalist-based food systems – a British-centric settler-nation "extensive" regime that existed from the late 1800s to the 1930s and a US-centric "intensive," food regime based on the industrialization of agriculture and the creation of "durable," manufactured, foods which lasted from the 1950s to the 1970s (McMichael 2013:5–6). McMichael (2005; 2013) and others (Burch and Lawrence 2009; Friedmann 2005; Otero 2014) have posited the emergence of a third food regime variously described as a corporate-environmental food regime, neoliberal food regime or financialized food regime. While its contours remain indeterminate, some features have been identified: the global integration of food supply chains, with the control of those chains having passed from food manufacturers to supermarkets; year-round availability of fresh foods; the "greening" of supermarkets – including a "quality turn" that is both forcing food retailers to be more conscious of food quality and safety issues, as well as creating new "spaces" for the emergence of local alternative food networks; the entrenchment of World Trade Organization (WTO) free-market principles; and the financialization of the entire agri-food system (Burch and Lawrence 2009; Burch and Lawrence 2013; Carolan 2011; Fairbairn this volume; McMichael 2013; Oosterveer and Sonnenfeld 2012).

Financialization is of particular significance in the emerging third food regime. The finance sector, which traditionally eschewed investment in land, has identified opportunities for speculation as food-producing resources such as prime farmland and water become scarce. Merchant banks have been purchasing farmlands both to take advantage of rising food prices and to achieve profits from speculation (Burch and Lawrence 2009). Sovereign wealth funds are investing in farmlands abroad not only to repatriate foods (especially in relation to oil-rich but land-poor countries in the Middle East) but also to produce biofuels (Burch and Lawrence 2009; McMichael 2013). According to McMichael (2013:117) "the general accumulation crisis, expressed in the conjunction of food, energy and financial crises, has resulted in international capital markets gravitating towards agriculture as a relatively safe investment haven for the relatively long-term, triggering the 'global land grab.'" Financialization is firmly embedded within neoliberalism and results in land, agri-food industries, and supermarkets being further integrated into financial circuits where profits can be generated via financial trading (Burch and Lawrence 2013; McMichael 2013).

Private equity firms and hedge funds have been involved in the purchase (often followed by asset stripping) of food manufacturers and retailers, as a means of delivering "shareholder value" to owners (Burch and Lawrence 2009; Fairbairn 2014).

Under neoliberal globalization, opportunities have arisen for the supermarket sector to expand its economic operations and influence. Supermarkets are now involved in insurance and banking with Tesco Bank, launched in 2009, having become one of the fastest growing finance providers in Europe (Tescopoly 2014). Supermarkets own service stations, liquor outlets and sell books, clothing, furniture and electronics. In 2013 Tesco launched its own personal computer – the "Hudl" (CEOWorld Magazine 2014). In Australia, Canada and the US shopper dockets from supermarkets such as Coles, Woolworths and Costco provide access to discounted petrol as part of "retail bundling" (Dixon 2007; Halsey 2013).

Some years ago, Wrigley and Lowe (1996) claimed that producer–consumer relations were becoming increasingly mediated by retail capital, with supermarkets being exemplars in this regard. Drawing on Bourdieu's (1984) theory of capital, it becomes clear that supermarkets operate as mediators or, more precisely, cultural economy actors, through accumulating and strategically using different forms of capital (economic, cultural, social and symbolic) so as to consolidate and reproduce their legitimacy in food systems and throughout society. Not only do supermarkets produce and sell goods for a profit, they also sell ways of living based upon those goods. To this end, supermarket firms must invest economic capital, employing armies of cultural intermediaries whose functions include consumer research to establish product ranges; devising campaigns to modify entrenched ways of living (for example, a move away from home cooking to home-meal replacement heat-and-serve); enrolment of celebrity chefs and other high-profile supporters to lend an aura of excitement and charisma; development of loyalty programs; and lobbying regulators and managing public opinion especially in periods of conflict with competition watchdogs and farmers (Burch, Lawrence and Hattersley 2013; Dixon 2007). Their investment in cultural capital (information, tastes, practices) and social capital (resources based on social networks and group membership, as in loyalty programs) is as important to their ongoing survival as is investment in cool chain technologies and other socio-technical systems which underpin the efficiency and safety of their supply chains. These forms of colonization of "the lifeworld," and hence the sphere of social reproduction, are made possible when cultural production becomes incorporated into the circuit of capital. For Harvey

(1996), there are "critical" cultural moments – discourse/language, power, beliefs/values/desires and institutions/rituals – which capital can mobilize and adapt. As neoliberal institutions, supermarkets have become adept at "economizing" spheres of life that were not, hitherto, part of the "economic calculation" (Lemke 2001).

While largely hegemonic, the supermarketization of food systems, described above, does not occur smoothly. According to food regimes analysis, food systems become stabilized through a constellation of forces across the spheres of production, consumption and state regulation (Friedmann and McMichael 1989). But they can be, and are, disrupted. Pockets of resistance are at work in an effort to insert greater political sovereignty into the food system (Johnston, Biro and MacKendrick 2009). For Friedmann (2005) and Campbell (2009) the resistance to food system corporatization and supermarketization is coming primarily from environmental movements and the environment itself, as the industrial model of agriculture on which supermarkets are based becomes less tenable (Carolan 2011; Weis 2013). This is discussed below.

## GROWING CONCERNS ABOUT GLOBAL SUPERMAKETIZATION

Supermarkets purchase foods from distant locations to satisfy the year-round demands for a variety of foods by western consumers. The so-called food miles required to transport food over vast distances both depletes energy and creates greenhouse gases (Lang, Barling and Caraher 2009). Although supermarkets have placed increasingly stringent environmental requirements on farmers supplying them, the very nature of much of industrial farm production (monocropping and the factory farming of animals in concentrated animal-feeding operations [CAFOs]) generates poor environmental outcomes including: pollution of streams and rivers with animal waste and toxic agri-chemicals; soil degradation; genetic pollution; biodiversity loss; and increased methane (greenhouse gas) production (Weis 2013). In CAFOs, environmental contaminants are responsible for a range of respiratory diseases affecting at least 25 percent of all workers (Carolan 2013:115). There are also many concerns raised about the welfare of animals, with practices such as de-beaking, toe-cutting, tail-docking and castration often performed in the absence of anesthetics (Oosterveer and Sonnenfeld 2012; Weis 2013:121).

While the major supermarkets have been adept at responding to the environmental challenge, they face other criticisms. First, they have been accused of cynically employing greenwashing techniques, another form of cultural capital-raising, which does little to address the major challenge of discouraging forms of hyper-consumption when current consumption patterns are unsustainable (Dixon and Banwell 2012). Second, they are contributing to the bifurcation of the food market which, in turn, reproduces existing forms of social stratification: environmentally oriented products are simply more expensive for consumers to purchase (Friedmann 2005). This particular contradiction of supermarketization arises because supermarkets have become hostage to the very basis of their original and ongoing success – the allure of product choice at a low price.

The issue of food waste has also drawn heavy criticism (Evans, Campbell and Murcott 2013). Globally, it is estimated that between 30 and 50 percent of all food is wasted (Government Office for Science 2011:93). While a good deal of this occurs in countries which have little capacity for on-farm food storage and which lack refrigeration, there is also a great deal lost in the supermarket-dominated food system of the developed nations (Carolan 2011; Evans, Campbell and Murcott 2013). The latter takes many forms. The first is the disposal, by farmers, of fresh fruit and vegetables deemed unacceptable for supermarket shelves – largely on the grounds that these foods do not meet aesthetic (cosmetic) standards (Gunders 2012). Farmers can feed some of this waste to animals but a considerable amount is also dumped. The second is the discarding of foods that have passed their designated use-by dates. Supermarkets now regularly provide charities with such foods for distribution to the poor and homeless and supply waste management firms with products to be converted into energy generation (Edwards and Mercer 2013) but large quantities still find their way into landfill, producing greenhouse gas emissions (Government Office for Science 2011; Gunders 2012). The third aspect of supermarket waste relates to packaging. Packaging is a marketing device employed by food manufacturers to differentiate products, making them appealing to consumers and fostering brand loyalty (Hawkins 2013). Of course, packaging helps protect food against contamination and spoilage, thereby extending the life of food – the packaging of food in plastic, glass, styrofoam, paper and cardboard has been the means of achieving this. Yet, as Hawkins (2013:69–70) has argued, while packaging foods might allow them to be protected (and not wasted), the "afterlife" of the packaging contributes to major waste-management problems. Packaging is the largest component of household waste and plastic containers, in particular, are non-biodegradable and have been implicated in widespread environmental pollution (Hawkins 2013:76).

Another major concern is that of population health. Among the important new strands of public health thinking is the extent to which industrial/corporate food systems can be health promoting. At present, their focus is on calorific content through cheap processed foods rather than the delivery of affordable dietary-diversity foods based on a wide array of nutritional qualities (Monteiro and Cannon 2012). "Cheap food" is a relative notion, which varies across and within countries, but generally refers to the proportion of household income spent on various foods. As supermarkets displace fresh markets, consumers become exposed to larger volumes of cheaper processed foods and more expensive fresh foods (Banwell, Dixon, Seubsman, Pangsap, Kelly and Sleigh 2012; Reardon, Henson and Gulati 2010). As a result, poorer populations are at risk of the phenomenon of being obese at the same time that they are undernourished in micro-nutrient terms (Wahlqvist, McKay, Chang and Chiu 2012). The health, social and economic consequences associated with "obesogenic" diets are profound (Friel and Lichacz 2010).

The risks and benefits of cheap food are not simply experienced at the household level. The process of national development which moves a country from peasant or agrarian societies to industrial and service sector economies is based on the availability of cheap calories (Friedmann and McMichael 1989; McMichael and Friedmann 2007; Timmer 2008). Cheap food allows the wages of factory and service sector workers to remain low, thereby increasing company profitability and investment in new ventures which, in turn, can generate growth in employment and national revenues. However, national development based on cheap calories is an approach which overlooks the needs of the global rural population (three billion people), 70 percent of whom work in agriculture. While agricultural households benefit financially from cheap food, they also need to derive decent/fair incomes from their agricultural activity in order to stay in farming and not flood into cities to become the urban poor. And, as suggested earlier, favoring cheap, processed, foods as central to the national food supply also ignores the environmental externalities generated by industrial chains geared only to greater efficiencies and economies of scale (Ingram, Ericksen and Liverman 2010).

## DISCUSSION AND CONCLUSION: THE FUTURE OF SUPERMARKETS

There is little doubt that consumers are attracted to supermarkets because of the product choices available, the lower prices (when compared to small retailers) and the convenience of "one stop" shopping (Gardner 2013). However, as has been argued above, the supermarketization of the food supply system can be seen to have negative impacts on the environment, on farmers and farmworkers, and on consumers.

Within the growing public health ecology movement, there are increasing calls for "healthy agriculture for a healthy population" (Dangour, Green, Hasler, Rushton, Shankar and Waage 2012; McMichael, Powles, Butler and Uauy 2007; Wahlqvist et al. 2012). This paradigmatic shift entails a move away from fossil-fuel-based inputs, monocultures, corporate control over inputs and pricing and a move towards agro-ecology principles, dietary variety and "fair trade" rather than "free trade." It entails food supplies produced in accordance with sustainable biophysical resources (Lang et al. 2009).

If supermarkets are serious about the public health outcomes of their activities they would agree to be independently audited to demonstrate that they, along with their suppliers, are promoting sustainability and wasting less. They would also encourage consumers to shop differently, which, in many cases, would mean recommending reductions in the consumption of processed foods and red meat (in particular). They would also have to incorporate the costs of the environmental resources used in commodity production and transport into their pricing structures, meaning that food prices would rise. However unlikely this type of response, it would constitute a potentially sustainable supermarket revolution!

In the meantime, the antipathy for supermarkets among cosmopolitan citizens who view shopping as an ethical practice appears to be growing. For affluent, educated shoppers who value the environment, animal welfare and fair trade, the support for alternative food systems appears to be gaining in importance (Dowler, Kneafsey, Cox and Holloway 2009). However, there is a contradiction, here, in these actions: while non-supermarket shoppers take pressure off the industrial food supply chain and provide incomes for greater numbers of small producers, their stance also takes pressure off supermarkets to change their procurement and retailing approaches – given the seemingly insatiable appetite for low-cost supermarket offerings by growing low-income populations.

The issue of supermarket regulation will not disappear, but greater clarity is needed regarding what aspects of supermarketization require regulation. At the global level, food standard harmonization has arisen in a context of the expansion of own brand products, with supermarkets joining food processors in actively supporting international food standards on additives and ingredients in order to be able to trade their products across national borders (Henson and Humphery 2009). Simultaneously, nations concerned about diet-related disease can be expected to become more active in international standard-setting fora, such as the World Health Organization's *Codex Alimentarius*, regarding salt, trans-fats and antibiotic use in foods. Foreign direct investment (FDI) in supermarkets has grown as another global-level issue. But, at this stage, it can be addressed only at the national level. So Thailand, for example, curbed the entry of foreign supermarket chains after the 2007 economic crash (Banwell et al. 2012), and India maintains a ban on FDI in supermarkets – although it allows FDI in food wholesalers who sell to small businesses (thus allowing firms like Wal-Mart to have a presence).

There are other national-level regulatory concerns, such as unrestrained supermarket concentration. Of the dozen or so inquiries launched throughout the world to investigate this issue, many have found evidence of the misuse of market power, including making changes to farmer contracts without proper notice, transferring risks to suppliers and passing auditing fees onto suppliers. Supermarkets can threaten removal from their list of guaranteed suppliers if discounts are not obtained (Gardner 2013). As a consequence of these and other practices, suppliers have been viewed as being "subjugated" and working in a setting which lacks transparency and accountability (Fox and Vorley 2004; Richards, Lawrence, Loong and Burch 2012). Yet, in no cases have these concerns led to the capping of supermarket concentration at lower levels: supermarket power – in line with corporate power, more generally (Mercuro and Medema 2006) – is currently untrammeled.

In British Columbia, Canada, there have been calls for the adoption of "regulatory pluralism" when it comes to advancing food systems which are designed to serve the public's health. It does not obviate the need for strong state protections in relation to food trade, food safety and fair supply chains, but regulatory pluralism provides a bigger role for civil society actors, especially in regard to local food sustainability (Seed, Lang and Caraher 2013). In this context, the current interest in community and cooperative controlled food hubs – which provide logistics and marketing support for an alternative to the supermarket supply chain – is noteworthy (Biggs, Ryan and Wiseman 2010). When these food hubs arise as part of a strategic social, environmental and economic planning approach, they have the potential to diffuse non-supermarket-based food systems to larger populations and to offer co-benefits to producers, the environment and public nutrition along the way. This may be one, progressive, means of at least challenging – if not eventually curtailing – supermarket domination.

## NOTE

1.  This study was part-funded by the Australian Research Council (Project Nos. DP 0773092 and DP 110102299). Professor Lawrence was also part-funded by the National Research Foundation of Korea (NRF-2010-330-00159) and the Norwegian Research Council (FORFOOD Project No. 220691).

# REFERENCES

Banwell, C., J. Dixon, S. Seubsman, S. Pangsap, M. Kelly and A. Sleigh. 2012. "Evolving Food Retail Environments in Thailand and Implications for the Health and Nutrition Transition." *Public Health Nutrition* 16(4):608–615.
Biggs, C., C. Ryan and J. Wiseman. 2010. "Distributed Systems: A Design Model for Sustainable and Resilient Infrastructure." VEIL Distributed Systems Briefing Paper N3. Melbourne: University of Melbourne. Retrieved April 12, 2014 (http://www.ecoin-novationlab.com/wp-content/attachments/305_VEIL.Resilient-Systems-Briefing-Paper.pdf).
Blythman, J. 2005. *Shopped: The Shocking Power of British Supermarkets*. London: Harper.
Bonanno, A. 2014. "The Legitimation Crisis of Neoliberal Globalization: Instances from Agriculture and Food." Pp. 13–31 in *The Neoliberal Regime in the Agri-food Sector*, edited by S. Wolf and A. Bonanno. London: Earthscan.
Bourdieu, P. 1984. *Distinction: A Social Critique of the Judgement of Taste*. London: Routledge.
Burch, D., J. Dixon and G. Lawrence. 2013. "Introduction to Symposium on the Changing Role of Supermarkets in Global Supply Chains: From Seedling to Supermarket – Global Food Supply Chains in Transition." *Agriculture and Human Values* 30:215–224.
Burch, D. and G. Lawrence. 2009. "Towards a Third Food Regime: Behind the Transformation." *Agriculture and Human Values* 26:267–279.
Burch, D. and G. Lawrence. 2013. "Financialization in Agri-food Supply Chains: Private Equity and the Transformation of the Retail Sector." *Agriculture and Human Values* 30:247–258.
Burch, D., G. Lawrence and L. Hattersley. 2013. "Watchdogs and Ombudsmen: Monitoring the Abuse of Supermarket Power." *Agriculture and Human Values* 30:259–270.
Busch, L. 2014. "How Neoliberal Myths Endanger Democracy and Open Avenues for Democratic Action." Pp. 32–51 in *The Neoliberal Regime in the Agri-food Sector*, edited by S. Wolf and A. Bonanno. London: Earthscan.
Busch, L. and C. Bain. 2004. "New! Improved? The Transformation of the Global Agrifood System." *Rural Sociology* 69(3):321–346.
Campbell, H. 2009. "Breaking New Ground in Food Regime Theory: Corporate Environmentalism, Ecological Feedback and the 'Food from Somewhere' Regime." *Agriculture and Human Values* 26:309–319.
Carolan, M. 2011. *The Real Cost of Cheap Food*. London: Earthscan.
Carolan, M. 2013. *Reclaiming Food Security*. London: Earthscan.
CEOWorld Magazine. 2014. "Tesco Launches Its First Android Jelly Bean Powered 7in Hudl Budget Tablet." Retrieved April 13, 2014 (http://ceoworld.biz/ceo/2013/09/23/tesco-launches-its-first-android-jelly-bean-powered-7in-hudl-budget-tablet-29920922).
Clapp, J. and D. Fuchs (eds.). 2009. *Corporate Power in Global Agrifood Governance*. Cambridge, MA: MIT Press.
CNBC. 2014. "The Costco Craze: Inside the Warehouse Giant." Retrieved May 3, 2014 (http://www.cnbc.com/id/46603589).
Competition Commission. 2000. "Supermarkets: A Report on the Supply of Groceries from Multiple Stores in the United Kingdom." London: Competition Commission.
Corporate Watch. 2014. "Corporate Control of the Food System." Retrieved April 7, 2014 (http://www.corporatewatch.org/?lid=3711).
Dangour, A., R. Green, B. Hasler, J. Rushton, B. Shankar and J. Waage. 2012. "Symposium 1: Food Chain and Health. Linking Agriculture and Health in Low- and Middle-Income Countries: An Inerdisciplinary Research Agenda." *Proceedings of the Nutrition Society* 71:222–228.
Davey, S. and C. Richards. 2013. "Supermarkets and Private Standards: Unintended Consequences of the Audit Ritual." *Agriculture and Human Values* 30:271–281.
Dixon, J. 2007. "Supermarkets as New Food Authorities." Pp. 29–50 in *Supermarkets and*

*Agri-food Supply Chains: Transformations in the Production and Consumption of Foods*, edited by D. Burch and G. Lawrence. Cheltenham, UK and Northampton, MA: Edward Elgar.

Dixon, J. and C. Banwell. 2012. "Choice Editing for the Environment: Managing Corporate Risks." Pp. 175–184 in *Risk and Social Theory in Environmental Management*, edited by T. Measham and S. Lockie: Victoria, Australia: CSIRO Publishing.

Dixon, J. and B. Isaacs. 2013. "There's Certainly a Lot of Hurting out There: Navigating the Trolley of Progress down the Supermarket Aisle." *Agriculture and Human Values* 30:283–297.

Dowler, E., M. Kneafsey, R. Cox and L. Holloway. 2009. "'Doing Food Differently': Reconnecting Biological and Social Relationships through Care for Food." *Sociological Review* 57:200–221.

Edwards, F. and D. Mercer. 2013. "Food Waste in Australia: The Freegan Response." Pp. 174–191 in *Waste Matters: New Perspectives on Food and Society*, edited by D. Evans, H. Campbell and A. Murcott. Oxford: Wiley-Blackwell.

Evans, D., H. Campbell and A. Murcott (eds.). 2013. *Waste Matters: New Perspectives on Food and Society*. Oxford: Wiley-Blackwell.

Fairbairn, M. 2014. "'Just Another Asset Class?': Neoliberalism, Finance and the Construction of Farmland Investment." Pp. 245–262 in *The Neoliberal Regime in the Agri-food Sector*, edited by S. Wolf and A. Bonanno. London: Earthscan.

Fox, T. and B. Vorley. 2004. "Stakeholder Accountability in the UK Supermarket Sector: Final Report to the 'Race to the Top' Project." London: International Institute for Environment and Development.

Freidberg, S. 2007. "Supermarkets and Imperial Knowledge." *Cultural Geographies* 14:321–342.

Friedmann, H. 2005. "From Colonialism to Green Capitalism: Social Movements and the Emergence of Food Regimes." Pp. 229–267 in *New Directions in the Sociology of Global Development*, vol. 11, edited by F. Buttel and P. McMichael. Oxford: Elsevier.

Friedmann, H. and P. McMichael. 1989. "Agriculture and the State System." *Sociologia Ruralis* XXXIX(2):93–117.

Friel, S. and W. Lichacz. 2010. "Unequal Food Systems, Unhealthy Diets." Pp. 115–129 in *Food Security, Nutrition and Sustainability*, edited by G. Lawrence, K. Lyons and T. Wallington. London: Earthscan.

Fuchs, D., A. Kalfagianni and M. Arentsen. 2009. "Retail Power, Private Standards, and Sustainability in the Global Food System." Pp. 29–59 in *Corporate Power in Global Agrifood Governance*, edited by J. Clapp and D. Fuchs. Cambridge, MA: MIT Press.

Gardner, B. 2013. *Global Food Futures: Feeding the World in 2050*. London: Bloomsbury.

Gertel, J. and S. Sippel (eds.). 2014. *Seasonal Workers in Mediterranean Agriculture: The Social Costs of Eating Fresh*. London: Routledge.

Government Office for Science. 2011. "The Future of Food and Farming: Final Project Report." London: Government Office for Science.

Gunders, D. 2012. "Wasted: How America is Losing up to 40 Percent of Its Food from Farm to Fork to Landfill." Washington, DC: NRDC.

Halsey, A. 2013. "AAA Thinks Pumps at New Costco May Drive Down Gas Prices." Retrieved 8 May, 2014 (http://www.washingtonpost.com/blogs/dr-gridlock/wp/2013/09/16/aaa-thinks-pumps-at-new-costco-may-drive-down-gas-prices/).

Harvey, D. 1996. *Justice, Nature and the Geography of Distance*. Cambridge, MA: Blackwell Publishers.

Hawkins, G. 2013. "The Performativity of Food Packaging: Market Devices, Waste Crisis and Recycling." Pp. 66–83 in *Waste Matters: New Perspectives on Food and Society*, edited by D. Evans, H. Campbell and A. Murcott. Oxford: Wiley-Blackwell.

Henson, S. and J. Humphery. 2009. "The Impacts of Private Food Safety Standards on the Food Chain and on Public Standard-Setting Processes." Rome: Joint FAO/WHO Food Standards Codex Alimentarius Commission.

Holmes, S. 2013. *Fresh Fruit, Broken Bodies: Migrant Farmworkers in the United States.* Berkeley and Los Angeles, CA: University of California Press.

Iba, H. and K. Sakamoto. 2014. "Beyond Farming: Cases of Revitalization of Rural Communities through Social Service Provision by Community Farming Enterprises." Pp. 129–149 in *The Neoliberal Regime in the Agri-food Sector*, edited by S. Wolf and A. Bonanno. London: Earthscan.

Ingram, J., P. Ericksen and D. Liverman. 2010. *Food Security and Global Environmental Change.* London: Earthscan.

Isaacs, B. and J. Dixon (in press). "Making it Local: The Rural Consumer, the Supermarket and Competing Pedagogical Authority." In *Food Pedagogies*, edited by R. Flowers and E. Swan. Aldershot, UK: Ashgate.

Johnston, J., A. Biro and N. MacKendrick. 2009. "Lost in the Supermarket: The Corporate-Organic Foodscape and the Struggle for Food Democracy." *Antipode* 41(3):509–532.

King Kullen. 2006. "About King Kullen Supermarkets." Retrieved April 4, 2014 (http://www.kingkullen.com/about-us/).

Konefal, J., C. Bain, M. Mascarenhas and L. Busch. 2007. "Supermarkets and Supply Chains in North America." Pp. 268–288 in *Supermarkets and Agri-food Supply Chains: Transformations in the Production and Consumption of Foods*, edited by D. Burch and G. Lawrence. Cheltenham, UK and Northampton, MA: Edward Elgar.

Lang, T., D. Barling and M. Caraher. 2009. *Food Policy: Integrating Health, Environment and Society.* Oxford: Oxford University Press.

Lawrence, G. and D. Burch. 2007. "Understanding Supermarkets and Agri-food Supply Chains." Pp. 1–26 in *Supermarkets and Agri-food Supply Chains: Transformations in the Production and Consumption of Foods*, edited by D. Burch and G. Lawrence. Cheltenham, UK and Northampton, MA: Edward Elgar.

Lemke, T. 2001. "The Birth of Bio-politics: Michel Foucault's Lecture at the Collège de France on Neo-liberal Governmentality." *Economy and Society* 30(2):190–207.

McCullough, E., P. Pingali and K. Stamoulis. 2008. "Small Farms and the Transformation of Food Systems: An Overview." Pp. 3–46 in *The Transformation of Agri-food Systems: Globalization, Supply Chains and Smallholder Farmers*, edited by E. McCullough, P. Pingali and K. Stamoulis. London: Earthscan.

McMichael, P. 2005. "Global Development and the Corporate Food Regime." Pp. 265–299 in *New Directions in the Sociology of Global Development*, edited by F. Buttel and P. McMichael. Amsterdam: Elsevier.

McMichael, P. 2013. *Food Regimes and Agrarian Questions.* Halifax, Canada: Fernwood Publishing.

McMichael, P. and H. Friedmann. 2007. "Situating the 'Retailing Revolution.'" Pp. 291–319 in *Supermarkets and Agri-food Supply Chains: Transformations in the Production and Consumption of Foods*, edited by D. Burch and G. Lawrence. Cheltenham, UK and Northampton, MA: Edward Elgar.

McMichael, A., J. Powles, C. Butler and R. Uauy. 2007. "Food, Livestock Production, Energy, Climate Change, and Health." *The Lancet* 370(9594):1253–1263.

Mercuro, N. and S. Medema. 2006. *Economics and the Law, Second Edition: From Posner to Postmodernism and Beyond.* Princeton, NJ: Princeton University Press.

Monteiro, C. and G. Cannon. 2012. "The Impact of Transnational 'Big Food' Companies on the South: A View from Brazil." *PLoS Medicine* 9(7):e1001252. doi:10.1371/journal.pmed.1001252.

Oosterveer, P. and D. Sonnenfeld. 2012. *Food, Globalization and Sustainability.* London: Earthscan.

Otero, G. 2014. "The Neoliberal Food Regime and Its Crisis: State, Agribusiness Transnational Corporations, and Biotechnology." Pp. 225–244 in *The Neoliberal Regime in the Agri-food Sector*, edited by S. Wolf and A. Bonanno. London: Earthscan.

Peck, J. and A. Tickell. 2002. "Neoliberalizing Space." *Antipode* 34(3):380–404.

Progressive Grocer. 2012. "New Frontiers of the 1950s." Retrieved April 4, 2014 (http://www.progressivegrocer.com/inprint/article/id2692/new-frontiers-of-the-1950s/).

Reardon, T., S. Henson and A. Gulati. 2010. "Links between Supermarkets and Food Prices, Diet Diversity and Food Safety in Developing Countries." Pp. 111–130 in *Trade, Food, Diet and Health: Perspectives and Policy Options*, edited by C. Hawkes, S. Blouin, N. Henson, L. Drager and D. Chichester. Oxford: Wiley-Blackwell.

Rees, E. 2011. "Tesco and Starbucks Feel the Heat in Battle against 'Clone Town Britain.'" Retrieved May 8, 2014 (http://www.theecologist.org/News/news_analysis/1026353/tesco_ and_starbucks_feel_the_heat_in_battle_against_clone_town_britain.html).

Richards, C., H. Bjorkhaug, G. Lawrence and E. Hickman. 2013. "Retailer-Driven Agricultural Restructuring – Australia, the UK and Norway in Comparison." *Agriculture and Human Values* 30:235–245.

Richards, C., G. Lawrence, M. Loong and D. Burch. 2012. "A Toothless Chihuahua? The Australian Competition and Consumer Commission, Neoliberalism and Supermarket Power in Australia." *Rural Society* 23(3):250–263.

Rodale Institute. 2005. "The Supermarket Turns 75." Retrieved April 4, 2014 (http://www. newfarm.org/news/2005/0805/080505/birthday.shtml).

Seed, B., T. Lang and M. Caraher. 2013. "Integrating Food Security into Public Health and Provincial Government Departments in British Columbia, Canada." *Agriculture and Human Values* 30(3):457–470.

Shaw, G., L. Curth and A. Alexander. 2004. "Selling Self Service and the Supermarket: The Americanisation of Food Retailing in Britain 1945–1960." *Business History* 46(4):568–582.

Supermarket News. 2014. "Top Global Food Retailers 2013." Retrieved April 4, 2014 (http://supermarketnews.com/top-25-global-food-retailers-2013).

Tescopoly. 2014. "Financial Services." Retrieved April 13, 2014 (http://www.tescopoly.org/ financial-services).

Thompson, L. and S. Lockie. 2013. "Private Standards, Grower Networks, and Power in Food Supply Systems." *Agriculture and Human Values* 30:379–388.

Timmer, C. 2008. "Food Policy in the Era of Supermarkets: What's Different?" Pp. 67–86 in *The Transformation of Agri-food Systems: Globalization, Supply Chains and Smallholder Farmers*, edited by E. McCullough, P. Pingali and K. Stamoulis. London: Earthscan.

Towill, D. 2005. "A Perspective on UK Supermarket Pressure on the Supply Chain." *European Management Journal* 23(4):426–438.

Vorley, B., A. Fearne and D. Ray (eds.). 2007. *Regoverning Markets: A Place for Small-Scale Producers in Modern Agrifood Chains?* London: Gower.

Wahlqvist, M., J. McKay, Y. Chang and Y. Chiu. 2012. "Rethinking the Food Security Debate in Asia: Some Missing Ecological and Health Dimensions and Solutions." *Food Security* 4:657–670.

Watt, E. 1982. *Authority*. London: Groom Helm.

Weber, M. 1947. *The Theory of Social and Economic Organization*. New York: The Free Press.

Weis, T. 2013. *The Ecological Hoofprint: The Global Burden of Industrial Livestock*. London. Zed Books.

Wrigley, N. and M. Lowe. 1996. *Retailing, Consumption and Capita: Towards the New Retail Geography*. Essex: Longman.

Young, E. 2012. *Food and Development*. London: Routledge.

# 12.  Finance and the food system
## *Madeleine Fairbairn*

## INTRODUCTION

The increasing power and prominence of finance has transformed the face of capitalism over the last four decades. The U.S., which had shifted from an agrarian to an industrial society in the early 20th century, began a new transition in the 1970s toward a post-industrial society revolving around financial markets (Davis 2009). Financial imperatives have come to shape the way that we see the world: national governments must worry about their credit ratings, the health of corporations is judged by their stock price, while our skills and relationships become so much human and social capital. This unfolding process is often referred to by the term *financialization*.

This pervasive re-orientation toward finance has transformed the agro-food system. Financial actors are increasingly investing in the food system and expecting good returns on their capital, while corporations involved in food and agriculture are themselves undertaking financial activities as a way to increase their profits. This growing focus on financial profitability does not benefit everyone, and in some cases it even comes into conflict with the food system's (presumed) purpose of food provision.

After a brief overview of the concept of financialization, this chapter will explore how finance is reshaping three areas of the agro-food system: agricultural derivative markets, food retail, and farmland ownership. In each case, financialization has concerning implications: financial speculation in derivative markets has been linked to high and volatile food prices, running supermarket chains so as to produce the highest possible returns for financial investors may mean firing employees and closing unprofitable locations, and financial investment in farmland may contribute to soaring land prices.

## WHAT IS FINANCIALIZATION AND WHY IS IT HAPPENING?

Financialization is a multi-faceted process that began around the 1970s. Epstein (2005:3) gives a widely cited umbrella definition of financialization as "the increasing role of financial motives, financial markets, financial actors and financial institutions in the operation of domestic and international economies." A narrower, and therefore slightly more useful, definition comes from Krippner (2011:4), who sees financialization as "the tendency for profit making in the economy to occur increasingly through financial channels rather than through productive activities." In other words, money lending and investment activities—in which profits take the form of interest payments, dividends, and capital gains on investments— are becoming increasingly prevalent, while commodity production and trade take the back seat.[1] Financialization can be seen simultaneously in both the expansion of the financial sector relative to other parts of the economy and in the growing dependence on portfolio income among non-financial firms (Krippner 2011).

There are several different ways of thinking about financialization, all of which overlap in important ways though they emphasize different factors. Marxist scholars see financialization as resulting from the systemic problems of capitalism (Arrighi 1994; Harvey 2010; Sweezy and Magdoff 1987). Arrighi (1994) describes financialization as a historically recurring phenomenon in which, midway through a "cycle of accumulation," capitalist accumulation shifts its emphasis from commodity production and trade to finance.[2] The U.S.-led cycle of accumulation that occurred in the 20th century, he argues, shifted into a phase of financial expansion in the early 1970s in response to increasing economic competition from other countries. Magdoff and Sweezy (1987) also trace financialization to the economic problems of the 1970s, but they attribute falling corporate profits to the stagnation tendency of "monopoly capitalism," rather than international competition. They describe this financial expansion essentially as a long-lasting economic bubble—the inflated financial sector brings in healthy profits even as the productive sector stagnates.

Other perspectives on financialization emphasize the role of the state in deregulating financial markets over the last few decades. The rise of neoliberal economic and political thought in the 1980s and 1990s provided an ideological justification for reducing the state's role in financial markets (Kotz 2011; Tomaskovic-Devey and Lin 2011). In the U.S., limits on credit card interest rates were lifted, as were restrictions on bank mergers and prohibitions on cross-industry activity that had formerly prevented banking, insurance, and investment activities from taking place within the same firm (Tomaskovic-Devey and Lin 2011). Krippner attributes the financialization of the U.S. economy to government action but sees it as an unintended consequence rather than part of a concerted neoliberal agenda. The government, she argues, in looking for the most politically expedient way to deal with the distributional conflicts and economic crisis of the 1960s and 1970s, unintentionally freed finance from its moorings.

Another very important dimension of the financialization process, and one that is stressed by organizational theorists, is the changing relationship between corporations and investors. Over the course of the 1980s and 1990s, institutional investors—organizations that manage enormous amounts of capital, such as pension funds, hedge funds, and insurance companies—grew to a previously unimaginable size, and investment power became increasingly concentrated in their hands (Useem 1996). Thanks largely to this consolidation of investor power, the "shareholder value" approach to corporate governance was popularized. According to this approach, the ultimate measure of a company's success is its ability to generate returns for investors, and maximizing these returns should be the priority of corporate managers. The value of a company was now no longer determined by its size, the number of people it employed, or the amount it produced, but by its ability to impress capital markets (Davis 2009; Fligstein 2001). The corporate takeover movement of the 1980s and the shift to compensating corporate executives in stock options helped ensure that companies got the message. Some researchers worry that, because of this intense pressure to perform, the shareholder value revolution may be leading companies to sacrifice long-term investment in productive capacity in favor of meeting the short-term demands of investors (Lazonick and O'Sullivan 2000).

The economic crisis that began in 2008 cast a spotlight on Wall Street, the City of London, and other financial centers. Metastasizing financial profits were suddenly called into question, and the lack of government oversight on multiplying financial instruments became the subject of scrutiny. But the increased prominence of finance has effects that go well beyond the financial sector itself. Its influence has fundamentally altered the agro-food system from the trade in agricultural inputs to the food on our plates.

## FINANCE AND AGRICULTURAL DERIVATIVES

Within the global agro-food system, the effects of financialization are most apparent in the market for agricultural commodity derivatives. Derivatives are financial assets whose price is based on the price of an underlying commodity, in this case agricultural crops. They arose because both farmers—who sell crops—and food traders and processors—who buy crops—want to protect themselves from price volatility. A wheat farmer, whose crop will not be harvested for some months to come, wants to know how much he will eventually earn from it. Meanwhile, a miller, whose business depends on raw inputs of wheat, would like to know his future expenses. These two parties can create a *forward contract*—the most basic type of agricultural commodity derivative—by agreeing now on a price for future delivery of the product. This gives them both some peace of mind: the farmer is protected against a fall in the price of wheat, while the miller is protected against an increase in the price of wheat (Clapp 2012).

Agricultural derivatives are nothing new. The first agricultural commodity exchange was founded in London in the 18th century (Clapp 2012), and the famous Chicago Board of Trade was established in 1848 (Cronon 1992). Over the years, the simple forward contract evolved into more sophisticated and standardized types of derivative, such as *futures, options*, and *swaps*. These derivatives are traded over exchanges, which means that the farmer and the miller no longer have any contact with one another, and the contracts can be settled in cash rather than through actual delivery, which means that people can invest in wheat derivatives even if they have no use for the wheat itself (Clapp 2012). The number of commodities for which derivatives can be purchased have also grown; in addition to grain crops like oats, rice, and soybeans, one can buy derivatives in coffee, cocoa, orange juice, sugar, eggs, beef, and pork bellies, to name just a few.

Until recently, despite their increasing sophistication, derivative markets still existed primarily to hedge the business risks of farmers and others in the food business—actors commonly known as *commercial traders*. Since those first derivative exchanges developed centuries ago, there have also always been financial actors who participate in the markets. These *non-commercial traders* invest in commodity derivative markets to speculate on price movements rather than to hedge business risk. In fact, some limited speculation is generally considered to be a positive thing for two reasons. First, it increases the liquidity of derivative markets—commercial traders who want to protect themselves from the riskiness of agriculture encounter demand for their derivatives in the form of speculators who see that risk as a potential source of profit. Second, it assists with "price discovery"—the price of a derivative represents traders' best information about future supply and demand, which, in turn, helps farmers make decisions about what and how much to plant (Clapp and Helleiner 2012).

In the U.S., laws have historically limited the level of speculation within commodity markets. The Grain Futures Act of 1922 stated that trading could only take place through qualified exchanges, and that these exchanges had to take steps to prevent market manipulation. The Commodity Exchange Act of 1936 allowed federal regulators to place "position limits" on non-commercial traders, restricting how many derivative contracts they could hold at a time (Clapp and Helleiner 2012). This regulation was not designed to eliminate speculation entirely, but rather to keep it in an auxiliary role and prevent it from distorting the market (Clapp and Helleiner 2012). With these regulations, finance was subordinated to the demands of production and trade.

This situation began to change, however, as the rapid financial innovation and deregulation of the 1980s and 1990s extended into commodity markets. In the 1980s, banks began selling commodity derivatives to clients "over-the-counter" (OTC), meaning that they bypassed the commodity futures exchanges. One new OTC investment vehicle was called the commodity index fund. Commodity indices are similar to general market indices like the Dow Jones Industrial Average, but rather than company stock, they measure the performance of a basket of agricultural and non-agricultural commodity derivatives. The commodities included range from corn to live cattle to crude oil to aluminum, with agricultural commodities generally composing 15–30 percent (Clapp 2012). Index funds, in turn, are composed of commodity derivatives designed to track the performance of a particular commodity index. Investors buy into an index fund directly through a bank, allowing them to get exposure to commodity futures markets without the knowledge or hands-on participation that this would have previously required (Clapp 2012).

As index funds increased in popularity throughout the 1980s and 1990s, banks began to petition federal regulators—the Commodity Futures Trading Commission (CFTC)—for exemptions to the position limits placed on non-commercial traders. In 1991 the CFTC granted the first position limit exemption, and many more followed. These position limit exemptions re-classified the banks operating in commodity markets from "non-commercial traders" to "commercial traders," dismantling the barrier between speculators and hedgers. In 2000 the Commodity Futures Modernization Act, formalized this deregulation by exempting all OTC derivative trading from CFTC oversight (Clapp 2012; Clapp and Helleiner 2012).

Throughout the first decade of the 2000s, commodity index funds grew in popularity, particularly among institutional investors. This was partly because of what was happening with alternative investments. According to De Schutter (2010), "other markets dried up one by one: the dotcoms vanished at the end of 2001, the stock market soon after, and the U.S. housing market in August 2007. As each bubble burst, these large institutional investors moved into other markets, each traditionally considered more stable than the last." Commodity prices had been steadily increasing, and the necessity of food and fuel to human survival made it unlikely that these markets would dwindle. Another big reason for the growing popularity of index funds was that investors began to favor commodities as a way to diversify their investment portfolios. The movement of commodities is thought to be relatively uncorrelated with the movement of the stocks and bonds that make up the bulk of most portfolios. Commodity investments are therefore seen as a way to reduce the overall risk of the portfolio (De Schutter 2010). As institutional investors, with their enormous coffers, embraced commodities, the amount of money invested in commodity index funds skyrocketed from U.S.$13 billion in 2003 to U.S.$317 billion in 2008 (Kaufman 2010).

The increasing participation of financial actors in commodity derivative markets is not the only indicator of derivative market financialization. Recall that financialization involves both an expansion of the financial sector and an increasing reliance on financial profits on the part of nonfinancial corporations (Krippner 2011). This is certainly true when it comes to agricultural derivatives. In recent years, the big grain traders—the so-called ABCDs: Archer Daniels Midland (ADM), Bunge, Cargill, and Louis Dreyfus—have increasingly branched out into financial activities. Grain trading companies have long been among the major commercial traders, using commodity derivative markets to hedge their business activities, but in recent years they have also come to see commodity markets as a source of speculative profits. The ABCDs have all opened financial subsidiaries that offer asset management services to third-party clients (Murphy et al. 2012). These make use of their parent companies' inside knowledge about supply conditions for the purposes of speculation; Louis Dreyfus' new hedge fund, the Alpha Fund, goes by the slogan "monetize our expertise" (Murphy et al. 2012). In short, the line between the ABCD's commercial hedging activities and their non-commercial speculative activities has become increasingly blurry, leading to questions about whether they should be thought of as "commercial" or "non-commercial" for the purposes of regulation (Isakson 2014; Murphy et al. 2012).

By the time the 2008 food crisis hit, financial speculators had come to dominate commodity markets, dwarfing the participation of those commercial hedgers for whose benefit the markets were originally created. Debate ensued about whether this speculation was to blame for soaring food prices in 2008 and again in 2011. Many attribute the increase in global grain prices to simple supply and demand, pointing out that global grain stocks were extremely low in 2007 and 2008 owing to biofuel subsidies, increasing meat consumption in China and India, and weather related shortfalls in production (Bobenrieth and Wright 2009; Irwin and Sanders 2011; Krugman 2010).

*Source:*   FAO (2013).

*Figure 12.1    FAO Food Price Index, 1990–2014 (2002–2004 = 100)*

Many others, however, argue that speculators—and particularly index fund investors—fueled a commodity market bubble that inflated food prices beyond what was justified by supply and demand (Ghosh 2009; Masters 2010; Wahl 2009; Wray 2008). They argue that in recent years speculation in commodity markets has changed both quantitatively and qualitatively; not only have commodity markets been flooded by an unprecedented amount of financial capital, but index fund investors behave in particularly troubling ways. While the traditional specula-tor in commodity markets is active—buying and selling in accordance with changes in the market—index investors take a much more passive approach. They make very long-term investments that are "long only," meaning that they only buy futures contracts and never sell them, and they continuously "roll over" these investments, meaning that they buy more futures as the old ones expire, irrespective of changes in the market (Masters and White 2008). Critics argue that this type of passive invest-ment has none of the positive functions of more active speculation in com-modity markets—it serves no price discovery function and actually drains liquidity from the market. Additionally, while active speculators may be said to smooth out market volatility by selling low and buying high, index investors engage in "momentum-based speculation," moving in the same direction *en masse*, which only adds to market volatility (De Schutter 2010). For speculators, volatility brings the potential for high profits, but for farmers and consumers, it is a threat to lives and livelihoods.

## FINANCE AND FOOD RETAIL

Over the last few decades, supermarket chains have consolidated and grown in scale so that they now exercise considerable power over other actors in agro-food supply chains (Lawrence and Burch 2007). They, along with other food retailers, establish private grades and standards that constrain the behavior of their suppliers (Busch and Bain 2004; Wiegel 2013). Meanwhile, the sale of own-brand, pre-packaged meals and other convenience foods extends supermarket influence into the realm of consumption (Lawrence and Burch 2007). Beginning in the 1990s, Northern supermarket chains rapidly extended their reach into Latin America and Asia, making them increasingly important transnational corporate actors and contributing to the Westernization of food practices (Reardon and Berdegué 2002; Reardon et al. 2009).

While this "supermarket revolution" has undoubtedly had far-reaching consequences, an exploration of the relationship between supermarkets and finance calls into question the dominance of food retailers (Burch and Lawrence 2013). Burch and Lawrence (2009; 2013) use a case study of the former UK supermarket chain Somerfield to explore the ways in which finance capital can exert influence over retail capital. Somerfield was taken over by a private equity consortium in 2005. Private equity investors buy out companies using private capital, increase company profitability, and then resell them. Burch and Lawrence point out that, because the primary purpose of private equity takeovers is to realize shareholder value, the transformations they effect do not necessarily lead to better supermarket services. The changes to Somerfield made by the new financial owners included selling a large number of the stores owned by the chain, reducing the number of products carried in its supermarkets by almost half, firing hundreds of employees, and outsourcing the company's IT functions to India. The new private equity owners also withdrew the supermarket from participation in an ethical trade initiative aimed at ensuring minimum labor standards from overseas suppliers. Finally, the new owners leveraged Somerfield's substantial real estate assets by splitting the retailer into two separate entities: an operating company, which continued to operate the supermarkets, and a property company, which now owned the real estate on which many of the supermarkets were situated. This "opco/propco" reorganization allowed the private equity consortium to "unlock" additional shareholder value by using the property value as collateral in a large bond sale. They were ultimately able to resell Somerfield for almost twice what they paid for it (Burch and Lawrence 2009; 2013).

As in other sectors of the economy, this increasing prioritization of financial profits is not limited to financial actors. Like the big grain trading companies, major supermarket chains such as Wal-Mart, Tesco, Carrefour, and Kroger have simultaneously become an object of interest for financial investors and have transformed into financial actors in their own right. Supermarkets began to branch out into financial services, offering customers everything from banking services to credit cards to insurance programs and home mortgages (Isakson 2014). Additionally, big retailers began reducing their real asset holdings in preference for more financial investments. Baud and Durand (2012) found that the ratio of financial assets to total assets held by major supermarket chains increased rapidly beginning in the late 1990s. By the early 2000s, many chains were up to a quarter or even a third financial assets, showing how reliant they had become on financial profits.

While the financialization of the supermarket industry clearly increases investor profits, it may not benefit other food-system actors as much. The changes made by Somerfield's private equity investors—closing branches, leveraging the property, and reneging on ethical commitments—were clearly aimed at extracting value for company shareholders, rather than improving the retailer's services (Burch and Lawrence 2013). Isakson (2014) argues that the pressure of financialization is leading to improved supermarket efficiency, thanks to labor reorganization and improved inventory management, but that these improvements often come at the expense of workers, farmers, and consumers. He also questions the impact of the new supermarket financial services: "Retailers such as Wal-Mart and Tesco champion their initiatives as offering financial services to underserved/unbanked populations . . . In doing so, they downplay the fact that they are often profiting from their customers' debt" (Isakson 2014:6).

## FINANCE AND FARMLAND

Until recently, the financialization of the agro-food system seemed to stop at the farm gate. However, the food and financial crises that hit simultaneously in 2008 changed this, suddenly turning farmland into an attractive

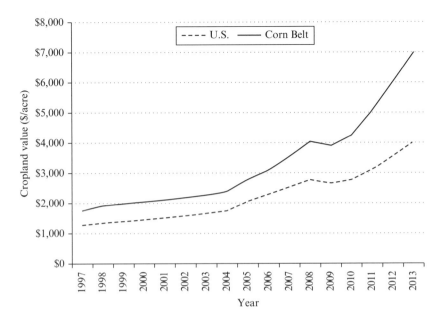

*Source:* USDA NASS (2013).

*Figure 12.2 Average U.S. cropland prices, 1997–2013*

investment option. When markets for stocks, bonds, and complex finan-cial derivatives like mortgage-backed securities were flourishing, financial investors had very little interest in buying farmland, which is illiquid and generally has relatively low returns. However, as the returns from other types of investments dropped off and high grain prices led to rising land values, farmland suddenly began to look much more attractive.

In addition to the capital gains from land price appreciation, investors like what farmland does for their overall portfolio. Farmland values have a high correlation to inflation but—like agricultural commodities—they have a low correlation to the stock market. Farmland is therefore seen by some investors as a good way to hedge against inflation and reduce port-folio risk through diversification (HighQuest Partners 2010). All of these qualities suddenly became very attractive in light of post-2008 food and financial insecurity. This newfound investor interest in farmland could be seen in high profile investments by celebrity investors like George Soros, Warren Buffet, and Lord Rothschild (Crippen 2011; O'Keefe 2009) as well as in stories about this hot "new" asset class in the mainstream finan-cial press (Gandel 2011). These new financial investments in farmland are truly global, spanning from Canada (Magnan 2011) to sub-Saharan Africa (Daniel 2012; Ducastel and Anseeuw 2013) to Russia and the former Soviet Union (Visser 2014).

The most significant development is that institutional investors have started adding farmland to their investment portfolios. For instance, the giant U.S. pension fund Teachers Insurance and Annuity Association – College Retirement Equities Fund (TIAA–CREF) suddenly began buying farmland in 2007. With over U.S.$500 billion in assets under management, this investment behemoth had the capital and the human resources to rapidly acquire an enormous portfolio of agricultural land. By 2012, just five years later, it had U.S.$2.8 billion worth of farmland in the U.S., Australia, Brazil, and Eastern Europe, and was one of the largest farmland owners and managers in the world (Minaya and Ourso 2012). With this capital, the fund had acquired over 400 individual farm properties totaling over 242,000 hectares (TIAA–CREF 2012). After several successful years of buying farmland for its own portfolio, TIAA–CREF also began acting as an asset manager for other institutional investors interested in farmland. In 2012 it reported the closing of a new fund, TIAA–CREF Global Agriculture LLC, with U.S.$2 billion in capital from third-party investors. This fund buys and manages farmland on behalf of other institutional investors including the Second Swedish National Pension Fund (AP2) and the British Columbia Investment Management Corporation (bcIMC) (TIAA–CREF 2012).

Growing investor interest in farmland has spawned a host of new farmland investment vehicles. These include private equity funds, hedge funds, venture capital, and specialized farmland funds operated by more mainstream asset managers. However, many of the new vehicles are private equity funds (Daniel 2012) or at least have a private-equity-like structure, meaning that their purpose is to acquire a portfolio of farmland or farmland-owning agribusinesses, upgrade, and resell them. Like most private equity funds, they operate for a fixed term—often of seven or ten years—after which they must have some kind of "exit" in order to return capital to investors. Common exit strategies include taking the entire fund public via an initial public offering on the stock market, selling off the properties to a strategic buyer, or rolling them over into a new fund, in which case the investors would retain ownership of the land after the fund's term (Daniel 2012; Fairbairn 2014). One estimate suggests that there are roughly 190 private equity funds operating in agriculture and farmland (IIED 2012). Investors now have a wide range of options, from NCH Capital's Agribusiness Partners Fund, which boasts 700,000 hectares of farmland in the former Soviet Union and Baltic States (Bergdolt and Mittal 2012), to Emergent Asset Management's African Agri-Land Fund, which focuses on sub-Saharan Africa (Daniel 2012).

Another new type of farmland investment vehicle is the publicly traded farmland real estate investment trust (REIT). This is essentially a method of securitizing farmland—turning it into a highly liquid, tradable financial asset similar to a stock (Fairbairn 2014). Securitization is most commonly associated with the aggregation of debt payments into a single income stream that investors can then buy into. This was the case with the now-infamous mortgage-backed securities that torpedoed the U.S. housing market in 2008. The income for farmland REITs, in contrast, comes from bundling together the rental payments made by tenant farmers on several farm properties. Shareholders receive regular dividend payments based on this rent and on the capital gains from farm sales (Fairbairn 2014). The U.S. has several publicly traded timberland REITs already (Gunnoe and Gellert 2011), but it gained its first public farmland REIT in January 2013 when Gladstone Land Corporation, a farmland-focused real estate firm, went public. As of late 2013, Gladstone Land owned 14 farms in California, Florida, Michigan, and Oregon, comprising 790 hectares (Gladstone Land 2014b). The company takes no part in farm operation, and its profits come from leasing the farm properties out to corporate and independent farmer tenants. It acquires land, in part, through sale-leaseback deals, in which the farmer sells land to the company in return for a long-term lease to continue as the farm operator (Gladstone Land 2014a). With farmland REITs, immobile, heterogeneous land becomes a fungible, liquid investment. This is the cutting edge of farmland financialization (Fairbairn 2014).

And, once again, it is not just financial actors that are coming to see land as an attractive investment. The financialization of farmland can also be seen in the changing behavior of agricultural producers. Farmland is simultaneously a productive asset and a financial asset; it creates income by growing crops but also appreciates over time, generating capital gains on the initial investment. Since 2008, even productive, nonfinancial companies are increasingly focused on those financial returns from land appreciation (Fairbairn 2014). Some large, agricultural operating companies have decided to capitalize on high rates of farmland appreciation by spinning off a part of their farmland portfolio into a separate business focused on farmland real estate (HighQuest Partners 2010). The publicly traded Brazilian agribusiness SLC Agrícola, for instance, recently created a separate agricultural property company called SLC LandCo. In order to construct LandCo., SLC took 60,000 hectares of its existing 200,000 hectare land portfolio and used it to raise ~U.S.$240 million from British asset management firm Valliance in exchange for a share of roughly 50 percent in LandCo. (SLC Agrícola 2012). These funds are used for purchasing additional agricultural land with potential for rapid appreciation.

This strategy bears a strong resemblance to the opco/propco strategy pursued by the private equity consortium that purchased the Somerfield supermarket chain. The farmland—formerly seen primarily as a capital asset necessary to conducting the company's business of agricultural production—becomes a source of capital gains and a way to raise additional financial capital from investors (Fairbairn 2014).

The financialization of farmland is still in its earliest stages, and it is not clear what the impacts will be. However, the influx of institutional capital into land markets could inadvertently contribute to land price inflation, further fueling the boom that made land attractive to investors in the first place. Rising land prices make land ownership more difficult for small farmers, who will rarely be able to outbid a multi-billion dollar financial institution. There is also the possibility of importing the short-termism of finance into land markets. Farmland private equity funds need an exit if the fund managers are to get paid, and an exit usually implies selling the land. While these multi-year funds are long-term commitments for most financial investors, who are accustomed to buying and selling stocks in an instant, they are short term from the perspective of most farmers, who measure land ownership in decades or generations. Although many private equity fund managers argue that their short tenure as landowner will involve soil quality or other property improvements as a means to increase profit on re-sale, it also seems likely that this short-term view could lead to careless environmental governance (Fairbairn 2014).

## CONCLUSION

Finance's increasing prominence in the global economy has reshaped many aspects of the global agro-food system. Agricultural commodity markets, once a way for food producers, processors, and traders to hedge their commercial risks, are now swamped with speculative capital. This speculation in food markets has likely contributed to the high and volatile food prices of the last few years. Supermarket chains, under pressure to generate impressive returns for shareholders, are offering financial services along with food products to their customers. Meanwhile, farmland is becoming a popular alternative asset class with financial investors. Beyond these developments, the influence of finance is at work throughout the food system, including the agricultural input industry, research and development in food manufacturing (Isakson 2014), and even the fight against food insecurity among peasant farmers (Breger Bush 2012). In general, the boundary line between financial activity and food provision has become extremely blurry, with financiers finding sources of profit in food and agriculture and food-system actors dab-bling in financial services and speculation (Isakson 2014). The expanded role of finance is key to understanding the transformations currently taking place within the global food regime (Burch and Lawrence 2009; McMichael 2012).

## NOTES

1. In defining financialization in this way, Krippner follows Arrighi (1994). He explains that, while under the capitalist system commodities generally act as intermediaries for turning money into more money (a type of transaction that Marx labeled MCM'), during periods of financial expansion, the commodity is cut out and money is used to create more money directly (MM'). Sweezy and Magdoff (1987) also characterize the "financial explosion" by a shift from productive to financial activities.
2. Each cycle is organized under a different hegemon. The four cycles of accumulation he discusses were led by the Genoese city-states (15th to early 17th century), the Dutch provinces (17th to late 18th century), Britain (the late 18th century to early 20th century), and the U.S. (the early 20th century to the early 21st century). Each is characterized by a period of material expansion, followed by heightened competition and stagnating profits, and finally a period of financial expansion in which firms switch from commodity production and trade to financial activities.

## REFERENCES

Arrighi, G. 1994. *The Long Twentieth Century*. London: Verso Books.

Baud, C. and C. Durand. 2012. "Financialization, Globalization and the Making of Profits by Leading Retailers." *Socio-Economic Review* 10(2):241–266.

Bergdolt, C. and A. Mittal. 2012. "Betting on World Agriculture: U.S. Private Equity Managers Eye Agricultural Returns." The Oakland Institute. Retrieved October 10, 2013 (http://www.oaklandinstitute.org/sites/oaklandinstitute.org/files/OI_report_Betting_on_World_Agriculture.pdf).

Bobenrieth, E. and B. Wright. 2009. "The Food Price Crisis of 2007/2008: Evidence and Implications." Food and Agriculture Organization of the United Nations. Retrieved December 3, 2013 (http://www.fao.org/fileadmin/templates/est/meetings/joint_igg_grains/Panel_Discussion_paper_2_English_only.pdf).

Breger Bush, S. 2012. *Derivatives and Development: A Political Economy of Global Finance, Farming, and Poverty*. New York: Palgrave Macmillan.

Burch, D. and G. Lawrence. 2009. "Towards a Third Food Regime: Behind the Transformation." *Agriculture and Human Values* 26(4):267–279.

Burch, D. and G. Lawrence. 2013. "Financialization in Agri-food Supply Chains: Private Equity and the Transformation of the Retail Sector." *Agriculture and Human Values* 30(2):247–258.

Busch, L. and C. Bain. 2004. "New! Improved? The Transformation of the Global Agrifood System." *Rural Sociology* 69(3):321–346.

Clapp, J. 2012. *Food*. Cambridge, UK: Polity Press.

Clapp, J. and E. Helleiner. 2012. "Troubled Futures? The Global Food Crisis and the Politics of Agricultural Derivatives Regulation." *Review of International Political Economy* 19(2):181–207.

Crippen, A. 2011. "CNBC Buffett Transcript Part 2: The 'Zebra' That Got Away."

*CNBC.com.* Retrieved October 10, 2013 (http://www.cnbc.com/id/41867379/ CNBC_Buffett_Transcript_Part_2_The_Zebra_That_Got_Away).

Cronon, W. 1992. *Nature's Metropolis: Chicago and the Great West.* New York: W.W. Norton and Company.

Daniel, S. 2012. "Situating Private Equity Capital in the Land Grab Debate." *Journal of Peasant Studies* 39(3–4):703–729.

Davis, G. 2009. *Managed by Markets: How Finance Re-shaped America.* Oxford: Oxford University Press.

De Schutter, O. 2010. "Food Commodities Speculation and Food Price Crises." Geneva, CH: United Nations Special Rapporteur on the Right to Food.

Ducastel, A. and W. Anseeuw. 2013. "Agriculture as an Asset Class: Financialisation of the (South) African Farming Sector." Retrieved May 7, 2014 (http://iippe.org/wp/wp-content/ uploads/2013/06/Antoine-Ducastel-Agriculture-as-an-asset-class.-Financialisation-of-the-South-African-farming-sector.pdf).

Epstein, G. 2005. "Introduction: Financialization and the World Economy." Pp. 3–16 in *Financialization and the World Economy*, edited by G. Epstein. Cheltenham, UK and Northampton, MA: Edward Elgar Publishing.

Fairbairn, M. 2014. "'Like Gold with Yield': Evolving Intersections between Farmland and Finance." *Journal of Peasant Studies* 41(5):777–795.

Fligstein, N. 2001. *The Architecture of Markets: An Economic Sociology of Twenty-First-Century Capitalist Societies.* Princeton, NJ: Princeton University Press.

FAO. 2013. "Monthly Food Price Indices (2002–2004=100)." Rome: Food and Agriculture Organization (FAO) of the United Nations (UN). Retrieved December 31, 2013 (http:// www.fao.org/worldfoodsituation/foodpricesindex/en/).

Gandel, S. 2011. "America's Hottest Investment: Farmland." *Time.* Retrieved May 7, 2014 (http://business.time.com/2011/06/01/americas-hottest-investment-farmland/).

Ghosh, J. 2009. "The Unnatural Coupling: Food and Global Finance." *Journal of Agrarian Change* 10(1):72–86.

Gladstone Land. 2014a. "Overview." Gladstone Land. Retrieved January 9, 2014 (http:// gladstoneland.investorroom.com/overview).

Gladstone Land. 2014b. "Portfolio." Gladstone Land. Retrieved January 9, 2014 (http:// gladstoneland.investorroom.com/portfolio).

Gunnoe, A. and P. Gellert. 2011. "Financialization, Shareholder Value, and the Transformation of Timberland Ownership in the US." *Critical Sociology* 37(3):265–284.

Harvey, D. 2010. *The Enigma of Capital and the Crises of Capitalism.* Oxford: Oxford University Press.

HighQuest Partners. 2010. "Private Financial Sector Investment in Farmland and Agricultural Infrastructure." Organisation for Economic Co-operation and Development. Retrieved October 10, 2013 (http://books.google.com/books?id=2v7hkQEACAAJ&dq=i nauthor:highquest+partners&hl=&cd=1&source=gbs_api).

IIED. 2012. "Farms and Funds: Investment Funds in the Global Land Rush." International Institute for Environment and Development. Retrieved October 10, 2013 (http://pubs.iied. org/pdfs/17121IIED.pdf?).

Irwin, S.H. and D. Sanders. 2011. "Index Funds, Financialization, and Commodity Futures Markets." *Applied Economic Perspectives and Policy* 33(1):1–31.

Isakson, S.R. 2014. "Food and Finance: The Financial Transformation of Agro-food Supply Chains." *Journal of Peasant Studies* 41(5):749–775.

Kaufman, F. 2010. "The Food Bubble: How Wall Street Starved Millions and Got Away with It." *Harper's Magazine.* Retrieved November 9, 2014 (http://frederickkaufman. typepad.com/files/the-food-bubble-pdf.pdf).

Kotz, D.M. 2011. "Financialization and Neoliberalism." Pp. 1–18 in *Relations of Global Power: Neoliberal Order and Disorder*, edited by G. Teeple and S. McBride. Toronto: University of Toronto Press.

Krippner, G.R. 2011. *Capitalizing on Crisis: The Political Origins of the Rise of Finance.* Cambridge, MA: Harvard University Press.

Krugman, P. 2010. "Nobody Believes in Supply and Demand." *New York Times*. Retrieved December 4, 2013 (http://krugman.blogs.nytimes.com/2010/12/28/nobody-believes-in-supply-and-demand/?_r=0).

Lawrence, G. and D. Burch. 2007. "Understanding Supermarkets and Agri-food Supply Chains." Pp. 1–26 in *Supermarkets and Agri-food Supply Chains: Transformations in the Production and Consumption of Foods*, edited by D. Burch and G. Lawrence. Cheltenham, UK and Northampton, MA: Edward Elgar Publishing.

Lazonick, W. and M. O'Sullivan. 2000. "Maximizing Shareholder Value: A New Ideology for Corporate Governance." *Economy and Society* 29(1):13–35.

Magnan, A. 2011. "New Avenues of Farm Corporatization in the Prairie Grains Sector: Farm Family Entrepreneurs and the Case of One Earth Farms." *Agriculture and Human Values* 29(2):161–175.

Masters, M. 2010. "Testimony of Michael W. Masters before the Commodities Futures Trading Commission." CFTC. Retrieved December 4, 2013 (http://www.cftc.gov/ucm/groups/public/@newsroom/documents/file/metalmarkets032510_masters.pdf).

Masters, M. and A. White. 2008. "The Accidental Hunt Brothers: How Institutional Investors Are Driving Up Food and Energy Prices." Masters Capital Management and White Knight Research and Trading.

McMichael, P. 2012. "The Land Grab and Corporate Food Regime Restructuring." *Journal of Peasant Studies* 39(3–4):681–701.

Minaya, J. and J. Ourso. 2012. "U.S. Drought Shouldn't Scorch Long-Term Farmland Investing." TIAA–CREF. Retrieved October 23, 2013 (https://www.tiaa-cref.org/public/advice-planning/market-commentary/market_commentary_articles/articles/mc_053.html).

Murphy, S., D. Burch, and J. Clapp. 2012. "Cereal Secrets." Oxford: Oxfam International. Retrieved May 7, 2014 (http://www.oxfam.org/sites/www.oxfam.org/files/rr-cereal-secrets-grain-traders-agriculture-30082012-en.pdf).

O'Keefe, B. 2009. "Betting the Farm." *CNN Money*. Retrieved February 23, 2014 (http://money.cnn.com/2009/06/08/retirement/betting_the_farm.fortune/).

Reardon, T. and J. Berdegué. 2002. "The Rapid Rise of Supermarkets in Latin America: Challenges and Opportunities for Development." *Development Policy Review* 20(4):371–388.

Reardon, T., C. Barrett, J. Berdegué, and J. Swinnen. 2009. "Agrifood Industry Transformation and Small Farmers in Developing Countries." *World Development* 37(11):1717–1727.

SLC Agrícola. 2012. "SLC Agrícola: Value from Both Farm and Land." Retrieved June 30, 2013 (http://www.mzweb.com.br/slcagricola2009/web/arquivos/SLCE3_PresentationInstitutional_201205_ENG.pdf).

Sweezy, P. and H. Magdoff. 1987. *Stagnation and the Financial Explosion*. New York: Monthly Review Press.

TIAA–CREF. 2012. "TIAA–CREF Announces $2 Billion Global Agriculture Company." TIAA–CREF. Retrieved October 23, 2013 (https://www.tiaa-cref.org/public/about/press/about_us/releases/articles/pressrelease422.html).

Tomaskovic-Devey, D. and K. Lin. 2011. "Income Dynamics, Economic Rents, and the Financialization of the U.S. Economy." *American Sociological Review* 76(4):538–559.

USDA NASS. 2013. "Quick Stats." U.S. Department of Agriculture (USDA) National Agricultural Statistics Service (NASS). Retrieved January 23, 2014 (http://www.nass.usda.gov/Quick_Stats/).

Useem, M. 1996. *Investor Capitalism: How Money Managers Are Changing the Face of Corporate America*. New York: Basic Books.

Visser, O. 2014. "Running Out of Farmland? Superb Soil, Land Value and the Sluggishness of Commoditisation in Russia." Retrieved May 7, 2014 (http://www.iss.nl/fileadmin/ASSETS/iss/Documents/Conference_papers/Food___farmland_Jan.2014/Visser-Land_value___superb_soil__commoditisation-FFF-conf.pdf).

Wahl, P. 2009. "Food Speculation: The Main Factor of the Price Bubble in 2008." Berlin:

Weltwirtschaft, Ökologie & Entwicklung (WEED). Retrieved May 20, 2011 (http://www2. weed-online.org/uploads/weed_food_speculation.pdf).

Wiegel, J. 2013. "A New Breed of Tomato Farmers? The Effect of Transnational Supermarket Standards on Domestic Cultures of Production and Trade." *International Journal of Sociology of Agriculture and Food* 20(2):237–254.

Wray, L.R. 2008. "The Commodities Market Bubble: Money Manager Capitalism and the Financialization of Commodities." Annandale-on-Hudson: Jerome Levy Economics Institute of Bard College. Retrieved May 7, 2014 (http://www.levyinstitute.org/pubs/ ppb_96.pdf).

# 13. The political economy of labor relations in agriculture and food
*Alessandro Bonanno*

## INTRODUCTION

The social, economic, and political relevance of labor relations has made this topic one of the most studied aspects of agriculture and food worldwide. Classical nineteenth- and twentieth-century studies tackled the fundamental phenomenon of the penetration of capitalist social relations in agriculture and the consequent transformation of the peasantry into the modern working class. Subsequent works documented the processes of expropriation, concentration, and redistribution of land that created capitalist farmers, independent family farm holders, part-time farmers, and wage workers of the contemporary era's agriculture. Arguably, the most decisive trait of the evolution of labor relations in the period leading to the second portion of the twentieth century was the massive rural to urban migration that significantly reduced the size of the agricultural labor force and, concomitantly, allowed the availability of labor for the expansion of the urban industrial apparatus. Interpreted by many as a physiological and necessary stage of the evolution of capitalism, the expulsion of workers from agriculture and their transformation into urban-industrial labor became a defining characteristic of capitalism and a central focus of investigation.

Post-World War II *High Fordism*[1] institutionalized mechanisms for the control and regulation of labor relations and the mitigation of the contradictions of mature capitalism (Antonio and Bonanno 2000). Measures that favored the gradual urbanization of agricultural labor but also the persistence of family farms were set in place accompanied by productivist policies that increased labor productivity and agricultural production. Following a general "management-labor accord," agricultural labor benefitted from state intervention and the consequent implementation of welfare-oriented social policies (Bonanno and Cavalcanti 2014; Bonanno and Constance 2008). Highly regulated labor relations became instrumental for the expansion of capital accumulation and social stability that characterized the period.

By the 1970s, the Fordist model had entered its final crisis. The income redistribution and welfare-supporting measures that it entailed, along with relatively high intervention of the state, became intolerable "rigidities" for the ruling capitalist class (Bonanno, Busch, Friedland, Gouveia, and Mingione 1994). The ensuing restructuring of the economy and society centered on the development of globalization and neoliberalism. Globalization brought about the reorganization of production and consumption along with the emergence of global networks dominated by transnational corporations (Bonanno et al. 1994; Bonanno and Constance 2008; Brown and Dias-Bonilla 2008; Inglis and Gimlin 2009). Featuring a much-reduced intervention of the nation-state in social matters, neoliberalism provided the theoretical and political tools for the deregulation of Fordist social relations and concomitant reregulation of production. This process engendered class polarization, the growth of corporate power, and increased exploitation of human and natural resources (Harvey 2005; Rosin, Stock, and Campbell 2012; Wolf and Bonanno 2014).

Adopting a political economy approach, this chapter analyzes salient characteristics of contemporary labor relations in agri-food. It opens with a brief analysis of the evolution and characteristics of labor relations under Fordism. Subsequently, it discusses the conditions and use of labor under Neoliberal Globalization. Emphasis is placed on the phenomena of the flexibilization of labor; the hypermobility of capital; the mobilization of the reserve army of labor, immigrant labor, feminized labor; gender discourses; the role and trajectory of trade unions; third-party production strategies; and the proliferation of contractual production arrangements and resistance. It concludes with a brief statement underscoring the significant transformation of labor relations created by neoliberal policies and global trends.

## LABOR IN AGRI-FOOD UNDER HIGH FORDISM

In pertinent agri-food literature, Fordism is seen as a period in which the "management-labor accord" characterized industrial relations (Bonanno et al. 1994; Kenney, Lobao, Curry, and Coe 1989). Social stability and economic growth were achieved through a "social pact" that allowed workers to obtain and maintain economic and political gains and the ruling classes to benefit from expanded capital accumulation, pacified industrial relations, and a supportive intervention of the state. In agri-food, Fordism signified the introduction of policies that augmented production and productivity and extended the control of multinational corporations over developing regions and their people, deepening the global South's economic and political dependency (Frank 1969). Fordism also generated an array of interventionist measures that supported the income of farmers and allowed the existence of permanently employed wage workers. It promoted the creation of infrastructure that, while benefitted corporations, also contributed to the wellbeing of rural communities and small- and medium-sized farm holders (Bonanno and Constance 2008). Fordist discourses centered on the idea that social stability and development could not be meaningfully achieved without strategies that contemplated the collective and balanced resolution of labor issues.

While socio-economic inequality and class divisions remained, processes of integration of the working class into mainstream society proceeded at a sustained pace. The application of Keynesian economic policies allowed the expansion of the middle class and the improvement of the working and living conditions of the lower classes. Family farm holders and peasants left farming at a record pace. Similarly, farmworkers were massively replaced by an intensive process of mechanization. Yet, the urbanization of these members of the agricultural labor force often translated into stable urban employment and a path toward urban middle class status. Arguably, the transformation of agricultural labor into the Fordist middle class was one of the salient aspects of the period. Labor that remained in farming and in the rapidly transforming agri-food sector enjoyed the support of state programs and the backing of powerful unions. Additionally, the diffusion of part-time farming allowed these workers to remain in agriculture despite inadequate and often declining farm income. While farmworkers, peasant, and small farm holders normally occupied the lower strata of the working class, employment opportunities in other sectors, union actions, and an expanded state-sponsored welfare system guaranteed their relative socio-economic stability. To be sure, in the Fordist era agricultural labor was among the most flexible forms of regulated work. The seasonally informal nature of farm work along with limited farm income made labor stability a less evident feature than in other sectors of production.

Under Fordism, agricultural labor played a double role. First, it was a pivotal factor in the expansion of the forces of production in farming. Increases in labor productivity contributed to the growth of production and the generation of inexpensive and abundant food that supported the expansion of manufacturing and urban areas. Second, agricultural workers represented a reservoir of labor for the development of the industrial/urban sector. Through rural to urban migration and supporting political economic measures, expelled agricultural workers provided the necessary labor power for the growth of manufacturing. Moreover, during periods of recession, farming absorbed excess labor, contributing to the maintenance of social stability. As economic growth resumed, workers were eventually released for participation in the urban-industrial labor market.

## AGRI-FOOD LABOR UNDER NEOLIBERAL GLOBALIZATION

By the early 1980s, Neoliberal Globalization appeared as a class response to Fordism (Harvey 2005; Robinson 2004; Krugman 2013). It restored the power of the ruling class after the gains obtained by subordinate groups during the Fordist era. Neoliberal Globalization significantly reduced state intervention in the social sphere, diminished the power of unions and political groups of the left, and created the availability of a cheaper and more docile labor force worldwide (Antonio and Bonanno 2000; Harvey 2005; Robinson 2004). The conditions that permitted the "management-labor accord" of the Fordist era were removed through structural changes that identified in the costs and power of labor some of the most fundamental *rigidities* that hampered capital accumulation (Bonanno and Constance 2008: Harvey 2005; Robinson 2004). Simultaneously, supporters of neoliberalism presented state intervention and programs for the working class and the poor as wasteful and ineffective. They were replaced by market-based mechanisms that benefitted the upper class, redistributed wealth upward, and eroded the socio-economic conditions of the working and middle classes (Harvey 2005; Gornick and Jantti 2013; Volscho and Kelly 2012; Krugman 2013; Stiglitz 2012). Labor stability – a feature of the Fordist era – was considered an unnecessary entitlement that distracted workers from accomplishing their labor tasks and working efficiently. Dwelling on pronouncements about the importance of meritocracy, individualism, and self-help, Neoliberal Globalization promoted discourses that viewed unions' actions as disadvantageous to labor and the intervention of the state in favor of subordinate classes as detrimental to economic development and social stability. Conversely, the view that more economic incentives for the upper class would translate into investment and enhanced economic growth became widely endorsed.

### Flexibilization of Labor

Neoliberal Globalization has fostered the *flexibilization of labor* whereby reduced wages, precarious and unstable employment, enhanced exploitation, and political weakness characterize the position of agri-food workers (Bain 2010a; 2010b; Harrison 2011; Wolf and Bonanno 2014). Flexibilization of labor consists of a number of interrelated aspects. It involves the *flexibility of work time* as workers are required to work a specific number of hours and/or periods with discontinuity; *flexibility of work activities* whereby workers perform a variety of different tasks involving varying skills; and *flexibility* of *employment conditions and duration* which refers to a situation when workers are hired and freely dismissed to fit production schedules and requirements set by management.[2] Flexibility also includes the introduction of *short-term employment contracts* that contemplate weekly and/or monthly work along with varying commitments whereby workers' requirements may change from week to week without a guaranteed minimum amount of worked hours. Production contracts and third-party contracts also promote the flexible use and control of labor (see below). Additionally, indicators of task performance determine wages rather than length of time worked and/or seniority. Finally, the ability of workers to move among work locations, or *mobility*, is employed as a condition of employment and pay. In essence, under Neoliberal Globalization, agricultural workers perform a number of new tasks that transcend the traditional sphere of cultivation. Workers are now required to be involved in many facets of the production process and of the transformation of farm products into food. In this context, low wages remain one of the primary characteristics of labor relations in the twenty-first century, and their exchange for a greater amount of, more sophisticated, and more specialized, work constitutes the norm. In agri-food, wages are lower than in other sectors as the use of marginal segments of the work force and informalization reduce them. Additionally, the dominant anti-labor climate allows the proliferation of wage compression strategies.[3]

**Hypermobility of Capital and the Mobilization of the Reserve Army of Labor**

Through the decentralization of production, plant relocation, and the creation of global networks, transnational corporations have been able to search for the most desirable factors of production worldwide. Global sourcing has emerged as one of the fundamental components of enhanced corporate mobility. It stands in sharp contrast with the overtly controlled mobility of labor. As distant labor pools are mobilized and placed in competition with one another, the hypermobility of capital alters established schemes of labor competition and neutralizes proven strategies to protect the rights and position of workers (Bonanno and Cavalcanti 2011:4–6; Gornick and Jantti 2013; Kubiszewski, Costanza, Franco, Lawn, Talberth, Jackson, and Aylmer 2013; Noah 2012; Volscho and Kelly 2012; Stiglitz 2012; Western and Rosenfeld 2011). As profit increases and labor remuneration stagnates, crises translate primarily into unemployment (Harvey 2010; Gornick and Jantti 2013; Vilscho and Kelly 2012; Krugman 2013; Stiglitz 2012). Under Neoliberal Globalization, enhanced mobility allows corporations to integrate weak segments of the labor force into global production networks. Women, minorities, immigrants, and other marginal groups from around the globe are sought to reduce costs of production and maintain a docile and highly controllable labor force. This process has mobilized an enormous reserve army of labor located in less developed and/or emerging economies. This labor force now participates in global production at costs that are fractional in comparison with those paid in more advanced countries. Its presence is a formidable barrier to the growth of wages worldwide as additional members of the reserve army of labor can be mobilized locally and/ or elsewhere. For instance, rising wages in China – the primary example of the integration of cheap labor into global production networks – have been accompanied with the relocation of production in other countries, such as Vietnam, where labor is even less expensive. Moreover, in these countries a large untapped reserve army of labor remains available to be mobilized: a situation that allows arguments about further compression of wages in the future (Bellamy Foster and McChesney 2012).

**Immigrant Labor**

The availability of the reserve army of labor is complemented by the mobilization of immigrant labor (Mize and Swords 2011; Preibisch 2012; Roman and Arregui 2013). Differing from the Fordist period (Holmes 2013; Friedland, Barton, and Thomas 1981), immigrant labor is, currently, one of the most common forms of labor employed in agri-food. The primary justification for its use is an economic one: immigrant labor is cheap and it is a suitable replacement for local workers who do not want these jobs (Roman and Arregui 2013; Mize and Swords 2011). Immigrant workers, it is maintained, are given the opportunity to have jobs that would be normally inaccessible to them. In this contest, these jobs are viewed as beneficial for all as they meet the desire of workers to find employment and firms' strategy to pay low wages. The discourse that contextualizes this argument views immigrants as "violators of established laws" and democratic principles and contemplates the criminalization of the immigration process and immigrants. The economically motivated desire and advantages to employing immigrants is, therefore, accompanied by the claim that military and/or police intervention is needed to protect national security, maintain social stability, and safeguard the economic wellbeing of local workers[4] (Cornyn 2013). Based on the neoliberal tenet of labor market impartiality, this discourse further assumes that firms' wish to pay low wages is a natural consequence of market mechanisms. Rejecting evidence that immigrants are fearful for their lack of papers, disciplined through their legal status, and, as a result, denied decent wages, working conditions, and employment, this discourse discounts the unfair use of these workers and legitimizes their exploitation.

In this context, as local workers' resistance has the potential to alter this trend, mechanisms that would generate the availability of inexpensive and highly controllable workers must be set in place (Holmes 2013; Roman and Arregui 2013; Preibisch 2012; Harrison 2014). Under Neoliberal Globalization these mechanisms are undocumented immigration and temporary immigration through guest worker programs. The availability of undocumented immigration is one of the most strident paradoxes of contemporary labor relations: virtually all sides of the political, economic, and social spectrum call for its elimination, yet very little is done in terms of legislative measures to address it (Bonanno and Cavalcanti 2011:5–6). This paradox, however, is explained by the fact that a reduction of the flow of undocumented immigrants would increase the cost of labor and labor strength and as such is resisted by anti-labor forces. In the United States – one of the most evident examples of this situation – the last reform of the immigration law was approved several decades ago in 1986 under President Reagan. This legislation allowed the proliferation of undocumented immigration despite the militarization of the border and vocal support to increase border security. Subsequent attempts to reform it failed in 2006 and 2007. More recent attempts resulted in the 2013 US Senate approval of a reform law that, however, never reached the US House of Representatives. Aside from domestic issues[5] that add layers to the reasons for its lack of support, the impact that this law would have on the availability of cheap and docile labor makes its future approval tenuous at best. The status quo that guarantees the presence of politically weak and economically inexpensive immigrant workers in the labor market is preferred to destabilizing alternative solutions.

Short-term immigration programs are heralded by many as desirable alternatives to undocumented immigration. However, their existence places immigrant workers in an equally weak and exploitable position. By tying the temporary legal immigrant status to a specific job, when this employment is terminated, the legal immigrant status is also lost. This situation prevents immigrant workers from exercising the rights to object to conditions and remuneration of work (e.g., strikes, grievances, and, in fact any form of dissent with the employer) and to be mobile within the labor market (e.g., find another and more suitable job). These are rights that are endowed to workers in a free labor market. Conversely, in the case of short-term immigration programs, the lack of these rights places virtually all the power in the hands of employers who for any reason can terminate employment. Being fired almost inevitably translates into deportation or degradation to illegal immigrant status (Preibisch 2007; 2012; Harrison and Lloyd 2012; Sanderson 2012; Bonanno and Cavalcanti 2014). In essence, these conditions perpetuate the availability of cheap labor that is highly controlled, not only through the availability of a large reserve army of labor, but also increasingly through political, cultural, and social mechanisms.

### Feminized Labor and Gender Discourses

The use of weak segments of labor in agri-food production includes the increased use of women. As in the case of immigrant labor, the use of women has grown because they can be paid lower wages, offer limited political resistance, and can be easily controlled (Bonanno and Cavalcanti 2012; 2014). These structural conditions are supported by an ideology that describes low paying and unstable employment as "convenient" for women and their families. This sexist ideology views women's work as complementary to that of men. Men are the family's breadwinners, while women contribute to the support of their families by taking secondary jobs. Particularly in the case of the expanding fresh fruit sector, these jobs are presented as uniquely suited for women as it is claimed that they require the delicate touch and care that only women can provide. While they remain poorly paid, they are described as a special recognition to women's attributes and desirable because they allow women to perform both domestic and work duties[6] (Lara Flores 2010; Bendini and Pescio 1996; Cavalcanti, Mota, and da Silva 2002). Disregarding historical evidence of women as breadwinners and about the hard work that they perform, pronouncements about the lack of mobility and the convenience of work near home are employed to create a climate conducive to increased exploitation. Additionally, such an understanding of femininity in the division of labor is accompanied by an equally sexist view of the work of men. Men are assigned to tasks requiring physical strength and technical expertise that are viewed as uniquely suited for this gender. They are better remunerated than the jobs assigned to women and contribute to the superior position of men in the organization of labor in the sector. Yet, they also add to the growth of labor exploitation as the segmentation of workers by gender divides them, increases their political weakness, and allows the introduction of restructuring measures that further worsen remuneration and working conditions (Bonanno and Cavalcanti 2012; Hirata 2002).

### Third-Party Production Strategies: Contracts

The proliferation of third-party production contracts has emerged as one of the defining features in labor relations in agri-food. It refers to the establishment of contracts for the delivery of production services to agri-food firms by third-party organizations. Relevant to this chapter are third-party contracts that involve companies that provide, and are responsible for, the provision of workers. For a fee, these companies deliver labor to agri-food firms by hiring, supervising, and paying workers. These workers are employed by the contracting companies and report to them. This process exonerates agri-food firms from having to follow requirements established by labor legislation and/or third-party certification protocols. These tasks fall under the responsibility of contracting companies (Bain 2010a; Bonanno and Cavalcanti 2014). Additionally, the use of contractors clears firms from paying labor taxes and workers' benefits. It also eliminates unwanted contacts with workers as claims and disputes are handled by contractors (Bain 2010a).

While firms gain by the use of contractors, workers are seriously penalized by this situation. This is primarily because, in agri-food, these contracting companies are often informal operations run by one or a few individuals who, also informally, recruit, manage, and pay workers. The precarious and frequently clandestine nature of these working arrangements exposes workers to many of the same negative conditions associated with the illegal immigrant status. They have virtually no ability to resist the power of contractors, negotiate better wages and working conditions, and demand more stable forms of employment.[7]

**Unions**

As flexibilization, feminization, and the overall exploitation of labor increase, an evident condition of contemporary agri-food is the diminished role and power of trade unions. Following trends typical of other spheres of the economy, unions have experienced a steady decline in membership and political power. While the decline of unions is particularly pronounced in North America, it is also visible in the traditionally union strong Europe and Latin America.[8] This weakness has been further accompanied by the shift to more centrist positions of labor parties, resulting in the diminished visibility and relevance of labor in political and social arenas (Bonanno and Cavalcanti 2014; Roman and Arregui 2013). According to some, these trends represent a positive way in which labor relations fit the requirements of a much more competitive and flexible global economy. They are much more desirable and practicable than Fordist arrangements and the costly concessions that they entailed for labor. Opposing interpretations read this situation as the result of the "defeat" of the labor movement by the forces that support Neoliberal Globalization (Harvey 2005; Lichtenstein 2013; Robinson 2004).

Also underscored are the limits of unions' strategies and vision.

Unions, it is argued, have not been able to transcend corporate centered protectionist postures that created hard to mend divisions between domestic and foreign workers and unionized and non-unionized labor (Roman and Arregui 2013). Additionally, unions have accepted the powerful entrepreneurial discourse that subordinates the wellbeing of workers to the growth of profit and the firm. According to this view, profitability and company expansion are necessary conditions that must be accomplished before actions leading to pay increases and the creation of new and "better" jobs could be set in place (Brady, Baker, and Finnigan 2013; Roman and Arregui 2013). By choosing this posture, unions have found themselves in a predicament in which improving firms' competitiveness and productivity has often translated into wage, working conditions, and employment concessions. The consequent loss of jobs, the concomitant creation of poorly paid and precarious new positions, and the continuous capital flight have weakened the power of unions and their appeal to a resigned working class. As production continues to globalize and more distant segments of the reserve army of labor enter the labor market, unions' ability to represent and defend workers continues to lessen.

**Resistance**

Despite the weakness of unions, the dominant agri-food system is resisted. This resistance, however, departs from labor-based forms of struggle that characterized the Fordist era. Because Neoliberal Globalization has been a powerful instrument against strikes and the ability of labor to negotiate at the political level, these strategies are now viewed as weak and ineffective. In this context, at least two aspects should be briefly discussed. The first refers to the shift of the primary locus of resistance from the sphere of production to that of consumption. Historically, resistance to dominant labor relations took place, first and foremost, at the level of production. Following the classical critique of "utopian socialism" initiated by Marx, the points that labor exploitation takes place at production, firms are most vulnerable during production, and, consequently, the ability of workers to be politically stronger derives from actions related to the production process were widely accepted within the labor movement. Accordingly, opposition to capitalist social relations was directed at the organization and structure of production and struggles occurred primarily in the factories and in the fields.

Through the decentralization of production and the enhanced use of the reserve army of labor, Neoliberal Globalization's attacks on labor and pro-labor Fordist arrangements have limited the effectiveness of traditional resistance at the level of production. Accordingly, opposition has shifted elsewhere and critical actions by consumers have emerged as desirable moves to counter corporate power. In this context, agri-food has been one of the sectors where this type of resistance has been most visible. Because it is located in the sphere of exchange, consumer-based opposition is primarily directed at improving the quality of products (e.g., better quality food and agricultural products) and the fairness of the formal production and exchange processes (e.g., respect of existing laws governing labor relations and commerce; protection of natural resources and the environment). Thus, consumer actions can only marginally affect important labor relation issues such as salary, employment length and stability, and employment growth. Moreover, consumers' concerns over labor have translated only into requests for the safeguarding and implementation of existing norms on working conditions, the rights of workers, and the use of labor. In effect, resistance through consumer actions has been viewed as defensive and as sharing individualistic and productivist postures that do not challenge dominant structural conditions and the neoliberal ideology that supports them (Johnston and Szabo 2011; DuPuis and Goodman 2005; Guthman 2003).

The second aspect of the shift away from labor-based resistance involves the multiplication of efforts for the development of alternative forms of production. Initiatives such as civic agriculture, farmer markets, organic production, and local food systems have emerged as popular new forms of resistance. These types of initiatives have grown significantly and, in some regions, represent a large portion of overall agri-food production. Yet, in many other countries – such as the United States – their contribution has remained fractional. While their novel and different dimension has been praised, these initiatives do not attempt to alter the dominant organization of agri-food. They, rather, provide a parallel system of production that finds in voluntary action, local embeddedness, reciprocity, and solidarity some of its mainstream alternative fundamental characteristics. Because they do not challenge existing social relations, they have not only had no effect on corporate power, but also a great number of these initiatives have been coopted by the very corporations that they wish to oppose. Most importantly, their availability to the weaker segments of society has remained quite limited. Accordingly, they have been charged with being "elitist" as they do not represent the interests, nor address the concerns, of the working class (Bonanno and Cavalcanti 2014).

## CONCLUSIONS

The chapter's brief illustration of the characteristics of labor relations in agri-food under Fordism first and Neoliberal Globalization later has shown the substantial changes that have occurred since the early 1980s. Contemporary labor relations in agri-food feature the significant flexibilization of the use of labor and its increased exploitation. The augmented use of weak segments of the labor force such as immigrants and women, the mobilization of a large reserve army of labor, and the crisis of labor unions add to the changes that characterize the sector. The implementation of neoliberal policies, which has fostered the decentralization of production and the mobility of capital and labor, has promoted the development of a sector in which corporate power and control have increased. The domination of neoliberal policies has been aided by the high level of legitimation that the ideology of neoliberalism has achieved in contemporary society. Even resistance movements have adopted postures that implicitly support neoliberalism's individualism and reliance on market mechanisms. Under these circumstances, significant short-term alterations of the conditions and use of labor appear problematic. Additionally, the widespread acceptance of neoliberalism and the implementation of policies that are inspired by this ideology suggest that alternatives to the overall status of labor relations in agri-food will be difficult to implement in the medium-run. This appears the case despite the existence of contradictions and the visibility of the worsening conditions of workers.

## NOTES

1.  High Fordism refers to the period between 1945 and 1979. It is differentiated from the overall Fordist period whose origins are identified with the years following World War I.
2.  In the literature on labor flexibility, one camp views it as the appropriate and successful response to exogenous events such as changes in the business and social environments and the introduction of neoliberal policies. See World Bank (2013); Auer and Cazes (2003); and Reilly (2001). An opposing camp stresses the socially constructed nature of these changes and labor flexibility as deliberate business strategies to further control and exploit labor. See Berhhardt, Boushey, Dresser, and Tilly (2008); Brown, Eichengreen, and Reich (2010); Ross (2009); Zeitlin and Tolliday (1992).
3.  Telling of this political climate is the debate on the proposed increase of the minimum wage level in 2014 in the United States. As the minimum wage has remained constant for years and does not allow workers and their families to rise above the poverty line, President Obama's proposal to increase the minimum wage has been met with the prevailing criticism that it would damage business and, accordingly, force firms to cut jobs. Central in this discourse is the concept that the satisfaction of workers' claims is detrimental to the wellbeing of companies, consumers, and the expansion of the economy.
4.  The contradictory dimension of this discourse is made evident by the diverging objectives that its supporters promote. Sharing the political conservative label, these groups call

for the continuous flow of inexpensive and docile immigrant labor but, simultaneously, they endorse protectionist and xenophobic postures that mandate restrictions to the flow of immigrant labor. In the United States, conservative political discourses and actions common in border-states (e.g., Arizona and Texas) are cases in point.
5. The immigration reform debate is often couched in terms of domestic politics. Accordingly, it is mostly addressed in terms of its potential impact on electoral results and benefits to the Democratic or Republican Party.
6. The power of this ideology can be seen by its use in analyses that aim at the improvement of the conditions of women. In these works, labor flexibility is seen as one of the consequences of the development of society and something that can and should be used by women to perform their many roles (see Gatta and McCabe 2005). For an analysis that criticizes the "convenience" and the assumed "individual choice" of these flexible jobs, see Presser (2005).
7. Contracts are used in a variety of different instances. In all of them, there is a direct attempt by firms to pass risks and costs onto labor regardless of whether this labor involves wage workers or family farm holders. For a discussion of the effects of contracts in agri-food production, see Bonanno and Cavalcanti (2014).
8. Among others, see the work of Antunes (2000) and Roman and Arregui (2013) for a discussion of the crisis of unions in Latin America. See also Fletcher and Gapasin (2008) and Brady, Baker, and Finnigan (2013) for a discussion about unions in the United States and Upchurch, Taylor, and Mathers (2012) for the case of Europe.

# REFERENCES

Antonio, Robert J. and Alessandro Bonanno. 2000. "A New Global Capitalism? From Americanism and Fordism to Americanization-Globalization." *American Studies* 41 (2/3):33–77.
Antunes, Ricardo. 2000. *Adeus ao Trabalho? Ensaio Sobre as Metamorfoses e a Centralidade do Mundo do Trabalho*. 4ª edição, Campinas: Editora da Universidade Estadual de Campinas.
Auer, Peter and Sandrine Cazes. 2003. *Employment Stability in an Age of Flexibility: Evidence from Industrialized Countries*. New York: International Labor Office.
Bain, Carmen. 2010a. "Structuring the Flexible and Feminized Labor Market: GLOBALGAP Standards for Agricultural Labor in Chile." *Journal of Women Culture and Society* 35(2):343–370.
Bain, Carmen. 2010b. "Governing the Global Value Chain: GLOBALGAP and the Chilean Fresh Fruit Industry." *International Journal of Sociology of Agriculture and Food* 17(1):1–13.
Bellamy Foster, John and Robert W. McChesney. 2012. *The Endless Crisis*. New York: Monthly Review Press.
Bendini, Mónica and Cristina Pescio. 1996. *Empleo y Cambio Técnico en la fruticultura del Alto Valle*. Bueno Aires: Editorial La Colmena.
Bernhardt, Annette, Heather Boushey, Laura Dresser, and Chris Tilly (eds.). 2008. *The Gloves-Off Economy: Workplace Standards at the Bottom of America's Labor Market*. Ithaca, NY: Cornell University Press.
Bonanno, Alessandro, Lawrence Busch, William H. Friedland, Lourdes Gouveia, and Enzo Mingione (eds.). 1994. *From Columbus to ConAgra: The Globalization of Agriculture and Food*. Lawrence, KS: University Press of Kansas.
Bonanno, Alessandro and Josefa Salete Barbosa Cavalcanti. 2011. *Globalization and the Time–Space Reorganization*. Bingley, UK: Emerald Publishing.
Bonanno, Alessandro and Josefa Salete Barbosa Cavalcanti. 2012. "Globalization, Food Quality and Labor: The Case of Grape Production in Northeastern Brazil." *International Journal of Sociology of Agriculture and Food* 19(1):37–55.

Bonanno, Alessandro and Josefa Salete Barbosa Cavalcanti. 2014. *Labor Relations in Globalized Food.* Bingley, UK: Emerald Publishing.
Bonanno, Alessandro and Douglas H. Constance. 2008. *Stories of Globalization: Transnational Corporation, Resistance and the State.* University Park, PA: Penn State University Press.
Brady, David, Regina Baker, and Ryan Finnigan. 2013. "When Unionization Disappears: State-Level Unionization and Working Poverty in the United States." *American Sociological Review* 78(5):872–896.
Brown, Clair, Barry J. Eichengreen, and Michael Reich (eds.). 2010. *Labor in the Era of Globalization.* New York: Cambridge University Press.
Brown, Joachim and Eugenio Dias-Bonilla (eds.). 2008. *Globalization of Agriculture and Food and the Poor.* New York: Oxford University Press.
Cavalcanti, Josefa Salete B., Dalva M. Mota, and Pedro Gama da Silva. 2002. "Mirando hacia al Norte: Clase Género y Etnicidad en los Espacios de Fruticultura del Nordeste de Brasil." *Areas* 26:161–181.
Cornyn, John. 2013. "Immigration Reform Starts at the Border. Security Provisions are Key to the Success of Any New Legislation." *Houston Chronicle.* June 27:B9.c.
DuPuis, Melanie and David Goodman. 2005. "Should We Go 'Home' to Eat? Toward a Reflexive Politics of Localism." *Journal of Rural Studies* 21(3):359–371.
Fletcher, Bill and Fernando Gapasin. 2008. *Solidarity Divided: The Crisis in Organized Labor and a New Path toward Social Justice.* Berkeley, CA: University of California Press.
Frank, Andre Gunder. 1969. *Latin America and Underdevelopment.* New York: Monthly Review Press.
Friedland, William H., Amy Barton, and Robert J. Thomas. 1981. *Manufacturing Green Gold.* New York: Cambridge University Press.
Gatta, Mary L. and Kevin P. McCabe. 2005. *Not Just Getting By: The New Era of Flexible Workforce Development.* Lanham, MD: Lexington Books.
Gornick, Janet and Markus Jantti (eds.). 2013. *Income Inequality: Economic Disparities and the Middle Class in Affluent Countries.* Palo Alto, CA: Stanford University Press.
Guthman, Julie. 2003. "Fast Food/Organic Food: Reflexive Tastes and the Making of 'Yuppie Chow.'" *Social and Cultural Geography* 4(1):45–58.
Harrison, Jill. 2014. "Situating Neoliberalization: Unpacking the Construction of Racially Segregated Workplaces." Pp. 91–111 in Steven Woolf and Alessandro Bonanno (eds.) *The Neoliberal Regime in the Agri-food Sector.* New York: Routledge.
Harrison, Jill. 2011. *Pesticide Drift and the Pursuit of Environmental Justice.* Cambridge, MA: MIT Press.
Harrison, Jill and Sarah Lloyd. 2012. "Illegality at Work: Deportability and the Productive New Era of Immigration Enforcement." *Antipode* 44(2):365–385.
Harvey, David. 2005. *A Brief History of Neoliberalism.* New York: Oxford University Press.
Hirata, Helena. 2002. *Nova Divisão Sexual do Trabalho? Um Olhar Voltado para a Empresa e a Sociedade.* São Paulo: Boitempo Editorial.
Holmes, Seth. 2013. *Fresh Fruit, Broken Bodies: Migrant Farmworkers in the United States.* Berkeley, CA: University of California Press.
Inglis, David and Debra Gimlin (eds.). 2009. *The Globalization of Food.* New York: Berg.
Johnston, Josée and Michelle Szabo. 2011. "Reflexivity and the Whole Food Market Consumer: The Lived Experience of Shopping for Change." *Agriculture and Human Values* 28:303–319.
Kenney, Martin, Linda Lobao, James Curry, and Richard Coe. 1989. "Midwest Agriculture and US Fordism." *Sociologia Ruralis* 29(2):131–148.
Krugman, Paul. 2013. "Austerity Doctrine Benefits Only the Wealthy." *Houston Chronicle.* April 26: B7.
Kubiszewski, Ida, Robert Costanza, Carol Franco, Philip Lawn, John Talberth, Tim Jackson, and Camille Aylmer. 2013. "Beyond GDP: Measuring and Achieving Global Genuine Progress." *Ecological Economics* 93(2013):57–68. Retrieved at http://dx.doi.org/10.1016/j.ecolecon.2013.04.019 on July 1, 2013.

Lara Flores, Sara M. (ed.). 2010. *Migraciones de Trabajo y Movilidad Territorial*. Ed. 1°. Mexico City: Consejo Nacional de Ciencia y Tecnología.

Lichtenstein, Nelson. 2013. *State of the Union: A Century of American Labor*. Princeton, NJ: Princeton University Press.

Mize, Ronald and Alicia Swords. 2011. *Consuming Mexican Labor: From the Bracero Program to NAFTA*. Toronto: University of Toronto Press.

Noah, Timothy. 2012. *The Great Divergence: America's Growing Inequality Crisis and What We Can Do about It*. New York: Bloomsbury.

Preibisch, Kerry. 2012. "Migrant Workers and Changing Work-Place Regimes in Contemporary Agricultural Production in Canada." *International Journal of Sociology of Agriculture and Food* 19(1):62–82.

Preibisch, Kerry. 2007. "Local Produce, Foreign Labor: Labor Mobility Programs and Global Trade Competitiveness in Canada." *Rural Sociology* 72(3):418–449.

Presser, Harriet B. 2005. *Working in a 24/7 Economy: Challenges for American Families*. New York: Russell Sage Foundation.

Sanderson, Matthew R. 2012. "Migrants in the World Food System: Introduction." *International Journal of Sociology of Agriculture and Food* 19(1):56–61.

Reilly, Peter A. 2001. *Flexibility at Work: Balancing the Interests of Employer and Employee*. Aldershot, UK: Gower.

Robinson, William I. 2004. *A Theory of Global Capitalism: Production, Class and State in a Transnational World*, Baltimore and London: Johns Hopkins University Press.

Roman, Richard and Edur Velasco Arregui. 2013. *Continental Crucible: Big Business and Unions in the Transformation of North America*. Halifax and Winnipeg: Fernwood Publishing.

Rosin, Christopher, Paul Stock, and Hugh Campbell (eds.). 2012. *Food Systems Failure: The Global Food Crisis and the Future of Agriculture*. Abingdon, UK: Earthscan.

Stiglitz, Joseph. 2012. *The Price of Inequality: How Today's Divided Society Endangers Our Future*. New York: W.W. Norton and Company.

Upchurch, Martin, Graham Taylor, and Andrew Mathers. 2012. *The Crisis of Social Democratic Trade Unionism in Western Europe*. London: Ashgate.

Volscho, Thomas M. and Nathan J. Kelly. 2012. "The Rise of the Super-Rich: Power Resources, Taxes, Financial Markets, and the Dynamics of the Top 1 Percent, 1949 to 2008." *American Sociological Review* 77(5):679–699.

Western, Bruce and Jake Rosenfeld. 2011. "Workers of the World Divide: The Decline of Labor and the Future of the Middle Class." *Foreign Affairs*. Retrieved at http://www.foreignaffairs.com/articles/137522/bruce-western-and-jake-rosenfeld/workers-of-the-world-divide on May 10, 2012.

Wolf, Steven and Alessandro Bonanno (eds.). 2014. *The Neoliberal Regime in the Agri-food Sector Crisis, Resilience and Restructuring*. New York: Routledge.

World Bank. 2013. "Doing Business: Measuring Business Regulations." Retrieved at www.doingbusiness.org/methodology/employing-workers on August 15, 2013.

Zeitlin, Johnathan and Stephen Tolliday (eds.). 1992. *Between Fordism and Flexibility: The Automobile Industry and Its Workers*. New York: Berg.

# 14. The political economy of alternative agriculture in Italy
## *Maria Fonte and Ivan Cucco*

## INTRODUCTION*

Modernization of the economy and agriculture in Italy occurred in a rapid but also unique manner following World War II. As in other Mediterranean countries, agriculture was long considered a backward sector afflicted by delays in its development. Notwithstanding the persistence of wide regional differences, farms across the country were generally small and were managed in accordance with a family farm logic, which was closer to the peasant model than to the economic rationality of the "American farmer." Well into the 1980s the small scale of the farms was still regarded as an insurmountable obstacle to modernization of the sector and organization of a modern agro-food and distribution system.

In the post-modernization era of the 1990s, when in Europe a new paradigm became the benchmark for agricultural and rural development, the gap in the industrialization of agriculture and food was transformed into an asset by many actors in the food system. Intended as a marker for variety in regional agriculture and food, "Made in Italy" was constructed as a quality brand and the basis for the "quality turn consensus" around which many conventional and alternative interests eventually coalesced (Brunori, Malandrin and Rossi 2013).

Within the same timespan, at the global level, a succession of changes shifted the dominant food regimes out of the era of Fordism and into the era of globalization (Friedman and McMichael 1989). In the agro-food system the globalization of supply chains brought about new forms of governance based on quality standards and certification systems. Broader struggles over the regulation of global markets framed the renegotiation of power and resources in global trade as a matter for private actors, eroding the role of public institutions (Marsden, Flynn and Harrison 2000).

In this new context social movements also changed their nature and shifted their strategies. In the Fordist period they were organized mainly as labor movements or in alliance with labor movements and were fighting to change relations of production in opposition to the State and the capitalist economy. Since the 1970s and the 1980s, with neoliberalism and global markets asserting themselves as the dominant organizing forces of the economy and politics, the new social movements have shifted their attention away from the State and towards global corporations and the market, determining a "merging of frontiers between markets and social forces" (Raynolds and Wilkinson 2007:43). Market- and consumption-based, rather than labor- or class-based movements (Eder 1993) sought to capture consumers' interest and to challenge conventional globalization and its negative repercussions. The proliferation of initiatives, such as campaigns for fair trade, consumer boycotts, community-supported agriculture, the promotion of alternative food networks, all indicate a shifting of attention away from production to consumption (Murray and Raynolds 2007:7).

Novel conceptual tools have been proposed as a necessary step towards grasping the complexities of this changing landscape. New social actors and new objects have been enrolled in the food economy of the post-Fordist era: not only farmers, workers and farms, but also the countryside and rural areas have become part of the new networks under construction. Biodiversity, the environment, natural resources, multifunctionality, supply chains, quality food, health, standards and certifications, (urban) consumers and urban areas have all become relevant subjects and key actors. Busch and Juska (1997) proposed using actor-network theory (ANT) for the purpose of overcoming the limitations of political economy (the reification of actors and the determinism of material structure) and improving our understanding of the globalization process. ANT would also open new "avenues for action" (p. 690) by analyzing how the "relationships among people, things, institutions and ideas are created, maintained and changed through time" (p. 701). A fruitful integration between ANT and political economy was also envisioned by Friedman (2009).

Writing from a socio-technical regime transitions perspective (Geels 2004 and 2010; Geels and Schot 2007 and 2010), other authors highlighted the relations between the "alternative" and "conventional" domains. As shown by Smith (2006) in the case of organic food in the United Kingdom (UK), such relations are not necessarily confrontational. Niche movements originally seeking radical transformation of mainstream regimes in the direction of sustainability can undergo a process of fragmentation whereby their more incremental elements are selectively appropriated and re-interpreted by actors with different interests and values. The most radical elements re-organize their "alternativeness" and the way they relate to the dominant regime, in a trajectory that evolves from "oppositional" to "incompatible." The objective is not necessarily to oppose the system in order to change it. It may be to construct a new one, starting from bottom-up autonomous economic initiatives based on a synergy of production practices and social resources and centered on such values as food democracy and social justice (Hinrichs and Lyson 2008; Hinrichs 2014; Furman et al. 2014).

In this complex and evolving scenario, defining what is alternative agriculture in Italy is a challenge. Actually, nobody seems to be defending an industrialized model of agricultural development, homogenization of products, standardization of agricultural practices and globalization of sourcing and tastes. Everybody would instead agree with the new rural development paradigm, which advocates the valorization of regional agro-ecological diversity in food and agriculture. As a result of this evolution, "alternative" and "conventional" social forces to a large extent intersect and overlap.

In this chapter we choose as point of entry into the blurred margins of Italian alternative agriculture the histories and strategies of the most prominent advocates of the "quality turn" and trace their evolving—and at times ambiguous—relations with the conventional agro-food system. We focus on a set of actors that represent a range of experiences and organizational forms which emerged at different stages between the 1970s and the 1990s: the organic movement, the "Campagna Amica" Foundation promoted by Coldiretti (the largest farmers' union in the country), Slow Food and the loose but growing network of Solidarity Purchasing Groups (Gruppi di Acquisto Solidale, GAS). Following Levidow (2014), the "alternative" character of these actors can be identified with their rejection of the "life sciences" and "decomposability" paradigms that characterize the dominant agro-food system. All the organizations examined proved to be supporters, albeit to differing extents and via differing means, of an "agro-ecological" approach and an "integral product identity" paradigm that "seeks to valorize distinctive comprehensive qualities" (Levidow 2014:4) of food and agriculture—pertaining either to production processes, product characteristics and territorial specificities or alternative models of producer/consumer relations. Of course, it remains a point of controversy as to how the new model might be sustained and which strategies might be best suited for sustaining it.

In order to elucidate the actual or potential implications of the different strategies for the political economy of Italian alternative agriculture, we have opted to take an eclectic stance and combine insights from different approaches. The political economy of food regimes, socio-technical transition paradigms, ANT and the theory of social practice all present some useful variables and suggest dimensions with a potential for guiding our investigation of the history and strategies of the selected organizations.

The reference here is to the socio-technical transition (STT) literature and to the multilevel perspective (MLP) for interpreting the evolving relations between niche movements and elements of the dominant regime. The degree of structuration of niches and regimes is not necessarily stable: a regime can be more or less structured and, in time, the degree of structuration of a niche can increase to the point where it becomes a competing alternative to the dominant regime. Fuenfschilling and Truffer (2014) suggest that the level of structuration of a socio-technical configuration can be assessed by its "degree of institutionalization," which is in turn linked to its duration, its scale and scope of diffusion, its resilience to innovations and controversies, its embeddedness in an institutional framework and its coherence with surrounding structures (pp. 774–775). Throughout this chapter we propose to regard the institutional stability and network structure of the organizations under examination as indicators of their level of structuration.

Given that all the movements under examination operate in the post-Fordist environment, the different architectures of producer–distributor–consumer relations proposed by each actor will be seen not simply as attempts to reshape circuits of accumulation in the agro-food system, but also as bearers of different bundlings of private demands, public norms and new social practices of consumption. The transition to a new social practice requires the reconfiguration of motivation and agency, through the construction of new collective subjectivities, but also a new cultural and value structure and a new material infrastructure (Reckwitz 2002; Shove, Pantzar and Watson 2012; Crivits and Paredis 2013).

In our analysis of the labeling schemes implemented by different actors we draw on the typology and critique of voluntary food labels proposed by Guthman (2007) to distinguish between the mechanisms employed for appropriation and distribution of the value associated with "integral product identity." Guthman detects an "important theoretical tension" (p. 457) in the relationship between voluntary food labeling schemes and neoliberalism. Labeling schemes may "protect"—in a Polanyian sense—land, labor and natural resources from the disruptions of self-regulating markets. On the other hand, voluntary food labels can themselves be seen as an expression of neoliberal modes of governance, given that they choose the market as the locus of regulation and actually create new markets (and property rights) for place- or labor-based values, capacities and ethical behaviors which are in this way fictitiously commodified.

Before presenting the actors involved with the "quality turn" of Italian agriculture, in the following section we introduce the reader to the peculiarities of the Italian agricultural modernization process. We will then present our analysis of the Italian movements and organizations mentioned above: Campagna Amica, the organic movement, Slow Food, the GAS movement. The main findings in the concluding section will highlight how the different dimensions taken into consideration are shaping alternative agriculture in Italy.

# FROM INCOMPLETE MODERNIZATION TO A NEW AGRICULTURE: THE CASE OF ITALY

In the 1960s, while the European Common Agricultural Policy (CAP) was pushing in the direction of modernization, Italian agriculture was still being represented as afflicted by a structural dualism between small peasant and big capitalist farms[1] (Fabiani 1978; Gorgoni 1978; Pugliese and Rossi 1978). One of the most lively debates counterposed the Leninist thesis of "differentiation and proletarianization" of peasant farms to the Kautskian thesis of their persistence and adaptation (through part-time work and pluriactivity) to the context of a capitalist economy (Bolaffi and Varotti 1978; Calza Bini 1978). According to Mottura and Pugliese (1975), "peasantization" and "modernization" policies were both functional to the industrial development of the Italian economy: the agricultural labor force functioned as a "reserve army" for industry and people underemployed in rural areas were available to be released as the demand for industrial labor increased.

In the 1980s this debate no longer reflected the reality of the agricultural sector: the idiosyncratic modernization process of Italian agriculture had already been accomplished through territorial concentration, specialization of production and adoption of mechanical and chemical innovation. The "entrepreneurial farm" had by then become the backbone of Italian agriculture, replacing the "peasant farm," an institution now conceptually linked with a backward system of production. Farmers acquired full legitimation as "entrepreneurs" and, however relatively small the average farm area (less than 5 hectares), displayed behavior analogous to that of the capitalist industrial firm (Cosentino and De Benedictis 1978). This led to increasing intensification and specialization but also, progressively, to the restructuring of the food system and loss of autonomy of the farm (van der Ploeg 2008; Fonte and Salvioni 2013).

The integration of agriculture into the food system took place initially (in the 1970s and 1980s) through the labor market and the stabilization of part-time work and of pluri-active farms, and later (in the 1980s and 1990s) through intensification of commercial relations with the food processing industry and the distribution system. The modernization of the processing industry and the distribution system had in fact proceeded in parallel with the developments in agriculture, with consolidation accelerating in the first decades of the new century (Brasili, Fanfani and Meccarini 2001;

Viviano 2012). Squeezed between an oligopolistic input industry and an increasingly concentrated processing and retailing industry, the farm lost its managerial and financial autonomy: only a small percentage of the final added value of food was flowing back into farmers' incomes (Sereni [1947] 1971; van der Ploeg 2008).

The process was neither thorough nor homogeneous. In a recent volume, Ortiz-Miranda, Moragues-Faus and Arnalte-Alegre (2013) stress how "the apparent common Mediterranean portrait" (p. 2) conceals manifold expressions of rural and agrarian pathways and paradigms, based on different mixes of traditional and productivist practices. The Italian case closely conforms to this view, given that agricultural modernization was incomplete or at least selective with regard to types of farms and geographical areas. Still, there is no agreement today as to how many "farms" there are in Italy and how many of them are "entrepreneurial" (Sotte 2006; Sotte and Arzeni 2013). This is a long-standing debate that seems difficult to resolve.[2]

Italian agriculture remains tightly linked to the agro-ecological features of the territories in which it is practiced, with differences in cultural specialization also implying differences in farm management. The majority of "professional" or entrepreneurial farms are engaged in stockbreeding and dairying (activities concentrated in the north of Italy). Such farms can employ stable labor forces. Small farms with mixed and perennial cultures are by contrast scattered over central and southern Italy, and their markedly seasonal working calendar encourages pluri-activity and diversification.

In the late 1970s, when the debate on the structure of Italian agriculture was in full swing, Barberis (1978) was quite an isolated voice when he pointed out that the specificity of the Italian agricultural sector and its "artisanal" form of production constituted the basis of the quality of Italian food. His views proved to be far-sighted when, in the 1990s, a different paradigm based on the so-called quality turn (Goodman 2003) started to characterize agricultural development. The turn was anticipated in Europe in the 1980s by the debates about the future of the CAP. The emergence of environmental discourse was accelerated by a series of scandals over industrial intensive agriculture (Fonte 2002). In Italy the most serious episode was the "methanol wine scandal" in 1986, which resulted in 23 deaths and left dozens of people poisoned and injured (Barbera and Audifreddi 2012), with devastating consequences for the wine market in Italy. In the same year a major problem of atrazine pollution of the aquifers emerged in the Po Valley. At the international level the Chernobyl disaster was followed a few years later by the explosion into prominence of the bovine spongiform encephalopathy scandal, both of these scandals being of vast extension and having deep implications for the food system (Ansell and Vogel 2006). This noteworthy series of scandals, along with the public debate on the diffusion of the new genetically modified organisms (GMO), triggered a reflexive behavior (Beck, Giddens and Lash 1994) among European consumers on the subject of food safety and health (Jaillette 2001; Fonte 2002 and 2004; Petrini and Padovani 2005).

GMOs met with a poor reception from consumers all over Europe but, apart from the shared fears of toxicity, allergies and modifications to people's immune systems, each country seemed to have its own additional rationales for contesting and refusing the new technology. Denmark, for example, stressed the risk of groundwater contamination; Austria was concerned to defend its organic agriculture; in Italy GMOs were perceived primarily as posing a threat to its most traditional products (Camera dei Deputati 1997; Fonte 2004) and to the quality of "Made in Italy" (Brunori, Malandrin and Rossi 2013).

It was above all around the threat to the safety and quality of Italian food that a coalition of "conventional" and "alternative" forces in the agro-food system was formed in the late 1990s. In their opposition to GMOs, "alternative" movements such as Slow Food, Legambiente (the national association for the protection of the environment), Greenpeace and AIAB (the Italian Association for Organic Agriculture—one of the associations for the promotion of organic agriculture) allied themselves with more "conventional" actors such as Coldiretti (the union of small farmers in Italy and incidentally the largest union of farmers), Confartigianato (the union of small artisan firms), a number of consumers' associations and most of the key supermarket chains (including Coop-Italia, Auchan-SMA and Carrefour).[3] Given that safety had begun to be linked conceptually to national production,[4] a "Made in Italy" consensus developed, uniting a wide coalition of interests in the agriculture and food sector. National production came to be seen not only as a guarantee of quality but also as a good marketing strategy with the potential to respond to consumer anxiety on food (Brunori, Malandrin and Rossi 2013).

The changes occurring in Italy were taking place within the wider context of reform of the CAP. In the frame of modernization, the European Union (EU) interpreted the "quality turn" as the need for further rationalization and control of industrial production through new and better management of safety rules. The reorganization of the EU's regulatory role in the food economy (Majone 1996; Marsden, Flynn and Harrison 2000) had to, however, take into account international pressures, given that the World Trade Organization (WTO) negotiations were pushing towards a policy of reduced agricultural subsidies and liberalization of market access.

It is in the context of the CAP reform (1992) and re-orientation away from the CAP's exclusive focus on productivity towards liberalization, on the one hand, and improvement of safety standards, food quality and environmental protection, on the other, that the European Union (henceforth EU) biosafety regulation on GMOs (based on the adoption of the Precautionary Principle), laws on hygiene (1991–1993) and regulation on the "traceability" of food (2002) were elaborated. The CAP reform also involved movement away from the sectoral emphasis towards a multidimensional concept of rural development. Together with cuts in the levels of price support and a re-focusing of subsidies on income support for farmers, the MacSharry reform of 1992 brought about a "quality turn" through its agro-ecological measures, for example provision of support for environmentally friendly organic practices and regulation for protection of geographic indications. The new orientation of the CAP, and particularly the establishment of its second pillar (the rural development policy), reinforced the shift towards food quality entailed by the "quality turn," creating opportunities and consensus among the big players in the agrofood system. It was during this period that the concept of a "European model of agricultural development" emerged, taking as its basis the valorization of difference and quality rather than productivity, specialization and standardization.

The "quality turn" and the way it was translated into EU policy introduced changes that generated tension for the actors engaged with Italian agriculture. Coldiretti, a staunch supporter of the modernization approach underlying previous CAP interventions, detected the change in the wind and accordingly reinvented itself, "gradually abandon[ing] the modernization discourse and corporatist defense of CAP price support and propos[ing] a new business model based on multifunctionality and a new agricultural policy. Tradition, locality and family farming became common elements of Coldiretti's concept of quality" (Brunori, Malandrin and Rossi 2013:23). Coldiretti also adopted an ambivalent stance towards liberalization. It thus emerged as one of the main actors in the construction of the alliance, with at times protectionist overtones, around a defense of products "Made in Italy." As for Slow Food, the recognition and protection of locally embedded quality within the EU framework was certainly a welcome development. Moreover, these organizations were able to enlist the support of the Italian State in their battle for identification and defense of traditional products whose survival was endangered by the promulgation of EU hygiene laws. Under the provisions governing the newly established Register of Traditional Products, products listed in it may be produced and processed in accordance with traditional practices, disregarding European hygiene regulations.[5]

The increased attention to the relation between food and health, safety, environmental protection and production practices was a contributing factor to the profound changes, which also took place on the demand side of the food sector. Consumers started to see alternative food economies as a way of avoiding risk and the concomitant anxiety. This lent new strength to alternative food networks, especially organic agriculture and networks based on a closer relationship between consumer and producers. The greater support given to organic production within the new EU framework was instrumental in expanding the sector, with all the ensuing tension derived from the scaling-up of operations and closer links to the large distribution systems.

It is within this context that the key actors of alternative agriculture in Italy make their appearance, elaborate their strategy and operate in competition or in symbiosis with the dominant food system.

## CAMPAGNA AMICA AND COLDIRETTI: THE TURN TO AN "ALL-ITALIAN FILIÈRE"

With a million and a half members Coldiretti defines itself as "the biggest farmers' federation at the national and European level" (Coldiretti 2014). The organization was founded in 1944 by Paolo Bonomi, who remained its President until 1980. Through its control over Federconsorzi[6] (also presided over by Bonomi), Coldiretti administered a considerable share of the public funds devoted to provisioning and agricultural policies prior to implementation of the CAP.

Coldiretti and Federconsorzi remained, until the mid-1990s, one of the main centers of economic and political power in the Italian countryside. They were political arms of the Christian Democracy (at the time, the major Italian political party) in rural areas. More than sixty Christian Democrat Members of Parliament were elected to the national Parliament through the influence of Coldiretti. At the local level thousands of officials were elected with support from the federation and formed a "pervasive web of power and social control" (Fanfani 2004:10; authors' translation).

Under its 1944 Statutes, Coldiretti's actions were to be inspired by "the history and principles of the Christian social school." Its purpose was to defend "rural people and . . . socially and economically elevate the farming classes through the promotion of initiatives for increase in agricultural production and the empowerment of family farms" (quoted in Occhetta and Primavera 2010:15; authors' translation). The guiding principle of the federation was that "the interests, needs and problems of small farmers are different from those of large farmers as well as from those of the salaried classes" (1st Coldiretti National Congress, 1946, quoted in Occhetta and

Primavera 2010:15; authors' translation). Coldiretti thus distinguished itself ideologically and politically from workers' organizations and from Confagricoltura, the association representing big landowners.

In reality things were far more nuanced than such ideological distancing would suggest. The interests of the "rural classes" were in fact mobilized by Coldiretti as part of a "green front" ruralist strategy aimed at shielding the whole agricultural sector (including landlords) from the negative effects of market-oriented capitalist development (Mottura 1987). Because of this corporatist approach, Coldiretti failed to propose an agricultural development model really oriented towards the defense of small and medium farmers. When the CAP came into effect, Coldiretti swiftly embraced a productivist logic based on agricultural modernization and the adoption of technical innovations. The new approach was in line with the economic interests of Federconsorzi, which had in the meantime asserted itself as the national leader in commercialization of agricultural machinery and intermediate goods.

At the beginning of the 1990s the organization faced a major crisis of legitimacy. The conflict of interests between Coldiretti's political and economic roles came under public scrutiny when Federconsorzi went into liquidation in 1991, starting what was to become one of Italy's biggest ever bankruptcy cases. The ensuing investigation highlighted the lack of transparency in the use of (largely public) funds. At about the same time, the Italian post-war party system was being shaken to its roots by the judiciary's anti-corruption "Clean Hands" campaign. Coldiretti's political patron, the Christian Democracy, was severely hit by the scandals and the party was disbanded in 1994. Calls for a radical reform of the CAP, which was regarded as being at the origin of endemic excess production, had meanwhile been intensifying since the early 1980s. The close association between Coldiretti and the CAP in Italy further contributed to the organization's crisis.

This confluence of events set in motion a deep renovation process. Coldiretti reinvented itself as an advocate of the quality turn: its "Covenant with Consumers" (2000),[7] launched a manifesto for an "all-Italian agricultural filière" and the federation became a promoter of genuinely "Made in Italy" products. Closer scrutiny of the new policy platform reveals some degree of continuity with the rural ideology of the previous phase. It remained, for example, unclear as to how the potentially conflicting interests of small and big farmers would be reconciled through the promotion of an all-Italian filière. However, the new Statute adopted in 2011 marks a clear discursive break from the previous productivist approach. In lieu of technical progress, Coldiretti elects as its new core themes the multifunctionality of agricultural enterprises, quality as an expression of local diversity, rural tourism, environmental services, the protection of territory and landscape and the promotion of public awareness campaigns (Coldiretti 2011).

The most innovative areas of the new policy agenda are assigned to the Campagna Amica Foundation (Friendly Countryside, hereafter CA), established in 2008. CA was in charge of a communication campaign aimed at increasing public awareness of agriculture's multifunctional role, promoting sustainable development and establishing linkages between producers and consumers as well as between rural and urban areas. Before even a year had passed, CA had turned into a national-level effort to nurture and co-ordinate the direct selling initiatives that were spontaneously spreading in response to growing consumer demand for trusted produce.

The core element in the CA campaign is the certification of producers' adherence to a code of conduct through a voluntary labeling scheme. The logo is owned by the foundation, which delegates the certification process to an external organization.[8] The labeling mechanisms implement and transmit the guidelines spelled out in the "Manifesto for an all-Italian agricultural filière." CA certification in fact guarantees that farmers sell only their own products and that these products are "Italian, agricultural and produced locally"; that farmers abide by a code of conduct based on rules for direct selling; and that prices are (in the case of the farmers' markets) lower than in local supermarkets.[9]

The novelty of the CA experience can be seen from the concurrent mobilization of Coldiretti's formidable organizational machine to promote the labeling scheme through the creation of a large distribution network directly managed by the CA Foundation. Certified producers in fact have access to reliable marketing channels, with the foundation providing services including the design of selling points, the scheduling of collective activities and the promotion of the logo and the values embedded in the certification. At the heart of the model are the CA Farmers' Markets, where CA-certified farmers sell their own products directly to urban consumers. Requirements concerning the origin of products offered for sale in CA farmers' markets are quite strict. In most cases CA farmers' market regulations state that farmers are only allowed to sell their own production and that all agricultural inputs that are not self-produced must come from the same region in which they are sold.[10] The network includes other distribution channels such as on-farm sales; farmhouses (*agri-touristic farms*); shops and so-called Italian shops that only sell CA products of fully traceable Italian origin; restaurants that only use CA products and CA urban orchards. CA also helps organize a procurement network for collective purchasing groups, including some GAS.

The CA network therefore involves both professional farmers and non-professional growers, restaurateurs, and citizens' and buyers' groups. The customer base is similarly varied. Unlike other alternative food networks, the CA has adopted a model aimed at catering for all consumer groups, not just to a specialized niche (organic, biodynamic, highbrow). By April 2014 the CA network had become the biggest direct sales organization in Europe with more than 7,000 selling points (Di Iacovo, Fonte and Galasso 2014:32–33). Besides engaging in sales activities, CA selling points have also begun to play host to a variety of sustainable development initiatives that leverage the connections between producers and consumers. CA selling points are often well embedded in their social environment: farmers' markets or CA shops have often become centers of renewal and revitalization in otherwise marginalized urban or suburban areas.

Apart from the development of its direct sales network, Campagna Amica seeks to protect and promote all-Italian products via traditional distribution channels through collective sales to supermarket chains. To this end it has established a second labeling scheme called *Firmato Agricoltori Italiani* ("Signed by Italian Farmers," hereafter FAI), which targets medium- and large-scale producers associated with Coldiretti and the CA Foundation. FAI certification covers oil, meat, salami, fruit, vegetables, rice and pasta; its core requirements are the strictly Italian origin of products, the agricultural character of all ingredients and a distribution of margins within the chain that is fair to agricultural producers.[11] FAI-labeled products are distributed throughout the country by major supermarket chains such as Carrefour, Coop, Conad, Despar and Iper. Beyond promoting FAI products, CA also collaborates with the large distribution networks, Iper and Coop, to develop all-Italian product lines sold under the distributors' own brand.[12]

Although the CA Foundation was officially founded only in 2008, its record to date in the six years of its existence must be seen as a success, attributable to the breadth and stability of the social and economic networks centered on Coldiretti, the longest-established of the organizations analyzed. Coldiretti's resilience has enabled the organization to survive a major legitimacy crisis and to re-emerge as one of the main actors in Italy's turn to quality. Its relations with the surrounding institutional environment have always been strong, exerting a strong gravitational pull. Some tokens of its success are its involvement in national- and EU-level policy, not to mention a history of often-preferential agreements with major corporate actors in the mainstream agro-food system. In terms of its networking features and degree of institutionalization, the CA Foundation represents a highly structured socio-technical configuration. In Guthman's taxonomy, the CA model rests on a private place-based labeling system whose specific focus of protection is the generic localism of products: their regional origin in the case of farmers' markets, or even their national origin in the FAI scheme. There are also redistributive elements in the CA system: the certification scheme seeks to appropriate value for producers not by setting higher price (which, on the contrary, have to be more favorably priced than standard products sold in local supermarkets), but by eliminating intermediaries and creating a protected market space alongside conventional distribution channels. Through the guarantee of lower retail prices at farmers' markets, some of the redistributive benefits accrue not only to producers but also to consumers.

## THE ORGANIC MOVEMENT IN ITALY: THE POLITICAL ECONOMY OF SOIL AND STANDARDS

The literature on the birth and evolution of the organic movement in Italy is very sparse and fragmented. There is no main character in this story— no equivalent of Petrini for Slow Food; the development of organic agriculture is associated with many lesser-known regional and local actors. From a socio-technical transition perspective (Smith 2006), the story of Italian organic agriculture can be told as the evolution of an innovation niche: the 1970s and early 1980s are the years of the pioneers; a process of "institutionalization" starts in the 1980s, when local operators formulate alternative rules for production, distribution and consumption; the 1990s are the years of stabilization through institutionalization backed by national- and EU-level regulations (Fonte and Salvioni 2013).

The pioneers of the organic movement came from different backgrounds: the radical left, the ecologist movement and the anti-conformist or alternative movements. The first group emerged from the experience of "agricultural communes" inspired by hippy counterculture. The second was more explicitly focused on environmental issues. The last called attention to the stresses and inconveniences of modernity and, following the precepts of Rudolf Steiner, proposed the recovery of traditional values and a lifestyle more in tune with nature. The heterogeneity of these roots hindered progress towards unitary national representation, even as its capacity to attract new farmers and consumers was steadily growing.

The pioneering phase was characterized by a multiplicity of regional-level and often unconnected initiatives. The first Italian organic association was Suolo e Salute (Soil and Health), founded in 1969 in Turin by a group of medical doctors, agronomists and farmers who opposed the use of synthetic chemicals in farming. Their objective was to reconcile the health of the consumer with the health of the soil. The first President of the association was a medical doctor, Francesco Garofalo, pioneer of a scientific approach to organic agriculture. Many similar initiatives were launched in the same period in different regions of Italy,[13] but the degree of cross-regional co-ordination remained low throughout the 1970s.

At the beginning of the 1980s there were still no official regulations on organic agriculture; such rules as there were were set only at the regional level (Cà Verde 2014). It was in this period that the process of "institutionalization" of the organic movement was set in motion. In 1982 the consumers' association "AAM Terra Nuova"[14] succeeded in amalgamating a number of regional initiatives to form a national committee *Cos'è biologico* ("What is Organic"), in which representatives of consumers and regional associations debated harmonization of rules for organic production.

In 1986 the committee approved the first national-level rules ("Norme italiane di agricoltura biologica"). The so-called *Libretto Rosso–Codice di Condotta Commerciale* (Red Booklet—Commercial Code of Conduct), produced by AAM Terra Nuova, spelled out the standards and fundamental ethical values that commercially oriented organic producers were supposed to abide by (La Primavera Coop 2014). In 1988 AMM Terra Nuova and many of the local consumers' and producers' groups scaled up the experience of the committee by forming the AIAB, a federation of regional groups which soon became the most representative body at national level. From a public relations perspective, the events that favored the institutionalization of the movement were the organization in 1989 of the first Natural Food Fair (Salone dell'Alimentazione Naturale, SANA) and the publication of the first national magazine entirely dedicated to organic agriculture (*BioAgricoltura*, started by AIAB in 1990), which became an important instrument for publicity and communication for extensionists, researchers and producers (Fonte and Salvioni 2013).

The institutional embedding of organic agriculture was fully achieved in the 1990s with the publication of European regulations, which transformed organic agriculture from an innovation niche to a market segment in the dominant socio-technical regime. In 1991 Regulation CEE 2092/91 established rules at the EU level for organic production and certification. The following year, implementing this regulation, the Italian Ministry of Agriculture recognized the first six national control agencies (AIAB, CCPB, Demeter, Suolo and Salute, AMAB, BioAgriCoop), followed by AgriEcoBio in 1993. In the same year the most important Italian organic agriculture organizations set up the Italian Organic Agriculture Federation (FIAO, later renamed FEDERBIO), which became the unitary representative body of Italian organic agriculture. Production protocols established the necessary conditions for differentiation of the organic niche. After that, and thanks to the financial incentives made available in accordance with the new CAP's agro-environmental measures, there was a rapid proliferation of organic farms and expansion of organic agriculture in all regions of Italy (Salvioni 1999; Fonte and Salvioni 2013). In 2010 there were more than 45,000 organic farms, with 9.7 percent of the total utilized agricultural area (about 1.25 million hectares) being cultivated with organic methods (Rete Rurale Nazionale 2013).

A further stimulus to the sector came from the many food scandals of the 1980s and 1990s, which led to greatly increased demand for organic products. The first larger-scale production and distribution initiatives started in this period (Santucci 2009): 1986 saw the establishment of the Fattoria Scaldasole, which specialized in dairy production; in 1987 a consumer co-operative upgraded itself into Gea, a company specializing in the distribution of organic products, which later, in 1998, became Ecor and in 2009 EcorNaturaSì, the most important national supermarket chain promoting the commercialization of organic products.[15]

But expansion had its costs. The ever-tighter integration of organic farming into the mainstream agro-food system, the growth in the size of firms and farms and the spread of organic products into the mainstream distribution system (especially in large-scale supermarkets) has resulted in a "conventionalization" of the sector. Organic agriculture has acquired a symbiotic relationship with the conventional socio-technical regime, involving a progressive erosion of the values and ideals that were at the origin of the organic movement.

In terms of political economy, this renewal of the agro-food regime is arguably predicated on a new relation between the farmer (and consumer) and nature, and especially the soil. The health of the soil and the health of consumers are at the core of the new techniques promoted by the organic movement. At the socio-technical level, a new class of technicians mediates the relation between farmers and nature and consumers, contributing to the diffusion of a new form of knowledge different from the "industrial-based" knowledge of private and public extensionists. The ambition of organic agriculture is to reaffirm the principles of traditional agriculture and traditional knowledge, to anchor them in scientific knowledge and to codify them in standards as an aid to communication with consumers.

The organic movement differs from other experiences such as Coldiretti and Slow Food specifically because of its approach to certification of the "integral" quality of organic products. The organic certification system is embedded in national and supra-national laws: the accreditation of certification bodies is legally sanctioned by the State. This approach is in stark contrast to the private and voluntary nature of the labeling schemes implemented by Coldiretti and Slow Food, which, according to Guthman, can be seen as the expression of a neoliberal mode of governance (Guthman 2007). It is significant that the definition of standards has become the battleground for the conflicts emerging around the identity of organic agriculture as part of a more conventional or more "alternative" food regime.

But the most acute conflicts in the European organic movement have to do with reconfiguration of relations with the mainstream food system, particularly the scaling-up of the sector through the retailing of organic food by supermarkets. Some adherents think that supermarkets are necessary allies in the up-scaling of organic agriculture; others think that they are incompatible with the principles of organic movements: health, ecology, fairness and care.

## SLOW FOOD AND THE POLITICAL ECONOMY OF PLEASURE

Slow Food is a complex organization and a social movement with great influence in Italian food politics. One indication of its success is the rich international literature that is flourishing around it (Leitch 2003 and 2005; Fonte 2006; Andrews 2008; Walter 2009; Sassatelli and Davolio 2010). But our interest in Slow Food here is not related to its character as an organization or the charges of elitism that are leveled against it: these have been thoroughly analyzed by, among others, Sassatelli and Davolio (2010). We will instead focus on Slow Food's role in the "quality turn" of Italian agriculture in the 1990s.

The origins of Slow Food cannot be understood without some knowledge of the movement's provenance in the traditional food and wine culture of the Langhe, one of the regions of Italian food excellence: Barolo wine and the Alba truffle are merely the internationally best known of the plethora of food products linked to this regional identity. The beginnings of the movement have also to be situated in the context of the broader transformations taking place in the global economy and in Italian political and cultural life between the 1970s and 1980s (Andrews 2008).

Globalization and liberalization have transformed the capitalism of late modernity. According to post-structuralist theory, in the process leading to the emergence of a post-materialist society, class has lost its centrality as an explicative concept of social organization and as an organizing framework for political struggle. In the transition from the "worlds of production" to the "worlds of consumption," culture and consumers (rather than production and the working class) are seen as the agents of social transformation (Baudrillard 1981; Miller 1995; 1997; and 2012; Miele 2001; Ritzer and Jurgenson 2010). In a new global economy conceptualized as an "economy of signs" (Lash and Urry 1994), culture becomes the basis for understanding new forms of collective action (Eder 1993) as well as an asset to be valorized and commodified (Ray 1998): "The growth of consumerist forms of identity-production in liberal democratic societies thus coincides with the development of new possibilities for consumer politics in which culture has become a favored idiom of political mobilization" (Leitch 2003:443).

As these changes were taking place, Italy was experiencing a significant decline in the cultural influence of institutions traditionally recognized as the political representatives of collective interests: political parties, labor unions and the Catholic Church. Their gradual waning opened up new spaces for civic engagement; new forms of collective action emerged, including new social movements and an independent non-profit sector. Trends towards the commodification of culture and the affirmation of post-industrial capitalism were also transforming the Italian left. Communist Party traditions of austerity were undermined; many intellectuals were redefining aspects of popular culture such as music, cinema and sports as forms of transformative cultural politics (Leitch 2003:451).[16] It is in this period that *Il Manifesto*—a radical left-wing newspaper—began publishing an eight-page monthly lifestyle supplement entitled *Gambero Rosso*, dealing with gastronomy, of which Carlo Petrini was one of the founders.

It is therefore important to stress that Slow Food was not born in a vacuum. When in 1986 McDonald's was opening a restaurant in Piazza di Spagna in Rome, Slow Food had not yet been born, but many intellectuals were giving expression to their disenchantment; they ranged from famous architects such as Portoghesi and Costantino Dardi, to urbanists and city planners like Bruno Zevi, to sociologists (Ferrarotti), journalists and politicians (Antonello Trombadori) (Petrini and Padovani 2005:91). Petrini recognizes as one of the most important influences in his education as a gastronome the famous journalist and writer Luigi Veronelli. As early as 1964 Veronelli had written a book entitled *In Search of Lost Food* (Veronelli 1964). He fought to save small vineyards from extinction and to protect local wines from the homogenization of techniques and tastes. In alliance with the radical movements of the young occupants of two Centri Sociali[17] ("La Chimica" in Verona and "Il Magazzino 47" in Brescia), in 2003 Veronelli founded an association called "Critical Wine" and inspired the creation of "terra/Terra" farmers' markets for local self-certified products (Terra e Libertà/Critical Wine 2004; Veronelli and Echaurren 2005). In 1998, in reaction to the blind application of EU hygiene laws in Italy, he was writing: "The European Community in which we placed our hopes has established subtle and falsely hygienist rules for the purpose of putting out of action, in favor of industry, preserves, sauces, cheeses and meats produced in a traditional way without any real long-term risk" (Rota and Stefi 2012:19–20, authors' translation). These views were to exert a great influence on the future platform of Slow Food.

Slow Food's Paris Manifesto was launched in 1989; the first Salone del Gusto (Taste Fair) was held in 1996: these are exactly the years of the great scandals in the European food system. Slow Food interpreted the many European food controversies of the 1980s and 1990s as the expression of crisis of the modernization model of the food system, based on industrial standardization, homogenization and globalization. It proposed to react to the crisis through "the political appropriation of food as symbol of collective or contested national identity," implying "the protection of threatened food and the diversity of cultural landscapes" (Leitch 2003:441).

At its birth Slow Food clearly identified itself as a new social movement. Its politics of pleasure implemented through the *convivia*, the group of territorial associates who promote dinners, food and wine tasting events and promotional campaigns, situates it firmly in the realm of critical consumerism. But the originality of the movement lies in the development of a *new*, post-hedonist, as it were, politics of pleasure, in which slowness "becomes a metaphor for a politics of place, concerned with local cultural heritage, regional landscapes and idiosyncratic material cultures of production, as well as international biodiversity and cosmopolitanism" (Leitch 2003:453).

Slow Food promotes the idea of cultural diversity and at the same time develops marketing strategies for encouraging consumers to buy local endangered foods. Its strategy is not oppositional to the food industry or food capital; it aims at educating consumer tastes, trusting that an educated consumer will be able to recognize quality and will support it with coherent market behavior. Individual behavioral change in response to information brought to consumers will thus bring about change in the whole food system.

As Slow Food sees it, the quality of a food product is first of all a narrative that starts from its place of origin (Slow Food 2014). Enogastronomy is transmuted into eco-gastronomy and the trajectory of the movement is from consumption towards the world of production. The defense of endangered food and biodiversity (through the Presidia) is systematically integrated into the politics of pleasure (Fonte 2006).

According to Leitch (2003), Slow Food is neither explicitly anti-capitalist nor anti-corporate; its mission is to promote a form of benign globalization in which members of minority cultures, including niche-food producers, are encouraged to network and thrive and in which industry is brought into conformity with Slow Food strategy: "We need to make industry understand that artisan food production must be supported and not boycotted. The quality of the latter has a positive return on the former" (Sassatelli and Davolio 2010:221). The practical realization of this strategy can be seen in Eataly, a chain of supermarkets developed with the support of Slow Food (Venturini 2008), and now with an international diffusion. In its department stores Eataly promotes the "endangered foods" listed by the Slow Food Presidia. It seeks to show that the asymmetry of power between the distribution firm and the small artisan farmers does not have to be an obstacle to defending good food and biodiversity.

Indeed, Sassatelli and Davolio (2010) detect a dualism of visions between the "centrally promoted endeavour to shift the varied and multiform set of SF [Slow Food] convivia on the Italian territory towards a more explicitly ethical and political outlook" and the outlook of local adherents to the movement who remain closer to traditional views of aesthetic appreciation and market orientation.

Centered on the Slow Food Presidia, the Slow Food certification system is furthermore clearly private in nature. In the typology proposed by Guthman (2007), Slow Food Presidia can be defined as promoters of a place-based labeling system aimed at protecting traditional tastes and traditional production methods through verification of the labor process. The Slow Food voluntary labeling system, and above all the "narrative labels" including additional information on the characteristics[18] of the food and how it is produced, provides a market-based mechanism for extracting the added value from "integral product quality," embedding the qualities of products in the producers' work and competences.

As in the case of Coldiretti, the labeling scheme goes hand in hand with the creation of a very effective marketing mechanism. However, apart from its reliance on the redistributive effects of cultural shifts taking place on the consumer side, no mechanism is in place, to ensure that the value extracted remains with producers.

## THE POST-ORGANIC MOVEMENT AND THE CIVIC FOOD NETWORK: THE POLITICAL ECONOMY OF NEW ETHICAL RELATIONS BETWEEN PRODUCERS AND CONSUMERS

The disappointment with the institutionalization and (according to many) conventionalization of organic agriculture led to the emergence of several grass-roots initiatives whose aim was to promote holistic sustainability in the food economy. Although ideologically rooted in the left, on one side, and in Catholic spirituality, on the other, these initiatives were novel. They were part of the wave of initiatives that have given rise to the new social movements, having rejected any links with traditional political parties or the Catholic Church.

In the international literature, the new grass-roots initiatives were initially perceived as being "local food networks" because they laid a great deal of emphasis on re-localizing the food economy. Following a sustained critical debate (Hinrichs 2000 and 2003; Allen et al. 2003; Ilbery and Maye 2005; Kirwan 2004; Allen and Guthman 2006; Kloppenburg and Hassanein 2006; Holloway et al. 2007; Fonte and Papadopoulos 2010; Goodman, DuPuis and Goodman 2012), the general feeling is now that they might better be designated "civic food networks" (Renting, Schermer and Rossi 2012; Furman et al. 2014). The core concern of "civic food networks" is not so much the quality of the product (local, traditional, typical, endangered, or simply good, food) as the social relations embodied in the product, which should become an expression of food citizenship, food democracy and food sovereignty. The main forms of "civic food networks" that have emerged in Italy include farmers' markets, urban gardens, the so-called social (or welfare) agriculture, and GAS. Among these, GAS certainly represent the most innovative experience.

Typically GAS are groups of households (between 30 and 80 in number) that co-ordinate their purchases in order to buy food and other goods on the basis of ethical principles, including solidarity. Food provisioning is organized through voluntary "co-ordinators" and orders are usually managed via the Internet. Building and maintaining personal relationships between all members of the group is considered important in most GAS. When a GAS grows too large, another group is often organized; sometimes the new group is placed under the supervision of the older one.

Since the first group was formed in Fidenza (Parma) in 1994, GAS have multiplied rapidly. As of March 2014, almost 1,000 GAS had registered with the national GAS network and 14 regional networks are currently active (www.retegas.org). Although it is hard to gauge the economic relevance of the GAS movement, data collected in an in-depth study of the GAS network in Rome can provide some indications (Fonte 2013). According to the budgets of 13 GAS in Rome, each member household spends about 700 Euros yearly. If the same were to hold for all GAS members in the Rome province, the total purchases in the province would be estimated at roughly 8 million Euros in 2010. Clearly this is still a "niche" in the food system.

GAS aim at establishing a new "economy of relations and places" and at implementing a different mode of food provisioning (and goods provisioning in general), through direct contact with producers. Their objectives include not only the promotion of environmentally friendly agricultural practices but also the reduction of greenhouse gas emissions in food logistics, the revaluation of local and seasonal food, the revitalization of the local food economy, the promotion of workers' rights and their fair compensation, the reconstruction of democracy in the food chain and the promotion of food sovereignty for producers and consumers.

The GAS movement emerged from the World Social Forum and anti- or alter-globalization movement milieu. Antecedents in Italy include the Catholic "Budgets of Justice" movement (Bilanci di Giustizia),[19] which saw hundreds of families questioning the prevailing model of consumption and re-orienting their expenditures towards more sustainable products, manufactured in an environment of justice. The variety of objectives and organizational forms in Italian GAS to some extent reflects the co-existence of different legacies: Centri Sociali, Fair Trade shops, Catholic spirituality groups, the Scout movement, leftist parties.

Perhaps it is from this heterogeneity of origins that the GAS's distinctive character is derived: they are the most decentralized of the several new alternative food networks to have emerged in Italy. They lack a central organization, but co-ordinate their activities at a number of different levels through a national network and several regional networks, the connections between which are horizontal rather than vertical. GAS are promoted by civil society, without any financial incentives from the State or from private firms. Most GAS emphasize the active participation of members as a contributing factor to democracy and political awareness.

The relationships between producers and consumers are crucial. Information on producers is collected through personal contacts, local investigations or exchange of information with other members of the GAS network. GAS prefer to buy from local small-scale organic producers. Organic production is often certified, although this is not necessarily required. Sourcing from local producers promotes ecologically sound production and distribution methods. At the same time it serves the even more fundamental objective of establishing direct, frequent contacts with producers, in this way sustaining local economies, local products and biodiversity. By establishing direct ties to producers (local farmers), each group creates a network of "consumer-citizens" and "producer-citizens" that co-produce not only food, but meanings and relations at each point in the food chain. Agriculture and food take on a social and political value that goes well beyond the production of commodities. Exchange relations are re-embedded in social relationships that combine the co-production of food with social values such as trust, respect for the environment and solidarity (Di Iacovo, Fonte and Galasso 2014). In keeping with this approach, standards and certification of food is not an important element in the movement strategy and it is not the main mechanism for distributing value in the food chain.

Solidarity is a key component of sustainability as articulated in the GAS discourse. Solidarity is practiced among GAS members, but also between GAS members, producers and agricultural workers. There are a number of instances of GAS having helped producers overcome difficulties, for example by committing themselves to advance purchases and in this way facilitating credit access.

The solidarity between consumer-citizens and producer-citizens finds economic expression in the notion of "just price." The aim of GAS is not to pay the minimum price, but rather a "just price" that can adequately cover all production costs—including environmental costs and the costs of paying fair wages to laborers. But prices must also be "just" for consumers, because it is only if socially, environmental and ecologically sustainable products can become affordable to the majority that the transition to a sustainable agro-food system will be achievable. In the vision projected by GAS, *access to sustainable food* is the key concept for transition to a more sustainable and just food system.[20] Restrictions on access to sustainable food, whether for physical (as in the case of food shortages) or economic reasons (organic food being too expensive) comprise very serious obstacles to sustainability. The energies of GAS are therefore channeled into constructing an alternative system of food provision and alternative practices of food consumption with the potential to ensure both physical and economic access to sustainable food (Fonte 2013).

A short food chain and a reconnection between producers and consumers are both essential to this endeavor. A short food chain is not only an organizational expedient serving economic purposes. It is also a means by which self-sustainable local economies can be created and sustained and the civic values of food democracy and food sovereignty affirmed.

## CONCLUDING REMARKS

We have presented and analyzed the strategies of what we think are the most important actors in Italian alternative agriculture. As the wealth of international literature on alternative food networks demonstrates, it is difficult to define what "alternative" agriculture is. Alternative may be intended to denote something different from the mainstream model for the agro-food sector, based on specialization, concentration of production, standardization and globalization. Sometimes "alternative" is applied to single agricultural practices, such as no-till agriculture (Goulet 2013). We have excluded this from our definition, taking into account only strategies and conceptions that, albeit with contradictions at times, entail transformation of the entire model for agro-food development, in accordance with an agro-ecological approach and supporting the "integral product identity" paradigm (Levidow 2014).

Because of their peculiarly Mediterranean characteristics, Italian agriculture and the agro-food system have struggled to adapt to an industrial development. The 1990s "turn to quality" fell on fertile ground precisely because of the persistence of a differentiated, diversified system of production and a rich diversity of food traditions. Furthermore, in the 1990s, the radical transformation of the political, social and economic context in Italy paved the way for the emergence of new social food movements, on the one hand, and a remodeling of the strategies of older organizations such as Coldiretti, on the other.

We see Coldiretti as a "borderline" organization situated halfway between the "incumbent" and the "alternative" food regimes. A traditional agricultural organization established after the World War II to represent the interests of smallholders, Coldiretti reinvented its strategy after the deep crisis that the political party system in Italy, and indeed Coldiretti's own organization, underwent in the 1990s. Its agro-food strategy now centers on the demand for an "all-Italian Filière," for a fight against agro-piracy and for a labeling system that would certify the national origin of all food ingredients. We see in this strategy a continuation of the ruralist policy of the past, which failed to discriminate among contrasting interests in the same agro-food sector (for example, big and small farms, or the big retailing industry and direct selling). But the new Coldiretti food politics also contains very innovative elements, which it has however delegated to a separate foundation, Campagna Amica (Friendly Countryside). Support is extended to a multifunctional model of agricultural development based on direct selling and a new alliance between producers and consumers with the capacity to ensure a fair income to producers and quality and transparency to consumers. There is unfortunately no emphasis at all, however, on environmental sustainability in agricultural practices.

Slow Food could also be considered a "borderline" organization: its innovative politics of pleasure with a view to valorizing a diversified agriculture and an agro-food culture and its reformulation of "gastronomy" as an instrument for the defense of biocultural diversity—both these characteristics qualify it for inclusion among the "alternative" movements. But it also includes neoliberal features: it entrusts promotion of the new model of a place-based agro-food system to a change in the behavior of individual consumers and to the goodwill of the dominant actors, the multinational food corporations.

The contradictions of the organic movement, as an alternative movement, are well known, and its conventionalization has been widely acknowledged and debated. Its alternative character is historically grounded in the vision of promoting sustainable agricultural practices and thus respect for the natural resource base of agriculture in contrast to the chemical agriculture of the era of modernization. It is also evident in the valorization of local and traditional knowledge in contrast to the dominant, public and private, extension service. It is still preeminent in the fight to promote public, and hence more democratic—as opposed to private—standards, at national and EU level, and it is still enmeshed in the contradictions that characterize the movement, part of which is mobilized in support of civic food networks and food sovereignty in Italy and internationally. The limits to "alterity" can be seen in the standardization of practices codified in European regulations, and above all in the determination of the mass market and big retailing industry to promote the organic food. The conventionalization of the organic movement is in a way an index of its success, its institutionalization and the willingness of its less radical elements (Smith 2006) to be co-opted, resulting in a re-orientation of the mainstream model.

Unlike other alternative initiatives, the GAS in Italy do not focus on any specific quality of a product (Italian, endangered, organic), or on new cultural values of food or a new technique. They focus on the social relationships around food. This is what qualifies them to be identified as part of the civic food networks flourishing all over Europe. The GAS seek to build a new "practice of food consumption," involving a transformation of subjectivities and agency, social-cultural values and norms and the material system of provision. If the attention of each of the other alternative actors mentioned here is primarily concentrated on one aspect of the overall equation—Campagna Amica on the local origins of food, Slow Food on the cultural value of food, the organic movement on the sustainability of agricultural practice—the GAS movement acts upon the food system as a whole, including all its numerous components. The GAS's challenge to the dominant regime is based on the establishment of a new practice in food production and consumption, implying empowerment of consumers and producers, transformation of the socio-cultural norms around food and transformation of the functional structure of food production and distribution. Producers and consumers are empowered through mutual reconnection and emancipation from the dominant regime. Transformation of socio-cultural values entails, for example, redefining "good food" or "a just price." Transformation of food production and distribution implies co-production of food and new values centered on sustainability and solidarity, a new division of labor and new competences.

The GAS movement might be seen as the latest dialectical response of the social movements to the conventionalization of other initiatives, in particular the organic food movement. Actually, while it is arguable that, in conformity with the multilevel transition theory, Campagna Amica, Slow Food and the organic movement have become well-structured institutionalized niches, the GAS movement is in its institutional infancy, with a very low level of structuration. It may well be that, in its trajectory towards a stronger structuration of the network, the less radical elements (i.e., a short food chain) will be appropriated by the dominant system, but it is notable that since its infancy it has prefigured a different organizational model for the food system as a whole, based on horizontal subsidiarity, solidarity between producers and consumers and co-production of goods and values, that is quite incompatible with the dominant food regime and the way it is organized.

## NOTES

\*  We wish to thank Marta Romeo, Gabriella Zampieri and Francesca Alfano for providing some bibliographic references and other materials on alternative agriculture in Italy. We thank also Wayne Hall for doing the language editing. The work has been financed by the University of Naples Federico II research funds.

1.  Farms with more than 50 hectares were generally considered capitalist.

2.  According to Eurostat, in 2010 Italy had 1,603,710 "agricultural holdings" of an average size of about 7 hectares (in Sotte and Arzeni 2013). Of these holdings, according to Istat statistics, only 64 percent sell goods on the market. Just to have some terms of reference, the UK, with a population and a total area quite similar to that of Italy, has 186,800 "agricultural holdings"; for France (with a comparable population to that of the UK and Italy, but about twice the total area) the figure is 516,000. To find comparable data we must turn to the Mediterranean (Spain, Greece, Portugal) or some of the Eastern European countries (Poland, Romania).

3.  See the coalition "Liberi da OGM" (Free from GMO), at the website http://www.liberidaogm.org/liberi/chisiamo.php. The enrolment of the distribution firms in the alliance against GMOs food is something peculiar to Europe; nothing similar had happened in the United States.

4.  The association between national production and safety is not unique to Italy; see, for example, Nygård and Storstad (1998).

5.  In the 14th revision of the register (June 2014) 4,813 products are listed (http://www.politicheagricole.it/flex/cm/pages/ServeBLOB.php/L/IT/IDPagina/3276).

6.  Federconsorzi is the National Federation of Consorzi Agrari, a second-degree cooperative linking the Consorzi Agrari (Agrarian Consorzia). Founded in 1892 in response to the agricultural crisis of the end of the 19th Century, it was conceived as a collective buying group for fertilizers and agricultural machinery, but its functions soon expanded to cover the collective marketing of agricultural produce and provision of extension services and technical assistance to farmers. In the Fascist period Federconsorzi became the implementer of the regime's stocking policy and the main provider of agricultural credit. The range of activities performed by the Consorzi Agrari remained vast throughout the post-World War II period.

7.  See the website: http://www.edizionitellus.it/patto.html.

8.  The certification of CA producers is delegated to CSQA, a private certification and inspection company with specific expertise in the farm and food sector. It was the first

authorized by the Ministry of Agriculture for monitoring of products with Registered Designation of Origin (Campagna Amica 2014b; CSQA 2014).

9. Under CA regulations, non-organic fresh produce sold in CA farmers' markets must be priced at least 30 percent lower than the local reference price. The local reference price is the lowest of a number of contending prices: (a) the price charged by local supermarkets, monitored at a minimum of three selling points and (b) the reference price provided by the SMS Consumatori service, jointly operated by the Ministry of Agriculture, ISMEA and several consumers' associations. SMS Consumatori monitors the daily average price (both wholesale and detail) for 84 agricultural products in three macro-areas: in the North, the Centre and the South. At the time of writing the SMS Consumatori service appears to have been suspended; we assume that the CA local reference price is now based only on local supermarket prices.

10. This is, for example, the case with CA farmers' markets in Trento province, in the North-East, where special exemptions had explicitly to be made from the regional origin rule for nomadic apiculture and for flours used in traditional baking and bread-making, since the local production of traditional wheat varieties was not large enough to cover the demand (Campagna Amica Trento 2013). Very similar rules apply at all CA farmers' markets, for which the official regulation is available online.

11. The "fairness" of margin distribution is mostly predicated on the reduction in the number of intermediate steps between farmers and distributors, and on the fact that CA and FAI aggregate large volumes and can therefore negotiate better terms for their associates.

12. The all-Italian product lines created with the involvement of CA are *VOI—Valore Origine Italiana*— for the Iper network, and *100% Italia* for Italian-produced pasta sold in Coop supermarkets (Campagna Amica 2014a).

13. In the Marche region of central Italy, for example, farmers who refused to convert to chemical agriculture decided in the 1980s to establish the Associazione Marchigiana per l'Agricoltura Biologica (AMAB, Association for Organic Agriculture in the Marche). The AMAB gradually spread all over Italy, and was eventually, in 1996, renamed the Mediterranean Association for Organic Agriculture (AMAB 2013). Several organic and biodynamic cooperatives emerged at around the same time in Veneto, in the North-East of the country, founded by groups of agricultural producers, technicians and students.

14. "AAM Terra Nuova" was founded in Bologna in 1977. The association edits a journal by the same name, dealing with themes related to organic food and agriculture.

15. See the website http://www.ecornaturasi.it/it/chi-siamo/storia.

16. The renewed attention of the Italian left towards culture in general and popular culture in particular was symbolically expressed in the "Roman Summers" organized between 1976 and 1985 by Renato Nicolini, an architect and city council member in left-wing administrations.

17. The self-managed Centri Sociali spread throughout Italy in the 1980s, in the wake of the crisis of the political movements in the 1960s and 1970s. Young people occupied abandoned buildings, often in the suburbs of big cities, and turned them into social youth centers engaged in cultural, recreational and political activities.

18. See http://www.slowfoodfoundation.com/narrative-labels#.U-xzrVY760c.

19. The "Budgets of Justice" (Bilanci di Giustizia in Italian) were started in the North of Italy from 1993 onwards, promoted by a number of groups and associations of Catholic inspiration. The basic idea has been to change the structure of family consumption in order to: (a) establish a fairer consumption model vis-à-vis the global South; (b) improve the quality of life; and (c) orient consumption models towards energy-saving and renewable resources (see http://www.bilancidigiustizia.it/chi-siamo/).

20. We can see here an original re-interpretation of Sen's concept of "access to food" and its importance for food security. In the vision of GAS, "access to sustainable food" is considered important for transition to a sustainable and just food system, that is food sovereignty (Crisci and Fonte 2014). This is in stark contrast to the vision of Slow Food, according to which consumers should pay a higher price to support quality food and endangered food.

# REFERENCES

Allen, Patricia, Margaret Fitzsimmons, Michael Goodman, Keith Warner. 2003. "Shifting plates in the agrifood landscape: The tectonics of alternative agrifood initiatives in California." *Journal of Rural Studies* 19 (1): 61–75.

Allen, Patricia and Julie Guthman. 2006. "From 'old school' to 'farm-to-school': Neoliberalization from the ground up." *Agriculture and Human Values* 23 (4): 401–415.

AMAB. 2013. "Chi siamo." Retrieved April 27, 2013 (www.amab.it/pagina.asp?Pag=2).

Andrews, Geoff. 2008. *The Slow Food Story*. London: Pluto Press.

Ansell, Christopher K. and David Vogel. 2006. *What's the Beef? The Contested Governance of European Food Safety*. Cambridge, MA: MIT Press.

Barbera, Filippo and Stefano Audifreddi. 2012. "In pursuit of quality: The institutional change of wine production market in Piedmont." *Sociologia Ruralis* 52 (3): 311–331.

Barberis, Corrado. 1978. "Le tre realtà dell'agricoltura italiana." Pp. 81–88 in *Azienda Contadina. Sviluppo Economico e Stratificazione Sociale*, edited by Paola Bertolini and Benedetto Meloni. Torino: Rosenberg & Sellier.

Baudrillard, Jean. 1981. *For a Critique of the Economy of Signs*. St. Louis, MO: Telos Press.

Beck, Ulrich, Anthony Giddens and Scott Lash. 1994. *Reflexive Modernization: Politics, Tradition and Aesthetics in the Modern Social Order*. Cambridge: Polity.

Bolaffi, Guido and Adriano Varotti. 1978. "La struttura capitalistica dell'agricoltura italiana e il problema dei contadini." Pp. 137–168 in *Azienda Contadina. Sviluppo Economico e Stratificazione Sociale*, edited by Paola Bertolini and Benedetto Meloni. Torino: Rosenberg & Sellier.

Brasili, Cristina, Roberto Fanfani and Elisa Ricci Meccarini. 2001. "Un'analisi strutturale ed economica delle industrie alimentari in Italia." Pp. 27–55 in *Il Settore Agroalimentare Italiano e l'Integrazione Europea*, edited by Roberto Fanfani, Elisa Montresor and Francesco Pecci. Milano: Franco Angeli.

Brunori, Gianluca, Vanessa Malandrin and Adanella Rossi. 2013. "Trade-off or convergence? The role of food security in the evolution of food discourse in Italy." *Journal of Rural Studies* 29: 19–29.

Busch, Lawrence and Arunas Juska. 1997. "Beyond political economy: Actor Networks and the globalization of agriculture." *Review of International Political Economy* 4 (4): 688–708.

Cà Verde. 2014. "Chi siamo." S. Ambrogio di Valpolicella (VR): Coop Agr A.R.L. 8 Marzo. Retrieved April 18, 2014 (http://caverde.com/index.php?route=information/information&information_id=4).

Calza Bini, Paolo. 1978. "Contadini proletari o basso ceto medio?" Pp. 189–204 in *Azienda Contadina. Sviluppo Economico e Stratificazione Sociale*, edited by Paola Bertolini and Benedetto Meloni. Torino: Rosenberg & Sellier.

Camera dei Deputati, XIII legislatura. 1997. "Indagine conoscitiva sulle biotecnologie." Retrieved July 25, 2014 (http://gnosis.aisi.gov.it/sito%5CRivista16.nsf/servnavig/10).

Campagna Amica. 2014a. "FAI." Roma: Fondazione Campagna Amica. Retrieved August 16, 2014 (http://www.campagnamica.it/fai/Pagine/default.aspx).

Campagna Amica. 2014b. "FAQ: Cos'è la Rete Nazionale dei Punti Campagna Amica?" Roma: Fondazione Campagna Amica. Retrieved August 13, 2014 (http://www.campagnamica.it/pagineCA/Pagine/FAQ.aspx).

Campagna Amica Trento. 2013. "Campagna Amica Mercato Contadino, circuito per la valorizzazione dei prodotti agricoli, Disciplinare Rev. 0.4.2 aggiornato al 30 gennaio 2013." Retrieved July 13, 2014 (http://www.comune.ala.trento.it/attivitaEconomiche/commercio%20su%20aree%20pubbliche/mercato_contadino/disciplinare%20campagna%20amica.pdf).

Coldiretti. 2011. "Statuto Confederazione Nazionale Coldiretti—Approvato dall'Assemblea della Confederazione il 15 febbraio 2011." Roma: Coldiretti. Retrieved July 13, 2014 (http://www.coldiretti.it/organismi/coldiretti/STATUTO%20CONFEDERAZIONE%20 approvato%20Assemblea%2015_02_11.pdf).

Coldiretti. 2014. "Chi siamo." Roma: Coldiretti. Retrieved July 13, 2014 (http://www.coldiretti.it/chisiamo/Pagine/default.aspx).

Cosentino, Vincenzo and Michele De Benedictis. 1978. "Forme di conduzione ed equilibrio dell'impresa agraria." Pp. 241–270 in *Azienda Contadina. Sviluppo Economico e Stratificazione Sociale*, edited by Paola Bertolini and Benedetto Meloni. Torino: Rosenberg & Sellier.

Crisci, Giacomo and Maria Fonte. 2014. "L'accesso al bio nella transizione verso la sostenibilità dei sistemi agro-alimentari." *Agriregionieuropa* 10 (37). Retrieved August 26, 2014 (http://agriregionieuropa.univpm.it/en/node/8863).

Crivits, Maarten and Erik Paredis. 2013. "Designing an explanatory practice framework: Local food systems as a case." *Journal of Consumer Culture* 13 (3): 306–336.

CSQA. 2014. "About CSQA." Roma: CSQA. Retrieved August 13, 2014 (http://www.csqa.it/CSQA/Overview/Profilo).

Di Iacovo, F., Maria Fonte and A. Galasso. 2014. "Agricoltura civica e filiera corta, Nuove pratiche, forme di impresa e relazioni tra produttori e consumatori." Working Paper No. 22, Gruppo 2013. Retrieved July 30, 2014 (http://www.gruppo2013.it/working-paper/Documents/WORKING%20PAPER%2022_luglio%202014.pdf).

Eder, Klaus. 1993. *The New Politics of Class: Social Movements and Cultural Dynamics in Advanced Societies*. London: Sage Publication.

Fabiani, Guido. 1978. "Aspetti strutturali e di tendenza nell'agricoltura italiana (1960–1970)." Pp. 109–136 in *Azienda Contadina. Sviluppo Economico e Stratificazione Sociale*, edited by Paola Bertolini and Benedetto Meloni. Torino: Rosenberg & Sellier.

Fabiani, Guido. 1986. *L'Agricoltura Italiana tra Sviluppo e Crisi (1945–1995)*. Bologna: Il Mulino.

Fanfani, Roberto. 2004. "Introduzione." Pp. 5–22 in Manlio Rossi-Doria, *Rapporto sulla Federconsorzi*. Napoli: L'Ancora del Mediterraneo.

Fonte, Maria. 2002. "Food systems, consumption models and risk perception in the late modernity." *International Journal of the Sociology of Agriculture and Food* 10 (1): 13–21.

Fonte, Maria. 2004. *Organismi Geneticamente Modificati, Monopolio e Diritti*. Milano: Franco Angeli.

Fonte, Maria. 2006. "Slow Food's Presidia: What do small producers do with big retailers?" Pp. 203–240 in *Between the Local and the Global: Confronting Complexity in the Contemporary Agri-food Sector*, vol. 12, edited by Terry Marsden and Jonathan Murdoch. Oxford: Elsevier.

Fonte, Maria. 2013. "Food consumption as social practice: Solidarity Purchasing Groups in Rome, Italy." *Journal of Rural Studies* 32: 230–239.

Fonte, Maria and Apostolos G. Papadopoulos (eds.). 2010. *Naming Food after Places: Food Relocalisation and Knowledge Dynamics in Rural Development*. Farnham, UK: Ashgate.

Fonte, Maria and Cristina Salvioni. 2013. "Cittadinanza ecologica e consumo sostenibile: dal Biologico ai gruppi di Acquisto Solidale." Pp. 81–103 in *Cibo Locale. Percorsi Innovativi nelle Pratiche di Produzione e Consumo Alimentare*, edited by Alessandra Corrado and Silvia Sivini. Napoli: Liguori.

Friedman, Harriet. 2009. "Discussion: Moving food regimes forward: Reflections on symposium essays." *Agriculture and Human Values* 26 (4): 335–344.

Friedman, Harriet and Philip McMichael. 1989. "Agriculture and the state system: The rise and demise of national agricultures, 1870 to present." *Sociologia Ruralis* 19 (2): 93–117.

Fuenfschilling, Lea and Bernhard Truffer. 2014. "The structuration of socio-technical regimes: Conceptual foundations from institutional theory." *Research Policy* 43: 772–791.

Furman, Carrie, Carla Roncoli, Donald R. Nelson and Gerrit Hoogenboom. 2014. "Growing food, growing a movement: Climate adaptation and civic agriculture in the Southerneastern United States." *Agriculture and Human Values* 31 (1): 69–82.

Geels, Frank W. 2004. "From sectoral systems of innovation to socio-technical systems:

Insights about dynamics and change from sociology and institutional theory." *Research Policy* 33: 897–920.

Geels, Frank W. 2010. "Ontologies, socio-technical transitions (to sustainability), and the multi-level perspective." *Research Policy* 39: 495–510.

Geels, Frank W. and Johan Schot. 2007. "Typology of socio-technical transition pathways." *Research Policy* 36: 399–417.

Geels, Frank W. and Johan Schot. 2010. "The dynamics of transitions: A socio-technical perspective." Pp. 9–101 in *Transitions to Sustainable Development: New Directions in the Study of Long Term Transformative Change*, edited by John Grin, Jan Rotmans and Johan Schot. New York: Routledge.

Goodman, David. 2003. "The quality 'turn' and alternative food practices: Reflexion and agenda." *Journal of Rural Studies* 19: 1–7.

Goodman, David E., Melanie DuPuis and Michael K. Goodman. 2012. *Alternative Food Networks: Knowledge, Practice and Politics*. Abingdon, UK: Routledge.

Gorgoni, Marcello. 1978. "Sviluppo economico, progresso tecnologico e dualismo nell'agricoltura italiana." Pp. 205–240 in *Azienda Contadina. Sviluppo Economico e Stratificazione Sociale*, edited by Paola Bertolini and Benedetto Meloni. Torino: Rosenberg & Sellier.

Goulet, Frédéric. 2013. "Narratives of experience and production of knowledge within farmers' groups." *Journal of Rural Studies* 32: 439–447.

Guthman, Julie. 2007. "The Polanyian way? Voluntary food labels as neoliberal governance." *Antipode* 39 (3): 456–478.

Hinrichs, C. Clare. 2000. "Embeddedness and local food systems: Notes on two types of direct agricultural market." *Journal of Rural Studies* 16: 295–303.

Hinrichs, C. Clare. 2003. "The practice and politics of food system localization." *Journal of Rural Studies* 19 (1): 33–45.

Hinrichs, C. Clare. 2014. "Transitions to sustainability: A change in thinking about food systems change?" *Agriculture and Human Values* 31 (1): 143–155.

Hinrichs, C. Clare and Thomas A. Lyson (eds.). 2008. *Remaking the North American Food System: Strategies for Sustainability*. Lincoln, NB: University of Nebraska Press.

Holloway, Lewis, Moya Kneafsey, Laura Venn, Rosie Cox, Elizabeth Dowler and Helena Tuomainen. 2007. "Possible food economies: A methodological framework for exploring food production–consumption relationships." *Sociologia Ruralis* 47 (1): 1–19.

Ilbery, Brian and Damian Maye. 2005. "Alternative (short) food supply chains and specialist livestock products in the Scottish–English borders." *Environment and Planning A* 37: 823–844.

Jaillette, Jean-Claude. 2001. *Il Cibo Impazzito. Il Caso Europeo della Contraffazione Alimentare*. Milano: Feltrinelli.

Kirwan, James. 2004. "Alternative strategies in the UK agro-food system: Interrogating the alterity of farmers' markets." *Sociologia Ruralis* 44 (4): 395–415.

Kloppenburg, Jack, Jr. and Neva Hassanein. 2006. "From old school to reform school?" *Agriculture and Human Values* 23 (4): 417–421.

LaPrimavera Coop. 2014. "Una storia lunga vent'anni." Campagnola di Zevio (VR): Cooperativa Agricola La Primavera Scarl. Retrieved July 13, 2014 (http://www.cooperati valaprimavera.it/pdf/Libretto%20forapan.pdf).

Lash, Scott M. and John Urry. 1994. *Economies of Signs and Space*. London: Sage.

Leitch, Alison. 2003. "Slow Food and the politics of pork fat: Italian food and European identity." *Ethnos* 68 (4): 437–462.

Leitch, Alison. 2005. "Why food matters: New perspectives on the politics of food." Paper presented at TASA Conference, University of Tasmania, 6–8 December.

Levidow, Les. 2014. "Contending agro-food transition in Europe: Prospect for agro-ecological transformation." Paper presented at the seminar *La grande transformation de l'agriculture, 20 ans après*. Montpellier, 16–17 June.

Majone, Giandomenico (ed.). 1996. *Regulating Europe*. London: Routledge.

Marsden, Terry K., Andrew Flynn and Michelle Harrison. 2000. *Consuming Interests: The Social Provision of Foods*. London: Ucc Press.

Miele, Mara. 2001. "Creating sustainability: The social construction of market for organic products." PhD dissertation, Circle for Rural European Studies, Wageningen University, Wageningen, the Netherlands.

Miller, Daniel. 1995. *Acknowledging Consumption: A Review of New Studies*. London: Routledge.

Miller, Daniel. 1997. *Capitalism: An Ethnographic Approach*. Oxford: Berg.

Miller, Daniel. 2012. *Consumption and Its Consequences*. Cambridge: Polity Press.

Mottura, Giovanni. 1987. *Il Conflitto Senza Avventure. Quarant'Anni di Strategia Ruralista nelle Campagne Italiane (1944–1987)*. Università degli Studi di Modena. Studi e Ricerche del Dipartimento di Economia Politica 47.

Mottura, Giovanni and Enrico Pugliese. 1975. *Agricoltura, Mezzogiorno e Mercato del Lavoro*. Bologna: Il Mulino.

Murray, Douglas L. and Laura T. Raynolds. 2007. "Globalization and its antinomies: Negotiating a Fair Trade movement." Pp. 3–14 in *Fair Trade: The Challenge of Transforming Globalization*, edited by Laura T. Raynolds, Douglas L. Murray and John Wilkinson. Oxford: Routledge.

Nygård, Berit and Oddveig Storstad. 1998. "De-globalization of food markets? Consumer perceptions of safe food: The case of Norway." *Sociologia Ruralis* 38 (1): 35–53.

Occhetta, Francesco and Nunzio Primavera. 2010. *Paolo Bonomi e il Riscatto delle Campagne*. Gorle, BG: Edizioni Velar.

Ortiz-Miranda, Dionisio, Ana Moragues-Faus and Eladio Arnalte-Alegre (eds.). 2013. *Agriculture in Mediterranean Europe between Old and New Paradigms*. Research in Rural Sociology and Development 19. Bingley, UK: Elsevier—Emerald Group Publishing.

Petrini, Carlo and Gigi Padovani. 2005. *Slow Food Revolution*. Milano: Rizzoli.

Pugliese, Enrico and Massimo Rossi. 1978. "Dualismo strutturale in agricoltura e mercato del lavoro." Pp. 169–288 in *Azienda Contadina. Sviluppo Economico e Stratificazione Sociale*, edited by Paola Bertolini and Benedetto Meloni. Torino: Rosenberg & Sellier.

Ray, Christopher. 1998. "Culture, intellectual property and territorial rural development." *Sociologia Ruralis* 39 (1): 3–20.

Raynolds, Laura T. and John Wilkinson. 2007. "Fair Trade in agriculture and the food sector: Analytical dimensions." Pp. 33–47 in *Fair Trade: The Challenge of Transforming Globalization*, edited by Laura T. Raynolds, Douglas L. Murray and John Wilkinson. Oxford: Routledge.

Reckwitz, Andreas. 2002. "Towards a theory of social practices: A development in culturalist theorizing." *European Journal of Social Theory* 5: 243–263.

Renting, Henk, Marcus Schermer and Adanella Rossi. 2012. "Building food democracy: Exploring civic food networks and newly emerging forms of food citizenship." *International Journal of Sociology of Agriculture and Food* 9 (3): 289–307.

Rete Rurale Nazionale. 2013. "Bioreport 2013. L'agricoltura biologica in Italia." Roma. Retrieved July 25, 2014 (http://www.sinab.it/sites/default/files/share/BIOREPORT_2013_WEB%5B1%5D.pdf).

Ritzer, George and Nathan Jurgenson. 2010. "Production, consumption, prosumption: The nature of capitalism in the age of the digital 'prosumer.'" *Journal of Consumer Culture* 10: 13–36.

Rota, Gian Arturo and Nichi Stefi. 2012. *Luigi Veronelli. La Vita è Troppo Breve per Bere Vini Cattivi*. Milano and Bra: GiuntiEditore/Slow Food Editore.

Salvioni, Cristina. 1999. "L'impatto del reg. 2078/92 sulla diffusione del biologico: il caso dell'Abruzzo." In *L'Agricoltura Biologica tra PAC e Mercato*, edited by F.M. Cantucci. Quaderno dell'Istituto di Economia e Politica Agraria di Perugia n. 25.

Santucci, Fabio Maria. 2009. "I circuiti commerciali dei prodotti biologici." *Agriregioneeuropa* 5 (17).

Sassatelli, Roberta and Federica Davolio. 2010. "Consumption, pleasure and politics: Slow

Food and the politico-aesthetic problematization of food." *Journal of Consumer Culture* 10: 202–232.

Sereni, Emilio. [1947] 1971. *Il Capitalismo nelle Campagne (1860–1900)*. Torino: Einaudi.

Shove, Elizabeth, Mika Pantzar and Matt Watson. 2012. *The Dynamics of Social Practice: Everyday Life and How It Changes*. London: Sage.

Slow Food. 2014. "The Slow Food approach to food labeling." Bra, Cuneo: Slow Food International. Retrieved July 25, 2014 (http://www.slowfood.com/sloweurope/fileman-ager/position_docs/INGLetichetta.pdf).

Smith, Adrian. 2006. "Green niches in sustainable development: The case of organic food in the United Kingdom." *Environment and Planning C: Government and Policy* 24: 439–458.

Sotte, Franco. 2006. "Quante sono le imprese agricole in Italia?" *Agriregionieuropa* 2 (5).

Sotte, Franco and Andrea Arzeni. 2013. "Imprese e non-imprese nell'agricoltura italiana." *Agriregionieuropa* 9 (32).

Terra e Libertà/Critical Wine (2004). *Sensibilità Planetaria, Agricoltura Contadina e Rivoluzione dei Consumi*. Roma: Derive Approdi.

van der Ploeg, Jan Douwe. 2008. *The New Peasantries: Struggles for Autonomy and Sustainability in an Era of Empire and Globalization*. London: Earthscan.

Venturini, Tommaso. 2008. "Our daily bread: Eataly and the reinvention of supermarket." Paper presented at the First International Conference on Economic De-growth for Ecological Sustainability and Social Equity, Paris, April 16–19.

Veronelli, Luigi. 1964. *Alla Ricerca dei Cibi Perduti. Guida di Gusto e di Lettere all'Arte del Saper Mangiare*. Roma: Derive Approdi.

Veronelli, Luigi and Pablo Echaurren. 2005. *Bianco Rosso e Veronelli. Manuale per Enodissidenti e Gastroribelli*. Viterbo: Stampa Alternativa.

Viviano, Eliana (ed.). 2012. "La grande distribuzione organizzata e l'industria alimentare in Italia." Banca d'Italia, Questioni di Economia e Finanza, Occasional Papers 119.

Walter, Lynn. 2009. "Slow Food and home cooking: Toward a relational aesthetic of food and relational ethic of home." *Provisions: The Journal of the Center for Food in Community and Culture* (1). Retrieved July 13, 2014 (http://www.uwgb.edu/cfcc/files/pdf/SlowFood&HomeCooking.pdf).

# 15. Animal welfare: The challenges of implementing a common legislation in Europe

*Mara Miele, Bettina Bock and Lummina Horlings*

## INTRODUCTION

The implementation of European Union (EU) legislation on animal welfare varies across the 28 member states in relation to the organization of the process and the results achieved (Evans and Miele 2007; Miele and Lever 2014). Recently, there has been an intensification of the non-compliance of several member states, as denounced by several influential animal welfare non-governmental organizations (NGOs).[1] In all member states, EU regulations have to be directly implemented; however, national authorities are in charge of the transposition of EU directives into national legislation and the follow up of EU regulations. Animal welfare issues have gained very different levels of attention in the political agenda of the EU members: in some countries, EU legislation is integrated into an already existing national policy for animal welfare, while in other countries there are no specific animal welfare policies. There are also considerable differences in the extent to which private actors such as farmers, processors, retailers and NGOs are invited to discuss and prepare the implementation of the EU regulation in collaboration with the national authorities or with regional authorities where regional governments are responsible for animal welfare policy. As a result, national and regional laws covering the EU directives may vary considerably. Recent studies have pointed out that the existence of a national animal welfare policy reflects the recognition of farm animal welfare as a matter of public concern and the political will to undertake a coordinated effort to organize its realization (see Kjærnes 2012; Miele and Lever 2014). It is, hence, not the national animal welfare policy as such, which facilitates efficient implementation. This chapter demonstrates that the level of commercialization of animal welfare plays an important role with regards to implementation as it encourages investments in animal welfare. Commercialization, moreover, coincides with an increasing involvement of private actors in the development and implementation of animal welfare legislation. The state is not displaced as the political regulatory authority but consciously chooses to share responsibilities with private stakeholders. This differs from traditional forms of neo-corporatist collaboration which are well known in agriculture through the involvement of new partners (NGOs and retailers), and the encouragement of collaboration between "former enemies" in the development of solutions to the problems resulting from more stringent animal welfare legislation. These new forms of collaboration fit into the idea of economization of society and, hence, the process of neoliberalization, as is described in the introduction to this book by Alessandro Bonanno and Lawrence Busch. Yet they also reflect how the politicization of a problem may force private actors "close to the problem" (Bonanno and Busch, this volume) to finally accept their responsibility for solving it (Bain, Ransom and Higgins 2013). In doing so a new political economy is formed, in which state, market and civil society collaborate, and where the economization of politics facilitates the incorporation of ethical issues, and at the same time redistributes responsibilities and liabilities between new parties, including not only politicians but also farmers, processors, retailers, scientists and, last but not least, consumers.

The data we present here are based on a project called EUWelNet,[2] funded by DG Sanco[3] and carried out in 2013. The project EUWelNet was dedicated to evaluating the feasibility and usefulness of a network that could assist the competent authorities and stakeholders in implementing EU legislation on animal welfare.[4] The empirical data have been collected in ten EU member states: Italy, France, Germany, the Netherlands, Poland, Romania, Slovakia, Spain, Sweden and the United Kingdom (UK). The study started by mapping the organization of the implementation process employed in the ten focus countries, the main public and private actors and agencies involved and the level of implementation achieved. Then we carried out a desk study, supplemented with a small number of interviews with the competent authorities in each of the ten study countries. The research then looked more in-depth at the situation in six of the ten countries (Italy, the Netherlands, Poland, Romania, Spain and the UK) by interviewing representatives of the competent public authorities, supply chain actors and relevant NGOs. The six selected countries represented the three main geographic areas of the EU and are of specific interest because of their diverse levels of implementation and investment in implementation procedures. The interviews focused on the identification of major bottlenecks in implementation and enforcement and corrective measures taken, while paying specific attention to knowledge gaps, the relevance of knowledge transfer and institutional arrangements.

This chapter is organized in the following way. First, we give an overview of the main challenges to the implementation of the EU animal welfare regulation in these ten study countries. Second, we present a "best practice" example of successful implementation in the Netherlands and the emergence of a new "governmentality" around animal welfare issues centered upon newly formed "private–public expert groups."

We conclude with some reflections about the challenges and opportunities for the harmonization of the implementation of the EU animal welfare regulation.

## CHALLENGES TO THE IMPLEMENTATION OF ANIMAL WELFARE REGULATIONS IN EUROPE

One of the main factors affecting the effective transposition and implementation of EU animal welfare regulations is the presence of a national set of rules and dedicated policies for improving and monitoring the welfare of farm animals. The differences in national legislation covering the welfare of farm animals across the ten countries studied are captured in Table 15.3. Importantly, the socio-economic context in which the implementation of the EU regulations in the EU member states takes place varies considerably. The ten European countries considered in this study differ decisively in the organization of the animal production sector, such as reflected in the level of food supply chain integration (higher for meat chickens compared to pig meat production, but highly variable in the countries), the level of production for the export market and the level of imports, as well as the presence of private certification schemes (ranging, for example, from seven in the UK to none in Slovakia, Spain and Romania – see Table 15.1 and Table 15.2). Particularly significant is the difference in the level of commercialization of animal welfare, by which we mean the use of animal welfare issues in the communication of product quality to consumers. Animal welfare, as well as a vast array of other ethical issues (Barnett, Cloke, Clarke and Malpass 2005; Barnett, Cloke, Clarke and Malpass 2011), is increasingly communicated on food products either on the packaging or through dedicated labels, especially in some of the older member states (Miele and Evans 2010; Evans and Miele 2012). The commercialization of animal welfare is based on the presence of quality certification schemes that differentiate between animal products in the market and may represent either a market entrance requirement, for example when large supermarket chains impose their schemes of production that include the achievement of certain animal welfare parameters (Miele, Murdoch and Roe 2005; Bock, Hacking and Miele 2014; Buller

*Table 15.1   Comparative assessment – national background for meat chickens*

| Country | Characterization | General structure of the retail sector | Consumption (kg per person p.a.) | Private farm assurance schemes | Presence and importance of organic schemes |
|---|---|---|---|---|---|
| France | 9,550 highly integrated farms. Clustered in the West. 100% self-sufficient. Exports to Europe and Middle East. | Four multinationals dominate. | 15.2 | 3 | The "Bio" scheme covers 1% of production. |
| Germany | 4,532 highly integrated farms. Clustered in the NW and SE. 108% self-sufficient. Exports to Europe, South Africa and Ukraine. | Four multinationals dominate. | 11.5 | 4 | Several organic associations with own labels. 1.8% of meat sales are organic. |
| Italy | 2,830 farms (100 + birds) which are highly integrated. Clustered in the North. 107% self-sufficient. Exports to Europe. | Three cooperatives and two multinationals dominate. | 18.5 | 2 | These account for much less than 1% of the national meat production. |
| Netherlands | 650 farms. No integration. Clustering of farms in South, North and East. Self-sufficiency is about 200% for chicken meat. | Three multinationals dominate. | 18.5 | 3 | A "Beterleven" welfare scheme exists. Organic meat is certified by SKAL, but has tiny market share (<1%). |

| Poland | 94,082 farms in total with 97.4 % having less than 500 birds. 2,444 farms (3,000+ birds) which are increasingly vertically integrated. No spatial clustering. 147% self-sufficient. Exports to Europe, Saudi Arabia, Hong Kong and China. | Four multinationals dominate. | 26 | 2 | Ekoland scheme exists but organic meat production remains very small. |
|---|---|---|---|---|---|
| Romania | 250 companies, 40 of which are highly vertically integrated. There is no spatial clustering. 72% self-sufficient. Exports to the EU and beyond. | Five multinationals dominate. | 19 | 0 | "Agricultură ecologică" scheme. Range of organic certifications. Organic meat: < 0.1%, but market increasing annually by 20–30%. |
| Slovakia | 10,430 farms dominated by 3 companies. Medium integration. Clustered in SW and E. 50% self-sufficient. No export markets. | Six multinationals dominate. | 19.9 | 0 | None. |

*Table 15.1*  (continued)

| Country | Characterization | General structure of the retail sector | Consumption (kg per person p.a.) | Private farm assurance schemes | Presence and importance of organic schemes |
|---|---|---|---|---|---|
| Spain | 8,826 highly integrated farms. Clustered in NW, NE, SW and SE. 98% self-sufficient. No export markets. | Four multinationals dominate. | 14.5 | 0 | 54 certified organic meat chicken farms (total 6074 organic farms). Some certification. Low demand. |
| Sweden | 120 medium integrated farms. Clustered in the South. 70% self-sufficient. No export markets. | Four multinationals dominate. | 18 | 2 | Organic (KRAV or EU organic): meat chicken meat: < 0.1 %. Organic meat: 1.4% of total retail food sales. |
| UK | 2,567 highly integrated producers. Clustered in SW, W and E. 88% self-sufficient. | Four multinationals dominate. | 27 | 7 | Soil Association Organic food scheme – sales of organic products in the UK grew by 2.8% in 2013 after four years of contraction. The UK organic market is now worth £1.79billion in sales. The rate of growth was above the annual inflation rate of 2%. |

Growth has been
particularly strong
in the dairy sector
(+4.4%): organic milk
sales grew by 3.4% and
yoghurt sales by 7%
while meat, fish and
poultry sales grew by
2.2%.

UK animals produced
under higher welfare
rise 52%, says RSPCA.
By Melodie Michel,
23-Feb-2012.
http://www.
globalmeatnews.com/
Livestock/UK-animals-
produced-under-higher-
welfare-rise-52-says-
RSPCA

*Source:* Bock et al. (2014). Grant agreement SANCO 2012/G3/EUWELNET/SI2.635078.

Table 15.2   Comparative assessment – national background for pigs

| Country | Characterization | Structure of the retail sector | Consumption (kg per person p.a.) | Private farm assurance schemes | Presence and importance of organic schemes |
|---|---|---|---|---|---|
| France | 11,500 increasingly vertically integrated farms. 3 produce 50% of the production. 4th just 6%. Clustered in NW. 106% self-sufficient. Exports to Europe. | Four multinationals dominate. | 34 | 3 | "Bio" scheme (1% of production). |
| Germany | 60,097 farms in highly vertically integrated systems. Clustered in N and NW. 110% self-sufficient. Exports to Europe, Russia and Hong Kong. | Four multinationals dominate. | 40 | 4 | 1.8% of meat sales are organic. |
| Italy | 100,000 farms which are generally less vertically integrated. Clustered in North. 60% self-sufficient. Negligible exports. | Three cooperatives and two multinationals dominate. | 35–37 | 2 | < 1% of national meat production. |
| Netherlands | 6,525 farms. Less integrated. Concentrated in S and E. Self-sufficiency is 200%, and live export of 20% of the finishers and 30% of the piglets. Exports to Europe. | Three multinationals dominate. | 41 | 3 | < 1% of national meat production. |

| Country | | | | | |
|---|---|---|---|---|---|
| Poland | 397,676 pig slowly vertically integrating farms. Clustered in central and East. 105% self-sufficient. Exports to Europe, Belarus, Hong Ukraine, Russia. | Four multinationals dominate. | 43 | 2 | Organic meat production "very small." |
| Romania | Only minor exports due to swine fever (2003–2011). None to Europe. | Five multinationals dominate. | 31 | 0 | Organic meat: < 0.1%. |
| Slovakia | 10,784 farms which are only lowly integrated and relatively evenly distributed. 38% self-sufficient. No export markets. | Six multinationals dominate. | 32 | 0 | None. |
| Spain | 93,000 highly vertically integrated farms. Clustered in NE, Central and S. 152% self-sufficient. Export markets in Europe, Russia, Hong Kong and China. | Four multinationals dominate. | 49 | 0 | < 0.1%. Low demand. |
| Sweden | 2,000 vertically integrated farms. Clustered in the South. 70% self-sufficient. No major export markets. | Four multinationals dominate. | 36 | 2 | 1.4% of total retail food sales. |
| UK | 4,000 highly integrated producers. Clustered along East coast. 50% self-sufficient. No major export markets. | Four multinationals dominate. | 25 | 7 | 1.0% of meat sales. |

*Source:* Bock et al. (2014). Grant agreement SANCO 2012/G3/EUWELNET/SI2.635078.

303

and Roe 2014), or a strategy for gaining a premium price, when animal welfare indicators are specified in schemes of production for quality and/ or organic products. The presence of these quality certification schemes raises issues about the validity of the welfare claims made and the actual market transparency on this matter (see Blokhuis, Jones, Geers, Miele and Veissier 2003; Blokhuis, Miele, Veissier and Jones 2013; Miele 2011), but they represent an answer to increasing consumer concerns about animal welfare and play an important role in promoting initiatives for improving farm animal welfare. They also signal the "importance" that producers and market operators attribute to improving animal welfare if they want to differentiate their products. However, as Tables 15.2 and 15.3 show, animal welfare is a competitive issue or, effectively, a "market entrance requirement," only in some countries, for example in the UK or the Netherlands (see Miele and Lever 2014; Miele et al. 2005; Freidberg 2004); in other countries animal welfare has no immediate role in market differentiation and is perceived by producers and the food industry only as "a set of rules" imposed by the EU. As discussed in Miele and Lever (2014), there are certain conditions that enable this "ethical" segmentation of the animal food markets: increased availability of consumers' information about animal production in general, animal welfare problems in current systems of production, lower relative food prices and a significant share of the population with enough disposable income to act upon political or ethical values and preferences (Koos 2012: 57). In the ten member states examined in this study there is a great variance in the average income and cost of food as a percentage of personal income (ranging, for example, from 8 percent in the UK to 34 percent in Romania). In those countries where the share of income allocated to buying food is low (which indicates relative low food prices in comparison to incomes), there are more opportunities for quality segmentation and the creation of food niches by communication of quality attributes considered desirable to specific groups of consumers.

Certification schemes that communicate the animal welfare status of farm animals are most frequently found in member states where animal welfare is a matter of high public concern. This is most often the case in countries where there are many resourceful NGOs that are actively fighting for farm animal welfare and promoting media attention given to farm animal welfare issues (Friedberg 2004). Eventually, and importantly, this influences the position of farm animal welfare on the national political agenda and the development of a national animal welfare policy (Miele and Parisi 2001; Kjærnes, Miele and Roex 2007; Kjærnes 2012; Bock and Buller 2013; Miele and Lever 2014). In addition, all these factors influence the production and transfer of the specific knowledge that is required for

Table 15.3  *National versus EU legislation in the ten study countries*

| Country | National Legislation | National vs EU Legislation – Status | National vs EU Legislation – Differences | Timing of transposition |
|---|---|---|---|---|
| Sweden | Yes. Various instruments. | Ahead of EU legislation for meat chickens, pigs and slaughter. | Includes a complete ban on slaughter without pre-stunning. | On time for both directives (1–4 years). |
| UK | Yes. Various instruments. | Ahead of EU directives for meat chickens and pigs. | Some stricter or more detailed national rules. | On time for meat chicken directive (2 years). Behind for slaughter. |
| Netherlands | Yes. Various instruments. | Ahead of EU legislation for meat chickens and pigs. | Tightens regulations a bit and may enable a higher level of production. | Meat chickens relatively short. Pigs longer. |
| Germany | Yes. Various instruments. | Ahead of EU regulation and directives. | Some stricter or more detailed national rules. | Meat chickens relatively short. Pigs very long. |
| Italy | National Plan for Animal Welfare (PNBA). | National legislation is at exactly the same level as the EU. | No difference. | Meat chickens and pigs long (3 years) |

*Table 15.3*   (continued)

| Country | National Legislation | National vs EU Legislation – Status | National vs EU Legislation – Differences | Timing of transposition |
|---|---|---|---|---|
| France | National policy on animal welfare closely aligned to EU regulation. | National legislation is at exactly the same level as the EU. | No difference. | Generally long. |
| Spain | National policy closely aligned to EU directives and the regulation. | National legislation is at exactly the same level as the EU. | No difference. | On time for both directives (1–4 years). |
| Poland | No specific policy on animal welfare. | National legislation is at exactly the same level as the EU. | No difference. | On time for both directives (3–4 years). |
| Romania | No specific policy on animal welfare. | National legislation is at exactly the same level as the EU. | No difference. | On time for both directives (3–4 years). |
| Slovakia | No specific policy on animal welfare. | National legislation is at exactly the same level as the EU. | No difference. | On time for both directives (3–4 years). |

*Note:*   The different shadings distinguish between countries with (white) or without (grey) farm national animal welfare policy. Italy and France have a long history of regulation against animal cruelty, however the focus of these early regulations was on pets, horses and generally non-farm animals (see Vapnek and Chapman 2010).

*Source:*   Bock et al. (2014). Grant agreement SANCO 2012/G3/EUWELNET/SI2.635078.

supporting the implementation and monitoring of the EU directives and regulations. It also affects the involvement of public and private actors and agencies and the degree of collaboration, as well as their relative power and status in this process. All these factors impact the speed of implementation of the EU regulation and the quality of monitoring.

In the next section we discuss the main challenges hampering implementation and monitoring in the study countries, and follow with a discussion of the elements that facilitated successful implementation in two cases of best practice. In looking at these issues we refer to the debate that has emerged in recent agri-food literature on emerging forms of governmentality and, more specifically, on the governmentality of animal foods centered upon the "commercialization" of animal welfare, by which we mean the use of animal welfare characteristics in the communication of product quality to consumers (as proposed by Miele et al. 2005; Miele 2011; Buller and Roe 2014). Our argument is based on the idea that institutions (the state, in its various manifestations, but also private organizations and NGOs) affect the ways in which animals become not only safe but also ethically "acceptable" foods (Ransom 2007; Miele and Lever 2014) via processes of economization and marketization (Busch 2007; Çalışkan and Callon 2009 and 2010). In this way, the concept of governmentality enables us to see how, in specific ways in all the examined countries, formal rules and regulations are negotiated, interpreted and internalized by the subjects (here the animal food chain stakeholders) which are the target of such rules.

## CHALLENGES AND FACILITATING FACTORS

The civil servants, members of NGOs and representatives of the supply chain stakeholders interviewed in all the study countries underlined the importance of socio-economic and political factors when asked what they considered important bottlenecks for the implementation of animal welfare legislation. Representatives of farmers explained that implementation at farm level was hampered by the extra long-term investments that new legislation often required and the higher production costs, which in farmers' perceptions threaten the *economic viability* of farming. They also pointed at the difficulties that arose from the incompatibility of animal welfare legislation with other legislation (e.g., environmental or food safety regulations) and the need for more involvement of farmers' organizations in the policymaking process. Many respondents, from different backgrounds, emphasized *political and cultural factors*, such as the level of public concern with animal welfare, that affected the importance of animal welfare in the political arena and the political will to invest in the implementation process; it also influenced, in their view, the market opportunities for animal friendly products. Looking more specifically at the implementation process, various respondents underlined *institutional bottlenecks*, such as the inefficiency of public control and enforcement. Monitoring practices are not harmonized in EU countries and there are significant differences across and within countries in terms of frequencies of control, use of indicators for measuring compliance and levels of tolerance before sanctioning. Such variances were related to differences in the attitude and behavior of individual inspectors but also to different interpretations of legislation at the level and organizational size of the central authorities.

Generally speaking, member states with a national animal welfare policy were more successful in implementing the three pieces of EU animal welfare legislation, as demonstrated in Table 15.3. The second column of Table 15.3 shows that there are two basic groups of countries in the study: those that have a national farm animal welfare policy that goes beyond EU legislation or was adopted before the EU developed specific farm animal welfare legislation (Germany, the Netherlands, Sweden, the UK and Italy) and those that do not (France, Poland, Romania, Slovakia and Spain). The last column of Table 15.3 indicates that adopting or "transposing" the EU directives into national legislation tends to be quicker in the countries where the national regulations are at the level of the new EU legislation or beyond. It is not surprising of course that implementation proceeds smoothly where the national regulations are at the level of the new EU legislation or even beyond. Here institutions needed to prepare, organize and follow up on implementation and enforcement are already in place, and they often have considerable resources at their disposal.

As mentioned earlier, a national animal welfare policy is, however, not a stand-alone factor but reflects the recognition of farm animal welfare as a matter of public concern and political decision to undertake a coordinated effort to organize its realization. Each policy may, of course, differ in content and ambition as well as approach. What resulted from the study conducted in these ten countries is that where the public authorities engaged with the meat supply chain actors, and involved public and private agents in the policymaking process at an early stage, they encouraged the collaboration of stakeholders in the development and implementation of the animal welfare regulation, promoting "ownership" of it by the subjects (farmers, retailers, etc.) who had to implement it.

The collaboration between public and private actors was generally considered the most important facilitating factor of successful implementation of EU regulations. It was supportive in itself but also played a crucial role in the development of other supporting practices, such as wide dissemination of knowledge and tailor-made information and training of target groups. It also helped to identify bottlenecks and to anticipate them, for instance through investment in knowledge production.

Some form of collaboration between public and private actors takes place in all study countries. There is, however, great variety in the level, scope and frequency of collaboration as well as in the composition and interconnection of networks.

There are *formal networks* that are promoted by the governments to participate in the implementation of either a specific piece of legislation (such as the broiler directive) or a general national animal welfare policy. Some of the networks function only temporarily; others are permanent. Some networks are public and include only or predominantly the relevant public authorities (e.g., the UK has the Advisory Committee on Animal Feedingstuffs in which the Ministry of Agriculture, or DEFRA, its agencies and the UK national government collaborate with scientists). Many networks, however, are mixed and also include agribusiness representatives (farm union, processing industry, breeding industry, slaughterhouses, etc.), NGOs, retailers and/or representatives of scientific authorities (universities). In all six focus countries the government may also initiate *temporary working groups*, focusing on specific issues (e.g., Campylobacter infections in the Netherlands), which they dissolve once the issue has been sufficiently dealt with. Besides public–private collaboration, *private–private collaboration* was also considered as crucial for facilitating implementation. Again, we can find some levels of this type of collaboration in all six focus countries, differing in formality and continuity as well as composition. Collaborations of private and public organizations are more frequent within a sector, while it rarely happens across sectors (with the exception of NGOs).

Many respondents underlined that close collaboration within the supply chain, and, hence, between farmers, slaughterhouses, the processing industry and retailers, promoted implementation and compliance, especially when legislation was included in farm assurance schemes. Farm assurance schemes contribute to the implementation of EU animal welfare legislation through training and education and by providing incentives for farmers to invest in animal friendly production methods. The schemes are often a requirement for selling products to the main supermarket chains. They also regularly inspect farms and slaughterhouses to check if they comply with the norms that are agreed upon as part of the scheme. The latter does not replace official inspection; still, the frequent control by the certifier indirectly supports compliance with legislation where certification rules go beyond or coincide with animal welfare legislations (domestic and supranational). This is, for instance, the case with the Dutch *Beter Leven*, the UK label *Freedom Food* and the German label *Für mehr Tierschutz*.

Such farm assurance schemes are, however, common only in some of the study countries and rare or even absent in others. The market share of, or the number of private schemes with, animal welfare indicates the extent of public–private collaboration in the promotion of animal welfare, which, indirectly, contributes to the implementation of EU animal welfare legislation as explained above. It goes too far, though, to say that they may be used as a proxy for successful implementation of EU legislation, as they do not always directly relate to specific legislation and may choose to include only animal welfare measures that are relatively easy to realize and which do not cover the whole piece of legislation (Buller and Roe 2012). However, they have paved the way for a large group of entrepreneurs to take new steps in implementing animal welfare measures.

When comparing the six focus countries (Italy, the Netherlands, Poland, Romania, Spain and the UK) in the second stage of our research, we can see that the public authorities in the UK and the Netherlands collaborate more frequently with a wider variety of public and private actors than public authorities in the other countries do, and they give these actors more opportunity to participate in policymaking, as will be explained below (see the example of the Netherlands in Table 15.4). The public authorities involve the public and private actors early in the implementation process of a specific piece of EU or national legislation and install working groups in which public authorities collaborate with the industry and knowledge institutes. The composition of these networks is also more mixed than in other countries and they bring together stakeholders with opposing views and interests, such as farmers' organizations and animal protection NGOs. As a result of the many interconnected networks, there are many occasions for the stakeholders to meet, also in an informal way. The Dutch respondents, especially, stressed how valuable such frequent meetings were not only for exchanging knowledge and identifying knowledge gaps, but also for encouraging further collaboration in knowledge production and transfer, as well as in the development of animal welfare oriented production schemes which are practical and workable at the business level.

The level of collaboration is much lower in the other countries. There are occasional meetings between agribusiness and government in Spain and Italy, but generally these meetings are organized per farm sector and do not involve retailers or NGOs. In both Spain and Italy the farm unions complain about their low involvement and the neglect of their interests and experience. Agribusinesses regularly collaborate with knowledge institutes, especially in the highly integrated broiler sector. Formally, NGOs

*Table 15.4  Collaborative working groups in the Netherlands*

| Network | Topic/goal | Participants | Scale |
|---|---|---|---|
| *Public* | | | |
| Formal working groups for implementation initiated by the Ministry of EZ (Direction DAD); among others on: the EU broiler directive and Interventions Decision, Covenant Castration, Revision Killing Regulation. | Discuss and decide how to implement, revise and monitor/control EU regulations. | Product Boards and sector organizations (LTO, NVP, NOP, NEPLUVI, COV), government, monitoring and control (EZ, NVWA, DR), research (WUR-ASG), NGO (DSPCA). | National |
| "Table of 11" meetings at the Ministry of EZ. | Investigate bottlenecks in implementation and improve compliance. | Stakeholders, EZ, NVWA, DR. | National |
| Formal juridical consultation of new laws. | Animal Law. | Legal consultation. | National |
| "Sustainable Animal Husbandry" convenant. | Formulate a vision for 2020 and discuss innovation. | COV, DSCPA, provinces (IPO), banks (Rabobank), LTO, EZ, The NGO Nature and Environment (*Natuur en Milieu*), Nevedi, NZO, GKC. | National |

*Table 15.4* (continued)

| Network | Topic/goal | Participants | Scale |
|---|---|---|---|
| *Public* | | | |
| Working group animal health and welfare within education installed by the Ministry of EZ. | Develop a policy strategy for animal welfare in education. | Green education institutes. | National |
| Alliance on "Sustainable meat 2020." | Develop agreements between retail and sector to improve animal welfare. | Supermarkets, cattle-breeders, supported by companies, NGOs and governments. | National |
| Working group Campylo-bacter. | Develop strategies to reduce animal diseases caused by this bacterium. | NEPLUVI, Ministry VWS, Chicken keepers, unions of animal keepers. | National |
| Council for Animal Affairs | Advice to the National Government. | Independent experts. | National |
| *Private* | | | |
| Unions of animal keepers. | NVP, NOP, NVV, COV, NEPLUVI. | Animal keepers, breeders. | National |
| Working Group "Curly tail." | Discuss and develop new strategies towards reduction and banning of pig tail cutting. | LTO, DSPCA, VIC Sterksel, etc. | National |
| *International public* | | | |
| Collaboration Working Group on Animal Health and Welfare research. | Research | Around 30 organizations (including the Dutch Ministry of EZ) in 20 countries. | EU |

*International private*

| | | | |
|---|---|---|---|
| Euro group for animals. | Cooperation, coordination and formulation of joint strategies of NGOs. | Most important NGOs on animal welfare in the EU members states. | Europe |
| Collaboration within the international Association of Poultry Processors and Poultry Trade in the EU countries (a. v. e. c.). | Cooperation between poultry processors. | Including the Dutch NEPLUVI 18 organizations. | EU |
| The European Forum for Farm animal Breeders (EFFAB). | Cooperation between animal breeding firms. | Including Hendrix Genetics BV 29 European breeders firms. | Europe |

*Note:* The abbreviations used in the table are as follows: COV The Dutch Meat Association; DSPCA The Dutch Society for Prevention of Cruelty to Animals; DR National Service Agency of the Ministry of Economic affairs; EZ Ministry of Economic Affairs; GKC Green Knowledge Cooperation; IPO Inter Provincial Consultation of Provinces; WUR–ASG Animal Sciences Group at Wageningen University and Research Centre; VIC The Pig Innovation Centre; LTO Nederland National Farm Union; NEPLUVI Association of the Dutch Poultry-Processing Industry; NEVEDI Dutch Organization of Animal Fodder Producers; NOP Dutch Union of Broiler Producers; NVWA Netherlands Food and Consumer Product Safety Authority; NVP Inion of the Dutch poultry farmers; NVV Dutch Union of Pig Producers; NZO The Dutch Dairy Association; VWS Ministry for Public Health, Welfare and Sports.

*Source:* Bock et al. (2014). Grant agreement SANCO 2012/G3/EUWELNET/SI2.635078.

are hardly involved in the implementation process. In both countries there are some public–private networks of collaboration; generally, however, these are separate and temporary networks that do not cut across the different stakeholders (primary and processing industries, retailers and NGOs).

In Romania and Poland public and private collaboration in the implementation of EU animal welfare legislation is almost absent. The government informs agribusiness which new rules and regulations have to be followed, once the legislation is applicable. There are hardly any NGOs working on farm animal welfare, as most NGOs focus on pet animals; those that do have very limited resources. They do not collaborate with the government, agribusiness or knowledge institutes. The government works with knowledge institutes, and the latter also cooperate with agribusiness, especially in the highly integrated pig sector, but these networks do not interconnect.

## IMPLEMENTATION AND EXAMPLES OF BEST PRACTICES IN THE NETHERLANDS

The Netherlands has one of the most productive systems of animal farming in Europe. The practical bottlenecks in implementation of EU regulation are partly related to this intensive way of production, such as the management of a maximum stocking density of chickens and the handling of mortality on a farm level. In relation to the pig directive, there are implementation problems regarding the permanent access to fresh drinking water and the interpretation of what can be considered appropriate enrichment material, as well as control of light requirements. The welfare monitoring body of the central competent authority of the Netherlands is the Netherlands Food and Consumer Product Safety Authority (Nederlandse Voedsel en Waren authoriteit – NVWA), which faces obstacles such as a lack of capacity for enforcement due to budget costs. For the directive on killing of animals, bottlenecks were identified in the control of slaughterhouses, the implementation of standard operating procedures and new killing techniques, and in the amount of information fed back to producers (more could be checked and fed back). Knowledge gaps included specific problems such as tail-biting in pigs, the development of a "social (non-pecking) chicken," and the interpretation of certain measures (enrichment material for pigs and the monitoring of footpad lesions in chickens) (Horlings and Bock 2013).

However, according to the respondents, most problems in the implementation of European animal welfare legislation are not caused by a lack of scientific or professional knowledge about how to improve animal welfare but are due to the low prices of meat and other animal products in the global market that lead to constant intensification. There are also issues related to farmers' attitudes and prioritization of production goals over the welfare of animals, and to the lack of a significant pull from consumer demand for welfare friendly produced products. Moreover, other, more technical issues have been mentioned, such as the lack of goal-oriented measures for the welfare achieved on farms and institutional problems such as a lack of effective monitoring/control/sanctioning and an ineffective division of responsibilities.

Compared to other EU countries, the Netherlands can be characterized as an early adopter. Implementation takes place at the national level, with the Ministry of Economic Affairs and the Netherlands Food and Consumer Product Safety Authority as the public authorities primarily responsible for implementation and monitoring of EU animal welfare legislation. Dutch animal welfare legislation is generally at the level of European legislation, with some additional amendments. Private quality assurance schemes, however, often include stricter animal welfare regulations. Public concern regarding animal welfare is high in the Netherlands. This is reflected in the high level of support for NGOs that are active in the field of animal welfare, and in the early development of a national animal welfare policy. The most prominent sign, however, is probably the existence of a political party for animals, which has been present in the parliament since the 2006 elections (Bock and Buller 2013) and had one of its candidates elected for the European Parliament in 2014.

The Dutch animal welfare policy is characterized by novel neo-corporatist collaborations that include not only policymakers, agribusinesses and researchers but also retailers and civil society organizations. It fits the Dutch "polder" model, with policymaking based on deliberation, compromise and conflict prevention. There are various formal and informal working groups that discuss animal welfare policy and the development of new national and EU directives – along with their revision and implementation – as well as the process of monitoring and control (see Table 15.3). Industry and researchers collaborate in the development of new technologies that improve animal welfare. There are also less institutionalized occasions where representatives of the industry, research, government, education and NGOs meet, discuss and collaborate.

The formal governmental working groups are initiated by the Ministry of Economic Affairs (before 2012 the Ministry of Agriculture). The working groups include the Product Boards and farmers' organizations, the government and public authorities for monitoring and control, and researchers as well as one of the prominent animal welfare NGOs, the "Dierenbescherming" (Dutch Society for Prevention of Cruelty to Animals – DSPCA). These groups focus on the development of animal welfare policy, discuss the scope and ambition of the national welfare policy and talk about how to prepare for new EU legislation coming up, in terms of implementation and monitoring. The government informs the stakeholders about developments "in Brussels" and, at the same time, deliberates with stakeholders about which position to adopt. In addition, stakeholders and governments exchange opinions regarding how to antici- pate new requirements by investing in research and development. This form of deliberative policymaking is common in the Netherlands and has characterized agricultural policymaking for a very long time. What has substantially changed, however, is the composition of the working groups, including the integration of former "enemies" – the farm industry and the DSPCA.

The integrative character of the formal working groups is important as it encourages further collaboration outside of the range of formal poli- cymaking. And this is indeed what happens. The collaboration between the food industry and the DCSPA is pushed and supported by the Dutch government, that prefers a (neoliberal) handling of farm animal welfare through market mechanisms instead of legislation. They offered financial support for new initiatives such as "the star system" of the *Beter Leven* (Better Life) label, but also used the threat of more stringent regulation as a stick to push the closing of private agreements between the food industry, retail and NGOs regarding, for example, piglet castration. In the following section we discuss the "Sustainable Meat 2020" agreement and the star system as examples.

### Public–Private Agreements on Sustainable Meat Production in the Netherlands

The association of food retailers (Central Bureau for Food Trade – CBL) played an important role in stimulating the collaboration of stakehold- ers in the development of an intermediary segment of animal friendly products, such as the *Volwaard* chicken in broiler production and the *Rondeel* stable for laying hens. They also figured prominently in a steering/ working group on "Sustainable Meat 2020." These negotiations have led to agreements with the supermarkets in 2013 to improve chicken and pig welfare. The working group "Sustainable Meat 2020" and the "Den Bosch Alliance" include supermarkets and cattle-breeders and are supported by companies, NGOs and the Ministry of Economics Affairs. They have promised to ensure that all the meat in Dutch supermarkets is produced sustainably by 2020.[5]

The recent retail agreement on chickens ("The chicken of tomorrow") includes the commitment to introduce a slower growing breed. Furthermore, the number of chickens per square meter will be decreased by 10 percent by 2015, extra enrichment material will be offered to lower animals' boredom and the use of antibiotics will be reduced. There are similar agreements regarding pork production, which grant pigs 25 percent more space and piglets up to 50 percent more space. This should also reduce boredom and turbulence in the stable. Requirements are set to keep the pigs tail as long as possible and interventions such as the grinding of teeth will be banned. The transport of pigs will be limited to a maximum of six hours and the piglets will be allowed to stay longer with their mothers (on average 28 days). Castration will be stopped earlier (2014 instead of 2015) and stringent quality checks on the drinking water of pigs will be introduced.

These agreements are comparable with one star in the *Better Leven* (Better Life) label for consumers, which was initiated by the DSPCA in 2007 (Commissie Van Doorn 2011; Min EZ and I 2013). Two stars means, for example, free range for chickens. For pigs the 2 star criteria include indoor range and the use of straw. Three stars indicates that the most stringent animal welfare requirements are met, which is generally ascribed to organic meat products. The ambition of the Ministry is that in 2020 half of the total pig meat offered in Dutch supermarkets is offered under this label. According to "Monitor Sustainable Food 2013" by the Ministry, the turnover of products under this label increased in 2012 by 47 percent and in 2013 by 13.4 percent (Ministerie van Economische Zaken 2014).

## CONCLUSIONS

As mentioned at the start of this chapter, the implementation of EU legislation on animal welfare varies across the 28 member states in relation to the organization of the process as well as the results achieved. The EUWelnet project, carried out in ten EU countries, showed important differences in the organization of the animal production sector, such as reflected in the level of food supply chain integration, the level of production for the export market and the level of imports, as well as the presence of private certification schemes. This last one, as shown in the chapter, is particularly significant because these schemes enable the "commercialization" of animal welfare, by which we mean the use of animal welfare issues in the communication of product quality to consumers, and the specific form of governmentality of animal welfare issues emerging from it.

This commercialization, a key aspect of the "marketization" process, is illustrated in the example of the Dutch Animal welfare polity, in which policymakers team up with agribusinesses and researchers as well as retailers and civil society organizations. This collaboration is expressed in formal national working groups, anticipating new legislation, informal meetings and public–private collaboration between industry and researchers. In this context, private quality assurance schemes have been developed which often include stricter animal welfare regulations than national policy. All these various forms of collaboration facilitate the dissemination of knowledge and aim at the implementation of regulation, the development of new production standards and agreements within the production chain for rearing methods that improve animal welfare in intensive systems of production, mainly by way of technological innovation. In doing so they are very successful. The cooperation between private and public organizations has led to a more effective implementation of the EU animal welfare regulation. Despite the high level of collaboration, communication about new knowledge in animal welfare science, the presence of private assurance farm schemes and monitoring and the high level of compliance with EU regulation, still the results obtained do not meet national policy ambitions (e.g., chicken, where the aim is to improve compliance for stocking density; light intensity; and data registration, for example on mortality). Moreover, one could argue that the current focus on somewhat more animal friendly intensive production methods diverts attentions from considering more fundamental changes in production systems and shifts towards less intensive systems of production.

The example discussed demonstrates that in the Netherlands farm animal welfare is increasingly interpreted under the processes of "economization" and "marketization" (Çalışkan and Callon 2009 and 2010); as a result it develops from a basic condition of legitimation and productivity to a set of specific product attributes requiring assessment and monitoring as well as scoring and qualification. As Buller and Roe have argued "over and above regulatory or assurance scheme compliance, welfare conditions and criteria are being used as a component or distinctive selling point for food products, brands or even particular manufacturers and retailers within 'value-added' marketing technologies" (2014: 141). However, this process involves a small number of production systems in Europe, and even in those countries where these processes of "marketization" of animal welfare are more developed, like the Netherlands, they remain a feature of dedicated market niches, while for the large majority of animal producers, animal welfare rules are a burden rather than a selling point.

This is partly due to the difficulties of applying animal welfare regulations in a context of intensive production with high stock densities at low cost. Low prices of meat and other animal products in the global market have stimulated a process of constant intensification, and the margins for improving farm animal welfare without compromising the economic viability of these types of production are small. This explains the great amount of attention on professional and efficient management at the farm level, as well as the high investments in innovation and knowledge dissemination in the Netherlands. Collaboration of public and private stakeholders is promoted by the government's preference for market solutions as well as by the opportunities given for market distinction in a society with a considerable middle class able to pay more for animal friendly products and high level of public concern about farm animal welfare. It is this politicization of animal welfare that forces the government as well as private actors to demonstrate to citizens, as consumers and voters, their willingness to invest time and effort in improving farm animal welfare.

## NOTES

1. For example, at the beginning of 2012 the European Commission sent a warning to non-compliant countries regarding the implementation of European Directive 1999/74/EC, which banned the use of barren battery cages for all laying hens in the EU from January 1, 2012 http://eurogroupforanimals.org/files/publications/downloads/Animals_in_Europe_-_issue_n%C2%B025_-_final.pdf.
2. For further information about the project EUWelNet please see http://www.euwelnet.eu. The data presented in this chapter are drawn upon Deliverable 4 of the project, a report edited by Bettina Bock, Nick Hacking and Mara Miele.
3. DG Sanco is the Directorate–General for Health and Consumers. Its mission is to ensure that food and consumer goods sold in the EU are safe and that the EU's internal market works for the benefit of consumers.
4. Further information about the projects is available at http://www.euwelnet.eu/euwelnet.
5. See http://www.retaildetail.eu/en/case-van-de-week/item/12898-dutch-meat-sector-to-become-100-sustainable-by-2020.

## REFERENCES

Bain, C., E. Ransom and V. Higgins. 2013. "Private Agri-food Standards: Contestation, Hybridity and the Politics of Standards." *International Journal of Sociology of Agriculture and Food* 20(1): 1–10.

Barnett, C., P. Cloke, N. Clarke and A. Malpass. 2005. "Consuming Ethics: Articulating the Subjects and Spaces of Ethical Consumption." *Antipode* 37: 23–45.

Barnett, C., P. Cloke, N. Clarke and A. Malpass (eds.). 2011. *Globalizing Responsibility: The Political Rationalities of Ethical Consumption*. RGS-IBG Series Book, Oxford: Wiley-Blackwell.

Blokhuis, H., B. Jones, R. Geers, M. Miele and I. Veissier. 2003. "Measuring and Monitoring Animal Welfare: Transparency in the Product Quality Chain." *Animal Welfare* 12: 445–455.

Blokhuis, H., M. Miele, I. Veissier and B. Jones (eds.). 2013. *Improving Farm Animal Welfare:*

*Science and Society Working Together: The Welfare Quality Approach.* Wageningen, the Netherlands: Wageningen Academic Publisher.

Bock, B.B. and H. Buller. 2013. "Healthy, Happy and Humane: Evidence in Farm Animal Welfare Policy." *Sociologia Ruralis* 53(3): 390–411.

Bock, B.B, N. Hacking and M. Miele. 2014. "Report on the Main Problem Areas and Their Sensitivity to be Addressed by Knowledge Transfer for each of the Specific Aspects of the Legislation Chosen for this Project." Brussels: EuWelNet Project (Deliverable 4). Retrieved November 16, 2014 (http://www.euwelnet.eu/euwelnet).

Buller, H. and E. Roe. 2012. "Commodifying Animal Welfare." *Animal Welfare* 21(S1): 131–135.

Buller, H. and E. Roe. 2014. "Modifying and Commodifying Farm Animal Welfare: The Economisation of Layer Chickens." *Journal of Rural Studies* 33: 141–149.

Busch, L. 2007. "Performing the Economy, Performing Science: From Neoclassical to Supply Chain Models in the Agrifood Sector." *Economy and Society* 36(3): 437–466.

Çalışkan, K. and M. Callon. 2009. "Economization, Part 1: Shifting Attention from the Economy towards Processes of Economization." *Economy and Society* 38(3): 369–398.

Çalışkan, K. and M. Callon. 2010. "Economization, Part 2: A Research Programme for the Study of Markets." *Economy and Society* 39(1): 1–32.

Commissie Van Doorn. 2011. "Al het vlees duurzaam: De doorbraak naar een gezonde, veilige en gewaardeerde veehouderij in 2020." Den Bosch.

Evans, A. and M. Miele. 2007. "Consumers' Views about Farm Animal Welfare, Part 2: Comparative Report Based on Focus Group Research." Welfare Quality® Reports No. 5. Cardiff, UK: Cardiff University.

Evans, A. and M. Miele. 2012. "Between Food and Flesh: How Animals Are Made to Matter (and Not to Matter) within Food Consumption Practices." *Environment and Planning D – Society and Space* 30(2): 298–314.

Friedberg, S. 2004. "The Ethical Complex of Corporate Food Power." *Environment and Planning A* 22: 513–531.

Horlings, L.G. and B.B. Bock. 2013. "Implementation of Three EU Directives on Animal Welfare in the Netherlands." EUWelNet Report Task 2.1: Mapping Implementation. Wageningen.

Kjærnes, U. 2012. "Ethics and Action: A Relational Perspective on Consumer Choice in the European Politics of Food." *Journal of Agricultural and Environmental Ethics* 25(2): 145–162.

Kjærnes, U., M. Miele and J. Roex (eds.). 2007. "Attitudes of Consumers, Retailers and Producers to Farm Animal Welfare." Welfare Quality® Reports No. 2. Cardiff, UK: Cardiff University.

Koos, S. 2012. "What Drives Political Consumption in Europe? A Multi-level Analysis on Individual Characteristics, Opportunity Structures and Globalization." *Acta Sociologica* 55(1): 37–57.

Miele, M. 2011. "The Taste of Happiness: Free Range Chicken." *Environment and Planning A* 43(9): 2070–2090.

Miele, M. and A. Evans. 2010. "When Foods Become Animals: Ruminations on Ethics and Responsibility in Care-Full Spaces of Consumption." *Ethics, Policy and Environment* 13(2): 171–190.

Miele, M. and J. Lever. 2014. "Improving Animal Welfare in Europe: Cases of Comparative Bio-sustainabilities." Pp. 143–165 in T. Marsden and A. Morely (eds.) *Sustainable Food Systems: Building a New Paradigm.* London: Earthscan.

Miele, M., J. Murdoch and E. Roe. 2005. "Animals and Ambivalence: Governing Farm Animal Welfare in the European Food Sector." Pp. 169–185 in V. Higgins and G. Lawrence (eds.) *Agricultural Governance.* London: Routledge.

Miele, M. and V. Parisi. 2001. "L'Etica del Mangiare, i valori e le preoccupazioni dei consumatori per il benessere animale negli allevamenti: un'applicazione dell'analisi Means-end Chain." *Rivista di Economia Agraria* LVI(1): 81–103.

Min EZ and I (Ministerie Economische Zaken Landbouw en Innovatie). 2013. "Agenda verduurzaming voedsel 2013–2016." Alliantie Verduurzaming Voedsel, Den Haag: Ministerie Economische Zaken.

Ministerie van Economische Zaken. 2014. "Monitor Duurzaam Voedsel." Den Haag: Ministerie van Economische Zaken.

Ransom, E. 2007. "The Rise of Agricultural Animal Welfare Standards as Understood through a Neo-institutional Lens." *International Journal of Sociology of Agriculture and Food* 15(3): 26–44.

Vapnek, J. and M. Chapman. 2010. *Legislative and Regulatory Options for Animal Welfare.* Rome: FAO Legal Office.

# 16. International political economy of agricultural research and development

*Leland Glenna, Barbara Brandl and Kristal Jones*

## INTRODUCTION

Many commentators are alarmed that publicly funded food and agricultural research and development (R&D), which in the third quarter of the 20th century was largely responsible for yield increases that helped feed the world as the population more than doubled, is stagnating in industrial nations (Piesse and Thirtle 2010; Pardey, Alston, and Chan-Kang 2013; Fuglie, Heisey, King, Pray, and Schimmelpfennig 2012; Pardey and Alston 2010). They warn that, as the world's population continues to increase, agricultural R&D will need to keep pace if the world is to avoid mass starvation. Despite the need for more public investment, however, they show that the growth rate of public spending in agricultural R&D began falling during the fourth quarter of the 20th century and continues to stagnate in the 21st century. Furthermore, they point out that the drop off in public funding has coincided with stagnating crop yields and a rise in food prices. Although there has been an increase in the private sector's investment in agricultural R&D, these commentators contend that it is not a substitute for the decline in public support (Fuglie et al. 2012). And although there has been a rise in public-sector support for agricultural R&D in emerging economies, such as Brazil, India, and China, they claim that support does not make up for the stagnation in public support in the Organisation for Economic Co-operation and Development (OECD) nations (Pardey and Alston 2010).

There are flaws in this narrative. First, the emphasis on financial investment in R&D overlooks research indicating that substantial advancements in food security could be achieved through policies promoting the diffusion of existing technologies and techniques (Godfray, Crute, Haddad, Lawrence, Muir, Nisbett, Pretty, Robinson, Toulmin, and Whiteley 2010). Even smallholder farmers in remote rural areas increase yields if policies are in place to provide input and output markets (Glenna, Ader, Bauchspies, Traoré, and Agboh-Noameshie 2012). Second, the emphasis on the role of R&D in feeding people privileges the supply side of agriculture and food provisioning over the demand side. It is important to keep in mind that people could be fed now if well-designed policies were put into place to deliver money to poor people, which would enable them to convert hunger into demand for food (Devereux 2011). For both of these critical points, the problem is not lack of public funding for agricultural R&D per se, but rather the lack of policies to enhance the productive capacity of farmers and the purchasing power of consumers.

Despite the validity of these critical points, there is still value in highlighting changes in the international political economy of food and agricultural R&D. After all, there are many current and emerging food and agricultural problems that require food and agricultural R&D if they are to be solved. However, we demonstrate here that an institutional framework is needed to enable the public interest to drive that R&D effort. We focus on three key trends that influence policies aimed at both the supply and demand sides of agricultural production. The first trend, which covers much of the previous four decades, is often referred to as neoliberalism and includes reductions in government spending, efforts to enhance international corporate trade, and efforts to undermine laws that protect labor, human health, and the environment (Moore, Kleinman, Hess, and Frickel 2011). More specifically, for food and agricultural R&D, neoliberalism describes efforts to convert public goods generated in universities into private goods that firms can sell for profit (Glenna, Lacy, Welsh, and Dina Biscotti 2007). However, it is important to recognize that political economies vary not just between industrialized and developing nations, but also among industrial nations and among developing nations. Hall and Soskice (2001) distinguish between liberal market economies and coordinated economies, and we suspect that the effects of neoliberalism are likely to be different in each. Liberal market economies, which include the United Kingdom, the United States, and Canada, tend to promote market self-regulation. Coordinated economies, which include Germany and France, tend to promote more state intervention in the management of the economy.

The second trend, which concerns funding for R&D in developing countries, is similar to the first. CGIAR Centers (formerly known as the Consultative Group on International Agricultural Research) have seen a rise in public–private and public–philanthropic partnerships that redefine the meaning of public and private investments and outputs (Brooks 2011). The impacts of these new partnerships and funding models are varied across countries and regions, but in general share common characteristics of an orientation toward technology and market development.

The third trend, which involves the rise of welfare states in emerging economies, has been called neo-Fordism (Fletes-Ocón and Bonanno

2013). Fordism is the term attached to the approach taken by nation-states between the 1930s and 1970s to manage contradictions in capitalism. It gained its name from the capitalist Henry Ford, who believed that the workers in his automobile factories should be able to purchase the cars they produced. The rise of neoliberalism in the 1970s, with its emphasis on reducing state regulation, was an attack on Fordism. Therefore, the return of state interventions to manage national economies is called neo-Fordism (Fletes-Ocón and Bonanno 2013). If neo-Fordism is emerging, we would expect evidence of a rise in public investments in food and agricultural R&D.

The goal of this chapter is to explore in more depth the implications of the general macro-level observations concerning changes in the public and private support for R&D and the potential consequences for innovation. First, we document trends in R&D in industrialized and developing nations. Second, we demonstrate that the changes in the international public and private support for R&D in and by OECD countries vary by internal political-economic structures and crop yield outcomes. And third, we critically assess the long-term benefits of efforts by emerging economies to expand public investment in agricultural R&D.

## DATA AND METHODS OF ANALYSIS

To measure changes in R&D funding, we use Alston, Andersen, James, and Pardey's (2010) data on public and private investment in agricultural and food R&D around the world (see also Pardey and Alston 2010; Fuglie et al. 2012; Pardey et al. 2013). These data are useful for our purposes because the starting point is 1981, which marks the beginning of neoliberalism. The elections of Margaret Thatcher as Prime Minister in the United Kingdom in 1978 and Ronald Reagan as President of the United States in 1980 are often highlighted as watershed moments in the emergence of neoliberalism (Wolff and Resnick 2012). Alston et al. (2010) also include data for the year 2000, which is well into the neoliberal transition. Two limitations in these data are that they only capture two years and that the most recent data is for 2000. However, the availability of this kind of data is scarce. The database that Pardey and his colleagues have developed took years to construct from various national and agribusinesses sources (Pardey et al. 2013).

We supplement these data with data on general trends in food and agricultural R&D spending at CGIAR Centers. The CGIAR Consortium was established in the mid-1970s as a network of publically funded research institutions meant to build on the initial successes of the Green Revolution in generating yield increases in key staple crops and decreasing rates of hunger in certain parts of the world (CGIAR 2011). The centers are publically funded through contributions by national governments and international institutions like the World Bank, and they also have had consistent support from private philanthropic foundations since their inception. The data we present below on changes in funding levels and sources over the course of CGIAR history was compiled from publically available annual financial statements that span from 1972 to 2012 (all amounts are in year 2000 US dollars to allow for inflation-adjusted comparisons across four decades). We analyze changes in funding internal to the CGIAR Consortium only, and not in comparison to funding for agricultural R&D in OECD and other countries, since the CGIAR system has always had a relatively small slice of overall global funding (Busch 2010).

Our third data source comes from the United Nations Food and Agriculture Organization (FAO STAT 2014), which maintains statistics on annual average crop yields and crop area by country. We use yield increase as an indicator of innovation activity focused on developing improved variety seed for the respective crop. Of course, yield changes are caused by more factors than improved seed, such as other inputs (e.g., fertilizers, irrigation, pesticides, and herbicides) and methods of cultivation. However, the quality of seed is regarded as the core factor for agronomic performance in terms of yield, and the development of improved variety seed has been a key focus of agricultural R&D over time (Fernandez-Cornejo 2004). We also recognize that agricultural innovation may be measured far more broadly than through just major crop yields. However, crop yield is a reliable, time-tested, and worldwide indicator of innovation. We are not aware of any comparable databases on the impacts of machinery, cropping practices, animal husbandry, or other types of agricultural innovations.

The argument we make is that there has been a shift in R&D emphasis on types of crops over the past 50 years. One potential explanation for those changes is that some crops are more commercially relevant than others. An important criterion for that relevance is physiological potential for hybridization. Another is the ability to secure a utility patent on a crop improvement. To compare transgenic, hybrid, and non-hybrid crops across nations, we chose three to five of the top crops produced in each respective OECD and emerging-economy country. We did not choose the same crops in all countries because each country specializes in different crops. Wheat is grown in each country. Maize and soybeans are the primary crops in the United States (US), but they are not significant in the United Kingdom (UK). However, we believe there is enough overlap among crops to make comparisons, and the emphasis on different types of crops is also an important point of comparison. We estimated the average yield increase within a given period by the slope of the regression line through the yield points in each year. We compared two periods, 1961 to 1981 (before neoliberalism) and 1982 to 2012 (after neoliberalism).

We use these two sets of data as indicators to gauge the relative influence of neoliberalism and neo-Fordism. First, the data on private and public funding sources indicate the relative reliance on private versus public funding for agricultural R&D in the study countries. Second, the data on crop yields and area harvested are indicators of neoliberalism to the extent that yield changes reflect both a decline of public investment and an increase in private investment in commercially interesting crops. What we mean by commercially interesting is that agribusinesses take a greater commercial interest in some crops than others. It has long been recognized that major crops are more commercially interesting than minor crops, because there is a greater opportunity to secure a profit from research investments (Welsh and Glenna 2006). However, the issue we explore here is whether agribusinesses take an even greater interest in some major crops than others because intellectual property or an integrated copy protection (hybridization) allows a more secure opportunity for capital accumulation.

## FOOD AND AGRICULTURAL R&D EXPENDITURES

Table 16.1 shows changes in public and private expenditures in selected industrial and emerging countries, as well as general trends for OECD member nations and developing nations. The key finding for the industrialized OECD countries is that the private sector accounted for a greater share of food and agricultural R&D in 2000 than in 1981. In 1981, the private sector accounted for 44 percent of food and agricultural R&D. By 2000, the private sector accounted for 54 percent. We interpret this to mean that neoliberalism has affected OECD nations to the extent that the private sector has taken on greater significance in what was previously considered the domain of the public sector. However, there is variation among those countries. France and the UK saw dramatic shifts in the private share of funding (from 44 percent to 75 percent in France between 1981 and 2000 and 56 percent to 72 percent in the UK between 1981 and 2000). Canada also saw a decline in public funding and a rise in share of R&D coming from the private sector (34 percent), but public funding still makes up the majority of the overall funding. The US made a far less dramatic shift (from 49 percent in 1981 to 51 percent in 2000). Germany was unusual because the private share of food and agricultural R&D declined

*Table 16.1*  *Public and private spending on agricultural R&D, 1981 and*
           *2000*

|  | Year | Public spending ($) | Private spending ($) | Private share (%) |
|---|---|---|---|---|
| United States | 1981 | 2,568 | 2,495 | 49 |
|  | 2000 | 3,882 | 4,118 | 51 |
| Germany | 1981 | 547 | 701 | 56 |
|  | 2000 | 758 | 877 | 54 |
| United Kingdom | 1981 | 533 | 676 | 56 |
|  | 2000 | 495 | 1,244 | 72 |
| Canada | 1981 | 520 | 109 | 17 |
|  | 2000 | 474 | 244 | 34 |
| France | 1981 | 478 | 377 | 44 |
|  | 2000 | 341 | 1,009 | 75 |
| *Total OECD* | *1981* | *8,339* | *6,478* | *44* |
|  | *2000* | *10,267* | *12,184* | *54* |
| Brazil | 1981 | 628 | NA | NA |
|  | 2000 | 928 | 36 | 4 |
| China | 1981 | 586 | NA | NA |
|  | 2000 | 1,762 | 73 | 4 |
| India | 1981 | 332 | NA | NA |
|  | 2000 | 1,159 | 128 | 10 |
| *Total Developing* | *1981* | *5,903* | *NA* | *NA* |
|  | *2000* | *10,030* | *686* | *6* |

*Note:*  All figures in millions of 2000 international dollars. NA = not available.

*Source:*  Alston et al. (2010).

slightly. However, when we move into the analysis of the crop yields, we will argue that these figures mask more profound changes within each country.

The emerging economies of Brazil, India, and China show a rather different trajectory. Their public expenditures rose dramatically between 1981 and 2000. China's and India's public expenditures more than tripled, and Brazil's also expanded. Unlike the OECD nations, private investments are not available for 1981 in China, India, and Brazil. However, we are able to note some modest private-sector investments in 2000, and we suspect that those investments have continued to increase since 2000.

There was also a substantial rise in R&D for all developing nations, as the public funding nearly doubled between 1981 and 2000. The private sector's share of R&D for all developing countries does appear in 2000, but it is very low when compared to the OECD nations. The growth of public funding for food and agricultural R&D in the three emerging economies may be an indicator of neo-Fordism.

## AGRICULTURAL RESEARCH IN DEVELOPING COUNTRIES

The CGIAR Consortium originated with the ostensible goals of generating goods that are relevant for the regions targeted by each research center and to safeguard the public availability of those goods (Pingali and Kelley 2007). Research in the CGIAR system is funded by a combination of contributions from national governments, international institutions (largely the World Bank), and private philanthropy. The Rockefeller and Ford Foundations were early supporters of the International Maize and Wheat Center where Norman Borlaug worked, and these two foundations were consistent contributors as the CGIAR system expanded. Until recently, however, philanthropic donations were small in comparison to contributions from other major donors. Figure 16.1 depicts the contributions of the top five donors to the CGIAR system from 1972 to 2012 and

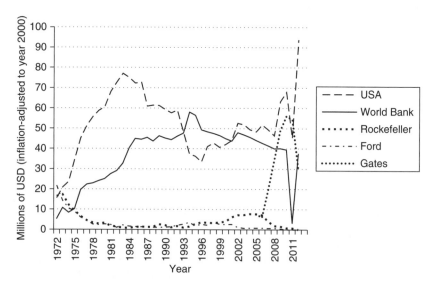

*Source:*   Data compiled from publically available CGIAR annual financial reports (CGIAR 2014).

*Figure 16.1    Top five contributors to the CGIAR Consortium, 1972–2011*

*Table 16.2   Overall operating budget and major donor dollar amounts,\**
*2005–2012*

| Year | Donor | | | | | |
|------|-------|------------|-------------|-------|-------|---------|
|      | US    | World Bank | Rockefeller | Ford  | Gates | Overall Budget |
| 2005 | 48,300,000 | 44,100,000 | 7,670,000 | 794,000 | 7,760,000 | 397,000,000 |
| 2006 | 51,800,000 | 42,700,000 | 7,180,000 | 854,000 | 5,980,000 | 364,000,000 |
| 2007 | 49,400,000 | 41,500,000 | 4,150,000 | 664,000 | 19,400,000 | 411,000,000 |
| 2008 | 46,400,000 | 40,000,000 | 1,840,000 | 720,000 | 34,400,000 | 425,000,000 |
| 2009 | 63,300,000 | 40,100,000 | 1,610,000 | 401,000 | 49,000,000 | 486,000,000 |
| 2010 | 67,900,000 | 39,500,000 | 790,000 | 0 | 56,100,000 | 531,000,000 |
| 2011 | 45,200,000 | 3,310,000 | 766,000 | 0 | 54,400,000 | 546,000,000 |
| 2012 | 93,800,000 | 37,500,000 | 0 | 0 | 29,900,000 | 417,000,000 |

*Note:*   *In inflation-adjusted year 2000 USD.

*Source:*   CGIAR (2014).

shows that after the first three years of the CGIAR's existence, the relative contributions of philanthropy were far less than those made by the US and the World Bank.

The establishment of the Bill and Melinda Gates Foundation in 2005, with a specific thematic focus on bolstering agricultural R&D for developing countries, has shifted the balance of CGIAR financial contributions. In 2012, as shown in Figure 16.1, the Gates Foundation was the third largest donor, after the US and the World Bank. As a percentage of the overall operating budget of the CGIAR, the Gates Foundation's financial contributions are still modest (see Table 16.2 for a budget breakdown). However, as Schurman (2011) and others (Brooks, Leach, Lucas, and Millstone 2009) have pointed out, the rhetorical impact of the Gates Foundations' entrée into international food and agricultural R&D has been substantial. The narrative of the new Green Revolution for Africa builds upon the supply side emphasis in agricultural R&D (see Toenniessen, Adesina, and DeVries 2008), but it also reinforces neoliberalism by emphasizing private philanthropic investment in agricultural R&D. As a major funder of both the CGIAR system and the development-oriented non-governmental organizations (NGOs) that work to diffuse innovations, such as research outputs from the CGIAR centers, the Gates Foundation has had a similar distorting effect on agricultural R&D to that of the private sector in OECD countries.

In addition to demonstrating the financial impacts of the Gates

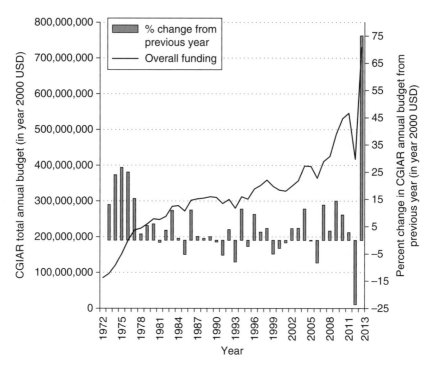

*Note:*    *In inflation-adjusted year 2000 USD.

*Source:*    CGIAR (2014).

*Figure 16.2    Total operating budget for CGIAR system and percent
change each year, 1972–2013\**

Foundation on CGIAR funding, Table 16.2 also highlights Busch's (2010)
point that even as the political economy of food and agricultural R&D
has changed over the past 50 years, the funding channeled to the CGIAR
system remains remarkably small compared to funding for other types of
research institutions. Many US research universities, for example, have
budgets larger than that of the entire CGIAR system. Figure 16.2 shows
that, adjusting for inflation, the total operating budget of the CGIAR
system and changes to it have largely followed the broader trends in the
political economy of agricultural R&D discussed in this chapter. Financial
resources grew rapidly in the first decade of the CGIAR system's existence,
as the Green Revolution gained steam and new research centers were established. Budget growth largely stalled from the mid-1980s to mid-1990s, in
part because of neoliberal policies that emphasized private investment

over public contributions. This period is often referred to as a lost decade in international agricultural development (Djurfeldt 2013). The uptick in funding from the late 1990s forward hints at a tacit recognition that publically supported food and agricultural R&D cannot be replaced by private enterprise. However, the recent reorganization of the CGIAR system (see CGIAR 2011) centralizes financial decisions and disbursements, emphasizes public–private partnerships, and focuses on research with high returns on investment. These changes, along with contributions from the Gates Foundation, increased the CGIAR operating budget to $1 billion in 2013, a figure that continues to pale in comparison to spending in OECD countries and increasingly in emerging economies. In addition, the consolidation of both funding sources and research program decision-making could detract from the generation of a wide range of public goods. Further research is needed to explore whether philanthropic contributions are promoting commercialization at the expense of public goods.

## CHANGES IN CROP AREA HARVESTED AND CROP YIELD

To explore the impacts of the neoliberal shift in food and agricultural R&D on food and agricultural innovation, we examine the trends in crop area harvested and crop yields in selected OECD countries and emerging economies. The data indicate important differences in agricultural crop area and crop yield between industrialized economies and emerging economies, as well as between liberal market economies and coordinated economies. We contend that agricultural innovations do not result from a purely technological logic, but that they are shaped by the type of funding and the institutional structure of an economy.

As we mentioned earlier, although the private sector's share of food and agricultural R&D passed the public sector's share in the late 1970s in the US, public support continued to increase. However, there was a shift in emphasis in the US towards diverting public research outputs to the private sector. As one might expect from such a shift, the crops that are increasing in production area and yield are soybeans, maize, and rice, which are commercially interesting to agri-biotechnology and seed firms. Although transgenic rice appeared on the market only recently in the US, hybrid rice has been available since the 1980s (Durand-Morat, Wailes, and Chavez 2011), which explains its commercial relevance. Area planted in soybeans rose dramatically over the past few decades, while the area planted in rice did not expand (see Figure 16.3). Furthermore, the average annual rate of yield in the commercially interesting crops (soybean, maize,

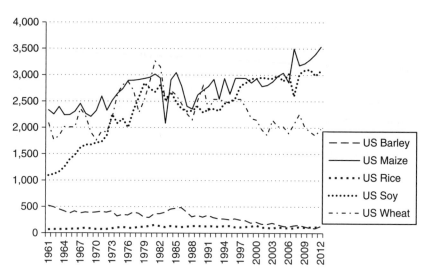

*Figure 16.3    US crop area harvested in 1,000 hectare*

*Table 16.3    Changes in major agricultural crop yields in the US in hectogram per hectare*

|  | Average yield increase per year | Average yield increase per year 1961–1981 | Average yield increase per year 1982–2011 | Change since 1982 |
|---|---|---|---|---|
| Maize USA | 1,160 hg | 1,230 hg | 1,260 hg | +2.44% |
| Wheat USA | 250 hg | 310 hg | 200 hg | −35.48% |
| Soybean USA | 270 hg | 200 hg | 300 hg | +50.00% |
| Rice USA | 750 hg | 450 hg | 870 hg | +93.33% |
| Barley USA | 340 hg | 410 hg | 340 hg | −17.07% |

and rice) rose while the average annual rate of yield increase for less commercially interesting crops, such as wheat and barley, declined (see Table 16.3).

The key difference we highlight is that, unlike maize, soybeans, and rice, wheat and barley are not hybrid or transgenic. Transgenic crops are especially commercially relevant because they bring intellectual property protections, which enable agricultural biotechnology and seed firms to secure returns on investment in these crops by making seed saving and replanting illegal. Another way of stating this is that companies having utility patents are able to convert the knowledge invested in them into private goods. The figures in Table 16.3 suggest that food and agricultural R&D has been directed at enhancing the crops that are commercially relevant to private firms at the expense of public goods. Because they are not yet hybridized or transgenic, scientific research to improve wheat and barley tends to remain a public good. And because the private sector is driving the research agenda, innovation is manifested as privatized knowledge.

A similar trend seems to be occurring in Canada (see Figure 16.4 and Table 16.4). Maize yield increased dramatically in Canada, but this is probably because maize was not widely grown prior to the 1980s. Where it is grown today, it has more investment in inputs. What is dramatic in Canada is the decline in area of production of wheat and barley, and the dramatic rise in production of rapeseed (Figure 16.4) and rapeseed yield (33 percent) (Table 16.4). Since nearly all rapeseed grown in Canada is transgenic, this further supports the point made about US trends. Food and agricultural R&D is being directed towards commercially relevant crops. It is important to note that much of the research that led to the creation of transgenic rapeseed (for canola production) was publicly funded, in effect subsidizing the creation of private goods.

The UK's approach to neoliberalism is different from the US's and Canada's. Rather than subsidize the private sector with public funding, the UK simply cut public funding. The resulting effect seems to be an overall decline in crop innovations in major staple crops of barley and

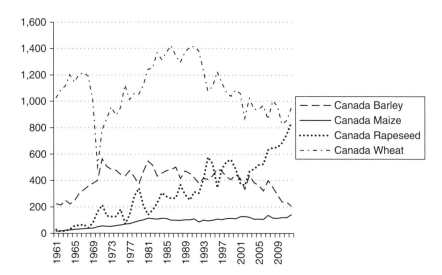

*Figure 16.4   Canadian crop area harvested in 1,000 hectare*

*Table 16.4    Changes in major agricultural crop yields in Canada in hectogram per hectare*

|  | Average yield increase per year | Average yield increase per year 1961–1981 | Average yield increase per year 1982–2011 | Change since 1982 |
|---|---|---|---|---|
| Maize Canada | 850 hg | 496 hg | 1120 hg | +124% |
| Wheat Canada | 260 hg | 310 hg | 350 hg | +12.90% |
| Rapeseed Canada | 180 hg | 180 hg | 240 hg | +33.33% |
| Barley Canada | 310 hg | 460 hg | 250 hg | −45.65% |

wheat. Area of barley production declined substantially after 1980 and wheat production has been flat (see Figure 16.5). Average annual yield increase in wheat and barley also declined dramatically in the UK (see Table 16.5). However, rapeseed production in the UK has increased (Figure 16.5), as has rapeseed yield (Table 16.5). The UK has not been open to transgenic crops, but as is the case with rapeseed in Canada, even non-transgenic rapeseed is a specialized, commercial crop that brings with it substantial commercial agribusiness interest.

Germany and France differ from the US, Canada, and the UK, since they are typically classified as coordinated economies. And the impacts of neoliberalism in France and Germany, in terms of crop production area

*Figure 16.5    UK crop area harvested in 1,000 hectare*

*Table 16.5    Changes in major agricultural crop yields in the UK in hectogram per hectare*

|  | Average yield increase per year | Average yield increase per year 1961–1981 | Average yield increase per year 1982–2011 | Change since 1982 |
|---|---|---|---|---|
| Barley UK | 560 hg | 430 hg | 300 hg | −30.23% |
| Wheat UK | 960 hg | 850 hg | 460 hg | −45.88 % |
| Rapeseed UK | 240 hg | 60 hg | 120 hg | +50.00% |

and crop yield, are quite different from those in the previous three countries. Germany saw a rise in rapeseed and maize crop area harvested, but a decline in barley crop area harvested (see Figure 16.6), which would be expected under neoliberalism. However, Germany also saw an increase in wheat area harvested, which is counter the neoliberal trend. Germany also had far more modest declines in crop yield rates when compared to the previous three countries (see Table 16.6).

Unlike Germany, and similar to the UK, France had a dramatic drop in public support for R&D. Similar to other countries, it also had a decline in barley crop area harvested, but an expansion in rapeseed crop area harvested (see Figure 16.7). Even though rapeseed is non-transgenic in France and Germany, just as it is in the UK, it is a commercially relevant crop. French maize area harvested increased slightly, but average yield

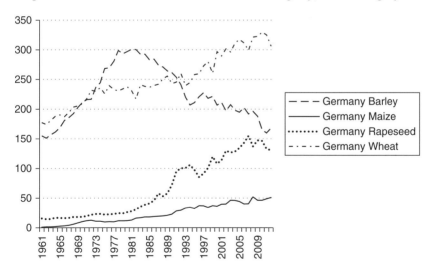

*Figure 16.6    German crop area harvested in 1,000 hectare*

*Table 16.6    Changes in major agricultural crop yields in Germany in hectogram per hectare*

|  | Average yield increase per year | Average yield increase per year 1961–1981 | Average yield increase per year 1982–2011 | Change since 1982 |
|---|---|---|---|---|
| Maize Germany | 1,290 hg | 1,490 hg | 1,290 hg | −13.42% |
| Wheat Germany | 980 hg | 870 hg | 720 hg | −17.24% |
| Barley Germany | 680 hg | 710 hg | 520 hg | −26.76% |
| Rapeseed Germany | 400 hg | 440 hg | 390 hg | −11.36% |

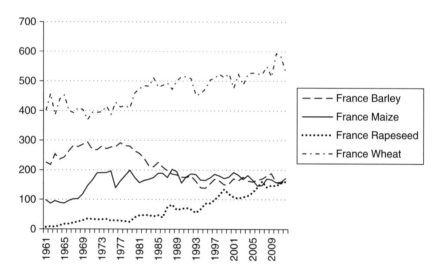

*Figure 16.7    French crop area harvested in 1,000 hectare*

increase declined. What makes France similar to Germany is that its harvested wheat area increased (Figure 16.7), even though its average annual yield increases in wheat declined substantially (see Table 16.7).

We interpret these results in Germany and France as evidence that coordinated economies have a stronger state with more clearly defined public interests, even during a period of neoliberalism, than liberal economies. As a staple crop that is not transgenic or hybrid, wheat declined in relevance in the US and the UK. The slight increase of wheat yields even after 1981 in Canada can be explained by the persistence of the publicly oriented agricultural sector in Canada. The eventual triumph of neolib-

*Table 16.7   Changes in major agricultural crop yields in France in hectogram per hectare*

|  | Average yield increase per year | Average yield increase per year 1961–1981 | Average yield increase per year 1982–2011 | Change since 1982 |
|---|---|---|---|---|
| Maize France | 1,310 hg | 1,240 hg | 1,100 hg | −11.29% |
| Wheat France | 934 hg | 1,200 hg | 472 hg | −60.66% |
| Barley France | 850 hg | 710 hg | 600 hg | −15.49% |
| Rapeseed France | 381 hg | 260 hg | 240 hg | −7.69% |

eralism in Canada may be evident in the demise of the Canadian Wheat Board in 2012. However, the rise in wheat production in the coordinated economies of Europe suggests neoliberalism affected these nations differently.

Trends in the emerging economies are more varied. Chinese maize crop area harvested has increased dramatically, while other crops declined or flattened in harvested crop area (see Figure 16.8). Average annual crop yield increases declined for everything but wheat (see Table 16.8). However, the dramatic increases in food and agricultural R&D in China

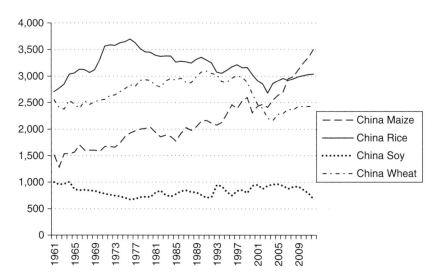

*Figure 16.8   Chinese crop area harvested in 1,000 hectare*

*Table 16.8    Changes in major agricultural crop yields in China in hectogram per hectare*

|  | Average yield increase per year | Average yield increase per year 1961–1981 | Average yield increase per year 1982–2011 | Change since 1982 |
|---|---|---|---|---|
| Rice China | 900 hg | 880 hg | 530 hg | −39.77% |
| Maize China | 930 hg | 940 hg | 710 hg | −24.73% |
| Wheat China | 880 hg | 710 hg | 770 hg | +8.45% |
| Soy China | 230 hg | 210 hg | 180 hg | −14.28% |

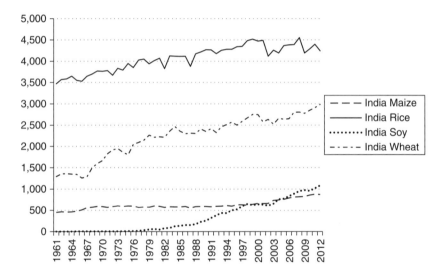

*Figure 16.9    Indian crop area harvested in 1,000 hectare*

does not seem to be translating into positive annual yield increases for crops other than wheat.

Indian crop production tells a story more consistent with neo-Fordism than Chinese production. India saw steady increases in crop area harvested in maize, rice, soy, and wheat production (see Figure 16.9). India saw dramatic increases in yield in rice and maize, and a modest decline in average annual yield increase for wheat. Average yield increase for soy declined substantially (see Table 16.9). Since maize is a commercially relevant crop that is used for industrial inputs and animal feed, its expansion in India may indicate a rise in meat consumption. However, neo-Fordism may be also evident in continued emphasis on staple food crops, like rice and wheat.

*Table 16.9   Changes in major agricultural crop yields in India in hectogram per hectare*

|  | Average yield increase per year | Average yield increase per year 1961–1981 | Average yield increase per year 1982–2011 | Change since 1982 |
|---|---|---|---|---|
| Rice India | 430 hg | 260 hg | 405 hg | +73.08% |
| Wheat India | 470 hg | 420 hg | 400 hg | −4.76% |
| Maize India | 290 hg | 60 hg | 420 hg | +600% |
| Soy India | 140 hg | 260 hg | 160 hg | −38.46% |

Brazilian crop production area tells a story more consistent with neoliberalism than neo-Fordism. This may be because Brazil adopted biotechnology earlier and more comprehensively than China or India (see Pray and Nagarajan 2014). Soybean production area increased dramatically, and maize production area increased modestly (see Figure 16.10). These transgenic crops are largely used as industrial outputs. Meanwhile, the rice and wheat production area declined. However, Brazil differs from all the other nations we analyzed in its dramatic progress in yield in rice, maize, and wheat, and modest progress in soy yield (see Table 16.10). Wheat yield increases may indicate some elements of neo-Fordism.

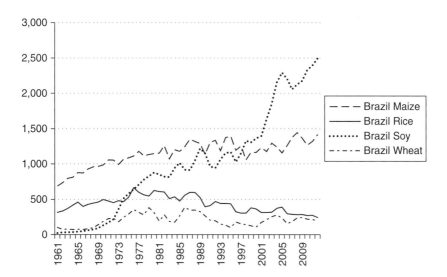

*Figure 16.10   Brazilian crop area harvested in 1,000 hectare*

*Table 16.10    Changes in major agricultural crop yields in Brazil in hectogram per hectare*

|  | Average yield increase per year | Average yield increase per year 1961–1981 | Average yield increase per year 1982–2011 | Change since 1982 |
|---|---|---|---|---|
| Rice Brazil | 0.60 hg | −10 hg | 1,050 hg | +10,600% |
| Maize Brazil | 0.60 hg | 200 hg | 950 hg | +375% |
| Soy Brazil | 0.38 hg | 360 hg | 450 hg | +25% |
| Wheat Brazil | 0.35 hg | 20 hg | 430 hg | +2,050% |

## CONCLUSION

Neoliberalism is evident across OECD countries, but its applications and effects in food and agricultural R&D and innovation vary by nation. Even in cases where countries are often categorized as similar, the impacts vary. For example, the UK, Canada, and the US are considered liberal market economies, and Germany and France are considered coordinated economies. However, the UK and France have taken a similar approach to reducing public funding for food and agricultural R&D. By contrast, public support in the US, Germany, and Canada has grown, even though the growth in spending has slowed over the years and the share of private funding has increased relative to public spending. These unexpected variations are informative. Whereas neoliberalism leads to reduction in state support in the UK, it leads to diverting public funds towards R&D that benefits the private sector in the US and Canada. This is evident in the yield increases in commercially relevant crops in the US and Canada. Despite the differences in public expenditures on food and agricultural R&D in Germany and France, they share a common focus on staple food crops. As a result, even though they have had some emphasis on commercially relevant crops, this has not been to the same extent as the UK, Canada, and the US. Despite these variations, neoliberalism is evident in each of these industrialized nations.

A similar trend is occurring in developing nations, but with the trend being driven more by private philanthropic support than by private industry. CGIAR Centers remain committed to public-goods research. However, evidence suggests that public-goods research is narrower in scope than it previously was and focuses primarily on market-driven diffusion strategies that reflect the neoliberal context from which the philanthropic funding comes (Brooks et al. 2009).

These trends in both R&D investment and crop yields have implications for the capacities of nations to solve food and agricultural problems. As we indicated in the introduction, public investment in food and agricultural R&D has been linked to productivity gains historically (Fuglie et al. 2102; Piesse and Thirtle 2010). More importantly, both variation in public research investment for food and agricultural R&D and variation in yields for multiple crops serve as indicators of each nation's commitment to the material wellbeing of its citizenry and the world's population.

The rise in public support for food and agricultural R&D and the dramatic rise in yield for staple food crops in emerging economies offer some evidence to support claims that neo-Fordism is nascent. However, the neo-Fordist nations are also clearly emphasizing commercially relevant crops that are of greater value to private agribusiness than to their nation's food supply. Although neo-Fordism may generate some positives, the social benefits for these nations and the world may take time to emerge. Pardey and Alston (2010) note that there are dramatic disparities in the education and skills of the scientific workforce and overall R&D budgets between OECD and emerging nations. They point out that the investment in time and finances would need to be immense to catch up with industrialized nations, and that there is likely to be a lag before these investments pay off.

Not all investments in food and agricultural R&D are the same. Private investment is not a replacement for the decline in public investment. And public investments directed at commercially relevant research lead to different outputs and outcomes than public investments directed at enhancing a nation's and the world's food supply. And although the rise in public investments in emerging economies are a welcome break from the neoliberal trends, they are unlikely to fill the gap left by the decline in public support in industrialized nations. Pardey and Alston (2010) note that even with the rising public investments in these countries, they pale in comparison to the losses in industrialized nations. They also note that there is a lag in payoffs from the initial investments in R&D. In other words, the rise in funding in China, Brazil, and India is not compensation for the stagnation of public R&D in the OECD nations.

One of the more intriguing ideas for promoting economic growth to emerge in recent years is the United Nation's Environment Programme's (UNEP's) Global Green New Deal. The UNEP's addition of "Global" to the proposed revival of the US President Franklin Roosevelt's "New Deal" expands the scale of the project. Furthermore, the term "Green" places an emphasis on the need for ecologically sustainable strategies, with focus on investment in sustainable agricultural production in developing nations. What remains consistent with the original New Deal is its emphasis on investing in public goods and people. Such grand thinking may be necessary to break from neoliberalism and to restore the role of the public sector in not only increasing agricultural productivity, but also in promoting the implementation of sustainable practices that enable people to feed themselves.

# REFERENCES

Alston, Julian M., Matthew A. Andersen, Jennifer S. James, and Philip G. Pardey. 2010. *Persistence Pays: US Agricultural Productivity Growth and the Benefits from Public R&D Spending*. New York: Springer Science and Business Media.

Brooks, Sally. 2011. "Is International Agricultural Research a Global Public Good? The Case of Rice Biofortification." *Journal of Peasant Studies* 38(1): 67–80.

Brooks, Sally, Melissa Leach, Henry Lucas, and Erik Millstone. 2009. "Silver Bullets, Grand Challenges and the New Philanthropy." STEPS Working Paper 24. Brighton, UK: STEPS Centre.

Busch, Larry. 2010. "Can Fairy Tales Come True? The Surprising Story of Neoliberalism and World Agriculture." *Sociologia Ruralis* 50(4): 331–351.

CGIAR. 2011. "The CGIAR at 40 and Beyond." Washington, DC: The CGIAR Fund.

CGIAR. 2014. "CGIAR Annual Financial Reports." Washington, DC: The CGIAR Fund. Retrieved February 4, 2014 at http://www.cgiar.org/resources/cgiarfinancial-reports/.

Devereux, Stephen. 2011. "Social Protection and Agriculture: Graduation or Dependency?" *Food Ethics* 6(4): 4–6.

Djurfeldt, Agnes Andersson. 2013. "African Re-agrarianization? Accumulation or Pro-poor Growth?" *World Development* 41(1): 217–231.

Durand-Morat, Alvaro, Eric Wailes, and Eddie Chavez. 2011. "Hybrid Rice and Its Impact on Food Security and the Pattern of Global Production and Trade." Selected Paper prepared for presentation at the Southern Agricultural Economics Association Annual Meeting, Corpus Christi, TX, February 5–8.

Fernandez-Cornejo, Jorge. 2004. "The Seed Industry in U.S. Agriculture: An Exploration of Data and Information on Crop Seed Markets, Regulation, Industry Structure, and Research and Development." Agriculture Information Bulletin No. AIB786. Washington, DC: United States Department of Agriculture.

Fletes-Ocón, Hector B. and Alessandro Bonanno. 2013. "Responses to the Crisis of Neoliberal Globalization: State Intervention in Palm Oil Production in Chiapas, Mexico." *International Journal of Sociology of Agriculture and Food* 20(3): 313–334.

FAO STAT. 2014. "Food and Agriculture Organization of the United Nations, Statistics Division." Rome, Italy: Economic and Social Development Department. Retrieved February 4, 2014 at http://faostat3.fao.org/home/E.

Fuglie, Keith, Paul Heisey, John King, Carl E. Pray, and David Schimmelpfennig. 2012. "The Contribution of Private Industry to Agricultural Innovation." *Science* 338(6110): 1031–1032.

Glenna, Leland, David Ader, Wenda Bauchspies, Abou Traoré, and Rita Afiavi Agboh-Noameshie. 2012. "The Efficacy of a Program Promoting Rice Self-Sufficiency in Ghana during a Period of Neoliberalism." *Rural Sociology* 77(4): 520–546.

Glenna, Leland L., William B. Lacy, Rick Welsh, and Dina Biscotti. 2007. "University Administrators, Agricultural Biotechnology, and Academic Capitalism: Defining the Public Good to Promote University–Industry Relationships." *Sociological Quarterly* 48(1): 141–164.

Godfray, H. Charles J., Ian R. Crute, Lawrence Haddad, David Lawrence, James F. Muir, Nicholas Nisbett, Jules Pretty, Sherman Robinson, Camilla Toulmin, and Rosalind Whiteley. 2010. "The Future of the Global Food System." *Philosophical Transactions of the Royal Society B* 365(1554): 2769–2777.

Hall, Peter A. and David W. Soskice. 2001. *Varieties of Capitalism: The Institutional Foundations of Comparative Advantage*. Oxford: Oxford University Press.

Moore, Kelly, Daniel Lee Kleinman, David Hess, and Scott Frickel. 2011. "Science and Neoliberal Globalization: A Political Sociological Approach." *Theory and Society* 40(5): 505–532.

Pardey, Philip G. and Julian M. Alston. 2010. "U.S. Agricultural Research in a Global Food Security Setting." Washington, DC: Center for Strategic and International Studies.

Pardey, Philip G., Julian M. Alston, and Connie Chan-Kang. 2013. "Public Agricultural R&D over the Past Half Century: An Emerging New World Order." *Agricultural Economics* 44(1): 103–113.

Piesse, J. and C. Thirtle. 2010. "Agricultural R&D, Technology and Productivity." *Philosophical Transactions of the Royal Society B* 365(1554): 3035–3047.

Pingali, Prabhu and Tim Kelley. 2007. "The Role of International Agricultural Research in Contributing to Global Food Security and Poverty Alleviation: The Case of the CGIAR." Pp. 2381–2418 in Robert Evenson and Prabhu Pingali (eds.) *Handbook of Agricultural Economics*. Vol. 3. Oxford: Elsevier.

Pray, Carl and Latha Nagarajan. 2014. "The Transformation of the Indian Agricultural Input Industry: Has It Increased Agricultural R&D?" *Agricultural Economics* 45(S1): 145–156.

Schurman, Rachel. 2011. "The New Culture of Philanthropy: The Bill & Melinda Gates Foundation, and the New Green Revolution for Africa." Conference Presentation, Rethinking Development Conference. Cornell University, NY. November 11–12.

Toenniessen, Gary, Akinwumi Adesina, and Joseph DeVries. 2008. "Building an Alliance for a Green Revolution in Africa." *Annals of the New York Academy of Sciences* 1136: 233–242.

Welsh, Rick and Leland Glenna. 2006. "Considering the Role of the University in Conducting Research on Agri-biotechnologies." *Social Studies of Science* 36(6): 929–942.

Wolff, Richard D. and Stephen A. Resnick. 2012. *Contending Economic Theories: Neoclassical, Keynesian, and Marxian*. Cambridge, MA: MIT Press.

# 17. Gender and the international political economy of agri-food
## Carolyn Sachs

Gender relations are key to agriculture and the political economy of food. Gender inequalities in employment, land ownership, access to technology, and access to markets disadvantages women, their families, and lessens food security. Understanding how these gender equalities shift with changes in the political economy of agri-food systems is important for scholars and policy makers.

Women provide much of the labor in agriculture in many regions of the world. Measuring the exact contribution of women and men as agricultural workers is difficult due to a number of factors such as poor sex-disaggregated data availability (Deere 2005), undercounting of women's work on family farms, and undercounting of casual or unauthorized workers. The most recent data suggests that women comprise 43 percent of the global agricultural labor force (FAO 2010) (see Table 17.1). Regions with the highest proportion of women agricultural workers are Sub-Saharan Africa (48.7 percent), Northern Africa (42.8 percent), and Asia (41 percent). Women comprise a smaller percentage of agricultural workers in Latin America and the Caribbean, Europe, and North America. Even more variation exists between countries within regions: in Africa women comprise 36 percent of the economically active population in Niger, 67 percent in Lesotho, and 65 percent in Mozambique; in Asia women comprise 47.9 percent of the economically active population in China, 32.4 percent in India, and 51 percent in Bangladesh; and in Latin America and the Caribbean, the percentage of women varies from 3.2 percent in Belize to 41.8 percent in Bolivia (FAO 2011). Women's and men's roles in agriculture vary by region of the world, the type of agriculture or livestock production, and the economic situation of the household. Men and women workers in agriculture work in a variety of circumstances, including on their family farms or as waged or unwaged laborers on other farms.

*Table 17.1* *Percentage of women economically active in agriculture by region*

| Area | Female share of economically active in agriculture 1980 (%) | Female share of economically active in agriculture 2010 (%) |
| --- | --- | --- |
| World | 40.4 | 42.7 |
| Sub-Saharan Africa | 46.0 | 48.7 |
| Northern Africa | 30.1 | 42.8 |
| Asia (excluding Japan) | 42.4 | 41.0 |
| Latin America and Caribbean | 18.6 | 20.9 |
| Europe | 44.9 | 32.4 |
| North America (excluding Mexico) | 22.5 | 28.9 |

*Source:* FAO (2011).

## WOMEN AGRICULTURAL WORKERS IN HIGH-VALUE EXPORT CROPS

With changes in trade policies, financial requirements, and increasingly corporate agriculture, many countries in the global South have switched their emphasis from traditional crops such as bananas, coffee, and tea to growing and processing non-traditional, high-value crops such as fruits, flowers, and vegetables. These products are typically grown for the export market and sold through value chains owned and operated by large international companies that supply fresh year-round produce to developed countries. These new crops require intensive labor in harvesting, selection, processing, and packaging, and the shift relies heavily on women's labor. As can be seen in Table 17.2, women constitute the majority of workers in fruit and flower production in many countries in South America and Sub-Saharan Africa. While these high-value crops are providing jobs and wages to poor women and men, there are a number of problems and gender-related issues in agricultural employment. The work is typically physically hard and taxing to people's bodies. Strong gender occupational segregation is typical, with men doing much of the work with equipment and machines and women doing hand labor. Stereotypical descriptions of women's dexterity, ability to work with their hands, and to be more careful with flowers and fruits are often used as the justification of gender segregated employment. Women agricultural wage workers are typically paid less than men and are more likely than men to work as part-time

*Table 17.2   Percentage of women wage workers in high-value crops in selected countries*

| Country | Crop | % Women workers |
|---------|------|-----------------|
| Northeast Brazil | Grapes | 65% of field workers |
| Chile | Fruit | 52% of temporary workers |
| Colombia | Flowers | 64% |
| Kenya | Flowers | 61% |
| Zimbabwe | Flowers | 87% |
| South Africa | Fruit | 69% of temporary workers |

*Source:*   Dolan and Sorby (2003).

and seasonal employees. In India, women's wages for casual agricultural work are 30 percent lower than men's and 20 percent lower for performing the same task (World Bank 2007). Women working in these casual or flexible jobs have limited job security. Gender discrimination in wages and employment is exploited by companies and contractors to lower costs of production (Barrientos 2013). As Barrientos argues, poor women who juggle productive and reproductive work and have few alternative sources of employment have weak bargaining positions and often have to accept such working conditions.

Agricultural laborers from poor regions in the global South also migrate for work in other countries in the global South. The demand for labor in non-traditional labor intensive crops in some countries in the global South has been met by employing women from even poorer countries in the global South. In Costa Rica, labor markets in agricultural processing are highly segmented by gender and citizenship. Lee's (2010) study of women workers in Costa Rica found that Nicaraguan undocumented women work in cassava production while cleaner and less physically demanding work in pineapple processing is predominantly performed by documented Nicaraguan women. The segmented labor market between men and women and documented and undocumented workers constrains possibilities for workers to organize for better working conditions.

## GENDER AND AGRICULTURAL WORKERS IN THE U.S. AND CANADA

In contrast to developing countries, recruitment of workers from the global South to work in agriculture in the U.S. and Canada has a masculine bias (Preibisch and Grez 2010). In the U.S., the majority of farmworkers in crops are men (79 percent), born in Mexico (75 percent), and not authorized to work in the U.S. (53 percent) (U.S. Department of Labor 2002). Canada is increasingly relying on migrant labor in agriculture and this sector is highly masculinized with women accounting for only 2 to 3 percent of the workforce (Preibisch and Grez 2010). Preibisch and Grez's fascinating study of Mexican women immigrant farmworkers in Canada points to multiple reasons that exist on both sides of the border for this highly masculinized workforce. Mexico did not allow women to participate in farmworker programs until 1989, and then only single mothers were eligible until 1998. Mexican women's mobility is constrained by gender ideologies and social norms that discourage women from leaving their children and/or husbands. Women who do migrate to work as farmworkers in Canada face similar gendered ideologies upon their arrival in Canada, where they are often perceived as bad mothers and sexually available. Also, Canadian farm owners and government officials perceive women as less appropriate than men as farmworkers (Preibisch and Hermoso Santamaria 2006). Preibisch's studies emphasize how racialized, sexualized and citizenship employment practices benefit agribusinesses and constrain farmworkers.

Men are preferred laborers as farmworkers in the U.S., while women are the preferred workers in lower echelons of food processing and dominate low-level, labor intensive jobs. In 2005, women comprised 75 percent of graders and sorters of agricultural products and earned three-fourths of men's earnings (U.S. Department of Labor and U.S. Bureau of Labor Statistics 2005). Women also comprise more than three-fourths (77 percent) of the 6.5 million workers in food preparation and service. Many of these jobs in food service are part-time, flexible positions with low wages and few benefits (Allen and Sachs 2007).

In the U.S., shifts in meat consumption from beef to poultry as well as concentration in the poultry industry has created numerous jobs in poultry processing factories. According to the National Center for Farmworker Health (2014), there are 250,000 poultry processing workers in 174 factories in the U.S. These jobs are what the International Labor Office classifies as 3-D jobs: dirty, demanding, and dangerous. About one-half of these workers are women, half are Latino, and about one-fourth of workers are undocumented. These workers work at high intensity and speed and are subject to numerous health injuries including carpal tunnel syndrome, musculoskeletal injuries, cuts from knives, and asthma and respiratory problems from poor quality air conditions. Despite these conditions, worker pay in the meat industry is low in these industries, averaging about U.S.$11 per hour with a mean annual wage of U.S.$24,000.

Exposure to pesticides is another health factor faced by both men and women in the horticulture industry. Exposure to toxic chemicals occurs through to early field re-entry following chemical spraying, inadequate training, and limited protective clothing. Exposure to chemicals is especially problematic in enclosed spaces such as greenhouses and packing sheds, where women workers tend to be concentrated. Short-term health effects include skin problems, respiratory conditions, nausea, and dizziness whereas longer-term effects include health concerns related to women's reproduction, including miscarriages (World Bank, FAO, and IFAD 2009).

Another serious problem faced by women agricultural workers is sexual violence. Violence and sexual harassment are common in workplaces with a high prevalence of women in low-paid positions with minimal security. A study in the Kenyan cut flower industry revealed that women reported that supervisors asked for sex in exchange for job security (Dolan, Opondo, and Smith 2002). Studies by Human Rights Watch and the Southern Poverty Law Center found high levels of sexual violence and sexual harassment of women farmworkers in the U.S. (Southern Poverty Law Center 2010). The Southern Poverty Law Center interviewed 150 women farmworkers and found that the majority had experienced sexual harassment. Women are particularly vulnerable to sexual assault and harassment by supervisors and labor contractors who often provide them with jobs, housing, and transportation. Many of these workers are unauthorized immigrants with little recourse for reporting violations due to language and cultural barriers. In addition to sexual abuse by their employers, migrant farmworker women also experience abuse by their husbands or boyfriends. Data from a study of 1,001 female farmworkers found that 19 percent had been physically or sexually abused by their husbands or boyfriends (Van Hightower et al. 2000).

## CHANGING GENDER RELATIONS ON FAMILY FARMS

Global agricultural policies clearly encourage the growth of agribusiness and corporate agriculture, but across the globe many men and women continue to produce food and agricultural products on family farms. Family farms in both developed and developing regions have a long history of patriarchal organization, with elder men owning the land, controlling the labor of other family members, and making the decisions in agricultural production. On many family farms, women played major roles as producers of specific commodities and in some contexts were the financial managers and chief marketers. However, these family farms are not static but are shifting in response to global shifts in the agri-food system. These shifts are accompanied by changing gender relations which in some cases involve disruption of existing patriarchal arrangements on family farms. On traditional family farms in many regions of the world, men claim the title farmer while women's identity and contribution to the farm is often downplayed or dismissed. Although men and women both work on family farms, women's work has often been viewed as secondary to men's work (Brandth and Haugen 2010). On traditional family farms, women are viewed and often view themselves as farm wives, helpers, or housewives. In both the U.S. and Europe, women are increasingly rejecting the position of farm wife and describing themselves as farmers, operators, or ranchers.

Agriculture in the U.S. is characterized by a bifurcated production system with large-scale, highly capitalized, often single commodity farms on the one hand, and smaller, labor intensive, and diversified farms on the other. The larger farms produce the five major commodities for the global agri-food system which include corn, cattle, dairy, soybeans, and broilers. Production of these commodities is becoming increasingly concentrated. Large farms dominate crop production, with most crop production occurring on farms with at least 1,100 acres (MacDonald et al. 2013). The U.S. Department of Agriculture (USDA) calculates the mid-point acreage as the best measure of farm size and this measure has doubled from 589 acres in 1982 to 1,105 acres in 2007. The mid-point acreages doubled in the five major field crops of corn, cotton, rice, soybeans, and wheat. The vast majority of these large commodity crop farms (96 percent) remain family farms and tend to have men as the principal operators (MacDonald et al. 2013). Increasing concentration of crop production has been facilitated by new technologies, separation of livestock and crop production, increased use of contracts, and federal commodity, loan, and tax policies. New technologies such as larger equipment for planting and harvesting, chemical pesticides, no-tillage techniques, and genetically modified seeds have reduced labor demands and facilitated the increase in size of operations. Concentration of production has been even steeper in dairy and livestock production. For example, the mid-point dairy herd size increased from 80 cows in 1987 to 570 cows in 2007. Concentration is perhaps most steep in hog production, with the mid-point size of hog farms increasing from 1,200 in 1987 to 30,000 in 2007 (MacDonald et al. 2013). Technologies in the form of large-scale animal facilities, integration with processors, and contracting practices have facilitated larger animal production facilities. Barriers of entry to large-scale capital intensive agriculture are steep and beyond the reach of most people unless they inherit farmland, structures, and equipment. For example, USDA estimates that to manage an average size corn and soybean farm in the Midwest would require 8 million U.S. dollars of land, equipment, and infrastructure (MacDonald et al. 2013). Because women are much less likely to inherit farms and become principal operators on family farms than men, men remain the principal operators and decision makers on the vast majority of these large-scale family farms.

## WOMEN FARMERS IN THE U.S.

Despite the male dominance of large-scale agriculture, more women in the U.S. are operating farms than in the past. The number of women-operated farms has doubled in the past 30 years. Data on the gender of farmers was first collected by USDA in 1978. At that time, only 5 percent of the principal operators were women, but by 2007 the number of women farmers increased and 14 percent of farms were woman-operated (Hoppe and Korb 2013). Women operate farms which are smaller and have fewer sales than men-operated farms. Nevertheless, between 1982 and 2007, women-operated farms increased in all sales classes, but the major increase in women-operated farms were in farms with less than U.S.$10,000 in sales. In fact, 78 percent of women-operated farms have sales of less than U.S.$10,000. Only 5 percent of women-operated farms had sales over U.S.$100,000 in 2007 (Hoppe and Korb 2013). The discrepancy in sales between men's and women's farms is large, with the average sales on women-operated farms about one-fourth of men's—U.S.$36,440 compared to U.S.$150,671. On average, women's farms are less than half the size of men's farms—210 acres compared to 452 acres (USDA 2007). Women-operated farms also raise different crops to men's farms. Almost half (45 percent) of women's farms specialize in livestock, including beef cattle, horses, sheep, and goats. The most economically successful farms of women operators in terms of sales were farms specializing in poultry, specialty crops, grains, and dairy. In addition to operating their own farms, many women farmers farm jointly with their spouses or other partners. The number of these women secondary operators has also increased. When both primary and secondary women farm operators are counted there are about 1 million women operators (Hoppe and Korb 2013).

Many women farmers are involved in agricultural operations that produce for local, sustainable, and organic markets and are actively involved in organic, sustainable, and local foods movements in the U.S. (DeLind and Ferguson 1999; Hassanein 1999; Meares 1997; Liepins 1998; Trauger 2004; Trauger et al. 2010). These three movements in agriculture have gained increased attention and have challenged the broader agroindustrial food system, but still represent a small proportion of agricultural production in the U.S. Women are more prevalent in organic farming than in conventional agriculture in developed countries. In the U.S. women make up 22 percent of organic farmers, in Canada they make up one-third of organic farmers, and in the U.K. they make up 50 percent of organic farmers (Jarosz 2011). Jarosz found that women predominated as community supported agriculture farmers in Washington. She argues that although they may be dismissed as hobby farmers or urban gardeners and not contributing to mainstream agriculture, they have consciously chosen to do this work because it nourishes themselves, their families, and their communities.

## WOMEN FARMERS IN THE GLOBAL SOUTH

In many developing countries, women play key roles in agricultural production at the household level. They produce food for their households and for local markets. Many development efforts are emphasizing improvements or upgrading of agricultural value chains as a policy to assist poor farmers and producers. These improvements in agricultural value chains can be at the production stage, such as irrigation or greenhouses, at the marketing stage, such as access to new markets, and at the distribution stage, such as cold storage for transportion. Efforts to upgrade value chains with an eye towards the empowerment of women usually focus on: (1) horizontal integration which improves the linkages between similar actors in a value chain, for example establishing women's groups and cooperatives, or (2) vertical integration which improves linkages between people in different positions in value chains, for example linking women with producers and buyers (Riisgaard et al. 2010). Some of the primary efforts here have focused on upgrading products—such as producing for certification standards such as fair trade and organic—and process upgrading—such as using new technology, reducing post-harvest loss. Women face barriers to participating in value chains such as limited education, limited mobility, limited access to assets and capital, and lack of connection to other actors in value chains. Women's time is often divided between productive and reproductive activities, and in regions with poor infrastructure for water, energy, and other basic services, women's reproductive work, especially that related to feeding their families, is quite time consuming and can limit their involvement in production activities. In their evaluation of various value-chain upgrading efforts, Riisgaard et al. (2010) find mixed results for increasing gender equity. The increased labor demands from organic and fair trade products often fall on women's shoulders. For example, in Uganda, conversion to organic coffee production at the household level significantly increased women's labor and had minimal effect on men's labor. Men largely controlled the income from coffee production, so they were the primary beneficiaries of participating in the upgraded organic coffee value chain (Bolwig and Odeke 2007). Women's participation in value-chain interventions does not automatically guarantee changes that lead to more gender equitable decision-making at the household level. Some efforts have specifically targeted women in organic value chains. For example, "Café Feminino" is the label of an organically grown coffee that began in Peru but has expanded to seven other countries in Central and South America. The program focuses on increasing women's participation in cooperatives, improving their technical production, and strengthening their leadership capacity (World Bank, FAO, and IFAD 2009). Women's groups can promote women to have their voices heard, learn participation skills, and may be more socially acceptable in certain cultural contexts. However, in some instances, the exclusion of men has resulted in acts of sabotage against women's groups. Mixed gender groups may provide more access to capital, assets, credit, and information, but women's participation must be more than marginal. While participation in upgraded value chains may offer opportunities for gender equity, without careful attention to how these upgrades are implemented, gender inequities may remain unchanged or may deepen.

Very small-scale women producers' contribution to local and household level food security is often overlooked, especially in urban areas. In many countries, women play key roles in urban agriculture through producing vegetables and meat in kitchen gardens and small plots of land in many cities in the global South, for example in India, the Philippines, Ghana, Kenya, and Peru (FAO 2011). However, many of these efforts go unrecognized, and more work is needed by city planners and officials to provide land and other resources to support women's efforts in urban agriculture (Sachs and Patel-Campillo 2014).

## DIFFERING GENDERED APPROACHES TO SOLVING HUNGER

The United Nation's Millennium Development Goal number one of eradicating extreme poverty and hunger is unlikely to be met by 2015. The target of the Millennium Development Goal was to halve the proportion of people suffering from hunger between 1990 and 2015. In 1990, 23.6 percent of people in developing countries were undernourished compared to 14.3 percent in 2011–2013, with some regions, especially Sub-Saharan Africa, not able to decrease the prevalence of undernourishment.

The Food and Agriculture Organization of the United Nations (FAO) now recognizes that gender is an important dimension of food security and that a narrow focus on food availability will not solve the problem. Their most recent framework addresses what they identify as four pillars of food security, which include availability, access, utilization, and stability, while recognizing that broader issues of health, water quality, and education, especially recognizing gender constraints, are essential for addressing food security. However, even within their gendered framework, FAO and other international institutions continue to emphasize market-based solutions such as upgrading value chains and emphasizing integration in the market.

By contrast to the approach of the United Nations, the food sovereignty movement, led by La Vía Campesina, comprises small and medium farmers, the rural poor, agricultural workers, and indigenous people. Vía Campesina also recognizes that that food insecurity is not caused by food scarcity. Rather, they argue that the main causes of hunger and malnutrition are the inequitable distribution of food, land, and other productive resources, including water and seed. Women within the food sovereignty movement at the grassroots level insist that the movement addresses gender issues, including valuing women's agricultural work, food provisioning responsibilities, and women's contributions to the household. Similarly, women within the movement emphasize the right to equitable access to culturally appropriate and healthy food on par with men and boys. At the core of the food sovereignty approach is an emphasis on the right of self-determination in agri-food systems, food choices and organization and sustainability of production and consumption, and the right to set priorities according to the needs of communities. However, this movement has yet to move gender issues to the core of their approach. Sachs and Patel-Campillo (2014) call for a feminist food justice approach for solving hunger and malnutrition. This approach involves recognizing and addressing the overlapping and conflicting dynamics of race, gender, class, sexuality, and citizenship related to food inequalities.

## PUSHING FOR CHANGE

Women are at the forefront of international, national, and local efforts to create environmental sustainability and social justice in agri-food systems. Women, such as Vandana Shiva, led the push for changes in food and agriculture issues in the anti-globalization struggle (Mohanty 2003; Shiva 2002). Women are also at the forefront in pushing for change through the consumer politics of food. They are leaders and make up the majority of participants in ethical buying, fair trade, humane, organic and local food. Barrientos (2013) points to case studies of how women oriented non-governmental organizations have pressured or collaborated with companies to improve working conditions in agricultural operations. She notes that women constitute a growing voice for a more caring commercial environment and that women are increasingly participating as informed workers, consumers, and activists in agriculture and food systems.

In the U.S., women farmers have formed agricultural networks to push for women's success as farmers in sustainable agriculture while simultaneously pushing for broader changes in the food system. These networks in Vermont, Maine, Iowa, and Pennsylvania support women farmers to learn production strategies and network with each other in order to succeed as farmers. For example, the Pennsylvania Agricultural Women's Network began in 2003 as a fledgling organization of women farmers and agricultural professionals and as of 2014 has 1,400 members.

Women have led the retail workers movement through filing a class-action suit for sex discrimination against Wal-Mart, the largest food retailer in the U.S. and one of the largest employers in many regions of the country. The suit charged Wal-Mart with discriminating against women in terms of pay, promotions, and job assignments and with being in violation of the Civil Rights Act (Featherstone 2004). The suit expanded to represent 1.6 million women and was the largest class-action suit in U.S. history. Fast food workers in the U.S. have recently gone on strike in seven U.S. Cities demanding 15 U.S. dollars an hour minimum wage. Many fast food workers are earning the federal minimum wage, which in 2014 is U.S.$7.25 per hour. While workers in the fast food industry were teenagers, this is no longer the case—50 percent of fast food workers are over 20 years of age and the median age of women in the fast food industry is 32. The majority of these workers are women, and of those women over 20, one-fourth are raising children. These campaigns have received national media attention, but movement for increasing wages has been slow.

Accessing and participating in value chains is one strategy for women's empowerment, but many women in developing countries continue to play a major role in producing food for their families and local markets. This agricultural work, often characterized as reproductive labor, continues to be invisible work to many policy makers and development projects, despite their major contributions to food security of households. Valuing women's reproductive labor in producing, cooking, and serving food is difficult in the increasingly market-driven framework for increasing food security. Promoting efforts to support women's reproductive efforts could easily result in the re-inscription of their subordinate status (Sachs and Patel-Campillo 2014) and add to women's workload. Another strategy is to involve men and boys more in food preparation and nutritional concerns.

Sachs and Patel-Campillo (2014) suggest a more radical strategy that involves the redistribution of labor and resources to ensure that all women and men have the time and resources to provide adequate food for their families. This trajectory involves rethinking and redefining heteronormative household models that lead to food inequality between and within households. Several possibilities for moving in this direction include new models of community kitchens, sharing cooking and food preparation across households, and a push for shaking up household divisions of labor to emphasize the joys and pleasures as well as the work of food provision.

# REFERENCES

Allen, Patricia and Carolyn Sachs. 2007. "Women and Food Chains: The Gendered Politics of Food." *International Journal of Sociology of Food and Agriculture* 15 (1):1–23.

Barrientos, Stephanie. 2013. "Corporate Purchasing Practices in Global Production Networks: A Socially Contested Terrain." *Geoforum* 44:44–51.

Bolwig, S. and M. Odeke. 2007. "Household Food Security Effects of Certified Organic Export Production in Tropical Africa: A Gendered Analysis." Research Report submitted to EPOPA (Sida).

Brandth, Berit and Marit S. Haugen. 2010. "Doing Farm Tourism: The Intertwining Practices of Gender." *Signs: Journal of Women in Culture and Society* 35 (2):425–446.

Deere, Carmen Diana. 2005. "The Feminization of Agriculture? Economic Restructuring in Rural Latin America." United Nations Research Institute for Social Development (UNRISD) Occasional Paper No. 1, Geneva.

DeLind, Laura and Anne Ferguson. 1999. "Is This a Woman's Movement? The Relationship of Gender to Community-Supported Agriculture in Michigan." *Human Organization* 58:190–200.

Dolan, C., M. Opondo, and S. Smith. 2004. "Gender, Rights and Participation in the Kenya Cut Flower Industry." Retrieved November 19, 2014 at http://www.dfid.gov.uk/pubs/files/tspgender.pdf.

Dolan, C.S. and K. Sorby. 2003. "Gender and Employment in High-Value Agriculture Industries." Agriculture and Rural Development Working Paper 7. Washington, DC: The World Bank.

Featherstone, Liza. 2004. *Selling Women Short: The Landmark Battle for Workers' Rights at Walmart*. New York: Basic Books.

FAO (Food and Agriculture Organization). 2011. *The State of Food and Agriculture, 2010–2011: Women in Agriculture Closing the Gender Gap*. Rome: Food and Agriculture Organization.

Hassanein, Neva. 1999. *Changing the Way America Farms: Knowledge and Community in the Sustainable Agriculture Movement*. Lincoln, NE: University of Nebraska Press.

Hoppe, Robert A. and Penni Korb. 2013. "Characteristics of Women Farm Operators and Their Farms." Economic Research Service, Economic Information Bulletin 111. Washington, DC: USDA.

Jarosz, Lucy. 2011. "Nourishing Women: Toward a Feminist Political Ecology of Community Supported Agriculture in the United States." *Gender, Place and Culture* 18 (3):307–326.

Lee, Sang E. 2010. "Unpacking the Packing Plant: Nicaraguan Migrant Women's Work in Costa Rica's Evolving Export Agricultural Sector." *Signs: Journal of Women in Culture and Society* 35 (2):317–342.

Leipins, Ruth. 1998. "The Gendering of Farming and Agricultural Politics: A Matter of Discourse and Power." *Australian Geographer* 29 (3):371–388.

MacDonald, James M., Penni Korb, and Robert A. Hoppe. 2013. "Farm Size and the Organization of U.S. Crop Farming." Washington, DC: USDA, ERS.

Meares, A.C. 1997. "Making the Transition from Conventional to Sustainable Agriculture: Gender, Social Movement Participation, and Quality of Life on the Family Farm." *Rural Sociology* 62 (1):21–47.

Mohanty, Chandra. 2003. *Feminism without Borders: Decolonizing Theory, Practicing Solidarity*. Durham, NC: Duke University Press.

National Center for Farmworker Health. 2014. "Poultry Workers." Retrieved November 19, 2014 at http://www.ncfh.org/docs/fs-PoultryWorkers.pdf.

Preibisch, Kerry and Evelyn Encalada Grez. 2010. "The Other Side of el Otro Lado: Mexican Migrant Women and Labor Flexibility in Canadian Agriculture." *Signs: Journal of Women in Culture and Society* 35 (2):289–316.

Preibisch, Kerry and Luz Maria Hermoso Santamaria. 2006. "Engendering Labor Migration: The Case of Foreign Workers in Canadian Agriculture." Pp. 107–130 in *Women, Migration, and Citizenship: Making Local, National, and Transnational Connections*, edited by Evangelia Tastsoglou and Alexander Dobrowolsky. Aldershot, U.K.: Ashgate.

Riisgard, Lone, Anna Maria Escobar Fibla, and Stefano Ponte. 2010. "Gender and Value Chain Development." Copenhagen: The Danish Institute for International Studies. Retrieved November 19, 2014 at http://eudevdays.eu/sites/default/files/45670567.pdf.

Sachs, Carolyn and Anouk Patel-Campillo. 2014. "Feminist Food Justice: Crafting a New Vision." *Feminist Studies* 40 (2):1–14.

Shiva, Vandana. 2002. *Sustainable Agriculture and Food Security: The Impact of Globalization*. Thousand Oaks, CA: Sage Publications.

Southern Poverty Law Center. 2010. "Injustice on Our Plates: Immigrant Women in the U.S. Food Industry." November.

Trauger, A. 2004. "'Because They Can Do the Work': Women Farmers and Sustainable Agriculture." *Gender, Place and Culture* 11 (2):289–307.

Trauger, A., C. Sachs, M. Barbercheck, K. Brasier, and N.E. Kiernan. 2010. "'Our Market Is Our Community': Women Farmers and Civic Agriculture in Pennsylvania, USA." *Agriculture and Human Values* 27 (1):43–55.

USDA. 2007. "Women Farmers: 2007 Census of Agriculture." Retrieved November 19, 2014 at http://www.agcensus.usda.gov/Publications/2007/Online_Highlights/Fact_Sheets/Demographics/women.pdf.

U.S. Department of Labor. 2002. "Findings from the National Agricultural Workers Survey 2001–2002: A Demographic and Employment Profile of United States Farm Workers." Washington, DC: U.S. Department of Labor.

U.S. Department of Labor and U.S. Bureau of Labor Statistics. 2005. "Highlights of Women's Earnings in 2004." Washington, DC: U.S. Department of Labor. Retrieved July, 2006 at http://www.bls.gov/cps/cpswom2004.pdf#search=%22%22highlights%20of%20women's%20earnings%22%22.

Van Hightower, Nikki R., Joe Gorton, and Casey Lee DeMoss. 2000. "Predictive Models of Domestic Violence and Fear of Intimate Partners among Migrant and Seasonal Farm Worker Women." *Journal of Family Violence* 15 (2):137–154.

World Bank. 2007. "World Development Report 2008: Agriculture for Development." Washington, DC: The World Bank.

World Bank, FAO, and IFAD. 2009. *Gender in Agriculture Sourcebook*. Washington, DC: The World Bank.

# Index